THE CONSTRUING PERSON

THE CONSTRUING PERSON

Edited by
James C. Mancuso
Jack R. Adams-Webber

PRAEGER

PRAEGER SPECIAL STUDIES • PRAEGER SCIENTIFIC

Library of Congress Cataloging in Publication Data

Main entry under title:

The Construing person.

Bibliography: p.
Includes index.
1. Personality.   2. Personal construct theory.
I. Mancuso, James C., 1928–   II. Adams-Webber,
Jack R.
BF698.C615   155.2   81-12101
ISBN 0-03-058691-7   AACR2

Published in 1982 by Praeger Publishers
CBS Educational and Professional Publishing
a Division of CBS Inc.
521 Fifth Avenue, New York, New York 10175 U.S.A.

23456789   145   987654321

Printed in the United States of America

CONTENTS

1

PERSONAL CONSTRUCT PSYCHOLOGY AS PERSONALITY THEORY: INTRODUCTION

James C. Mancuso
Jack R. Adams-Webber

Mary Stone, the mother of a 19-year-old son, sporadically employed as a bookkeeper, married for the first time at the age of 40 to a man who was ten years her senior. He died of heart disease shortly after the birth of her second child, a daughter named Sally. Their five-year marriage had been a torment to both partners. It was filled with charges and countercharges of infidelity, and Mr. Stone stated publicly that Sally was not his child. He was arrested for promoting gambling. Further, their problems were exacerbated by Mr. Stone's frequent abuse of alcohol.

Following her husband's death, Mary and Sally moved into the home of another man, Paul, with whom Mary had been acquainted for many years. They lived together for about two years, and then Paul moved out, although he returned regularly to the house. He saw reasons to become worried about both Mary and the child. The mother rarely left the house and spoke to no one. At times, she would begin to act and speak as if she were playing the role of another person. Paul contacted the local children's services and, claiming that he was Sally's father, persuaded the officials to intercede on the basis of child neglect. As a result, Mary was removed to a psychiatric center, and Sally was placed in foster care by a family court.

Another woman, Elena Ferro, who is about 50 years old, lives with her husband who manages a prosperous shoe store. They have remained married for 26 years and have reared two children, both of whom have finished university and are beginning careers. Elena works as an administrative assistant for a superintendent of schools. She and her husband maintain steady contact with a small circle of intimate friends. At home, they share the housework and preparation of meals, often arranging to share meals with friends. They travel frequently, visiting historic sites and museums, attending concerts, and relaxing at out-of-the-way resorts. During the summer months, they regularly attend horse race meets and turn over a tidy sum by rather heavy betting. They try to avoid separations. For example, when Mr. Ferro schedules a buying trip, he usually arranges to have Elena accompany him. In short, the Ferros share a busy and mutually satisfying existence and foresee no change in their relationship.

Assume that a psychologist were called upon to explain the lives of these two women, Mary Stone and Elena Ferro. Obviously, whatever explanation he* offered would reflect the personality theory that he holds either explicitly or implicitly. That is, he would attempt to interpret the available data on the basis of a set of related assumptions concerning human nature. At the same time, a philosopher of science could conduct an analysis of the psychologist's personality theory, looking for those elements that should be included in any system of explanation. The philosopher might ask about the rules of evidence that guided the psychologist's selection of assumptions, or what ideas about time or causality are incorporated in the theory. Theoretical psychologists might feel no obligation, however, to address these metaphysical questions, leaving them to philosophers who are viewed as the competent commentators on such issues. On the other hand, there are specific issues that are of central importance to any theory that is intended to explain the behavior and experience of individual persons such as Mary and Elena. Thus, personality theories in general can be evaluated in terms of the adequacy with which they address and resolve these issues.

FIVE ISSUES FOR PERSONALITY THEORY

Our consulting psychologist would find it difficult to talk about personality without making a statement about the relative _continuity_ of the behavior of each woman. For example, he might indicate that he does not believe that Mary will persist in her excessive "seclusiveness." He might assume that Elena is a "sociable" person, implying that certain related behaviors are continuously available in Elena's repertoire.

Our consulting psychologist might implicitly take a stand on the second major issue. In commenting on Elena's "sociability" and Mary's "seclusiveness," he would thereby reveal that he thinks that behavior reflects underlying traits. In other words, this psychologist may have selected the trait as the _basic unit of analysis_ in describing the structure of personality. Alternatively, he may have chosen responses, schemata, expectancies, drives, personal constructs, or some other units.

---

*Editor's Note: Throughout the book, in an attempt to avoid the awkward "he/she" or "his or her" constructions, the masculine gender is usually used in referring to individuals. This does not mean that the contents are *not* relevant to both males and females.

As the psychologist developed an explanation of the behavior of either Mary or Elena, he should say something also about *how persons relate their conduct to "real" events*. He might do this indirectly, for example, by asserting that "Mary has lost contact with reality." Or he might specify more directly that "Elena has a useful set of cognitive dimensions for processing information input from the external world."

A psychological explanation of Mary's and Elena's different patterns of behavior should also contain some propositions relevant to a fourth basic issue, *motivation*. If our psychologist subscribed to a psychoanalytic approach, he might, for example, speculate that Mary's childhood experiences had mitigated against her having developed defense mechanisms that adequately allow for the modification and control of her aggressive impulses. Statements about impulses would suggest also the psychologist's point of view with respect to another central theme that is closely related to the motivation issue. We might inquire whether the psychologist believes that impulses are somehow represented in the form of *emotions* such as love and anger. If he were to emphasize Mary's anger, we might infer that he thought that the anger was a direct expression of an underlying energetic force. A psychologist who adopted a different personality theory might formulate the problem in other terms. For example, a personal construct theorist might hypothesize that when Mary's husband did not behave in the way she expected, Mary attempted to resolve her own anxiety — her arousal — by resorting to actions that were intended to force him to conform to her anticipations.

If the consulting psychologist wishes to give a complete explanation of either Mary's or Elena's conduct, he must come to grips with at least one more significant issue, *the origins of new behaviors*. For example, Elena might decide that on Tuesday evenings she would go bowling with some of the teachers at the school where she works. The psychologist's account of the acquisition of this novel behavior would, perhaps, be formulated in terms of modeling. Elena watches the other bowlers and, somehow, the visual input informs those neural patterns that regulate the movements by which she launches a nine-pound ball down a runway, albeit at first with modest results, which gradually improve.

The psychologist's specific position on each of these issues can be seen as deriving from a set of assumptions that underlie his theory of personality, whether or not he can state them explicitly.

METAPHYSICAL ASSUMPTIONS AS THEORETICAL CONSTRAINTS

Anyone who undertakes to develop a theory of personality can select a wide variety of criteria to assess its adequacy. This choice of criteria, in itself, will shape the evolution of the theory. If, for example, we believe that the science of personality should be based on "natural laws," a model of which might be the "law of effect," then we might be more satisfied with the concept of response as our basic unit of analysis than with the notion of construct. We would believe that a response can be charted precisely in terms of spatial and temporal dimensions. Moreover, we could propose to relate responses in time and space to other events, which we call stimuli. Those psychologists who assume a priori that spatiotemporal locations constitute our most accurate map of events are likely to use the response as their unit of analysis.

Thus, a metaphysical assumption, whether or not it is frankly examined, can impose specific constraints on a theory of personality with respect to the issues we have outlined. Also, our epistemological presuppositions, both explicit and implicit, define limits for our attempts to resolve each of these issues. For example, we may be satisfied only with certain types of proofs or, if we accept another notion of sophistication, disproofs. As a result, we may consider only those kinds of propositions that can be evaluated by the methods we have adopted. Unfortunately, problem and method often pass one another by.

Whatever their criteria of validity, or utility, most theorists would use a coherence test to evaluate their theory. That is, most of us would be embarrassed to discover that our attempt to resolve one issue resulted in a proposition that contradicted one or more propositions we have used to resolve other related questions. On the other hand, it is doubtful that any theory can be both wholly consistent and complete (Hofstadter, 1979).

Psychologists who try to explain the conduct of persons should address at least the five basic issues: the continuity of personality, the basic unit of analysis, the way in which a person's actions relate to other events, motivation and emotion (activation and direction), and the origins of new behaviors. A theory of personality should deal with these issues as completely as possible, while remaining as coherent as possible. Certain metatheoretical presuppositions can impose specific constraints on our attempts to resolve each of these issues.

PERSONAL CONSTRUCT THEORY

George Kelly (1955) developed his psychology of personal constructs within the explicit framework of a Fundamental Postulate and 11 corollaries. The structure of this volume is built on that basic framework. Each of the 12 remaining chapters takes one of these basic propositions as a specific point of departure in discussing current problems in the field of personality. Thus, it is useful to offer a foreview in which we consider, at the outset, the ways in which one might use the axiomatic principles of personal construct theory to address the five issues explicated in the foregoing paragraphs.

The first personality theory issue that we considered relates to matters of the continuity of personality. Kelly emphasized the regularities we encounter in our own experiences, including our experiences of others. These regularities reflect the fact that we systematically impose formal structure on all our personal experiences, that is, "Each person characteristically evolves, for his own convenience in anticipating events, a construction system embracing ordinal relationships between constructs" (Kelly, 1955, p. 56). Thus, when we interpret the conduct of others we assume that their actions are based on organized anticipations, or hypotheses, that function as do those that guide our own conduct. We make inferences about an individual's personality as we attempt to explain his or her behavior in terms of the unique system of personal constructs that informs it. Similarly, as personality theorists we explain an individual's continuity in terms of that person's organized system of personal constructs.

In attempting to make sense out of Mary Stone's relations with the men in her life, a personal construct theorist might focus primarily on how she construes her "core role." If seeing herself as sexually desirable is a central aspect of her self-concept, we can attempt to understand the implications of this within the context of her own construct system. For Mary, the alternative to desirable person, in her relations with men, might be exploited person. Thus, if Mary, at this point in her life, begins to have evidence that she is unwanted by Paul, she might be required to make a desperate reorganization of her system in order to be assured that Paul has not exploited her situation.

In terms of the second issue, Kelly adopted the personal construct as his basic unit of analysis. Each construct represents a single bipolar distinction, such as happy-sad. The form of the distinction is dichotomous. For example, if the same behavior could be interpreted simultaneously as expressing happiness and sadness in the same respect, then this construct would have no definite meaning. Kelly also assumed that each construct is useful for representing a single feature of a limited domain of events. Outside of this "range of convenience" the construct is not applicable.

For example, Elena Ferro may have developed a system of constructs that contains the distinction loyal-disloyal, which includes interpersonal relationships within its range of convenience. She can derive specific anticipations concerning her own behavior from her view of herself as a "loyal wife." On the other hand, when she loses money on a horse at the track, she does not construe the animal as disloyal. The situation is outside the range of convenience of that particular distinction. The success of the Ferros' marriage may depend, in part, on the extent to which Elena's husband understands what she means by loyalty and what specific expectations, concerning his behavior, she has based on this construct.

When Kelly adopted the construct as his basic unit of analysis, he also assumed a position on the third issue: the significance of "real" events in relation to human conduct. He assumed that the event in itself does not directly reveal its meaning to us. We, as construing persons, create the shared and the private meanings of events. In short, our systems of constructs allow us to assimilate and to represent our versions of events. We do not merely respond to stimulus input.

If we were to say that poor Mary is no longer in touch with reality, we are admitting that her actions are unintelligible to us, in terms of our own construing of her situation. Her behavior seems "irrational" in the sense that we ourselves cannot give any "rational" account of it. It is possible that we could understand her conduct, and even predict it, if we could discover which specific distinctions, within her own personal construct system, have guided her psychological processes.

Kelly's position with respect to our fourth issue is somewhat perplexing since his writings contain passages that specifically eschew the concept of motivation as a formal aspect of personal construct theory. Nonetheless, the fundamental postulate has definite implications relative to the motivational principles that inform the theory. The postulate contains this assertion: "A person's processes are psychologically channelized by the ways in which he anticipates events" (Kelly, p. 46). Thus, our personal constructs are fundamentally anticipatory in nature, that is, their function is to anticipate events. The person continually "moves" toward more and more successful prediction of his or her world of experience. It might also be said, within the framework of personal construct theory, that the person continually "moves" away from ultimate anxiety (see Chapter 7).

According to Kelly, anxiety is experienced whenever one is confronted with events that are outside the range of convenience of one's personal constructus, that is, one has no basis for anticipating them. In short, anxiety is being "caught with one's contructs down." He points out that, "from the standpoint of the psychology of personal constructs, anxiety, per se, is not to be classified as either good or bad. It represents the awareness that one's construction system does not apply to events at hand. It is, therefore, a precondition for making revisions" (p. 498).

If Elena were suddenly to find herself a widow, she might experience considerable anxiety. Within the framework of her personal construct system, her core role — her "self-concept" — is defined primarily in terms of her relationship with her husband. He serves as the main source of "validation" for her anticipations of her own behavior in terms of the personal constructs that are most important to her. Without him, she no longer knows what to expect of herself; that is, she is confused about how she can continue to enact the part of Elena Ferro without her husband playing his "supporting role." She may begin to isolate herself from others, because she no longer knows how to act, even in familiar situations or with old friends. In short, the death of her husband might transform her happily ordered world, in which she knows what to expect of Elena Ferro, into chaos. Her former poise and self-confidence might be replaced by confusion and anxiety.

If, at this point, Elena is ready to attempt to restructure her existence as a "widow," she must experiment with some novel behaviors. How does personal construct theory explain the origins of new behavior? As a theory of personality, it should provide some basis for developing a coherent account of how new patterns of action can become part of a continuing personality. According to Kelly, "new" ways of interpreting events permit us to deal with them in novel ways. That is, we can conduct experiments, using our own behavior as the "independent variable," to test hypotheses that are formulated by the rearrangement of constructs, within the hierarchic organization of our systems. We can then revise our hypotheses in light of the outcomes of our experiments. If we change our hypotheses in response to this "feedback," then we can design different experiments to test these new constructions. In short, new behaviors are seen as reflecting changes in the structure and, ultimately, in the content of our personal construct systems. Thus, new behavior emerges from our attempts to accommodate our constructs to events, thereby enhancing our capacity to anticipate our experience.

For example, Elena, as a widow, might undertake a "research project" in which she assumes the direction of her husband's business. At the outset, she might rely primarily upon her own understanding of the specific constructs that Mr. Ferro once had brought to bear on this task. Thus, in the beginning, she may frequently ask her assistants to explain how he typically had handled certain situations. Later on she might find that she can apply her own constructs to conducting the retail shoe business. As she gains confidence in her role as manager, she might become more interested in testing her own hypotheses than in replicating her husband's previous experiments, regardless of how successful their outcomes. In the course of this active program of experimentation, Elena could successfully elaborate a new core role for herself. Specifically, the role of "creative businesswoman" may evolve within her self-construing to replace that of "loyal wife."

The preceding brief analysis sketches the argument that personal construct psychology provides a comprehensive theoretical framework for the study of human personality. In the 12 chapters that follow, Kelly's basic principles are extensively elaborated in light of recent research and clinical studies concerned with the development of personality. The organization of this volume follows the formal structure of Kelly's Fundamental Postulate and 11 corollaries. Chapter 2 deals with the Fundamental Postulate itself; each of the other 11 chapters takes one of its corollaries as a point of departure.

Much of the work discussed in this volume derives from direct applications of the principles of personal construct theory to various clinical problems and to issues that are related by tradition to personality study — personal change, person perception, interpersonal relations, and child development. On the other hand, recent experimental and theoretical research in the areas of psycholinguistics, decision making, memory processes, problem solving, and other "cognitive" processes is reviewed in terms of its specific implications for the further elaboration of Kelly's Fundamental Postulate and corollaries. The analysis of these 12 propositions, in light of more than 25 years of research in human psychology since their initial formulation, provides a basis for extending the range of convenience of personal construct psychology with respect to the variety of problems to which it is applicable. At the same time, these analyses serve to enhance the overall coherence of Kelly's basic theoretical system.

2

ANTICIPATION AS A CONSTRUCTIVE PROCESS: THE FUNDAMENTAL POSTULATE

James C. Mancuso
Jack R. Adams-Webber

The Fundamental Postulate: A person's processes are psychologically channelized by the ways in which he anticipates events.

Kelly's (1955) theory of personality — personal construct theory — forthrightly focuses on a person's representation of events, taking overt response as one subset of representation. According to his Fundamental Postulate, all of our representations, including the represented action elements, are anticipatory. Human action, from the standpoint of Kelly's theory, flows from an intention to bring about a correspondence between a person's constructions of the future and his mental representations (personal constructions) of information-producing events. To perceive the source of human action a constructivist/contextualist psychologist construes events occurring "inside" the person.

When Kelly initially formulated his position, in 1955, he promoted a constructive alternative to the paradigm that underlay the "scientific behaviorism" then dominating psychology. When Kelly emphasized internal psychological functioning, rather than external parameters of action, he joined a minor faction of the world's psychological scientists. Piaget (1952, 1971a, b), whose long and prolific career totally spanned Kelly's professional career, provided a similar alternative to mechanistic behaviorism. Piaget's theory of cognitive development contains many elements that parallel those embodied in personal construct theory. As we shall see, Kelly and Piaget were in accord with Bartlett (1932), whose pioneering contributions to the understanding of perception, memory,

8

and thinking fared poorly in the mechanist ambience until they were incorporated into the influential works of Miller, Galanter, and Pribram (1960) and Neisser (1967). These latter works now represent the turning points in the "cognitive revolution," which has brought constructivist conceptions into psychology to rival seriously the concepts that guided mechanistic behaviorism.

RADICAL BEHAVIORISM AS A MODEL

In 1919 J. B. Watson systematized a position that focused on the proposition that behavior scientists could adequately explain all human action in terms of the mechanics of "stimulus-response" relationships. From this position psychologists were to develop the principal tenets of the school of psychology called "radical behaviorism" (Fodor, 1981). In a very short time, psychological scientists all over the earth, vigorously pursuing behavioristic formulations, pushed aside extant constructivist conceptions and elevated mechanism to the leading position. The implications of behaviorism have been developed most completely, both methodologically and philosophically, in the work of B. F. Skinner (1938, 1957). He submits that all behavior — even his own "verbal behavior" as a scientist (a point to which we shall return in a moment) — can be understood fully in terms of external events. These events are described as stimulus inputs to the organism, and these stimuli channelize its behavior. Skinner maintains that behavior can be completely predicted and controlled on the basis of present inputs to the organism, in that the organism's responses are related to its past history of inputs.

In his incisive critique of Skinner's model of "verbal behavior," Chomsky (1959) showed that such strict stimulus-response (S-R) formulations are of very limited theoretical significance from the standpoint of explaining human action, thought, and speech. Chomsky pointed out, among other considerations, the following basic dilemma. If, on the one hand, any external event to which the organism is capable of reacting is called the stimulus, and any part of the organism's activity is designated as the response, then it never has been demonstrated that behavior, in general, is lawful, when lawfulness demands probabilistic specifications of S-R relationships. If, on the other hand, only an event to which the organism does in fact respond is identified as a stimulus, and only that part of the organism's activity that is shown to be connected to that stimulus is considered a response, then behavior is lawful by definition. From this standpoint, however, most of what the organism does cannot then be called behavior. In a similar vein, Deese (1969) notes that psychology is the study of behavior only in a trivial sense, since if we limit the focus of our investigations to behavior per se, we will be forced to ignore altogether many important facts of experience. Perhaps the most important of these are the cognitive acts by which we represent and anticipate events.

A FUNCTIONAL APPROACH

Kelly, like Skinner, accepted the epistemological position that relates the truth statements in the behavioral sciences to successes in prediction and control. Kelly, however, took the novel step of eschewing the distinction between behavioral scientist and subject. He suggested that "it is not that Man is what Skinner makes of him, but rather what Skinner can do, Man can do — and more" (Kelly, 1969, p. 136). That is, our model of human nature should not be Skinner's model of a behaving organism, which Bannister (1966) characterized as essentially "a ping-pong ball with a memory." Rather, our model should be based on the conduct of Skinner himself; the person-as-scientist, whose processes are channelized by his attempts to predict and control events. In short, Kelly set out to develop a model of persons that can account for scientific activity as well as all other cognitive activities. In this sense, Kelly's theory is essentially self-referential (see Hofstadter, 1979). That is, personal construct theory is a system for anticipating events through prediction and control, which tries to explain how we go about anticipating events through prediction and control.

In formulating the basic assumptions of his model, Kelly returned to the prebehavioristic tradition of "functionalism" represented in British psychology by Francis Galton, and in American psychology most notably by William James and John Dewey. In his critical analysis of the reflex arc concept, Dewey (1896) had pointed out that, although the nominal stimulus usually can be identified as a "physical event" external to the person (that is, adequately described by a physicist), the functional stimulus (that which is of primary concern to the psychologist) is constituted by the anticipatory processes of the organism itself (see Koffka, 1935; Rotter, 1954). Kelly (1955, p. 129) noted that "Dewey emphasized the anticipatory nature of behavior . . . the psychology of personal constructs follows Dewey in this respect." Kelly (p. 157), however, went considerably beyond Dewey in interpreting the significance of anticipation in human action: "Where Dewey would have said that we understand events through anticipating them, we would add that our lives are wholly oriented toward the anticipation of events."

From the standpoint of personal construct theory, it is our own anticipations that define the meaning of events in relation to our behavior. "The subject of psychology is assumed at the outset to be a process" (p. 47), and as theorists, "we are conceptualizing processes in a psychological manner rather than something else" (p. 48). According to Kelly, a person's processes can be viewed as "channelized" within a "network of pathways" leading toward the future, that is, as fundamentally anticipatory.

> Here is where we build into our theory its predictive and motivational features. Like the prototype of the scientist that he is, man seeks prediction. His structured network of pathways leads toward the future so that he may anticipate it. This is the *function* it serves.

Anticipation is both the push and the pull of the psychology of personal constructs (Kelly, 1955, p. 49, italics added).

This argument is, as was noted above, clearly self-referential. Personal construct theory is itself a system of personal constructs, developed by a scientist, for anticipating events. In short, personal construct theory also refers to itself as a theory (see Bannister, 1969).

ANTICIPATION AS A PSYCHOLOGICAL CONSTRUCT

A psychological theory that presumes that the anticipation of events channelizes a person's processes should provide a useful construction for the term *anticipates*. Specifically, the Construction Corollary (see Chapter 3) asserts that "a person anticipates events by construing their replications" (Kelly, 1955, p. 50). This proposition does not necessarily imply that the "same" event actually ever repeats itself. The Construction Corollary does assert, however, that a person's anticipations are a matter of his ascribing certain recurrent "themas" as he successively construes events.

Schemata

Our understanding of the process of successive construction might be facilitated by a detailed analysis of the concept schema and its use in related theories of cognitive activity, namely those of Bartlett, Piaget, and Neisser. This concept, first introduced into psychology by Head (1920), has proved useful in the explanation of processes as disparate as motor action (Schmidt, 1976) and the use of metaphor (Ortony, 1979). Of particular relevance to the present discussion is the way in which Bartlett employed the notion of schema in his classical analysis of memory. He defined the term *schema* as follows:

"Schema" refers to an active organization of past reactions, or of past experiences, which must always be supposed to be operating in any well-adapted organic response. That is, whenever there is any order or regularity of behavior, a particular response is possible only because it is related to other similar responses which have been serially organized, yet which operate, *not simply as individual members coming after one another, but as a unitary mass* (Bartlett, 1932, p. 201, italics added).

According to Bartlett, any perceived similarity between two or more events must depend on underlying tendencies (active schemata), which lead to the grouping together of items of input, which possess a welter of diverse sensory characteristics. It must be the case that whenever two or more events, separated by an interval of time, are perceived as the "same," some kind of information is retained during the interval. From the perspective of personal construct theory, Bartlett's primary contribution to our understanding of this process was his insight that "in all cases recognizing is rendered possible by the carrying over of orientation, or attitude, from the original presentation to the representation" (Bartlett, p. 193).

He assumed that the perception of events involves both the simple registration of sensory patterns (input) and the use of these sensory data in the construction of something that has significance that extends beyond their immediate sensory character. Although a given stimulus may possess some degree of "reactive significance" at the level of neurophysiological analysis, as soon as the reacting person becomes aware of the material with which his or her reactions deal, there is meaning. Bartlett referred to the process of connecting a particular stimulus input with some preformed setting (schema) as an "effort after meaning." In this sense, even the most elementary perceptual acts involve anticipation.

Reconstruction and Recognition

As Kelly (1955) put the case, events do not directly reveal their meanings; rather it is a person's anticipations — his or her "effort after meaning" — that lend whatever significance objects may have in relation to one's activities. In short, it is always one's anticipations that determine the meaning of an event. The question is how can people recognize a given event as the "same" as or as "different" from that which they had anticipated. For example, let us suppose that a person recognizes a currently perceived event as the "same" as one he had observed on a previous occasion. Since this kind of recognition is frequently quite detailed, there must be some way in which specific "information" is preserved within the perceiving system from the first to the second occasion.

The traditional solution to this problem appeals to the notion that recognition of the "same" event on a subsequent occasion requires the re-exitation of a specific "trace" or comparison with a preserved template or abstract copy of the previous sensory input. A short logical exercise shows that this solution begs the question. As Asch (1969) points out, it still leaves open the issue of how the present stimulus input can make contact with the correct trace or template without prior recognition, which is what we wish to explain in the first place.

It seems clear that, in order for a person to recognize the "same" event on a second occasion, the new sensory data (input) must exert some control over the perception of similarity. That is, there must exist common properties in the two stimulus patterns that the processes of cognition are prepared to seize upon and elaborate (Neisser, 1976). Thus, even if perception on each occasion involves certain inferential constructions, the input information must play a role in accurate recognition. In short, whenever there is repeated perception of the "same" event, the stimulus patterns that activate sensory neurons are presumed to have something in common (Neisser, 1967). Nonetheless, something more is required.

Cognitive Structures and Input

Bartlett (1932) suggests that there is a gradual building up of cognitive structures (schemata) that are nonspecific but organized representations of a great many previous acts of construction. Despite the fact that these structures consist of the residue (traces) of previous cognitive acts, they do not represent these separate acts individually. Nor are they dormant copies of events, which are revived from time to time. They are residues of previous cognitive acts that are organized in that they have regular and controlling interrelations that are elaborated in the course of our ongoing cognitive activities. In short, cognitive structures are used, not aroused (see Neisser, 1967).

Following Bartlett, Neisser (1967) submits that a psychological system stores information about its own constructive processes rather than the products of those constructions. That is, the information that is retained consists of traces of similar acts of construction, and it is organized in ways that correspond to the structure of those acts. These cognitive structures (schemata) control the fate of information that is to be stored and are themselves information of a similar kind. Thus, they are integral parts of all of our memories, and they also provide articulate patterns into which new material can be assimilated. In the latter sense they are fundamentally anticipatory. As Kelly (1955, p. 79) notes, "one does not learn certain things merely from the nature of the stimuli which play upon him . . . [but] only what his cognitive framework is designed to permit him to see in the stimuli."

Perceiving and Remembering

It follows that "stimulus input" does not appear directly in awareness. Events do not impose their impressions upon a passive receptor, nor are they reproduced in overt or covert responses. As Bartlett points out, even the most elementary perceptual processes involve inferential constructions that go beyond the available stimulus data.

Similarly, to think of the recall of an event we cannot think of reviving a veridical trace that has been stored and that remains in the psychological system. Memory is also a constructive process in which there is the creation of something new in each act of remembering. Nor do we think of the same construction repeatedly appearing and reappearing. Rather we think of an elaborate process of reconstruction that makes use of stored information consisting of traces of prior acts of construction. This stored information is not simply retrieved as a whole, but rather it is used to support a new construction. The memory is manufactured out of the active schemata of the moment.

Both recall and recognition depend on the use of certain schemata for the reason that the original perceptions were elaborated in terms of similar schemata. In Kelly's (1955, p. 74) words, "Thus, the recurrent themes that make life seem so full of meaning are the original symphonic compositions of a man bent on finding the present in his past and the future in his present." It follows that learning, which is the main concern of behaviorists, does not consist merely of acquiring specific responses in connection with specific stimuli. A new construction can be synthesized with the aid of information about a prior act of construction, but the two constructions are rarely, if ever, identical. Constructions are wholes whose ends are prefigured (anticipated) in their beginnings. To borrow a phrase from Piaget (1960), a construction is a "gestalt with a history" or, in more precise terms, "Perception itself does not consist in a mere recording of sensorial data, but includes an active organization in which decisions and preinferences intervene and which is due to the influence of perception as such on this schematism of actions or of operations (Piaget, 1971a, pp. 86-87).

In short, constructions are not organized as, nor do they arise from, chains of connected stimulus-response units. "Associations in the sense of connections between reappearing traces or responses do not exist" (Neisser, 1967, p. 97). Although the sequential use of similar constructions allows either the recognition or the recall of the "same" event on different occasions, our successive constructions of events are not necessarily derivable from one another. As Neisser (1967) notes, the whole conception of structured cognitive processes is quite different from that of a response sequence. In Kelly's (1955, p. 83) terms,

> new constructs are not necessarily derivatives of, or special cases within, one's old constructs. . . . It should make even clearer the assumed necessity for seeking out the regnant construct system in order to explain the behavior of men, rather than seeking merely to explain each bit of behavior as a derivative of its immediately antecedent behavior.

Our personal constructs, together with available stimulus data and overt actions, are integral parts of a continually flowing psychological context. A person's evolving constructions — "The organism's picture of itself and its universe" (Miller, Galanter, and Pribram, 1960, p. 7) — are the stuff by which input is anticipated.

SCHEMATA AS ANTICIPATIONS

In a contextualist model of persons, where schemata are a central strand in the context, one's anticipations are nothing other than the schemata that are assembled to incorporate, integrate, or assimilate the incoming information. In that all input becomes input only by its integration to a person's construction system, then one's processes are, indeed, channelized by his anticipations of events.

To demonstrate the utility of the foregoing robust assertion, one may draw upon the large literature on memory and retrieval that has developed from information processing approaches to recall and recognition. Additionally, numerous studies of prose processing have demonstrated the utility of thinking about signal interpretation in terms of a person's imposing of his own personal structure on input. Some illustrative examples will contribute to the development of this treatise.

Schemata, Recall, and Recognition

Spiro (1980, 1977) provides valuable direction and clarification of the place of schemata in current theory. Spiro would agree with Greeno (1980, pp. 718-19) in conceptualizing schemata as "data structures or procedures that are used to organize the components of specific experience and to expand the representation of an experience or message to include components that were not specifically contained in the experience but are needed to make the representation coherent and complete in some important sense." Specific experience involving an interaction between immediate input and the knowledge network of the person are to be discussed as constructive processes. Spiro (1980, p. 84) distinguishes these processes from reconstruction, "a process of inferring the past rather than reproducing stored traces of past experience." Both processes, nevertheless, would be regarded as memory processes. Construction and reconstruction involve the use of stored knowledge to organize specific experience.

Spiro, having concluded that experimental work (see, for examples, Anderson and Ortony, 1975; Bransford, Barclay and Franks, 1972) had amply shown the utility of constructivist concepts, sought to establish more firmly his conceptions about reconstruction. Spiro's thinking begins with an effort to clarify the conditions that affect accuracy in recall and reconstruction. Following Bartlett, various researchers have taken inaccuracy in long-term recall to be an indication that the person draws from his existing memory store to reconstruct an event; often infusing the reconstruction with elements that were not in the event's context, but that, nevertheless, fit into the recall schema. "Remembering the old information would then require constructing an interpretation that coheres with the relevant knowledge available in the present. It is this attempt to accommodate the past to imperfectly cohering present knowledge that should produce gross recall error" (Bartlett, 1932, p. 85).

Spiro set out to show that a change in a person's knowledge network could retroactively affect a prose sequence that had been construed earlier, so that recall of that prose should contain coherence-enhancing distortions and importation. Spiro worked with prose that described events that would be subsumed by people's implicit personality theories, so that the persons who participated in the study would build schemata that derived from their underlying assumptions about the workings of interpersonal relationships. The study's participants heard varied stories about a young engaged couple who talked about their views on having children. The man did not want to have children. In some stories the social situation was balanced, in that the woman held the same negative view. In others there was imbalance, in that the woman wanted to have children. It was assumed that those who heard the stories would construct schemata, in the initial experience with the prose, that would contain inferences imported from the person's general implicit personality theory. If the structure was balanced, those hearing the story would use their existing constructs to infer a positive relationship. If the structure was imbalanced, the anticipation would be that the relationship between the couple would be negative.

Subsequent to hearing the original prose passage, some of the subjects who heard "balanced stories" were told that the couple were happily married and living together (married outcome). Others were told that the couple had terminated their engagement to marry (unmarried outcome). Thus, some of the "balanced" participants heard the congruent outcome, whereas others heard incongruent outcomes. The same generalization would be made about those who heard the unbalanced outcome. Participants who heard about the couple's having disagreed heard an expected outcome — separation — whereas others heard an unexpected outcome — continued association. Finally, other participants were given no information about outcome.

Spiro (1980, p. 86) reasons, "If the accommodative reconstruction hypothesis is correct, three sources of information will be blended over time: remembered details from the story, the subsequent information, and general knowledge about interpersonal relations. . . ." One would expect that having heard the incongruent outcomes (balanced-unmarried, unbalanced-married) would promote the operation of reconstructive processes that would increase coherence. For example, a participant who had heard an unbalanced-married story, providing he retains the same structure to his implicit personality theory, should erroneously recall elements describing a reconciliation of the couple.

The results of Spiro's study clearly validated the reconstructivist position as he had developed it with respect to his study. When subjects had been led to believe that the study was focused on problems entailed in understanding interpersonal interactions, recall errors appeared with high frequency in the recall efforts made by those participants who had heard outcomes that were contradictory to outcomes that would have been anticipated from the context that had generated the participants' schematization of the story. Furthermore, with increases in the time interval between the original experience and the recall efforts, there was an increase in the number of participants' stories that included errors that "corrected for" incoherence between expectation and outcome.

Some examples illustrate the "reschematization" that resulted from incongruencies. A participant who had heard a story in which the couple disagreed about having children and then were reported to have been married successfully made the following recall error: "They discussed it and decided they could agree on a compromise, adoption" (p. 91). Another participant, who had heard a balanced story, made sense of the incongruent failure of the couple's relationship by recalling that they had *disagreed* about having children.

One could argue that the participants' final reconstructions of the stories, that is, their "anticipations" of the outcomes, represented a process of filling in gaps in a conscious storytelling exercise. Spiro collected data on participants' certainty that they had heard the "erroneous" details they had reported. Participants, in fact, were more certain of having heard the erroneous details than of having heard the confirmable "true" details.

Spiro concludes as follows:

> It would appear that recall is, at times, not based on the retrieval of stored traces of interpreted experiences. Rather, recall involves a process of accommodating details of what is to be remembered to what is known at the time of recall. In other words, the past is not reproduced, but is reconstructed, guided by one's knowledge-based principles of coherence (p. 94).

From a personal construct theory perspective, one could say that the schemata constructed to integrate the recall experience have been derived from a context that includes the person's construction system. The participants would anticipate the "true" story to be a match of that which they have created. Thus, the ways in which participants anticipate interpersonal events is shown to have channelized the process of reconstructing the story of the engaged couple's relationship.

Schemata in Prose Processing

When one adopts a constructivist position and enters any area of psychological study one would be unable to exclude memoric processes from consideration. If input is always processed in terms of a person's existing knowledge structures, then memory processes are always involved in the retrieval of constructions that are impressed on to input. Thus, studies of text or prose processing would be conducted from the assumption that "reading is externally guided thinking" (Neisser, 1967, p. 136), during which a person brings to bear his or her construction system to develop schemata that will account for the material to be comprehended. In this way, the schemata, built from the contents of long-term memory and imposed on the text, represent the reader's anticipations of events.

A constructivist would believe that a reader looking at a word in a text draws from his own construction system to impose a particular meaning on the word. One of the more forthright demonstrations of this process was devised by Anderson and Ortony (1975). They had their participating people process, among a series of other sentences, the sentence, "The apples are in the container." The word *container* may have many meanings in this sentence. Among other things it might mean, simply, an amorphous box. It can be shown, however, that recall of this sentence will be raised considerably if the cue word *basket* is presented to participants. The word *bottle* does not facilitate recall of the "apple sentence." Other results are obtained if participants process the sentence, "The cola is in the container." In this case, *basket* does not facilitate recall, whereas *bottle* does. One may believe, then, that readers actively impose specific anticipatory schema on to polysemous words. The word itself does not contain the meaning.

Such activity goes on in all discourse interpretation, and the success of conversation depends on the narrator's skill in framing his prose to fit the knowledge network of his communication partner. (Kelly [1955] incorporated this principle in the Sociality Corollary, "To the extent that one person construes the construction processes of another, he may play a role in a social process involving the other person" [p. 95].) Winograd (1977, p. 78) cites some examples.

- Examining the cabinet, we noticed that a door was marred.
- When the presidential plane arrived at Dulles airport, the reporters were greeted by (a/the) sullen and snappish Henry Kissinger.

In the first example, the narrator will assume that the processor will build a schema around the belief that one of several possible doors was marred. The same kind of conclusion would be extracted if *a*, rather than *the* were used in the second example sentence. Many Henry Kissingers may be schematized! *The* one that was at the airport was *a* Henry K. — the sullen and snappish one. Of course, in a very special circumstance a speaker might say, "Well, when we were there, we met the sullen and snappish Kissinger," providing the kind of inflection that would lead the listener to conclude that this was only one of the many Kissingers that might have been encountered. Thus, inflection as well as the phonetic pattern of the word stimulates the prose processor to bring his semantic memory system to the comprehension of narrative.

In addition to providing schemata for individual words, readers carry a larger structure to prose passages. In the course of their experience with stories, people develop and use anticipatory schema regarding structure of the text. People take to a story a previously learned organizational framework, which is then used to comprehend and encode information in a particular text. People construe stories as they do sentences, processing the context within a framework of structural formalities that might be spelled out as one would define syntax rules. People expect to find narrative dependencies, such as cause and effect relationships, goal seeking, and conflict resolutions, and these expectancies are imposed on the narratives to guide comprehension. Further, if the use of these kinds of anticipatory schemata do aid comprehension, then memory and recall would be enhanced, since the ability to relate new information to existing structure will influence storage and retrieval from long-term memory.

An active group of investigators (Kintsch, 1977; Mandler and Johnson, 1977; Rumelhart, 1975; Thorndyke, 1977; van Dijk, 1977) have reported studies of the ways in which schemata representing these macrostructures are imposed on narrative. Thorndyke's report is illustrative. He assumed that a schematic grammar would be brought to bear by participants who would read simple, prototypical narratives. Using an analysis reported by Rumelhart, Thorndyke extracted a story grammar that he believed would be the kind of representational framework that would be used by those who would process the stories he presented.

On a more general level, Thorndyke follows the reasoning chain that states that such stereotypical narrative frameworks underlie the processing of all discourse. These schemata can be modified to fit the particulars of any story by enumerating the concrete deatils — the variables — that map into the abstract and general schemata.

Thorndyke set out to validate the utility of these concepts by showing that comprehension and recall of a story would be deteriorated if the people attempted to process stories in which the rules of narrative grammar had been violated. He devised four versions of two different stories. Each version of each story was intended to represent a variation in the level to which the narrative concurred to the inferred narrative framework that underlay the stories. One version, of course, was the straight story, which clearly contained propositions stating the setting, theme, plot, and resolution of the narrative. Another version represented gross variation from the standard macrostructure, in that the principal goal of the story's protagonists was completely deleted from the passage.

After the participants had been presented the stories, they were asked to rate the comprehensibility of the narrative they had processed. In addition, participants were tested for recall of the story by a variety of techniques. Analysis of the findings of this study leads to the unequivocal conclusion that "memory and comprehension were best when an incoming text matched up readily with a standard, well-learned structural hierarchy of goal-directed episode sequences" (Thorndyke, 1977, p. 95). Participants rated the stories as being more comprehensible if they more clearly adhered to the expected narrative grammar. They also recalled greater percentages of the propositions in the story if it were more reflective of the structure that the participants were assumed to have brought to the story. Similarly, the adherence to expected structure facilitated the recognition of true statements from the story.

Thus, Thorndyke has produced results that indicate that people take "macropropositions" to their reading of a text. These macropropositions, which follow from the person's implicit theory of how stories work, allow inferences from the propositions that are directly cued by the language of the text. Such inferences serve to provide summary structure to the text, and allow for long-term memory storage in terms of abstract frames or scripts, so that the gist of a story is easily recalled by cuing the abstract frame along with specific variables that fit the frame for the narrative under discussion.

Development of Macrostructure

Two other studies (Kintsch, 1977; Mandler and Johnson, 1977) provide an extension of the concepts by which one may discuss macrostructure in narrative. Both are important because the investigators asked questions about the developmental history of the schemata by which narrative is structured.

Kintsch and his associates set out to demonstrate the ways in which macrostructures affected story processing in four-year-old children enrolled in a preschool. The investigators used pictures to induce storytelling among these nonreading children. They used a procedure that paralleled that used by Thorndyke (1977). They took the pictures from two children's storybooks. The children were asked to describe the pictures. In one condition the pictures were presented in the order in which they had appeared in the books. In another condition the pictures were scrambled. After completing the picture descriptions the children were asked to tell a story. Their performance on this part of the task was used as a measure of recall.

These investigators assumed that the children's existing and implicitly used macrostructure would be important to processing the story input. The preschool child's story grammar would not be readily applicable to the scrambled picture. Thus, description and recall would be hindered.

To provide a base of comparison Kintsch's group asked 24 adults to write one or two brief sentences for each picture. They were instructed to describe the portrayed events that would be central to the story associated with the pictures. After analysis of the adult productions, about 25 "core propositions" were obtained for each story. By using these statements as a baseline, the investigators could ask a variety of questions about how the children's narrative-defining macrostructure would affect the children's processing of the stories.

When the pictures were presented in a normal order, that is, following the story as presented, the average child used about 10 of the adult core propositions to describe the pictures. They used about 7.5 core statements to describe the scrambled pictures. At the same time they used more (5.8) spurious propositions when telling about the scrambled pictures than when telling about the normal pictures. The data regarding "story propositions" and recall more clearly showed the effect of macrostructure. Story propositions are statements that do not derive directly from the pictures, but are drawn as inferences through implicitly relating the pictures. The children responding to the normal-ordered pictures used an average of 10 "correct" story propositions to describe the normal-ordered pictures, and an average of 14 "correct" story propositions in recall of these pictures. The children responding to scrambled pictures used an average of 5 core story propositions to describe and 2 such propositions to recall the story.

These and other data reported by Kintsch further validate the hypothesis that four-year-old children profit from being able to impose their narrative-interpreting systems to schematize input. Their findings complement those that show the use of macrostructure in adults, and they are enhanced by the work of Mandler and Johnson (1977). These latter investigators had children listen to stories and then asked for recall of what had been heard. First-graders, compared to fourth-graders, recalled relatively fewer "story nodes" describing attempts and endings, while doing relatively well with settings, beginnings, and outcomes. Nevertheless, the first-graders functioned as did the fourth-graders and the adults in that they retrieved more setting, beginning, and outcome nodes than they retrieved attempts, endings, clauses, and reactions nodes.

The point to be made is as follows: Processing of narrative is guided, facilitated, and organized by the person's anticipations with regard to story structure. If his experiences have led to the development of a narrative grammar that allows him to anticipate the progress of the prose, he can more readily process, store, and recall the story's contents.

Constructions, Learning, and Adaptation

The foregoing studies of the development of macrostructure proceed from the assumption that one acquires macrostructure through "learning." Experience with stories allows the anticipatory structures used to process stories. Kelly (1955, p. 75) contends that "when we accept the assumption that a person's construction system varies as he successively construes the replication of events [Experience Corollary — see Chapter 9], together with the antecedent assumption that the course of all psychological processes is plotted by one's constructions of events [Fundamental Postulate], we have pretty well bracketed the topic learning." Viewed in this light, learning is not a special class of psychological process, but rather is synonymous with all psychological process.

> Construction is systematic in that it falls into a pattern having features of regularity. Since construing is a kind of refinement process involving abstraction and generalization, it is a way of looking at events as having a kind of identity with each other and as not being wholly unique. These features of identity and regularity are given shape through construction which itself has been shaped up as a system (Kelly, pp. 72-73).

In the same vein, Bartlett (1932) pointed out that if we retained the effects of experience in unchanged form, we could not adapt at all. Indeed, adaptive variation is the rule in perception and recall (Neisser, 1976). The same can be said in problem solving. That is, we do not solve problems by reviving relations that already exist, but by constructing new ones (Neisser, 1967). From the standpoint of contextualist psychology, life can be viewed as the continuous play of adaptation between our own changing constructions and environmental variation. The way in which Kelly formulated his Fundamental Postulate makes the problem of adaptation the central issue in personal construct psychology:

> If we are to see a person's psychological processes operating within a system which he constructs, we need also to account for the evolution of the system itself in a similarly lawful manner (p. 77). . . . Since our Fundamental Postulate establishes the anticipation of events as the objective of psychological processes, it follows that the successive revelation of events invites the person to place new constructions upon them whenever something unexpected happens. *Otherwise one's anticipations would become less and less realistic.* . . . The constructions one places on events are working hypotheses which are about to be put to the test of experience. As one's anticipations are successively revised in the light of the unfolding sequence of events, a construction system undergoes a progressive evolution (p. 72, italics added, though we hedge at the use of the word *realistic*).

Thus, according to Kelly, variations in the organization of our psychological processes occur primarily in response to "invalidation" of our anticipations by events. It follows that, in the normal course of development of a "personal construct system," it is the novelty of those events that do not "fit into" current psychological structure that stimulates change in its organization. That is, new structure evolves within a person's construct system to accommodate to events that lie outside the range of convenience (see Chapter 8 on Range Corollary) of its existing structure.

Kelly (p. 533) specifically refers to "the awareness that the events with which one is confronted lie outside the range of convenience of his construct system" as anxiety. Thus, the concept anxiety plays a central role in adaptation according to Kelly (p. 498): "From the standpoint of the psychology of personal constructs, anxiety, per se, is not to be classified as either good or bad. It represents the awareness that one's construction system does not apply to events at hand. It is, therefore, a precondition for making revisions." It would seem to follow that without anxiety, as defined by Kelly, our psychological processes could not accommodate to events in a constantly changing environment.

Piaget's basic "motivational" concept, the need-to-function, appears to play a role that is analogous to the role played by the concept anxiety in Kelly's theory. Piaget assumes that a need-to-function arises from the temporary instability of schematic organization (disequilibration) following an attempt to assimilate a novel event into a psychological system in which there has not developed the schemata that can be accommodated to that event. The novelty of the event, in terms of existing schematic organization, will precipitate a "circular reaction" of reciprocal assimilation and accommodation, producing modifications of structural relations within schematic organization, until the latter has become accommodated to the characteristics of the new event and the system as a whole has become equilibrated.

According to Piaget (1960) the ideal end-point of psychological adaptation is a hypothetical level of development at which the introduction of novelty does not create any disequilibrium in schematic organization. That is, any newly assimilated event will no longer alter mental structures that refer to it, nor the relations of mental structures to each other. Thus, "the structure of operational wholes is conserved while they assimilate new elements" (p. 108).

Piaget (1969, p. 165) views the function of every schema within a psychological system as "the part (i.e., the sector of activity or functioning sector) played by a sub-structure in relation to the functioning of the total structure and, by extension, the action of the total functioning on the functioning of substructures." In a similar vein, Kelly (1955) contends, "We can be sure only that the changes that take place from old to new constructs do so within a larger system (p. 83) . . . [and] one's personal constructs can only be changed within subsystems of constructs and subsystems within more comprehensive systems" (p. 79). In other words, adaptive variation involves the progressive evolution of the system as an integrated whole, not simply the acquisition of new responses.

ANTICIPATION, SURPRISE, AND MOTIVATION

In his lucid effort to promote a psychology of purposive systems, Powers (1973, 1978) distinguishes between sensory inputs and reference inputs. The comparator is an essential feature of Powers' cybernetic model of a behavioral control system. Sensory input is compared to the reference signal that has been preset and established in the comparator. Behavior might then be instigated to "correct" the external environment so that the stimulus pattern from the altered "out there" matches the reference signal in the comparator. Powers (1973, p. 419) says specifically:

The information reaching the subtractor or comparator by that path [reference input] is by definition and function the *reference signal*. Engineers show reference signals as inputs because artificial control systems are meant for use by human beings, who will operate the system by setting its reference input to indicate the desired value of the controlled variable. In nature control systems are set by processes inside the organism and are not accessible from the outside.

In the language we have established in the foregoing sections of this chapter, Powers would be saying that a person's internally set anticipations represent his purpose. Persons *intend* to produce environmental change that, in turn, alters available sensory input so that there is a match between the sensory input and the schemata that the workings of the person's system has devised as the reference signal. One can say in everyday terms: people try to avoid excessive surprise.

The Concept of Surprise

Mancuso (1977) reviewed the then current motivational concepts applicable to personal construct theory. He summarized a series of studies on novelty and attention and then made a statement that parallels Powers' propositions.

A person's processes — his conduct — are directed toward those events which are incongruent with the internalized structures against which information has been monitored. Resolution of discrepancy occupies the major part of a person's life activity. At the same time, prolonged immersion in a state approaching absolute absence of discrepancy also "motivates," in that attention is diverted toward low-discrepancy material following periods of high redundancy (pp. 65-66).

The concept of moderate discrepancy as the major motivational notion has been explored and analyzed to the point that Berlyne (1978, p. 133) was able to say:

Bearing all this in mind, we can see that the principal collative variables can be interpreted in terms of, at least, subjective information theory. For instance, a stimulus that is novel will have had low frequency of occurrence either among all events that the subject has ever encountered (when long-term novelty is involved) or among the events that have been perceived in the recent past (when it is a matter of short-term novelty). It will, therefore, have a high information content. A surprising event is one that has low probability in a particular context or following a particular signal that generates a particular expectation, so that high information can once again be inferred.

Surprise, Arousal, and Attention

From this conclusion Berlyne goes on to elaborate the connections between the concept of surprise and arousal. In this posthumously published analysis of motivation, Berlyne brought to bear a large body of work to show a direct, positive relationship between the level of subjective uncertainty and general arousal. Furthermore,

as Lindsley [1957] has put it, rises in arousal have repercussions on efferent processes, afferent processes, and central processes. In other words, they tend to mean increases in the vigor, speed, and efficiency of bodily movements (the amount of effort invested in them — Kahneman, 1973), in the sensitivity and information-gathering capacities of the sense organs, and in the ability of the brain to discriminate, analyze, and base decisions on incoming and stored information. There are plenty of indications that all these functions are at their peak when arousal is moderately high but decline when arousal approaches its upper extreme, thus conforming to the inverted-U-shaped curves that have been much discussed in the relevant literature (p. 152).

Thus, the line of thought connecting subjective uncertainty, arousal, and attention leads directly to the proposition that a person's processes are channelized by the schematizations that he can bring to bear to reduce high levels of subjective uncertainty. So long as a person is "certain," that is, so long as he can impose schemata that allow him to anticipate appropriately, he need not attend to the constantly arriving sensory input.

AROUSAL AND STANDARD BUILDING

To this point in this treatise we have spoken of schema building, representation, encoding, surprise, arousal, and so forth. The evidence for the utility of these concepts has been drawn from observations of people's psychological functioning, and our discussion contains no effort to anchor these concepts in concrete neurological concepts. The progress is built on a principle that is in agreement with Neisser (1967, p. 6) when he says, "But psychology is not just 'something to do until the biochemist comes.' " Nevertheless, a psychological system that is built on a Fundamental Postulate that ultimately attributes attention to a person's failure to anticipate would benefit from useful physiological explanation of the context that includes anticipation, failure, arousal, attention, and action. At least, it would be helpful to know that one may build a physiological model that parallels the psychological model and to know that the physiological model is something more than a science fiction fantasy.

There has been a neurophysiological tradition to support concepts like those used by Berlyne. Following models developed by Sokolov (1963), neuroscientists have validated the conclusion that the orienting reflex is a function of a match between a neuronal "model," or a patterned memory trace, and sensory input. Investigations (Grandstaff and Pribram, 1972) have shown that the arousal reaction is obtained by either increase or decrease of stimulus intensity, following the organism's having developed an expectancy. In a later section, we shall refer to Pribram and McGuiness' (1975) review of the physiological concomitants of failure to anticipate. These concepts remain broad and nonspecific.

Grossberg (1980, p. 7) became much more specific when he laid out the foundation of a recent paper:

The central theoretical theme will be, How can a coding error be corrected if no individual cell knows that one has occurred . . . erroneous cues can accidentally be incorporated into a code . . . and will only become evident when our environmental expectations become more demanding. . . . Furthermore, we never have an absolute criterion of whether our understanding of a fixed environment is faulty, or the environment that we thought we understood is no longer the same.

If a coding pattern, or schema, is activated, how can the central nervous system "know" that the schema is or is not an "error?"

It will be useful to observe some of Grossberg's effort to describe "how does the brain build a cognitive code?" Grossberg (p. 9) begins by positing fields of neural cells, and lets one field, $F^{(1)}$, represent the field at a distal level (sensory, lateral geniculate body) and another field, $F^{(2)}$, represent a more central coding. In addition to the straight-line $F^{(1)}$ to $F^{(2)}$ neural paths, Grossberg postulates a learned feedback from $F^{(2)}$ to $F^{(1)}$. The pattern of cells at $F^{(2)}$, designated as $X_1{}^2$, is the schematization of what is expected at $F^{(1)}$, which stands ready to receive the feedback. "The feed-forward data sensory input, for example to $F^{(1)}$ and the learned feedback expectancy, or template, from $F^{(2)}$ to $F^{(1)}$ are thereupon compared at $F^{(1)}$ [Powers' (1973) comparator]."

The second design problem that Grossberg (p. 10) overcomes is stated as follows: "How does the mismatch of patterns across a field $F^{(1)}$ of cells inhibit activity across $F^{(1)}$?" Grossberg carries forth a logic chain built on his own resolution to the noise-saturation dilemma (see Grossberg, 1977, 1978) and reaches the conclusion that "mismatched input patterns quench activity, whereas matched patterns amplify activity across a field $F^{(1)}$ that is capable of noise suppression" (p. 12). The next step in Grossberg's reasoning takes up the matter of suppressing the activity of $F^{(2)}$, the point at which the nonuseful schema is represented. In the neural system envisioned by Grossberg, $F^{(1)}$, the comparator, has no way of "knowing" which part of the erroneous schema at $F^{(2)}$ is the source of mismatch. Thus, the detection of mismatch at $F^{(1)}$ must be associated with a general effect on all of the field, $F^{(2)}$. "How does a mismatch and subsequent quenching of activity across $F^{(1)}$ elicit a nonspecific signal (arousal!) to $F^{(2)}$" (p. 12)? Grossberg draws on the long-available work of Hebb (1955) and Moruzzi and Magoun (1949). He concludes (p. 13): "Sensory inputs to $F^{(1)}$ bifurcate before they reach $F^{(1)}$. One pathway is specific: It delivers information about the sensory event $F^{(1)}$. The other pathway is nonspecific: It activates the arousal mechanism that is capable of nonspecifically influencing $F^{(2)}$." If activity at $F^{(1)}$ is associated with sensory input, however, and if sensory input is associated with nonspecific arousal, what prevents arousal at $F^{(2)}$ during *any* sensory input? Grossberg returns to his earlier conclusion that mismatch of the feedback (from $F^{(2)}$) and feedforward patterns (from sensory input), at $F^{(1)}$, quenches activity at $F^{(1)}$. He decides that arousal at $F^{(2)}$ is present when there is a mismatch at $F^{(1)}$ but is not present when there is straightforward sensory activity at $F^{(1)}$. This happens because "activity at $F^{(1)}$ inhibits the arousal pathway, and quenching associated with mismatch of this activity disinhibits the arousal pathway" (p. 13). Thus, at any time that a mismatching pattern quenches activity at $F^{(1)}$, the arousal action is disinhibited so that high arousal is developed at $F^{(2)}$, the field in which the "erroneous" pattern had been evoked.

The next problem in the model building process is stated as follows: "How does the increment in nonspecific arousal differentially shut off the active cells in $F^{(2)}$" (p. 13)? A differential suppression at $F^{(2)}$ is required. The active cells led to the failure-to-anticipate situation. These must be shut off when the nonspecific arousal arrives at $F^{(2)}$. Furthermore, these cells must be blocked until a new pattern of cell firings can be established at $F^{(2)}$. The blockage must take place in real time, for there must be retrieval from long-term memory to build a new cell field at $F^{(2)}$. Thus, a given paradox must be resolved in a way that allows us to continue to view Grossberg's model as sane and logical. The paradox can be crudely stated as follows: How can arousal shut down active cells in a field while incrementing activity in other cells in the same field?

To resolve this paradox Grossberg carefully develops the conception of antagonistic rebound. For our purposes, let us simply summarize this highly significant concept by referring to that notion which so insistently recurs in psychology, namely, dialecticism (see Chapter 6, and Mancuso, 1976 for commentary on Kelly's Dichotomy Corollary relative to dialecticism). Figuratively, every thesis must have an antithesis. Grossberg adduces the proposition that all neural transmitters are organized as competing network patterns or dipoles. Cells are organized in agonist-antagonist pairs, so that offset of the agonist input will evoke rebound in the antagonist cells. Grossberg then mathematically demonstrates that arousal enhances antagonistic rebound. Thus, it can be concluded that the disinhibition of arousal, generated by a mismatch at $F^{(1)}$, increments rebound of antagonists in the dipole organizations at $F^{(2)}$. In this way the previously active, "erroneous," pattern, $X_1{}^2$, is superseded by its previously suppressed antagonists. From this conclusion, Grossberg elaborates his neural model to discuss new code building, the development of long-term memory, and so forth. The needs of this chapter are satisfied by accepting his neurophysiological formulations about cognitive codes and the functioning of arousal in the building of these codes. We turn elsewhere to elaborate the concept of arousal.

Arousal and Attending

Can one credibly propose that attention can be traced through a conceptual network that involves neurophysiological processes associated with the concept of arousal that Grossberg intricately weaves into his model? Pribram and McGuiness (1975) have addressed this question. They accept Berlyne's (1960) view. Arousal is produced by "collative variables"; that is, by a failure in a match of input and "some residual in the organism of his past experience" (Pribram and McGuiness, p. 117). They then organize the work from approximately 200 neurophysiological and psychological experiments that led them "to identify three basic attentional control processes: One regulates *arousal* resulting from input; a second controls the preparatory *activation* phase, and a third operates to coordinate arousal and activation, an operation that demands *effort*?" (p. 116). Our reading of their review leads us to believe that there is now sufficient demonstration that the arousal process, which is intricately related to effortful attention, can be described in neurophysiological terms.

Reprise

This section contains an argument aimed, primarily, at affirming the presence of a neurophysiological dimension in the anticipation-surprise-motivation context. We have tried to enhance the view that a recordable neurophysiological state follows the person's failure to anticipate. Persons are motivated to attain an adequate match between neural fields activated by distal stimuli and the more central fields that are constructed to "absorb" the input pattern at the centrally located field. An "erroneous" construction at a central field involves a mismatch and incremented arousal. The person is motivated, often to the point of requiring controlled *effort*, to create the conditions that eliminate the mismatch. His processes are directed toward successful anticipation.

SOME RELATED CONSIDERATIONS

Anticipation in Action

Some recent efforts to discuss *self* can illustrate the utility of the concepts explicated in the foregoing sections. Carver (1979) wrote a theory to explain how various "self-standards" are brought into attentional focus. Relying heavily on the negative feedback models developed by Miller, Galanter, and Pribram (1960) and Powers (1973, 1978), Carver describes a process leading to one's attention to self-attributions. The making of self-standards, that is, the development of a schema that assimilates the self-involving situation, can be conceptualized by using those notions about memory and cognition that are described earlier in this chapter. Self-defining schemata and self-stories are developed as schemata just as are all schemata. (See Mancuso and Ceely, [1980] for an extended discussion of self-standards as memory processes.) Carver (1979, p. 8) develops the central proposition that through the process of evoking and applying recognitory schemata "the context evokes in a person a behavioral standard" relative to self-involving situations.

One can see that Carver's theory and the idea of self-standard construction as memory processing are related to studies (Cantor and Mischel, 1979; Gara and Rosenberg, 1979) of prototypes in person perception. Investigators in this latter area have developed a useful technology for extracting and exploring the ways in which person perception involves "prototypical persons;" those people who are used as standards in the process of person perception. With the concept of prototype, in that it has been shown to be a concept that is quite compatible to constructionist conceptions of memory processes, one may move into explorations of how self-standards, or roles, are placed on long-term storage, stored, and retrieved for use in behavioral contexts. From an assumptive base that uses these notions, one can then talk about self-standards in the anticipation-surprise-motivational cycle. A centrally located self-standard, that is, a self-defining schemata, is evoked by sensory input. If the self-standard does not match the pattern at the input-containing field, the person moves into an arousal-attention progression. Thereupon, behavior is directed toward producing conditions that reduce the discrepancy of the input and the standard. The person's conduct is his representation of the environment-changing sequences that will produce input for which he can create a self-defining construction.

In everyday language the person in this disequilibrated condition would be described as being in an emotional state. The diffuse neurophysiological changes that prevail in the activation condition are associated with changes in visceral muscle tension, vascular supply, and skin condition. Each of these kinds of changes can be recorded by a broad array of sensory systems. Thereupon the person's knowledge systems are brought to bear to construe these arousal-associated sensory inputs. Having been acculturated in a particular world of prose, poetry, and song, the person can bring to bear a particular set of constructs to build schemata that assimilate these inputs. In the northern part of North America, he might make the attribution that he is "angry," or "annoyed," or "frightened," or "infuriated," or "guilty," or "in love." If the arousal-produced stimulation persists over an inordinate period, the person might apply the self-standard labeled by the term *neurotic* and could take himself to a behavior change expert. The expert, of course, will apply his constructions to the disequilibrated person's reports. The outcome of the consultation would depend on the paradigm the expert would use. The inordinately aroused person might be told that he is experiencing the inappropriate release of frustration-produced anger. He might be told that his unconditional anger responses have been inadvertently conditioned to women's shoes (now a conditional stimulus for his anger response). From our view, the expert would be advised to look for the mismatch between evoked self-standard and sensory input regarding the self.

Our point now deserves stress: The most profound of psychological functioning, that is, self-image maintenance, can readily be conceptualized as an anticipation-surprise-motivation process. Maintenance of self, like all processes, is channelized by the ways in which a person anticipates events. One's self-involving behavior is "caused" by the propensity of the person (as a system) to maintain surprise at a systematically acceptable level.

Anticipation in a Real World

The Fundamental Postulate is the central assertion in a theory intended to explain how our psychological processes, including our overt conduct, gradually become adapted to recurring and novel events in our environment. To use the theory of personal constructs without considering adaptation leaves us with the logical conclusion that one of any possible constructions is as valid as is any other. The concept of adaptation relates to the idea of convenience in antici-pation. The Range Corollary states explicitly that a construct is convenient for the anticipation of a finite range of events only. If this were not the case, adapta-tion, as discussed above, could not occur. That is, if our constructions were not anticipatory in the sense that they are open to positive and negative feed-back from events, then psychological development would not be constrained by the environmental parameters that are the source of sensory input.

Yet, having taken this position, we need not conclude that people's psycho-logical processes are mechanistically shaped by the events themselves. The Fundamental Postulate, explicated as in the foregoing, can lead to the conclusion that a pattern of construction that is not informed in any way by relations between external events cannot be useful for successive anticipations of those events. Persons tend to reconstruct those feature-embedding schemata that have proved useful for anticipating events in the past, and to "forget" those that have failed to produce convenient anticipations. A major conclusion developed by Bartlett (1932) was that memory does not literally reproduce past events. Instead, current input from events is assimilated to reconstructed schemata that had been used in the perception of similarly experienced input. In this sense past constructions anticipate our current constructions, which, in turn, anticipate future reconstructions.

The philosopher Theodore Mischel (1964) has raised the following question as an epistemological issue: How can anticipations ever be "invalidated" if one assesses feedback from the environment in terms of the same system of constructs that originally had been used to formulate those anticipations; One cannot simply check one's representations of events against an "external reality." This would be logically impossible, within the theory, since a person cannot step outside of the frame of reference set by one's own personal construct systems to compare the constructions with the extant events. Warren (1964, p. 11) elaborates this problem, as follows:

> Taking a more general view, I consider the point Mischel raises here to be a basic problem for all psychological theories which attempt to take "perception" seriously. It is a matter of the veridicality of percep-tion or construction and how this is checked by the perceiver. It crops up under headings like "The Selectivity of Perception" or the "Trans-formation of the Information Input." All theories using the concept of "hypotheses" or "expectation" run into this issue sooner or later.

Warren notes that Kelly's solution to this epistemological problem coincides with the solution that Pepper (1942) identifies as a standard test of "truth" among contextualist theorists. Kelly subscribes to an internal consistency criterion of validity, and this "truth test" is expressed quite directly in the Choice Corollary.

> He [Kelly] makes the business of validation of constructs also a matter of construing, either at a different level of construing from the original construing or by employing different but systematically related constructs. . . . [the] criterion for a person's assessment of the outcome of his anticipations [is] the internal consistency of the present constructions within the person's construction system. . . . truth becomes a matter of coherence within a system rather than of correspondence with reality (Warren, p. 11).

It is important to observe that Kelly did not assert that people always function as if they were exact replicas of the hallowed model of the competent scientist. People do not always rely only on well-designed, carefully controlled experiments to test hypotheses. For example, a person may resort to hostility, defined as "the continued effort to extort validational evidence in favor of a type of social prediction that has already been recognized as a failure" (Kelly, 1955, p. 533). For example, if one construes his neighbors as hostile toward him, but the neighbors' behavior provides little support for this hypothesis, he might then throw rocks at their dog to elicit evidence of their hostility. On the other hand, it may be difficult for the rock thrower then to maintain a construction of himself as the innocent victim of their hostility, and this may lead him to question some other related aspects of his "self-concept."

In general, we presume that we cannot specify the precise relationship between events and a person's representation of them. We can infer, however, that whenever a person improves his capacity to anticipate events, the overall pattern of his experience will become more coherent, and he will encounter less arousal. To paraphrase Schopenhauer, even if we cannot prove that our waking life is not entirely a dream, it appears to be, at least, far more coherent than the shorter dreams that punctuate it from time to time.

CONCLUSION

The concept of anticipation may be written into a theory of the functioning of persons. To do this a theorist takes a totally constructivist position. Explanations of perception, memory, and all else that is discussed as cognition proceed from the assumption that sensory input is integrated into a person's knowledge network. A person's "knowing" of an event is understood as the construction, built on elements retrieved from long-term memory store, that immediately assimilates the input. Anticipations, in these terms, are nothing other than the schemata that are assembled to assimilate the incoming information.

"A person's processes are psychologically channelized by the ways in which he anticipates events" (Kelly, 1955, p. 46), in that a person is continuously activated toward imposing an assimilating schemata onto input. Behavioral scientists who have been working with constructivist/contextualist models have produced a variety of demonstrations of the ways in which a person's processes are enhanced or disrupted through having or not having structures that may be imposed on events. Additionally, investigators have invented plausible neurophysiological models to account for the mobilization that is observed that persons are incapable of building anticipatory schemata through assimilative or accommodative activity. The bases of these "emotional" states are to be found in each person's constant efforts after meaning.

Taking personal behavior as the event-to-be-construed, we judge the construct anticipates to be a suitably integrating term. This construct's utility, however, depends on how well we can incorporate the concept construction — or schema — into the total knowledge network we will use to explain personality.

3

CONSTRUCTION OF EXPERIENCE:
THE CONSTRUCTION COROLLARY

Lars Nystedt
David Magnusson

The Construction Corollary: A person anticipates events by construing their replications.

The task of psychology is to explain and to understand why, how, and what people think, feel, and behave. Different views have been and are held on the nature of man and his reactions in a complex environment. One very common school of thought, associated with associationism, holds that a person's behavior depends on what happens around him. Consequently psychological problems have been studied by systematically varying the situation and observing or measuring the variability of the person's reactions. The situation has been defined and measured as objectively as possible. The relationship between the variation in the objective characteristics of the situation and the variation in the person's reactions is used to draw conclusions about the mediating process between the input and the output.

Another view is that a person's behavior depends on how he interprets or imposes meaning on the world around. With this view in mind, associated with constructivism, it is essential to define the situation in terms of psychological variables (Kelly, 1955; Lewin, 1936; Murray, 1938). It is the person's perception and construction of the situation that defines the situation. The physical characteristics of the situation are not relevant in themselves, but only with

This study was supported by a grant from the Swedish Council for Research in Humanities and Social Sciences.

respect to their meaning to the person. In using this approach the latent cognitive and affective structures underlying behaviors and the inference process must be a central concern of research. The focus is on how and why the person selects, interprets, and treats the information available in a situation and the factors that influence this process.

CONSTRUCTIVISM

It is fundamental to the constructivist's view that the environment can never be directly known but that conception determines perception. We know reality only by acting upon it. This means that knowledge is neither a copy nor a mirror of reality, but the forms and content of knowledge are constructed by the one who experiences it. The active interaction between the individual and the environment is mediated by the cognitive structures of the individual. What we learn in interaction with the environment is dependent upon our own structuring of those experiences. Thus according to this view, man does not merely respond to the environment, he construes it.

The constructivist approach to psychology is not new. According to Neisser (1967) it goes back at least to Brentano's Act Psychology and Bergson's Creative Synthesis. Brentano held that psychic phenomena are to be thought of as acts: conception of meaning and content. Each psychic phenomenon is directed upon an object, whose significance the psychic phenomena makes intelligible. When, for example, one sees a color, the color itself is not mental. It is the seeing, the act, that is mental. The act as such implies an object and refers to a content. Brentano's Act Psychology was an alternative to, at that time, the predominant empiricist-associationistic theory. Brentano's psychology had importance for Gestalt psychology, phenomenological psychology, and existentialism. This does not mean, however, that Gestalt psychology and constructivism can be used interchangably. As Cofer (1977, p. 319) has pointed out, "in *Gestalt* theory the forces responsible for organization are not located in the activity of the organism, whereas in constructive theory the Kantian view of an active synthesis or construction is paramount." As mentioned above, in constructive theory it is assumed that things in themselves are unknowable. The "things" are part of our "apparatus" of perception. We apply our mental constructs to whatever we experience, but there is no reason to suppose that they can be applicable to things in themselves.

The relationship between constructivism and some part of Bergsonian philosophy is seen from the following quotation from Russell (1961, p. 757):

> Bergson's philosophy unlike most of the systems of the past is dualistic: the world, for him, is divided into two separate portions, on the one hand life, on the other matter, or rather the inert something which the intellect views as matter. The whole universe is the clash and conflict of two opposite motions: life, which climbs upward, and matter, which

falls downward. Life is one great force, one vast vital impulse, given once for all from the beginning of the world, meeting the resistance of matter, struggling to break a way through matter, learning gradually to use matter by means of organization; divided by the obstacles it encounters into diverging currents, like the wind at a street-corner; partly subdued by matter through the very adaptations which matter force upon it; yet retaining always its capacity for free activity, struggling always to find new outlets, seeking always for greater liberty of movement amid the opposing walls of matter.

Thus in Bergson's (1910) view, reality is given in immediate experience as a continuous process of becoming and is grasped by sympathetic insight. The concept used by the person to break up the continuous flow of reality gives us nothing of the life and movement of reality, but an artificial reconstruction of reality. However, the antiintellectual philosophy of Bergson is not related to constructive theory.

The aim of the following parts of the chapter is to discuss constructivism as it has been expressed within personal construct psychology, especially in the Construction Corollary in Kelly's (1955) theory of personal constructs, and to present a short overview showing that constructivism as a school of thought has influenced theory building and research in different fields of psychology.

PERSONAL CONSTRUCT THEORY: THE CONSTRUCTION COROLLARY

In Kelly's (1955) constructive theory of personality, the man is regarded as man the scientist. A person's experiences or thoughts about reality are regarded as a tentative hypothesis about reality that may or may not be true. Every man is assumed to have the capacity to represent the external environment. It is this representation that guides the person's interaction with the environment. The assumption that the man is free to construe the environment, but that he is bound by his constructions, implies also that the person does not react to external stimuli, but to his interpretations of them. Consequently, knowledge of the stimulus is not sufficient for predicting a person's behavior; one needs to know the person's subjective reality. This view also implies that there is not merely one possible act corresponding to given antecedents, but that the same series of events can be interpreted in several different ways, all equally possible. This has been referred to by Kelly as constructive alternativism, and it seems to be related to Bergson's view of free will. Personal construct theory is based on one Fundamental Postulate and 11 corollaries. In this chapter we are concerned with the Construction Corollary.

The Construction Corollary in personal construct theory deals with how the psychological process is anchored to an ever-changing reality. The corollary states that a person anticipates events by construing their replications. To understand the tenor of the corollary one has to consider three of the four assumptions behind personal construct theory, two about the universe and one about the nature of man. One assumption is that the universe really exists. It contains real events and objects, and it is not merely a function of the imagination. Man comes to know this reality by making successive interpretations of it. These interpretations, images, thoughts, mental events, and so on, also really exist. Another assumption is that the universe exists by virtue of activity, or, more precisely, it exists by continual change with respect to itself. Thus Kelly regards reality as a process consistent with the Heraclitean theme, that only change is real.

In this assumption we see the relationship between construct psychology and contextualism. In discussing the root metaphor of contextualism, Sarbin (1977, p. 6) says

> contextualism asserts change and novelty. Events are in a constant flux; the very integration of the conditions of an event will alter the context of a future event which appears to have similarity to a preceding event. The texture of an event, argues the contextualist, can be understood by noting the integration of the conditions of the event within the context of the event.

The third assumption is that the most fundamental characteristic of man is his creative capacity to represent the external environment; that man is free to construe the situation in alternative ways, but that he is bound by his constructions. He develops a model of the external reality and tests this model by predicting what is going to happen in the future.

Keeping these assumptions in mind, we can briefly consider the key concepts of the Construction Corollary: anticipate, construe, event, and replication.

Anticipate: Kelly used the concept anticipate to furnish the theory with its predictive and motivational features. The motivational aspect of the theory will be dealt with in other chapters. Suffice it here to state that if man lacked the capacity to anticipate or to predict future events, it would be hard to understand how he could be an active participant in a continuously changing world.

Construe: The act of construing is a process of abstraction in which one attributes properties to an ongoing stream of events. By the process of construing, a person imposes meaning on events. "He erects a structure, within the framework of which substance takes shape or assumes meaning. The substance which he construes does not produce the structure; the person does" (Kelly, 1950, p. 50). This is another way of saying that the external events do not tell the person how or what they are. This the person has to find out for himself, and he does so by attributing properties to events. Furthermore, in the act of construing "the person notes features in a series of elements which characterize some of the elements and are particularly uncharacteristic of others" (p. 50). Thus, the construed events are assumed to reflect the external events.

Event: As mentioned before, one basic assumption behind personal construct theory is that the environment is real and our knowledge about the environment is based on our personal version of the environment. This means that events exist without our perception of them, but we come to know the events only by construing them. Thus, the term *event* is used with two different meanings: the meaning of the real event, that is, the event that exists without the person's perception of it, and the meaning of the construed event, that is, the reflection of the event as it is constructed by the person.

Replication: Replication of events is the basis for prediction, since replication implies that something that happens now has happened before and may happen again in the future. A necessary requirement for discussing replication is that events can be separated from each other. According to personal construct theory the person detects replicative aspects in the stream of events by construing the beginnings and endings of events and by abstracting the common intersect of a certain set of common properties. Thus it is assumed that what a person predicts is not the event itself but the construed common intersect of these properties.

In summary, the basic tenet of personal construct theory is that in the interaction with the environment the person develops a mental model of the environment, and these mental representations of phenomena are acquired and employed through mental manipulation of the internal models of events to predict future events.

CONSTRUCTIVISM IN COGNITION

When Kelly presented his constructive theory of personal constructs, mechanistically oriented theories dominated psychology. However, constructivism as a school of thought has become more and more pronounced in modern cognitive psychology. The aim of this section is to sketch some of the influences that constructivism has had on cognitive theories and research.

The view that man thinks by manipulating internal models of reality is found in Newell and Simon's (1972) theory of human problem solving. Ohlsson (1980) has called such a theory the Enacting Theory of thinking. According to Ohlsson, there is a lot of evidence from studies on human problem solving and mental rotation supporting the enacting theory. He concludes, "In summary, then, the Enacting Theory has considerable support from the success with which it has been applied to human data. Also there is independent evidence that people think by manipulating internal models" (p. 48). Similarly, Neisser (1967, p. 3) argues for a constructive view of perception and memory in that "the world of experiences is produced by the man who experiences it" and that "whatever we know about reality has been *mediated*, not only by the organs of sense but by complex systems which interpret and reinterpret sensory information." Tulving (1972) presents a similar idea in his discussion of memory cells. According to Tulving, the record of personal happenings is not of the order of external happenings, but rather of the order of our own thoughts at the time.

In his later book Neisser (1976) argues even more convincingly for a constructive view of perception and memory.

> Not only reading but also listening, feeling and looking are skilful activities that occur over time. All of them depend on pre-existing structures, here called schemata, which direct perceptual activity and are modified as it occurs (p. 14). At each moment the perceiver is constructing anticipations of certain kinds of information, that enable him to accept it as it becomes available (p. 20).

Constructivism is also represented in cognitive approaches to developmental and social psychology. Piaget, for example, held the view that to know is to produce in thought and that we interact with the environment through our cognitive structures by means of processes of assimilation and accommodation. Piaget, then, suggests that man "actually *constructs* his world by assimilating it to schemas while accommodating these schemas to its constraints" (Flavell, 1963, p. 71). A constructivist-interactional approach is also found in Hunt's (1980) approach to developmental psychology and to personality (Endler, 1977). Weizmann (1977), in an article entitled "Praxis and Interaction: The Psychology of J. McVicker Hunt," concludes that most developmental theories "imply a growing independence from, and the seeming devaluation of, the importance of the ongoing environment" (p. 18). This is a viewpoint that shares much of the constructivist orientation.

The resemblance with this position is also found in Uzgiris' (1977) work. In her discussion of environmental conditions and experience, she says

> it is the individual who has to construe those conditions (environmental) as opportunities for these activities (psychological). The same environmental conditions may be construed differently by different individuals. Moreover, the same individual may construe the same environmental conditions as offering different opportunities at different periods in development (p. 91).

A constructivist view of the development of perception, attention, and memory has recently also been discussed by Collins and Hagen (1979). Furthermore, the notion of an active partnership between the individual and the environmental conditions is also characteristic of work on styles in cognitive development (Fowler, 1977).

Constructivism is also reflected in the attribution approach in social psychology, in which the person is considered "as a constructive thinker searching for causes of the events confronting him and acting upon his imperfect knowledge of causal structure in ways that he considers appropriate" (Jones et al., 1972, p. x). Furthermore, in Kelley's (1973) attribution theory the term *causal schemata* reflects the individual's notion of reality and his assumptions about the external world. Thus the causal schemata is regarded as a general conception held by a person about how certain kinds of causes interact to produce a specific kind of effect.

In person perception research the notion of implicit personality theory is also a constructivist one. It refers to the categories a person invents and uses in perception of another person's personality (Bruner and Tagiuri, 1954; Rosenberg, 1977; Wegner and Vallacher, 1977). There is a lot of evidence (Schneider, 1973) suggesting that a person's implicit personality theory is important in determining that person's impression of another person. Moreover, most research on social cognition, that is, the ways in which we conceptualize other persons' feelings, intentions, and so on, uses a constructivist approach (Gruen and Doherty, 1977).

The essential meaning of the Construction Corollary in personal construct theory is that a person's immediate experiences must be construed as being both similar to and different from what has previously been construed and that the person uses the construed replication of an event to predict what will happen in the future. Thus, one necessary condition for the "truth" of the Construction Corollary is that past experience leaves some effects. The person does not start construing without some earlier knowledge, but uses some preexisting schema (Neisser, 1976) that enables him to attend to or to notice certain aspects of the environment rather than others.

As an early proponent of a constructivist theory of memory, Bartlett (1932) marked out the directions that would be followed by current investigators. His definition of the term *schema* (cited earlier in the discussion of the Fundamental Postulate) has stood as a foundation of the vast revision in thinking regarding memory function (see Cofer, 1977, for a discussion of the constructivist approach to memory).

From a modern constructivist point of view (Bannister and Fransella, 1971; Kelly, 1955; Landfield, 1977; Mancuso, 1977; Sarbin, Taft, and Bailey, 1960) the memory process is considered as a creative construction, by which is meant that the input from an event is located within a person's existing construct system. It is the abstracted features or attributes that are represented in memory and not the event per se. Thus, a representation is a system of classificatory features and of relationships among these features.

Several modern theories of the memory process are based on this idea. Collins and Quillian (1972) and Collins and Loftus (1975) have presented a semantic network model in which the memory process is treated as a construction process, that is, the stimulus input from the event is integrated with the person's existing knowledge system and thereby becomes a part of the construct system. Other similar models of memory have been presented by Anderson and Bower (1972), Rumelhart and Ortony (1977), and Tulving and Thomson (1973).

The assumption that man is an active participant in the construction of experience, that he uses schemata for organizing the situation, and for predicting and controlling the future, suggests we direct our attention to the research literature on memory for evidence of an integrative and constructive perspective. Jenkins (1974) has analyzed the results from experiments on learning and memory from two perspectives: associationism and contextualism. The experiments concern free recall, event recognition, and integration of information. Jenkins' analysis shows that the efficiency of free recall is dependent on contextual factors, that recognition of events is dependent on the quality of the event that the person *constructs* from the stimuli during the acquisition part of the experiment, and that when persons are to consider each sentence in a set of sentences as the events, they learn very little, but when the subject is instructed to integrate the whole set of sentences into a single event the learning is efficient. Jenkins' conclusion is that

> what is remembered in a given situation depends on the physical and psychological context in which the event was experienced, the knowledge and skills that the subject brings to the context, the situation in which we ask for evidence for remembering, and the relation of what the subject remembers to what the experimenter demands (p. 793).

Cofer (1973, 1977) has reviewed a number of studies that also support an integrative and constructive view of memory. The research reviewed by Cofer deals with such problems as the processing and meaning of isolated words, integration of input with existing memory structure, the duration of learned material, and the retention of inferences drawn from input. One conclusion from this review is that

> comprehension or understanding of an input or the learning or retention of it is heavily dependent on the context in which that input occurs. This context may be provided by the situation, but it may also be constructed by the individual; in construing a plausible context, the individual integrates incoming information with the knowledge that he or she possesses and that is engaged by the context (Cofer, 1977, p. 322).

In support of this conclusion Cofer refers to studies performed by Anderson and Ortony (1975) that have shown the meaning of a word to be dependent on the context. Cofer also refers to Dooling and Lachman (1971) and to Bransford and Johnson (1972), who have shown that otherwise meaningless material can be integrated with a person's existing knowledge, if the material is described by means of a title or picture. Cofer also mentions a number of studies supporting the evidence "that the memory for the form of the material studied erodes with time, while memory for the gist of the material may persist" (Cofer, 1977, pp. 324-25), and that the person draws inferences from the input material that are often remembered as well as the input material itself. Cofer (1977, p. 325) concludes his review by saying that

> the knowledge one gains from an experience goes beyond what is shown in accurate recall and recognition, that what is remembered from the input depends on how one processes that input, and that memory for the gist of meaningful material, verbal or pictorial (Kintsch, 1974), is likely to be far more complex and longer lasting than memory for the wording, the syntax, and other formal properties of the material.

The main conclusion of the results presented is that a person's construction of input is a product of an interaction between contextual factors and the person's knowledge of the situation. This brings us to another important field of psychology in which the constructivist position and the implications from the Construction Corollary in personal construct theory is central, namely, models of personality.

PERSONALITY

As Kelly himself insisted, his theory was not merely a theory of cognition. He belongs rather to the tradition of researchers interested in models of molar, social behavior, and this makes him a central figure in the field of personality.

In defining Kelly's place in the history of personality theorizing and research, one notes that Kelly also was a child of his time: Not all of the ideas that he integrated into his theory were new. For example, the central idea of cognitive construction and representation had been used by theorists before him, using different terms. This in no wise detracts from Kelly's merit, since his contribution was to integrate prevalent ideas with new ones in a creative way to produce a comprehensive, coherent theory. The central concepts of his theory later became incorporated in the mainstream of psychological theory to an extent that obscured their origin.

Both the influence of earlier ideas on Kelly's theoretical formulations and the role of these formulations for later theorizing and research can be illustrated with reference to theorizing in what has been called interactionistic models of personality.

Early Interactional Formulations

A central idea in interactionistic models of personality is that a consideration of person factors is insufficient to understand and explain why individuals feel, think, and act as they do. It is also necessary to consider both the situational conditions under which an individual's behavior is observed and the interplay between the sets of person and situation factors (Endler and Magnusson, 1976; Magnusson and Endler, 1977).

For most theorists advocating this view it is not the environment as it is, in its physical and sociocultural manifestations, that presents the important situational factors; it is the environment as it is perceived, interpreted, and construed by the individual. This idea has been elaborated, in different ways and using different terms, by the most influential theorists interested more in social, molar behavior than in specific responses in the S-R tradition (compare, for example, Angyal, 1941; Lewin, 1951; Murphy, 1947; Murray, 1938; Tolman, 1951). Two examples should suffice to illustrate the importance of cognitive construction and representation of the outer world for theorists prior to Kelly. Lewin (1938) entitled one of his influential papers "The conceptual representation and the measurement of psychological forces," and Tolman (1948) underlined the importance of cognitive construction and representation for the formation of actual behavior when he stated, in his discussion of cognitive maps in rats:

> The stimuli, which are allowed in, are not connected by just simple one-to-one switches to the outgoing responses. Rather, the incoming impulses are usually worked over and elaborated in the central control room into a tentative, cognitive-like map of the environment. And it is this tentative map, indicating routes and paths and environmental relationships, which finally determines what responses, if any, the animal will finally release (p. 192).

Modern Interactional Formulations

In the renewed discussion on the person-situation interaction issue during the past decade, the concepts of cognitive construction and representation and of prediction and anticipation have come to play a decisive role (see Magnusson, 1976; 1981).

According to an interactional model, individuals differ mainly with respect to their partly unique, cross-situational patterns of stable and changing behaviors. For each type of behavior, an individual is best characterized by two parameters: the mean level of intensity of the behavior and the partly unique cross-situational profile of the behavior. The interindividual differences in cross-situational patterns of manifest behaviors are explained with reference to interindividual differences in the momentary perceptions, interpretations, and cognitive constructions of the outer situation and the predictions and anticipations about possible outcomes and about their consequences that the individual continuously makes. The perceptions, interpretations, constructions, and predictions are supposed to be steered by the more persistent system of cognitions and abstractions about the outer world that an individual has built up in the continuous interaction with his environment, in a process of learning and maturation, during the course of development. The following quotation from Bowers

(1973, p. 328) is one among many examples of formulations, underlining the basic role of the individuals' systems of cognitive constructions: "The situation is a function of the person in the sense that the observer's schemes filter and organize the environment in a fashion that makes it impossible even to completely separate the environment from the person observing it." The importance of hypotheses and expectations, in the sense of predictions and anticipations advocated by Kelly, has been underlined particularly by Mischel, one of the most influential debaters of the person-situation interaction issue. In his 1973 article, a classic in the field, in which he strongly advocates the role of cognitions in the process underlying actual behavior, he stated:

> For many years personality research has searched for individual differences on the psychologist's hypothesized dimensions while neglecting the subject's own expectancies (hypotheses). More recently, it seems increasingly clear that the expectancies of the subject are central units for psychology (for example, Bolles, 1972; . . .). These hypotheses guide the person's selection (choice) of behaviors from among the enormous number which he is capable of constructing within any situation (p. 267).

(It is interesting to note that a reference is missing to the one who more clearly and more strongly than most other researchers had formulated this idea earlier.)

The concepts of anticipation and of anticipatory reactions, in the sense of replication in Kelly's terminology, are also central to theorizing in the increasingly important area of stress and anxiety research (see, for example, Lazarus, Averill, and Opton, 1974; Lazarus and Launier, 1978). A basic concept in the theory presented by Lazarus and his coworkers is cognitive appraisal of the continuous flow of situational information. In the discussion of stressful primary appraisal, *threat* is defined as harm or loss that has not yet happened but is anticipated, and in the discussion of secondary appraisal — which deals with coping resources and options as they are subjectively accessible to and evaluated by the individual — anticipation of possible alternative situational outcomes and anticipatory, cognitive coping with the different anticipated outcomes are fundamental elements.

SUMMARY

The aim of this chapter has been to sketch briefly the rise of constructivism in psychology and to relate the basic tenor of the Construction Corollary in Kelly's (1955) theory of personal constructs to theories and research in cognition and personality.

Constructivism as a general view of psychological processes is an alternative to the naive realism found in mechanistically oriented psychological theories. Even if constructivism as a school of thought can be traced back long before

Kelly's presentation of his theory, his contribution to the mainstream of constructivism in psychology was to integrate constructivistic ideas into a coherent theory of personality.

The Construction Corollary deals with the process whereby man anticipates and construes an ever-changing environment. The idea that the act of construing is a process of abstraction in which man notes features in a series of events is now a common assumption in several modern theories of memory. The view implied by the Construction Corollary that man's mental representations of the reality are acquired and employed through mental manipulation of internal models of events is also reflected in modern theories of perception, human problem solving, and cognitive development.

Finally, it was observed that Kelly's theory has been very influential on later theorizing and research in the field of personality. This has been the case especially for formulations in modern interactional models of personality and theories and research on stress and anxiety.

4

BACK TO BASICS IN PERSONALITY STUDY – THE INDIVIDUAL PERSON'S OWN ORGANIZATION OF EXPERIENCE: THE INDIVIDUALITY COROLLARY

Michael A. Gara

The Individuality Corollary: Persons differ from each other in their construction of events.

From the standpoint of personal construct psychology, the individual's *own* organization of experience is the most fertile starting point for the process of understanding his or her conduct. There are alternative starting points, to be sure. Currently available personality theories, for one, provide several frameworks for the comprehension of an individual's conduct and "knowings." However, the distinctive images of the human condition offered by any given personality theorist can be shown to be bound up in that theorist's *own* personal reality (see Stolorow and Atwood, 1979, for current work on this old idea). Nonetheless, constructs offered by personality theorists (for example, locus of control, self-efficacy) are often used in personality research as universally applicable scientific constructs, convenient for anticipating the conduct of individuals. Personal construct psychology invites us to remain skeptical of the utility of these so-called scientific constructs.

Using personal construct theory reflexively would, of course, invite skepticism about the constructs offered by the theory itself. Kelly's (1955) two-volume work on personal construct theory is replete with his own personal

The writing of this chapter was supported in part by a National Science Foundation Grant BNS-7906853 to Seymour Rosenberg. I would like to thank Seymour Rosenberg for his helpful comments concerning earlier drafts of this chapter.

constructs, the ways by which he made sense out of the behavior of the clients and the students whom he had encountered in his dual role as professor/ therapist. He also organized his constructs for us when he wrote the theory, just as he claimed that everyone organizes his personal constructs in some fashion (Organizational Corollary). By the way Kelly organized his theory, it is readily apparent that "constructive alternativism" is a superordinate construct in the theory; the other constructs (corollaries) in the theory imply constructive alternativism: one is always free to revise one's construction of an event. A construct is only a convenient device for anticipating events; if need be, the construct can be revised or abandoned. On constructive alternativism, Kelly (1955, p. 15) wrote: "No one needs to paint himself into a corner; no one needs to be completely hemmed in by circumstances; no one needs to be a victim of his biography."

A would-be Kellian personologist would become an unknowing victim of Kelly's own biography if he did not first recognize that constructive alternativism, superordinate in the theory, was also superordinate in Kelly's personal system. Once the personologist recognizes the personal origins of Kelly's idea, he is, of course, free to share the conception — make it an integral part of his *own* system for the construing persons. The fact that constructive alternativism permeates Kelly's writing suggests that he had invented the rudiments of constructive alternativism (the philosophical position) in his own personal context and that his personal construct (something like painted into a corner-free to be anything) had become superordinate in his own personal system, thus enabling him to embrace the philosophical position as superordinate in his theory without reservation.

We are given insights into the fundamental position the construct painted into a corner-free to be anything held in Kelly's own personal context by Holland's (1970) essay: "George Kelly: Constructive Innocent and Reluctant Existentialist." Kelly simply refused to allow his theory to be labeled as phenomenological, or one of its subcategories — existentialism. Assuming Kelly *owned* his theory and, in some sense, *was* his theory, we might infer from this "protection" of the theory that Kelly had a personal concern that he should not be labeled. Thus he grew a personal distaste for preemptive labeling per se. "Unlike those people who are tormented by the ambiguities and uncertainties of life he finds himself in trouble over the very opposite — those things he once thought he knew with certainty" (Holland, 1970, p. 114). Holland then goes on to quote Kelly: "a world jam-packed with lead pipe certainties, dictionary definitives, and doomsday finalities strikes me as a pretty gloomy place."

RECAPITULATION AND FOREWORD

No theory of personality is complete. A given author, being human, faces issues in experience that some persons may share, but other persons do not.

Often a theorist will give his issue ontological status (Stolorow and Atwood, 1979) as if all persons must somehow face and resolve that issue in the course of becoming a person. Kelly himself had certain issues in his experience, which I abstracted in terms of the construct painted into a corner-free. Some of his conduct, especially with regard to how his theory was received by the academic community, could be construed as an attempt to maintain his view of his theory (himself) as free from labeling: No replica of his theory (himself) has ever been devised. From his own experience, Kelly makes a statement concerning the meaning of being human: No one needs to paint himself into a corner. Interestingly enough, Kelly saw everyone as having his own particular issues in experience, although he never played down his belief that each person could always revise the way he looked at his world. Maybe he can. However, to understand the conduct of a person, Kelly maintained, we must try to understand how that person organizes his experience. Focus on the individual's own organization of experience is, I think, the major thrust of personal construct theory and the essence of the Individuality Corollary. The remainder of this chapter will focus on the utility of examining *own* organization in the context of psychological research. That context includes something of what is believed about "scientific" research.

A THEORY IN SEARCH OF ITS ZEITGEIST

Can there be a nomothetic science of personality study, if we are to take the Individuality Corollary seriously? The answer depends on what one means by nomothetic. If nomothetic means the finding of general laws of behavior, we would need to ask whether or not we were following the most useful course for psychology, or at least for personality-social psychology (Gergen, 1973; Sarbin, 1977). However, the process of coming to know the individual's *own* organization, which we believe *is* the most useful course for personality psychology, requires a series of assumptions about what to look for and where to look for it. There is no a priori reason for rejecting the belief that the methods and ideas that guide us in our search cannot be developed so that they are substantially the same (nomothetic) regardless of the individual in question. Likewise for the historian: "the historian, in contrast to the chronicler, also derives general laws and principles which run through the mass of events that have happened. If he did not, he would be hopelessly bogged down in his newspaper files" (Kelly, 1955, p. 42).

The latter view of nomothetic is at odds with the prevailing way of talking about a nomothetic science of personality — the zeitgeist — which is to invent and measure personality variables and state laws that interrelate these variables to others (often traits). A study (Rosenberg and Gara, 1980, n. 1) of the perceptions that social and personality psychologists (members of APA Division 8) use to survey the history of their discipline(s) suggests that we have reached the end of a dominant cycle in our short history: social psychology has become experimental and personality psychology has turned into testing and measurement.

Personal construct researchers themselves can be seen as slipping into this prevailing view of what constitutes nomothetic personology. Kelly advanced the Rep Grid as a series of techniques to start the personologist on the venture of studying an individual's *own* organization. Judging from Adams-Webber's recent review (1979a) of personal construct research, the Rep Grid appears to be the sine qua non of personal construct theory. Actually, I think, the Rep Grid is peripheral to the theory. Nonetheless, investigators are already scoring the Rep Grids for determining the degree of organization (Landfield, 1977) of a construct system, degree of organization clearly being a personality variable. It will not be long before the personologists' vocabulary of "traits" will include "loose organization" and "tight organization," complete with a compendium of tests to measure these. These events may come to pass probably because Kellian theory is a theory in "search of its Zeitgeist" (Rosenberg, 1980).

SOME POINTS TO CONSIDER IN STUDYING OWN ORGANIZATION

In moving toward a nomothetic science of personality study that begins and ends with the Individuality Corollary, it is essential that we develop a systematic approach for ascertaining an individual's own organization of experience. In this section we will work toward some points to consider in developing such an approach for the experience of persons. To do so, we will draw on some work by social psychologists on person perception — especially implicit personality theory — since that work shares many of the substantive interests and methods of personal construct psychology.

Implicit personality theory (IPT) refers to a person's everyday beliefs about personality. This belief system includes the traits that they perceive as characteristic of themselves and others — traits having to do with intelligence, integrity, sociability, attractiveness, maturity, and so on — and their beliefs about the interrelations among these traits (Bruner and Tagiuri, 1954; Cronbach, 1955; Rosenberg and Sedlak, 1972b; Wegner and Vallacher, 1977). The theory is "implicit" because it is inferred from the individual's characterizations of people rather than being stated by the individual in any explicit way.

A large portion of the research on IPT has focused on "culturally shared" dimensions for perceiving persons. This research is important since individuals, while ultimately possessing their own organization of perceptions about people, can have components or features in their own systems that other individuals may share. The fact that the belief systems of several individuals may share certain components may be, but often is not, accidental. In order to establish some degree of communal process, human beings may need to share a system of construing experience, including the experience of persons (see Chapter 12 on the Commonality Corollary). The semantic structure of the language may afford this "shared system" to some extent, but not exclusively (Gara and Rosenberg, in press; Shweder, 1977). Ultimately, however, at least in the case of belief systems, what is truly shared by an individual is also owned by him or her.

A prototypical study in this large corpus of IPT research involves the selection by the investigator of a set of trait terms and then obtaining a matrix of trait similarities (or dissimilarities) based on the aggregated judgments of a sample of subjects. The judgments made on the trait terms can take several forms, for example, sorting (see Rosenberg and Sedlak, 1972b). A multivariate technique such as factor analysis or multidimensional scaling is then used to determine the multidimensional structure of the trait terms. Once the trait terms have been plotted in a multidimensional space, it is the task of the investigator to determine what the dimensions of the space mean psychologically. For example, the semantic differential model, originally proposed as an affective theory of meaning (Osgood, Suci, and Tannenbaum, 1957) and later applied as a multidimensional scheme for person perception (Osgood, 1962), construes the "shared" dimensions of person perception to be evaluation, potency and activity (EPA).

Social psychologists have also begun to study implicit personality theory in a way that is directly relevant to the Individuality Corollary (Gara and Rosenberg, 1979; Kim and Rosenberg, 1980; Rosenberg, 1977; Rosenberg and Sedlak, 1972a; Shikiar, Fishbein, and Wiggins, 1974; Wiggins and Fishbein, 1969). The Kim and Rosenberg study is especially noteworthy because it assumes that an individual has his own way of organizing beliefs about persons, and sets out to determine what components (dimensions) of individual belief systems are truly shared by the comparison of individual belief systems. In contrast, studies that support the semantic differential model of implicit personality theory essentially assume that individuals share a common system for perceiving persons and thus aggregate individual data. Research on the semantic differential also relies on trait scales and trait lists provided to the subjects by the investigator, rather than a vocabulary that the subject freely generates, thus reflecting the trait-sampling biases of the investigator to an unknown extent. Kim and Rosenberg examined whether these two factors (aggregation of individual data; trait vocabulary provided by the investigator) had any effect on what conclusions an investigator would reach about what is shared in person perception.

We will review here some relevant aspects of the Kim and Rosenberg study. In that study, ten subjects (the F group) described persons in their lives with their own trait vocabulary, while another ten (the C group) described persons using a vocabulary provided by the experimenter. All subjects rated each of their trait terms on nine marker scales, of which three scales (for example, good-bad) constituted evaluative markers, three constituted potency markers (strong-weak) and three constitued activity markers (active-passive). Two separate factor analyses were performed on the nine marker scales, one for the F group and one for the C group. For both the F and C groups, the first factor was clearly evaluation, although it accounted for more variance in the F group. For the F group, the second factor was activity and the third factor potency, while for the C group, the third factor was activity and the second factor was potency. These results support the semantic differential model, especially the variant where potency and activity are considered "fused" to turn a "dynamism" dimension (Osgood, Suci, and Tannenbaum, 1957).

The relations among E, P, and A were also examined on the individual level. For each subject three ratings (one each for E, P, and A) were calculated to describe each trait; that is, each dimension (EPA) rating was the average of the three scales used to mark that dimension. The correlations among E, P, and A for each subject were then calculated.

The average correlation for subjects in the C group (experimenter's traits) was .08 between E and P and .06 between E and A. On the basis of that result, one would be led to conclude that E and dynamism were orthogonal, as proposed by the semantic differential model. However, for the F group (own traits), the average correlation between E and P was .20, and the average correlation between E and A was .32. Further, all average correlations were significantly larger for the F group than for the C group. Orthogonality between E and dynamism, then, is more likely to emerge with an experimenter-selected vocabulary.

Additional analyses reported in Kim and Rosenberg show that the average correlations among E, P, and A are misleading in representing the correlations at the individual level. The individual correlations between E and P vary from −.34 to +.60 for the F group and −.33 to +.59 for the C group. The correlations between E and A vary from .08 to .57 for the F group and from −.21 to +.37 for the C group. Further, tests for homogeneity of correlations show that individual correlations are heterogeneous in both the F and C groups.

The nine marker scales also were used by the subjects to rate their people and all of the above analyses were also performed on these ratings. The picture is the same. The semantic differential model holds up when subjects' ratings are aggregated; it fares less well at the individual level. Further, the EPA model is more adequately supported when subjects use an experimenter-selected vocabulary than when they use their own.

Thus, in accordance with the Individuality Corollary, subjects are using their *own* organization of the constructs by which they perceive people, especially when they are given the opportunity to describe people in their own words. If given an experimenter-selected vocabulary, not necessarily their own, a subject's organization might better approximate the "shared" organization posited by the semantic differential model. However, even in this case, the emergence of EPA as a shared system is partly artifactual; that is, it is due to aggregation of individual ratings.

However, one would look for some "shared" organization, if we are to take the Commonality Corollary seriously. Kim and Rosenberg's multidimensional evaluative model suggests that the only dimension that is common to all individuals is an evaluative dimension. The proposed model is multidimensional, however, in that it assumes additional dimensionality resulting from a set of content areas not independent of evaluation, such as attractiveness, integrity, intelligence, maturity, sociability, and so on. The particular content areas that compose this evaluative structure have been shown, by Kim and Rosenberg, to vary among individuals.

Certain groups of individuals could, of course, share a particular content area in their perceptions of persons. The subjects in the Kim and Rosenberg study, all college students, in general share a concern with intelligence and maturity in their perceptions of others. The concern with maturity, however, may not be present in older adults and younger children. The concern with intelligence may reflect a particularization of a ubiquitous concern among human beings about competence or success (Rosenberg, 1977); "competence in certain other occupations may be reflected in traits other than (or in addition to) intelligence, such as agility, strength, political savvy, and so on" (Kim and Rosenberg, 1980, p. 388).

Although the evaluative model shares with the EPA model the assumption of a general evaluative dimension, it is not a special case of the EPA system. In fact, the reverse is true if potency and activity are not assumed to be orthogonal to evaluation. In this case, potency and activity may be viewed as two content dimensions that are assumed to be present in the implicit personality theory of all individuals. Moreover, as a special case of the evaluative model, the poles of these two hypothesized "universals" need not be oriented the same way for all individuals; for example, some individuals may perceive certain active traits as good, whereas other individuals may perceive certain passive traits as good (Kim and Rosenberg, 1980, p. 377).

Returning now from the preceding discussion of research on person perception to what was promised at the beginning of this section, what points should be considered in ascertaining how an individual uniquely organizes the experience of persons — more specifically, beliefs about persons?

• People often try to figure out how other human beings view the world (see Chapter 13 on the Sociality Corollary). The person may not share in (ultimately own) the other's construction, but he can "get it." In Gara and Rosenberg (in press), subjects were asked to make fine distinctions among 20 trait terms in terms of a provided list of "features" of traits. (Saves old things is an example of a "feature" of the trait sentimental; crys at weddings is another.) However, another group of subjects, when describing people with the 20 trait terms, clearly did not use all those fine distinctions among the traits in the way they ascribed the traits to different people. While there is little evidence, in general, that persons share making such fine distinctions in their trait descriptions, they "get" that they can be made. Similarly, subjects can "get" all of the distinctions an investigator makes in the vocabulary that the investigator provides to them for the purpose of describing persons and yet use only a minority of those distinctions in their everyday perception of people. In fact, people are usually more timid (in terms of extremity of ratings) about using constructs provided by the investigator than they are when using their own constructs (H. Bonarius, 1977). Taking the Sociality Corollary seriously, it makes little sense to pursue own organization of beliefs about persons using anything but the individual's own vocabulary. Taking the Sociality Corollary seriously is not just a good idea for research on own organization in person perception; it has immediate application in the real world exchange between client and professional in the clinical setting, as we shall see later.

   •   For those of us interested in what people share in their perception of persons, we take the Individuality Corollary very seriously. Kim and Rosenberg's (1980) study amply demonstrates the pitfalls of aggregating person descriptions across individuals in order to determine what is truly shared in person perception.

Own Organization and Conduct: Two Case Illustrations

If one paints a picture of an individual's own organization of his beliefs about persons, using, for example, Rep Grid methodologies (Bannister and Mair, 1968; Fransella and Bannister, 1977) or related techniques (Rosenberg, 1977), and their associated methods for data analysis, what kind of insight does one gain into the person's conduct, if any? Do we have just a pretty picture?

To explore these issues, two case studies will be examined. The first case is Theodore Dreiser, because his life has been extremely well documented. The second involves a male who was a student at Rutgers University at the time of the study and who completed a person description task (see Rosenberg, 1977, for a description of the task) as part of an independent study project. This subject provided extensive descriptions of various significant events, problems, and choices that he was confronting in his life, and he has agreed to allow a piece of his story to be told.

The Case of Dreiser

Theodore Dreiser never completed a Rep Grid. However, his writing was rich in characterization of persons, and since much was known about his life, the characterizations that he made in *A Gallery of Women* were analyzed by Rosenberg and Jones (1972). The procedures involved in this analysis are too technical to report here; interested readers can refer to the published study.

Two dimensions are seen to underlie Dreiser's characterizations of persons: male-female and conforms-does not conform. The presence of sex as a significant dimension in Dreiser's characterizations appears to be explicable in terms of his deep involvement with women, which was often scandalous. "He often carried on affairs with several women at a time. One such affair, with a 17-year-old girl, was instrumental in his loss of the lucrative editorship of Butterick Publications" (Rosenberg and Jones, 1972, p. 384).

The theme of conformity, which showed up Dreiser's characterizations in *A Gallery of Women*, appears, by several accounts, to be a major theme in his life. Dreiser viewed himself as "nonconformist" and sought out nonconformists of all sorts as companions. Consider "Dreiser's Law": "Beliefs held by the multitude, the bourgeois and their leaders, are likely to be wrong per se. . . . Beliefs held by unconventionalists which fly in the face of orthodoxy are in all probability right," (W. Swanberg, quoted in Rosenberg and Jones, 1972, pp. 384-85).

Demonic Possession and Other Matters

A strong evaluative dimension was found in the person descriptions of our second case study. Moreover, a potency dimension was found to be highly related to this good-bad dimension; that is, traits that were perceived as belonging to strong people were good; traits that were perceived as belonging to weak people were bad. This close correspondence of potency and evaluation is particularly instructive for understanding various problems that this individual faced in his life.

This particular individual reported that he gravitated toward powerful and/or dynamic people in both his informal and work-related social relations and avoided those whom he perceived to be weak or dependent. This report would seem to be a restatement of his belief that powerful people were desirable. On the other hand, his intimate relations were with people he considered to be dependent and not self-directed. He himself felt powerful in relation to these dependent persons. However, he felt inadequate in the presence of figures perceived to be powerful, although, as stated above, he gravitated toward such figures. I observed that the subject described his ideal self as powerful-good, his negative self as weak-bad, and his present self as both powerful and weak; everyone else was described as either one or the other. I queried the subject with regard to this quality of his self and other descriptions: Did he see himself as simultaneously powerful and weak? His answer was "no": He vacillated in his perception of himself as either very powerful — almost grandiose — and extremely inadequate, depending on whom he was with.

As I interpret it, the subject's reliance on a potency-evaluative dimension in his perception of self and other created some deleterious effects in his life experience, in addition to a vacillating self-in-relation-to-other image. One troubled experience occurred three years before this individual had become a subject in this study. After seeing the film *The Exorcist*, he experienced a period of extreme anxiety, coupled with fears of being possessed. This experience was intense and debilitating for a period of about six months and continued, albeit with less intensity, for a period of another year. Basically I was able to relate this troubled period to his inability to integrate the concept of Satan (very powerful yet very bad) into his overall conceptual framework. It seems conceivable that he saw the possibility of a future self in the demon; that is, if he became too powerful he might become evil; he might destroy the others around him. His conceptual framework had never before allowed for the co-occurrence of badness and power. It could be that the possibility of a powerful-bad self, heretofore never allowed by his conceptual framework, was symbolized in the fear of being possessed, that is, becoming the demon.

During this troubled period, he underwent no formal "therapy"; instead he seemed to develop a new pathway for experience and conduct. Actually, as I see it, he disentangled the construct school-play from his superordinate dimension and immersed himself in both academic affairs and recreational activity (mostly gambling). He kept his academic friends and gambling friends physically and conceptually apart, and moved back and forth between the two domains with increasing regularity. The shifting back and forth on this dimension had no implications for a shift back and forth on the superordinate evaluation-potency dimension, and gradually the intensity of the experience evoked by *The Exorcist* diminished.

Gradually the school-play dimension became again superordinated by his good-bad dimension: He started to view academic concerns as positive and his gambling as negative, probably because he began losing large sums of money. One year before this individual became our subject his gambling decreased noticeably, although to this day he flirts with it occasionally. He views gambling as bad, but views the enterprise of prediction involved (for him) in gambling as implying that he is powerful. Thus his flirtations with gambling can be seen as an attempt to explore the personal meanings of being bad but powerful, although on a less threatening scale than the experience that was thrust upon him when confronted with the concept demon. It still seems as if he has failed to integrate bad-yet-powerful into his overall framework: To this day he has a sense of discontinuity when returning from gambling activity to other, say academic, activities. It could be said that he experiences fragmentation (see Chapter 11 on the Fragmentation Corollary) upon starting or ending gambling activity.

Another notable aspect of this subject's implicit personality theory is seen in his use of a dimension that Kim and Rosenberg would call a "content dimension" — large-small. This dimension was strongly related to his overall evaluative-potency dimension. Being large was viewed as having an impact on someone or something, that is, being powerful and good. Being small was bad. Since preadolescence, up to and including the point in his life where he completed the Rosenberg (1977) "version" of the Rep Grid, this subject was large (300 pounds, 6 feet, 2 inches tall); in fact, he was obese.

The subject had made several attempts to lose weight. Prior to seeing *The Exorcist*, he had lost 40 pounds. However, after seeing *The Exorcist*, he regained the weight. (Did becoming small and thin, like the little girl in the movie, imply that he would be possessed — become powerless?) Two years later he lost another substantial amount of weight, started to feel "weird," and regained it. It seems that if he reconstrued his body along the large-small dimension, somehow he would become small, weak, and powerless. Yet he would also become "good" (he did not like being fat) — but good and weak constituted for him an experience that could not be integrated into his overall conceptual system, just as bad and strong (symbolized by the demon) could not be integrated.

He perceived that people treated him differently whenever he lost weight. He thought that they were treating him as if he had less impact, even though they also praised his efforts. In my interpretation, every time he regained weight, he was literally moving his "body" along the large-small dimension so as to again see himself as having impact.

Actually, for the subject, the relationships of the constructs about body size with other superordinate constructs were implicit: He could not spell out these relationships. He had attempted to construe other explicit constructions of his weight problem (and there are many, "scientific" and otherwise). For example, he thought about the idea that fat people were simply lazy. This made no sense to him because when he lost weight he felt lethargic; he felt energetic when he was fat.

When he completed Rosenberg's (1977) person description tasks and examined the various (see Rosenberg, 1977) representations of his implicit personality theory, he was struck by the fact that large was equated with powerful and small was equated with weak. By making the implicit connections between body size and having impact explicit to the subject, the subject could suddenly explain his feeling of "weirdness" in previous attempts to lose weight. Certainly other factors were involved in what then ensued, but following his "insight" the subject successfully lost weight; moreover, he has maintained his weight at 175 pounds for four years. Interestingly enough, making the implicit explicit is the essential feature of cognitive therapy (Beck et al., 1979) that has compared favorably with treatment by means of antidepressants.

Notes on Implications for Therapy Based on the Second Case

In Kellian theory, the Individuality Corollary emphasizes the importance of own organization. In the above case we have a cogent illustration of how the implicit parts of a person's own organization have to be understood and made explicit to that person in order for that person to make a significant change in his life, or at least understand some of the chaotic experiences confronting him. Borrowing the constructions of others, which this subject could do, just as subjects in the common-vocabulary group in Kim and Rosenberg's study (1980) could do, did not necessarily make his experiences more meaningful to him (give him "insight") or allow him to make any significant changes, such as losing weight.

Although each of us has the ability to share momentarily another's (that is, a reference group's) organization of experience, it would seem that own organization, essentially the interrelations among personal constructs, is what really matters in an individual's day-to-day psychological processes.

If it is own organization that really matters, then it is a clinician's role, first of all, to construe the personal construct system of his client. A reader familiar with Kelly's approach to psychotherapy will readily recognize this idea as central to his approach. Second, the clinician opens to the client the possibility of generating alternative ways of construing self and other.

However, any effort to provide the client with alternatives will fall on deaf ears if those alternatives have little or no (implied) relationship to the client's own organization. For example, if a clinician were to have suggested to the subject discussed in this chapter that his overeating was an attempt to recover a lost love object, the client would have been side-tracked. Guided by the therapist, the client would have been engaged in efforts to recover "memories" of that loss. Moreover, although "loss" was not an integral thread in this subject's personal experience, the client (presumably because he had been trained to make sense out of another's constructions) might find himself trying to reconstrue his past in terms of what he understands to be loss. An interesting spectacle might be understood in terms of loss, and the clinician's construction would be confirmed. For this particular case, I doubt that any harm would have been done, unless, of course, the client had well-elaborated constructs revolving around the notion of "wasting time."

Of course, it is relatively easy to generate cases in which the alaternatives provided by the clinician can be clearly harmful. If the construct I control versus they control is a superordinate construct in the client's system, assembling a behavior modification program for that individual could well result in catastrophe, especially if the client can tell a rather bleak story centering on the notion that he controls. Even if the client does not kill himself, we have validated the very same superordinate construct that has given the client his set of adjustment problems. We have frozen his system; we have helped him make himself a victim of his own biography.

The foregoing section should not be viewed as an attempt to sell Kellian therapy, or any therapy for that matter. The point we are making is simple. Since we have claimed that own organization of experience is an important consideration to any psychological process, it follows that own organization is central to understanding and implementing the interpersonal process that is involved in therapy. However, since we are cavalier in stating that own organization is what matters in any psychological process, we will not linger on the topic of therapy. We will now discuss the Individuality Corollary as it is relevant to prototypes in person perception.

THE INDIVIDUALITY COROLLARY AND
THE STUDY OF PROTOTYPES

Many personologists have sought to establish that there are "types" of personalities. A reader with only a passing familiarity with personality theory and research will easily recognize these personality types: the anal personality; the extrovert; the authoritarian personality. The discussion thus far, which centers on the utility of examining own organization for understanding an individual's conduct, would suggest that we focus not so much on how an individual fits into an existing typology, but rather on what typologies individuals employ in their perceptions of persons.

If we are to focus on the categories or types of personalities that an individual believes to exist, then important matters to consider are the configurations of attributes that are believed to be prototypical (ideal examples) of a given personality category (Cantor and Mischel, 1979), and the persons in an individual's life who best fit a given prototype.

The notion of a prototype has appeared in the cognitive literature as a way of understanding memory phenomenon (Bartlett, 1932; Posner and Keele, 1968, 1970). When subjects are shown a series of patterns, even random dot patterns, they seem to abstract — build a schema for — a prototypical visual pattern and use it as a standard for subsequent memory tasks. They indicate in the memory phase that they "had seen" patterns that resembled their standard, even though such patterns were never shown (Posner and Keele, 1970).

Cantor and Mischel (1977) argue that individuals also organize — build a schema for — trait descriptions (for example, bold, outgoing, energetic) by subsuming them under a "more abstract superordinate trait that functions as a unifying category label" (p. 45). Such superordinate schema have properties similar to prototypes in memory tasks. Cantor and Mischel (1977) have shown that when subjects are shown a series of statements that represent an introvert, they misidentify, in a later recognition task, some introvert statements that were never previously seen as having been original introvert statements.

Rogers, Kuiper, and Kirker (1977) argue that the construct self-not self acts as a prototype, a standard against which incoming data about persons are interpreted or coded (see also Carver, 1979; Mancuso and Ceely, 1980; Markus, 1977 for further discussion of self-standards). They report a study (Rogers, Rogers, and Kuiper, 1977, n. 2) in which subjects filled out self ratings on 84 adjectives. Two and a half months later the same subjects participated in a recognition task. First they saw a set of 42 adjectives randomly selected from the 84 originally presented items. Then subjects were required to recognize these 42 within the total set of 84. Subjects made more false alarms (reported that the adjectives were in the set of 42 when they had not been) for adjectives that were self-descriptive than for adjectives that were not. The superordinate schema self appears to serve as a prototype, just as the schema introvert had been used as a prototype in Cantor and Mischel (1977) and as the abstracted visual pattern had served as a prototype in Posner and Keele (1970).

The special utility of Rogers, Kuiper, and Kirker's (1977) notion of the self as a prototype is that self may be a widely used personal prototype: It seems to reflect any individual's own organization of person perceptions. Cantor and Mischel (1977) suggested that the superordinate category introvert is a prototype; however, we would expect that the category introvert only acts as a prototype when it is in fact used by subjects in organizing their perceptions of people. Self seems a more likely candidate for a "universally used" personal prototype.

From the extant discussions of prototypes it seems that prototypes must be superordinate schemata. In fact, the ideas of superordinate schemata and prototypes are often used interchangeably. The idea of superordination, as Kelly (1955) used it, can be conceived in terms of asymmetric implication. For example, assume that good is superordinate to other constructs in an individual's personal construct system. That means that when the perceiver detects one quality (say intelligent) in another person, that quality implies that that person is a "good" person. However, it does not mean that the perceiver views all good people as intelligent. In other words, intelligent implies good "more" than good implies intelligent: asymmetric implication!

Gara and Rosenberg (1979) have developed a methodology for determining which persons (not descriptors) in a subject's life show asymmetric implications. Subjects chose persons in their lives who fit certain roles (parents, siblings, close and distant relatives, close and casual friends, lovers, public figures, mythical figures, and disliked people) and described those people using their own vocabulary. If Persons A and B were described such that everything A had, B had, but not vice-versa, then A → B more than B → A. B was thus a superset of A, and A was a subset of B. Further, from the above discussion, B was superordinate to A.

Using this line of reasoning, they identified the persons that were supersets (superordinate) to many other persons that the individual described. The self and mother were identified as supersets in 8 of 14 cases. Therefore the idea that self is a widely used superordinate schema is not a bad one; however, it is not universally used. Consistent with the Individuality Corollary, different supersets emerged from the person descriptions of different subjects. Some subjects had only parental figures as supersets, whereas other subjects had nonparental figures (lover, best friend) as supersets. A third group of subjects had both parental figures and nonparental figures as supersets. For all subjects, mythical, public, or disliked role figures were never found to be supersets.

Gara and Rosenberg (1979) suggest that supersets act as standards to which other persons that an individual might know or meet are compared; that is, the individual sees other persons as partial replications of his supersets. In other words, supersets are ptototypes, albeit personal prototypes.

The idea that supersets serve as prototypes can be illustrated in the clinical phenomenon of transference. Transference refers to the situation in psychotherapy where the therapist is seen as a partial replication (subset) of a significant person (say mother) in the patient's life, and the patient acts and reacts with the therapist on the basis of his perceptions of mother. Something about the therapy context may call to mind dependency constructs, which may very well instantiate the construction mother for the patient, whereupon the patient subsequently makes attributions to the therapist consistent with his perceptions of mother, even though such attributions are inappropriate. Transference, then, is a naturally occurring analog of the use of prototypes in laboratory settings: In laboratory settings subjects retrieve from memory items that are consistent with their prototypes, even though such items are inappropriate; that is, they were never presented in the memory task.

The idea that transference involves the use of prototypical persons, coupled with the fact that two such persons discussed in classical accounts of transference (self and mother) are often identified as supersets in Gara and Rosenberg (1979), is consistent with the idea that supersets are prototypes. The validity of the idea is further strengthened by the fact that self was also found to act like a prototype in memory for personality descriptions. The procedures for identifying supersets reported in Gara and Rosenberg (1979) may then be viewed as ways to identify personal prototypes. The study also shows that rating sclaes can be used as short-cut methods for identifying such personal prototypes or supersets.

Supersets, then, comprise the set of persons that an individual *generally* uses as standards to which he compares other persons (and new persons) in his life. We emphasize the qualifier *generally* because often individuals compare another person to a standard that involves only one content category, and the supersets discussed in Gara and Rosenberg (1979) really span many content categories. However, if a man is looking for a date in a single's bar, and is accustomed to using the content category physical attractiveness to determine the suitability of another for a date, he really does not need to use a superset that spans many content categories. He can and probably does use a person that spans only the content category physically attractive; such a person would be a superset for that category but not an overall superset. From Gara and Rosenberg (1979) we know that such a person (call it a content specific superset) would probably not be a significant person in the individual's life; it may even be a public figure. Yet, in this context, the content specific superset is used as a prototype.

To summarize this section, the Individuality Corollary offers an important consideration for the growing numbers of researchers interested in prototypes. It invites them to look at personal prototypes. Although research on personal prototypes is sparse to date, it is promising enough to warrant further investigation, especially when the focus is on individuals and their day-to-day psychological processes.

THE INDIVIDUALITY COROLLARY IN MEMORY RESEARCH

We have been maintaining throughout that an individual's own organization of experience is a fundamental consideration in the study of any psychological process. However, the psychological processes that have been discussed so far essentially have to do with the perception of persons. There is some evidence, however, that research in the area of memory process is beginning to consider own organization as an important thread in the context of memory phenomena.

Studies of memory completed by Jacoby (1978), Slamecka and Graf (1978), and Graf (1980) have clearly shown the working of a "generation effect." This term refers to the finding that retention for verbal material is consistently worse when subjects simply read the material than when they generate the same material according to some rule. Such an effect could be simply due to the fact that generating verbal material requires more effortful and elaborative processing than simply reading it. McFarland, Frey, and Rhodes (1980), however, maintain that effortful versus effortless processing is not the entire story. The greater memorability of subject-over-experimenter-generated words (to fit a specified context, for example, what word means the same as *cave*?) also has to do with the "personal reference attribute of the generation operation per se" (p. 210). That is, when subjects generate a word to fit a semantic context (what means the same as *cave*?) they are using their own semantic network (see Collins and Loftus, 1975; Collins and Quillian, 1972, for discussion of semantic networks) in storage, and they are likely to retrace that network in recall. When they read experimenter-generated words that fit a semantic context, they may not share the experimenter's semantic network and thus will not have that particular semantic network available to them in the retrieval phase. In other words, because subjects are more likely to use the *same* semantic network (their own) in both the encoding and retrieval phases of memory when they generate the to-be-remembered material, than when they read experimenter-generated material, memory performance is enhanced. Again, McFarland et al. (1980) have shown that the generation effect is not simply due to the fact that generating verbal material requires more effortful processing than simply reading it. Own organization is an important consideration in memory process.

SUMMARY

The Individuality Corollary invites a close examination of an individual's own organization of experience for an understanding of his conduct. This chapter has focused on methods for assessing own organization of beliefs about persons, how determinations of shared organization of beliefs about persons are better served by examining own organization first, and how an individual's conduct can make sense to an observer if we allow ourselves glimpses into his experiential world. This chapter has also touched briefly upon the possibilities that a focus on own organization of experience would offer to ongoing inquiry into psychological processes such as memory and psychological representation (prototypes). The point that we arrive at is probably less modest than Kelly's statement that persons differ in their construction of events: Own organization of experience is an important matter to consider in the understanding of any psychological process. I wonder what a personality theory would look like if it made the Individuality Corollary the Fundamental Postulate?

5

THE ORGANIZATION OF CONSTRUCT SYSTEMS:
THE ORGANIZATION COROLLARY

Walter H. Crockett

The Organization Corollary: Each person characteristically evolves, for his convenience in anticipating events, a construction system embracing ordinal relations between constructs.

Sarbin (1977) conjectured that George Kelly's theoretical ideas were rooted in a world view that Pepper (1942) would call contextualism. Though Sarbin (p. 12) doubted that Kelly took the implications of that world view as far as he might have, he concluded that when Kelly wrenched free from the mechanistic metaphor that was prevalent during his time, he moved to a concern with how psychological events affect and are affected by the social context in which they occur. However, the Organizational Corollary and related conceptions emphasize an aspect of personal construct theory that does not rest easy under the contextualist mantle. Instead, the corollary implies another root metaphor, one that Pepper termed organicism.

It is not the purpose of this chapter to argue at length that Kelly was an organicist. Mancuso (1979) has joined Sarbin in categorizing him as a contextualist. Likely they are right. On the other hand, when Delia (1976, 1977) elaborated a theoretical system that combined many of Kelly's ideas with those of Werner, Piaget, and G. H. Mead, he explicitly adopted an organismic position. Whatever root metaphor Kelly may have preferred, by the corollary here discussed he was committed to the importance of organization as well as of context. The corollary asserts the fundamental importance of interdependence and hierarchic relations among constructs. It requires advocates of the theory

62

to pay attention to developmental and organizational properties of systems of constructs.

In what follows, I will first try to lay out some basic concepts about organization. This will be followed by a discussion of research into the organization of systems of constructs: their development, the relationships among constructs, and the effects of organizational properties upon how others are construed. The final section will sketch out some directions in which I believe future research and theory might profitably move.

BASIC CONCEPTS

Kelly (1955) contended that an individual's unique system of constructs is what is distinctive about that individual's personality. The system is hierarchically organized, in the sense that some constructs subsume others. It continuously evolves and changes so as to minimize incompatibilities and inconsistencies. The function of the system is to assist the individual to anticipate events. When events are not adequately anticipated, the system changes. While we understand events in terms of our systems of constructs — "we can look at natural events any way we like" (p. 20) — when the way we look at a set of events produces incorrect anticipations, something in the system has to change.

Extensions and Related Concepts

The corollary's implications are extended by other aspects of the theory, many of which are discussed in other chapters of this book. The Modulation Corollary (Chapter 10) asserts that some constructs are permeable; that is, they can readily be extended to new events or constructs, while other constructs are impermeable. Bannister and Fransella (1971, p. 32) assert that it is not the constructs that have those properties, it is we who use the constructs in a permeable or impermeable way. This means that constructs or sets of constructs may change from permeable to impermeable and back, depending upon the effectiveness of the person's anticipations and the changes in either constructs or anticipations that may be implied when a person extends a construct to embrace new elements.

According to the Fragmentation Corollary (Chapter 11) an individual may employ, at different times, constructs from subsystems that are inferentially incompatible. Thus, personal construct theory does not require the entire system of a person's constructs to be internally consistent, only the subsystem of elements that is operative at a particular time. So long as they are not simultaneously invoked, two subsystems can be mutually inconsistent without disturbing unduly either the person involved or Kelly's theory.

Except to assert that constructs change as a consequence of ineffective anticipations, Kelly did not analyze in detail the development and change of construct systems. Presumably, such changes might involve the addition of new constructs, changes in the events to which a construct or set of constructs is applied, changes in the relations among constructs, or changes in how the individual uses the construct system. However, Kelly did discuss in some detail (pp. 877ff) how an individual's use of the construct system may change by the dilation or constriction of constructs or sets of constructs.

"Dilation" involves extending a construct or set of constructs to a wider range of events. If this does not cause inconsistency with other constructs or the invalidation of anticipations, the extension may persist; the construct becomes more permeable. If dilation leads to inconsistency or invalid anticipations, however, it will have produced anxiety, by Kelly's definition. One of two outcomes is likely. First, the person may pull back from the potential change, either by constricting the range of applicability of those constructs or by avoiding the unpredictable elements. Alternatively, the person may set out to revise the constructs, using propositional constructs to try to make sense of the elements, or "loosening" present constructs by making them less precise.

In any case, some constructs are easier to change than others. Core constructs, those by which the person maintains identity, are resistant to change. Peripheral constructs can be altered without seriously modifying the structure.

Even this cursory summary of Kelly's comments about the organization of constructs leaves no doubt that he conceived them as falling within organized, systematically related systems; but he did not carry out a detailed analysis of the effects of such organization or of how it influences the development and change of constructs. Many of the concepts by which Kelly dealt with change or resistance to change — dilation versus constriction, tightening versus loosening, and the like — are metaphorically rich. Clinicians who work within Kelly's systems seem easily to adopt them as tools to understand how and in which directions their clients might want to, or are likely to, change. What the concepts offer in richness of associations and in clinical insight, however, they take back in lack of precision. It is difficult to define them operationally and to put them to empirical test. Before turning to research on the organization of constructs, we will develop a few general concepts about organization and will consider how they pertain to personal construct theory. Many of these are already implicit in personal construct theory.

Some Concepts about Organization and Change

What keeps personal construct theory from being a full-fledged contextualism is its assertion that the context is interpreted through a perceiver's constructs. Changes in the way one construes events depend in part, but only in part, upon changes in the context. When one's anticipations do not work, the construct system must change; but the changes do not simply mirror changes in the context; they also depend upon the way the system is organized. Changes in one or a few constructs often require changes in other constructs. To accept one change — for example, to come to accept the theory of evolution — may imply changes the individual cannot accept in other parts of the construct system — for instance, rejection of constructs about a personal God who will care for and protect us. To understand how a person will respond to exposure to a set of events presented in a particular way, we often need to know more than just how the person construes those specific events. We must also know how that construal is related to other important constructs and sets of constructs in the individual's system.

Elements of the System

Any organized system consists of a set of elements in relation to each other. The elements of a construct system are personal constructs and psychological representations of the events to which the constructs are applied. The distinction between constructs and representations of events will be developed in the last section of this chapter. For present purposes, we can consider a construct to be a cognitive-perceptual discrimination of some aspect of an event or events. Most of the work of personal construct theorists has dealt with events relative to people; the constructs that were studied have mostly referred to the attributes of people. As an approach to cognition, the viewpoint can easily be extended to other domains (see Adams-Webber, 1979a, Chapter 8); however, present attention will focus upon constructs about people.

The constructs of different individuals, or of the same individual at different times or in different conceptual domains, may differ in a number of ways. Some of these include the content of the constructs — differences between people in the content of their constructs implies differences in the way they will construe events; the number of constructs that are employed to deal with the events of a domain — presumably, the more constructs one employs for a given set of events, the more carefully one is able to discriminate among those events; the preciseness of the constructs — whether they are vague and cloudy or relatively clear and carefully delineated. Changes in the vagueness or precision of the constructs an individual employs constitute one aspect of construct development.

Relations among Constructs

Our concern will be with implicational relations among constructs. These are relations that permit a person to infer the presence of some constructs from a knowledge of others. Implicational relations may rest upon a number of different bases. Three will be considered here.

The basis for relations among constructs that Kelly emphasized was superordination-subordination. He discussed two forms of superordination (1955, pp. 479ff). In the first, a superordinate construct includes every element that the subordinate construct includes and more, too. Thus, any element that falls within the range of convenience of courteous-discourteous might also be included within the range of right-wrong; however, right-wrong might contain other elements that do not fall within the range of courteous-discourteous. The other sense of superordination is one in which both a construct and its contrast are subsumed under one pole of another construct, as when the "evaluative" pole of evaluative-objective subsumes both poles of right-wrong. Ryle (1975) pointed out that the latter type of superordination is seldom applied to the construal of other people; it is mainly applied to other constructs. For the most part, in the following, we will use superordination in the first sense.

In a doctoral dissertation that was carried out under Kelly's direction, Hinkle (1965) presented the most extensive analysis that has yet been made of implicational relationships among constructs. Some of its details will be discussed below. Consider Hinkle's definition of superordination: One construct, A, is called superordinate to another construct, B, if A is implied by B; A is called subordinate to B if it implies B. The definition follows from Kelly's first sense of the term "superordinate."

It is too restrictive to contend that superordination-subordination exhausts the possibilities of implicational relations among constructs. There are at least two other bases for implicational relations among constructs. One of these is similarity in the kinds of events that evoke the constructs. Consider, for example, the constructs helpful-not helpful and sympathetic-unsympathetic. For at least one perceiver, neither of these constructs is superordinate to the other; that is, neither includes all of the elements that are subsumed by the other and more, too. Nor are they synonymous, for the perceiver can and does ascribe one construct, but not the other, to different individuals. Still, the constructs are mutually implicative. If that perceiver knows how someone else falls on one of the two constructs, he is likely to draw inferences to the second construct. The reason seems to be that, for this perceiver, the behaviors of other people that elicit the ascription "helpful" (or "not helpful") overlap to a considerable extent with the behaviors that elicit "sympathetic" (or "unsympathetic"); but neither construct subsumes the other.

A third source of implication among constructs is a perceiver's belief that one construct requires another in some causal sense. For another perceiver, knowing how a person could be characterized on anxious-not anxious permitted inferences to the construct perceptive-imperceptive. For this perceiver, a person who was anxious could not be perceptive, but had to be imperceptive. Whether one agrees or disagrees with this implication, it can hardly be thought to reflect either superordination-subordination or similarity of actions. Instead, it rests upon the assumption that the presence of one quality, anxious, prohibits the other, perceptive, or at least greatly reduces its likelihood.

Patterns of Relations between a Pair of Constructs

Hinkle (1965, pp. 18-19) reported that four patterns of implication between pairs of constructs are commonly observed. One of these, which Hinkle termed parallel, occurs when each pole of one construct, A-$\overline{A}$, implies the corresponding pole of another construct, B-$\overline{B}$. This is the pattern that would be expected of a superordinate-subordinate pair of constructs, such as right-wrong and courteous-discourteous. It may also occur when two constructs are conceived to be causally related.

A second, reciprocal type of relation occurs when A-$\overline{A}$ implies B-$\overline{B}$, as in the parallel form, but, in addition, B-$\overline{B}$ implies A-$\overline{A}$, in return. Hinkle suggested that pairs of constructs of this type may be functionally equivalent. It is also possible that they refer to distinct, but empirically related, events as in the example of helpful-not helpful and sympathetic-unsympathetic. Again, the pair of constructs may be causally related, as in happy-unhappy and relaxed-nervous.

A third pattern of relations Hinkle termed orthogonal. There are two types: both A and $\overline{A}$ imply B, as in Kelly's second form of subordinate-superordinate relations, described above; A implies B but $\overline{A}$ does not imply $\overline{B}$, as in the case of the causal implication, above, in which "anxious" implied "imperceptive" but "not anxious" did not necessarily imply "perceptive."

Finally, Hinkle labeled a fourth common pattern ambiguous. In it either A or $\overline{A}$ implies both B and $\overline{B}$. He gave as an example a subject for whom "fun-loving" and "serious" each implied both "desired behavior" and "undesired behavior." Hinkle called the pattern an "implicative dilemma"; he said it either fails to differentiate the contexts in which the constructs are used (for example, does not separate "fun-loving in Context A" from "fun-loving on Context B"), or it employs a single construct label to identify two different constructs. He remarked, "psychological movement, conflict resolution, and insight depend on the locating of such points of ambiguous implication and the resolving of them into parallel or orthogonal forms" (p. 19).

Relations within Larger Sets of Constructs

The preceding refer to patterns of implication between pairs of constructs. The problem becomes more complicated when the relations among several constructs are considered. To take one complication, some people employ constructs that can alter the expected pattern of relations between other pairs of constructs. One subject employed the construct attentive-inattentive as a "switching" construct in this manner. According to this subject, if a person is attentive, then the constructs helpful-not helpful and sympathetic-unsympathetic are in a reciprocal relation to each other. However, if a person is inattentive, then the other two constructs are deemed to be unrelated. Such complications have yet to be investigated in detail. Also largely uninvestigated is the extent to which the implications within a set of constructs are logically consistent, and the effects of inconsistency when it exists. In short, there remains a great deal of theoretical and empirical work to be accomplished in the analysis of the patterns of relationships among constructs.

Impermanence of Structure

It is difficult to think about the structure of a system without imputing to it greater permanence than it possesses. It is important to remember that structural properties — elements and their relations — change from time to time. Sometimes the change involves the addition of new constructs, the revision of old ones, or the alterations of relations among constructs. Such changes will be discussed shortly. There are other sources of fluctuation, as well. Kelly's reference to dilation-constriction and to tightening-loosening has already been mentioned. Those terms refer to processes that reflect the effects of the success of one's anticipations upon structural aspects of one's construct system.

The matter is still more complex. According to Kelly, the relation between constructs may reverse itself from time to time. For example, for a particular person, the construct intelligent-stupid may, at one time, be subordinate to good-bad, while both intelligent-stupid and good-bad may be subordinate, in the second sense of that term to the "evaluative" pole of evaluative-descriptive. Yet, at another time, " 'intelligent' may embrace all things 'good' together with all things 'evaluative,' and 'stupid' would be the term for 'bad' and 'descriptive' things; or, if the other kind of subsuming is involved, 'intelligent' might embrace the construct *evaluative vs. descriptive* while 'stupid' would be the term for the *good vs. bad* dichotomy" (Kelly, 1955, p. 58). It is open to debate whether the constructs that are indexed by the terms *intelligent, stupid, good, bad, evaluative,* and *descriptive* are used in different ways in the preceding passage. What is clear, however, is that the relationships among constructs in a person's system are likely to be fuzzy and impermanent. It must constantly be borne in mind that the apparent preciseness of a correlation matrix, a Repertory Grid, an Implication Grid, or some other measure of relationships among constructs will often mask great ambiguity of the relationships in an actual system of constructs.

Constructs and Words

We are often reminded to distinguish between constructs and words. A construct is a discrimination that one makes about events or things. Most people who have completed the Role Repertory Test will have found themselves, at least once, knowing very clearly how two people were alike and different from a third but being unable to find a word or a phrase that satisfactorily represented the construct they had in mind. Sometimes both poles of a construct are not easily verbalized. At other times, one pole may be expressed and the other "submerged." Not only are some constructs not verbalizable, but a particular word may be used with different meanings to index quite different constructs. Clearly, then, words and constructs are not the same things.

Just as clearly, constructs and words are closely related. They are related because words (or, more generally, verbal and nonverbal symbols) are the vehicles by which people communicate their constructs to friends, to psychotherapists, to psychological researchers, and, in all likelihood, to themselves.

No doubt people often fuse words and constructs in their own minds. A perceiver who attributes "intelligent in school" to another person may almost automatically ascribe "intelligent in social relations" to the same person, even though the same perceiver later insists upon distinguishing between the two kinds of intelligence. It is rash to dismiss words as mere verbal labels, considering only constructs as the real thing. Words can have real effects, too, because: they make it more likely that a perceiver will employ a construct; they aid in the storage of past experience in memory; and perceivers, themselves, often mistake the word for the construct. The quotation from Hinkle about ambiguously related constructs makes this last point clear. A perceiver who fails to distinguish fun-loving-versus-serious-in-Context-A from fun-loving-versus-serious-in-Context-B may mistake his own words for the underlying constructs and become hung up on the examination of "inconsistencies" that result more from the confusion of words with constructs than from contradictions within the construct system itself. A large share of the time spent in psychotherapy seems to be devoted to unraveling such ambiguities.

RESEARCH INTO THE ORGANIZATION OF CONSTRUCTS

The study of how an ongoing, changing system is organized has to be concerned with how the system developed. This section will begin by considering the development of construct systems. It will then examine, as one aspect of the structure of a construct system, the number of constructs it contains. This will be followed by a review of research and theory into relations among constructs.

The Development of Construct Systems

An infant does not come equipped with an elaborate system of personal constructs; therefore, how construct systems develop is of fundamental importance. Within the general framework of personal construct theory, the problem has been addressed in some detail by Adams-Webber (1970, 1979a) and by Salmon (1970). From a somewhat different perspective, Delia and his associates (Swanson and Delia, 1976; Delia, 1976, 1977; Applegate and Delia, 1980) have combined the approaches of Kelly, Werner, Piaget, and G. H. Mead to the analysis of personal constructs and their role in interpersonal communication. The general theoretical view that will be outlined here draws heavily upon those sources.

Some Theoretical Conceptions

Developmental theorists such as Werner (1957), Piaget (1960), or Riegel (1979) view development as a kind of dialectical process. An individual with a unique, organized system of ideas, intentions, adaptive patterns, and related processes meets an environment with a particular unique set of objects, people, and demands. If events in the environment can be interpreted and dealt with by the system as it is (in Piaget's terms, can be "assimilated" to the system) there need be little development or change in the system. However, if intractable aspects of the environment cannot easily be handled by the system, then aspects of the system must change (in Piaget's terms, the system must "accommodate") so as to deal more effectively with the environment. In this view, the continued elaboration of a more complex system depends upon some degree of incompatibility between the system and the environment. Little or no incompatibility will mean little or no development; too much incompatibility may overwhelm the system by requiring changes that are too great for the system to undertake given its present form of organization.

The compatibility between this scheme of development and personal construct theory is obvious. Constructs and relations among constructs develop and change because of the individual's difficulties in anticipating events effectively. When unexpected outcomes occur, people revise and extend their constructs in the interests of accounting for past events and anticipating future ones. In the process, three things happen in the system of constructs: New constructs are differentiated; abstract, dispositional constructs appear; and a pattern of hierarchical relationships among constructs is elaborated.

An infant's constructs are global, diffuse, and unverbalized. Over time, these vague and imprecise constructs become more precise. A global construct is differentiated into a number of specific, more clearly articulated ones that enable their user to make more, and more precise, discriminations about relevant aspects of the environment. In an area a person knows little or nothing about, an adult's constructs are also likely to be global and diffuse. Continued experience by an adult with a new set of events will produce changes in the construct system that follow the same formal developmental principles as in children: increased differentiation of constructs; the generation of abstract, dispositional constructs; and the formation of hierarchical patterns of relationships among constructs.

The function of abstract constructs is to help a perceiver deal with what might be an overwhelming mass of details from the environment. People come to identify "dispositional" qualities of objects and events. These are qualities that are presumed to be relatively constant attributes of the objects or to refer to recurrent patterns in sequences of events (Heider, 1958). Dispositional constructs commonly refer to such things as abilities, personality traits, attitudes, beliefs, emotions, short-term intentions, and long-range goals. While constructs are being elaborated, they are tied together in patterns of relationship that become, with development, increasingly complex.

Soon, an individual enters new situations with a rather detailed set of constructs and, consequently, of anticipations. When the individual meets a new acquaintance, the construct system will affect the qualities in the stranger's appearance and behavior that the individual will attend to. Even more, the construct system will affect how the stranger's behavior and appearance are interpreted — the constructs that are applied to the perceived behavior, the other constructs that are inferred, and the way the stranger is expected to behave in future encounters. Additional experience with that person will yield a more elaborate construal. Often, construals of the new acquaintance will change as expectations about his behavior are disconfirmed. Such a change often involves only a reconstrual of the other person in terms of other constructs in the perceiver's system; that is, some constructs are no longer ascribed to the person and other construct attributions are made. Less often, the change will bring about a revision of some part of the construct system by the differentiation of existing constructs, the generation of new ones, or changes in relations among constructs.

These developments are facilitated by the simultaneous development of language. Children begin with an egocentric view of the world, then develop one in which external objects — including, especially, people — are seen as independent of oneself, with stable, dispositional characteristics that persist over time and across situations. All of these developments are affected not just by the person's own direct experiences with others but also by discussions with family and other acquaintances, by reading books or viewing movies and television plays, by any number of other indirect experiences with others, and by the person's reflection upon these experiences.

According to the Individuality Corollary (Chapter 4) the construct systems of different people will develop in different ways and to different degrees of complexity. The same person will often show different degrees of complexity in different content domains. The same person may even reveal different degrees of complexity in the same content domain at different times. Despite this individuality, members of the same cultural community are likely to present a certain degree of similarity in their construct systems because they experience a similar set of events and they spend a great deal of time talking to each other about how those events should be construed.

Research into Developmental Changes in Constructs

A dozen or more studies have been carried out to explore differences in the kinds of constructs that people of different ages employ to describe others whom they know. Researchers consistently find an increase with age in the total number of constructs that children employ (Livesley and Bromley, 1973; Peevers and Secord, 1973; Scarlett, Press, and Crockett, 1971). In addition, there are qualitative changes with age in the nature of children's constructs.

Little (1968) reported a decline with age in children's use of constructs that described physical appearance, along with an increase in the use of psychological constructs. Brierley (cited in Adams-Webber, 1979a) found a similar age decline in children's use of role- and appearance-related constructs and an increase in constructs that referred to behavior and personality. Barratt (also cited in Adams-Webber, 1979a) reported much the same results except that constructs that described behavior also declined in the older age groups while those referring to personality increased.

Peevers and Secord (1973) developed a number of different ways of classifying constructs. They reported a change with age: from general, undifferentiating constructs to dispositional ones; from constructs that related the other person to the child, himself or herself, to those that are independent of the child; and from general ascriptions about another person to constructs that account for why one person is the way he is. Livesley and Bromley (1973) found a very similar pattern of results. Similarly, Scarlett, Press, and Crockett (1971) found a shift with age from the use of egocentric constructs to nonegocentric ones and from constructs that described concrete behavior to constructs that referred to abstract, dispositional qualities. Duck (1975) reported a similar decrease with age in factual and physical constructs and an increase in psychological constructs. Duck also found that children tended to form friendships with others who formed constructs similar to their own; this was especially true with "fact" constructs.

In short, a number of investigators have reported a consistent pattern of change in constructs with age; however, the precise ages at which particular changes in constructs were observed varied somewhat from study to study. Young children's constructs are quite concrete. Even when they are dispositional, they tend to be global and diffuse ("she's a nice girl," or "he helps me"). Young children also tend to describe others in terms of how the others are related to the describer ("we play together a lot" or "he's always hitting me"). With increasing age, a child's constructs become more abstract and dispositional, and they refer to more precisely defined qualities. Thus, "nice" may be differentiated into "helpful, quiet, funny, sharing, artistic, . . ." It should be noted that concrete, physical, factual, and self-oriented constructs do not disappear from the descriptions of older children and adults. However, their role in the description changes: They come to be subordinated to, to be organized and interpreted by, the more abstract, dispositional constructs.

Developmental Changes in Social Perception and Interpersonal Communication

As the construct systems of children change in the ways described above, their ability to adapt their behavior to different characteristics in others increases. Delia and his associates have carried out a program of research into age differences in the strategies children adopt in communicating to people with different characteristics. Clark and Delia (1976) asked children to produce persuasive messages in a variety of familiar situations, each involving different people. They developed a way of scoring children's responses according to whether their messages acknowledged the perspective of the others and adapted to it. Age was highly correlated with such ability in perspective taking (Clark and Delia, 1976; Delia, Kline, and Burleson, 1979). A similar result was obtained using Alvy's (1973) measure of listener-adapted communication (Delia and

Clark, 1977). With increasing age, children's communications show greater responsiveness to differences in the other child's feelings (Delia et al., cited in O'Keefe and Sypher, in press). The dependence of these changes upon aspects of children's personal construct systems will be discussed below.

Rosenbach, Crockett, and Wapner (1973) varied, in a factorial design, subjects' age and whether or not they were in a positive, a negative, or a neutral relationship to another person. Subjects were then given information about both desirable and undesirable actions by that person. There was a consistent increase with age in the differentiation of subjects' impressions of that person and also in the extent to which they were able to reconcile the ambivalent information in a comprehensive, integrated impression. Other aspects of this experiment will be discussed below.

The Number of Constructs as an Aspect of Structure

If constructs develop in the manner sketched out above, then one variable that should distinguish the construct systems of different individuals is the number of constructs they contain. Crockett (1965) reasoned that differences in the number of constructs available to different people represented differences in the degree of differentiation of their personal construct systems. On the proposition that the differentiation and hierarchic integration of construct systems increase simultaneously, it seemed reasonable to assume that the number of constructs in a person's system would reflect its degree of complexity. Hence, the measure that was ultimately developed was termed "cognitive complexity." This was not a happy choice of terms because it fostered a confusion that has continued to this day between the number of constructs subjects employ and other measures that go by the name *complexity*; many of those measures have been shown to be uncorrelated with one another.

The Measure

Clearly, there is no way to identify and count all of the constructs in any person's system. At the same time, the Role Repertory Test, or any other device that requires a person to describe other people, provides a sample of the describer's constructs. If such samples are obtained in a standard manner for a set of people, then differences in the number of constructs those people employ may be assumed to reflect differences in the total number of constructs that are available to them. Crockett's measure of complexity grew out of this assumption. Note that this measure counts all types of constructs as equal: Relatively concrete descriptions of another person's behavior are given equal weight to abstract, dispositional constructs.

In the first study that was based on this measure, Mayo and Crockett (1964) had subjects generate constructs from a constant number of sorts on the Rep Test, then took the number of different constructs that were produced as the index of the subjects' relative complexity. Subsequent research indicated that asking subjects to describe eight acquaintances who were known to them — half of them male and half female, half peers and half superiors, half liked and half disliked — was easier than administering the Rep Test and produced much the same ordering of subjects. There is a high correlation between the number of constructs subjects used to describe one of those eight acquaintances and the number they used to describe the others. Therefore, subsequent researchers using this method have asked subjects to describe only four acquaintances (liked and disliked, male and female peers) or sometimes only two acquaintances (a liked and a disliked peer of the same sex as the subject).

Reliability and Validity

A study by Judith Supnick (reported in Crockett, 1965) showed a four-month test-retest reliability of .95 for this measure. In a large number of investigations, rater reliability in scoring responses to the measure has consistently approached or exceeded .90.

The chief reservations about the measure have concerned its validity. Leitner, Landfield, and Barr (quoted in Adams-Webber, 1979a) asserted that the measure is "contaminated by artifacts such as verbal fluency and writing speed." In fact, such has been shown *not* to be the case in half a dozen studies. When the number of constructs subjects employ is correlated with the number of words contained *in the same descriptions* (Powers, Jordan, and Street, 1979) the correlation is substantial, as would be true for any part-whole correlation; but such correlations are artificially inflated. Correlations of scores on this measure with scores on independent measures of verbal fluency have hovered around zero and have never attained statistical significance (Crockett, 1965; Rosenkrantz and Crockett, 1965; Scarlett, Press, and Crockett, 1971). Similarly, correlations of this measure with a variety of measures of intelligence have uniformly been nonsignificant (Crockett, 1965; Rosenkrantz and Crockett, 1965; Press, Crockett, and Rosenkrantz, 1969; Delia and Crockett, 1973). We may conclude, then, that the measure is *not* correlated with general loquacity nor, for subjects who are normally intelligent or brighter, with standard measures of intelligence.

Relationship to Communication Behavior

In most of the developmental studies reviewed above, Delia and his associates have employed this measure of complexity as an individual-differences variable. It has been shown to correlate with children's adaptation of their communications to the perspective of other persons (Clark and Delia, 1976, 1977; Delia and Clark, 1977) and with their performance on a variety of referential tasks and tasks that require adaptation to the feelings of others (Delia et al., cited in O'Keefe and Sypher, in press). It was also correlated with the flexibility of the strategies children used to persuade others (Delia, Kline, and Burleson, 1979).

Burleson (cited in O'Keefe and Sypher, in press) reported similar patterns of correlations except that, in the older age groups, the *number* of constructs subjects used on this measure was less highly correlated with the dependent variables than was the *proportion of abstract constructs* to the total number of constructs given. In all of this research, correlations between indexes of communication flexibility and this measure of complexity remained significant when the age of the subjects was partialed out. Sometimes complexity effects within a group exceeded the effects of age differences betweeen groups that were two years apart.

As would be expected from results of the developmental studies, the complexity measure is also positively correlated to indexes of communication behavior in adults. Hale and Delia (1976) reported that the measure correlated significantly with a measure of social perspective taking. O'Keefe and Delia (1979) found that the measure correlated significantly with subjects' strategic adaptation of their arguments and appeals in persuasive messages. Hale (1980) showed that the measure predicted subjects' effectiveness in communicating the characteristics of visual stimuli and in the Password game. Delia, Clark, and Switzer (1979) had subjects carry out ten-minute conversations with others they did not know; those who scored high on the complexity measure focused their conversations upon the characteristics of the two interactants; those who scored low on the measure concentrated their conversation on topics external to the interaction.

Relation to Reconciling Inconsistency in Impression

A number of experiments have been carried out into the effects of differences on the complexity measure upon how subjects deal with potentially contradictory information in forming impressions of others. Mayo and Crockett (1964), Nidorf and Crockett (1965), Delia, Clark, and Switzer (1974), and O'Keefe, Delia, and O'Keefe (1977) have all reported that complex subjects were more likely than noncomplex ones to integrate the potentially contradictory qualities in impressions that represented and reconciled the inconsistent elements. Later research has shown that a variety of factors can reduce or eliminate the effects of differences in complexity upon the resolution of inconsistency in impressions of others.

Rosenkrantz and Crockett (1965) and Meltzer, Crockett, and Rosenkrantz (1966) found the expected effects of complexity upon resolution of inconsistency so long as subjects agreed with the central values of the other person; however, when they were in basic disagreement with the other person's central values, complex subjects were no better than noncomplex subjects at reconciling the inconsistency. Delia (1972) reported a similar result in impressions of speakers: When the other person's speech dialect was similar to the subject's own, the relationship between complexity and resolution of inconsistency was found; however, when the other person's dialect revealed a different regional background from that of the subject's, complexity was not related to the resolution of inconsistency. Crockett, Mahood, and Press (1975) and Press, Crockett, and Delia (1975) found the expected effects of complexity upon resolution of inconsistency when subjects were oriented toward understanding the other person; however, when they were oriented toward evaluating the other person, complex subjects did no better than noncomplex ones.

The developmental experiment by Rosenbach, Crockett, and Wapner (1973) did not employ a measure of cognitive complexity. However, it showed that subjects who were emotionally involved with another person, either positively or negatively, were less likely to attend to and reconcile inconsistent qualities in that person's behavior than were subjects who were not involved with the person. Disliking led to univalent negative impressions, while liking led to univalent positive impressions of the other person; in both cases, subjects' impressions revealed little resolution of inconsistency, especially as compared to the impressions of uninvolved subjects. The magnitude of this effect increased with age, principally because the capacity to reconcile the inconsistency also increased with age; that is, emotional involvement has a greater potential disorganizing effect for adults than for children.

Relation to Other Aspects of Social Cognition

Press, Crockett, and Rosenkrantz (1969) studied the learning of balanced and unbalanced social structures. They found that complex subjects were less likely than noncomplex ones to persist in applying the balance schema to unbalanced structures. Delia and Crockett (1973) replicated the preceding finding and found the same effects of complexity upon the rate of learning dominance relations in linear-ordered and nonordered structures: Complex subjects did not cling as long as did noncomplex ones to the linear-ordering schema. In an altogether different experimental context, O'Keefe (1980) found that complex subjects were less likely than noncomplex ones to display consistency between their attitude toward another person and their behavioral intentions toward that person.

Summary and Conclusions

A substantial amount of research converges on the conclusion that the number of constructs subjects employ in describing a standard set of persons affects the way they construe other people. Subjects who use relatively many constructs are likely to differentiate relatively precisely among the characteristics of other people. They are also relatively more likely to employ abstract, dispositional constructs in their descriptions of others. Such individuals show greater flexibility than noncomplex subjects in adapting to differences in the perspectives and feelings of others. This, in turn, promotes increased flexibility in interpersonal communication. Complex individuals are relatively unlikely to rely on simple rules or principles when they construe others: They identify and reconcile potentially incongruent qualities in others; they are not tightly bound to organizing schemata, such as balance or linear ordering; and they do not unequivocally express their attitudes toward others in their behavior.

It is important to note, in addition, that the way such subjects employ their relatively complex construct systems may vary with changes in their relations to other people. The effects of complexity were wiped out by strong emotional feelings toward a person, by an orientation to evaluate, instead of to understand a person, by disagreement with a person on important values, or even by recognizing from a person's accent that he belonged to a disvalued out-group.

RELATIONSHIPS AMONG CONSTRUCTS

Two methods are employed to study relationships among constructs. One is to ask subjects directly to state which constructs imply others; the other is to infer relations among constructs from the way subjects use them to describe people. Research using the two types of measures will be discussed separately. There have been few studies of the development of relationships among children's constructs; therefore, no special attention will be given to that topic.

Research Using Direct Measures of Relations among Constructs

Hinkle (1965) employed a grid technique in which 20 constructs were obtained for each subject. These were arrayed in a 20-by-20 matrix, with the same constructs in the rows as in the columns. For each construct in one row of the matrix, the subject was told, "Suppose you were to change back and forth from one side to the other of this construct. What other constructs would also be likely to change?" Constructs that were judged to change were said to be implied by the first construct.

A variety of concepts can be defined from such a matrix. Hinkle defined a "core" construct, for instance, as one whose removal would eliminate a large number of implications from the matrix and a "peripheral" construct as one with few implications. Obviously, it would be possible to apply factor analysis or multidimensional scaling to such matrixes. It is also possible to compare different individuals according to how extensive a set of relationships their matrixes contain.

Superordination and Resistance to Change

Hinkle proposed that subjects would be more resistant to change on core constructs than on peripheral ones. To obtain a measure of resistance to change, he presented subjects with all possible pairs of their 20 constructs, in turn. For each pair, subjects were to suppose they would have to change from their preferred pole to the opposite pole on one of the two constructs; their task was to choose which change they would be most willing to make. Most subjects preferred to change on the construct with the fewest implicational relations. For the 28 subjects, the rank order correlations between the two variables varied from −.25 to +.92, with a median of +.58. For more than three-fourths of the subjects, the correlation was significant at <.05.

Hinkle also expected that superordinate constructs would have more implicational relations than would subordinate constructs. To identify superordinate constructs, Hinkle invented a technique that has been called "laddering." Ten constructs were first obtained for each subject by standard Rep Test procedures. One of these constructs were selected, and the subject indicated the pole of the construct that he would prefer to occupy. The subject was then asked what made the preferred pole better than the other one. The resulting quality was taken to be a new construct, for which the subject provided a contrasting pole. Again, the subject indicated what made the preferred pole of the new construct better than the other pole, thereby identifying still another construct. This procedure continued until ten new constructs were identified or the subject could produce no new ones. In the latter case, another construct was taken from the first set of ten and the laddering procedure was carried out with that one. Eventually, ten new constructs were generated. Hinkle reported that, whichever initial construct was chosen as the starting point, "the chain of superordinate constructs in the hierarchy generated from the first subordinate was almost invariably repeated in the hierarchies of the remaining subordinates" (p. 34). By Hinkle's definition, the ten laddered constructs should be superordinate to the others. As he expected, for about three-fourths of the subjects, the ten constructs obtained in the laddering process had more implicational relations than the ten initial constructs.

To summarize, Hinkle's results suggest that people will be less willing to change the way they are characterized on core constructs than on peripheral constructs and that superordinate constructs are more likely to be core constructs (that is, to be tied to other constructs with implicational relations) than are peripheral ones.

Relations among Constructs and Reactions to Disconfirmation

Levy (1956) proposed that how people react to disconfirmation of expectancies should vary with the pattern of relations among their constructs. For each of a group of subjects, Levy identified five "constellatory" constructs (they all had high loadings on a general factor obtained from a Rep Grid) and five "propositional" constructs (all had nearly zero loadings on the general factor). Subjects formed an impression of two hypothetical persons, using their constructs as the checklist. Each subject was then told that one of the impressions was less accurate than the average prediction while the other impression was more accurate than average. Subjects were allowed to change their impressions if they wanted to. On impressions they thought were inaccurate, subjects changed their judgments on constellatory constructs more than on propositional ones, presumably because substantial changes in an impression required changes in the constellatory constructs. On impressions they thought were relatively accurate, subjects made very few changes on either constellatory or propositional constructs.

Crockett and Meisel (1974) argued that the overall pattern of implications among a person's constructs should affect how that person would react to disconfirmation of expectancies. Suppose, for instance, that the constructs of one person are massively connected by patterns of implication while, for another person, the implicational relations among constructs are much less extensive. For the first person any change in one aspect of an impression would induce change throughout the system. For the second person, however, a change in one part of an impression could be accomplished without extensive implications for other parts of the impression. Two hypotheses follow:

- Impressions formed by people whose constructs are massively interrelated will be resistant to change; otherwise, the person's impressions must vacillate back and forth with every slight disconfirmation.
- Clear disconfirmation of expectancies should produce greater change in the person whose constructs are massively interconnected than in the person whose constructs are selectively related.

To test these hypotheses, the Rep Test was used to generate 20 constructs for each subject. Implicational relations among each subject's constructs were obtained using Hinkle's grid procedure. Two measures were obtained from each implication grid: the total number of implications among constructs and the most central construct (defined as the construct with the largest number of implicational relations to and from others).

After these measures had been obtained, subjects were asked to form an impression of a young man from minimal information, using their own constructs as the checklist. The experimenter ostensibly scored each impression for accuracy. The subject was told that the impression was very inaccurate and was given a chance to change it. Subjects in one group also received strong disconfirmation of a core construct. They were told that the judgment on their most central construct was wrong. In that group, the greater the connectedness among subjects' constructs, the more changes they made in impressions ($r = +.54$). A second group received weak disconfirmation; they were told they had done very poorly, but were given no further information. In that group, the greater the connectedness among subjects' constructs, the fewer the changes in their impressions ($r = -.78$). A third group received "predictive" disconfirmation. They were told that their predictions of an action related to their most central construct was wrong. In this group, the degree of connectedness was inversely related to changes in impressions, but the correlation was not significantly different from zero ($r = -.30$).

These results strongly supported the hypotheses: Individuals whose construct systems were massively connected needed unambiguous disconfirmation of expectations before they changed their impressions very much; however, when they did change, they changed a great deal. On the other hand, individuals whose constructs were selectively interrelated changed their impressions a moderate amount whether the disconfirmation was general or was directed specifically at a central construct.

Psychotherapy and Changes in Patterns of Relations

Fransella (1972) used a version of the Implication Grid to monitor the effects of psychotherapy with a group of stutterers. At periodic testing sessions, clients were administered Rep Tests that provided two sets of constructs, one for "me as others see me when I am stuttering," the other for "me as others see me when I am not stuttering." Clients then completed two Implication Grids, one for the me-as-stutterer constructs, the other for the me-as-nonstutterer constructs. Fransella then developed a measure of the magnitude of implicational relations among constructs in those grids.

Fransella's therapy consisted in helping clients work out a more elaborate construction of situations in which their speech was fluent (all stutterers apparently experience episodes of fluent speech). Fransella proposed that these clients construed in detail, and could anticipate effectively, what would happen in stuttering situations, but their constructs for dealing with fluent episodes were so sparse they could not effectively anticipate others' reactions. Therefore, client and therapist reviewed each fluent episode in great detail to help the client "build up a set of constructs and implications to make fluency more meaningful" (p. 69). As a group, the clients improved considerably in verbal fluency. For our purposes, it is of greater interest to examine changes in the patterns of their stutterer and nonstutterer Implication Grids.

At the beginning of therapy, the stutterer grids had significantly more implications among constructs than the nonstutterer grids, which contained very few implicational relations. As therapy progressed, the number of implications in the nonstutterer grids increased significantly; the number in the stutterer grids declined somewhat. At the end of the study, there were significantly more implicational relations between nonstutterer constructs than between stutterer constructs. Improvement in verbal fluency was correlated significantly with increase in the number of implications among nonstutterer constructs. Clients who entered therapy with almost no construal of fluent episodes did not improve as much as those who initially had some ability to construe such episodes.

Fransella concluded that this form of therapy increased the meaningfulness of fluency for clients. Adams-Webber (1979a) suggested that the results also indicate that the clients developed a more differentiated set of constructs about verbal fluency. He cited evidence from Fransella's report that her clients entered therapy with very undifferentiated construals of their fluent episodes. In time, they came to apply a much more extensive set of constructs to the fluent episodes and to develop a relatively complex pattern of relationships among those constructs. Thus, Fransella's results probably do not suggest that the clients' nonstutterer constructs became massively interrelated. Instead, clients seem to have progressed from little differentiation about fluency to a highly differentiated, complexly integrated construal of fluent episodes.

Adams-Webber's interpretation suggests a curvilinear relationship between effective construal and the number of implicational relations among one's constructs. At the two extremes are people whose constructs are connected by few or no implications and those whose constructs are massively related to one another. One sort of person draws few inferences from information about others; the other cannot change an impression without altering a substantial part of it. Between the extremes are relatively differentiated systems of constructs that are tied together by complex, but not monolithic, patterns of relations. This type of system should provide the most effective construal.

Assessment

These procedures require the subjects to judge which constructs imply others. Seldom is more than one judgment made of the relation between a pair of constructs. This makes one suspicious of the stability of the judgments and of the reliability of the measure; few reliability statistics are available to quiet that suspicion. The problem is compounded by the fact that a given word can index different constructs when the verbal context varies. Add to this questions about whether subjects can, or are willing to, report accurately on their own inferential processes, and one is left with grave doubts about the reliability and validity of direct measures of relations among constructs. Nevertheless, the implications of the research are exciting enough to warrant further development of these methods.

Patterns of Relations Inferred from the Use of Constructs

Another way to infer relations among constructs is to analyze how they are used to describe others. The most popular technique for this purpose among researchers in the construct-theory tradition is the Repertory Grid, or Rep Grid. Respondents rate a number of different individuals on a set of constructs.* Depending upon the interests of the researcher or the clinician, the subject's own self may be among the individuals rated, along with other people who are

---

*Just as constructs might be obtained from descriptions of nonhuman objects, so they might be applied in ratings of such objects. For that reason, it is conventional to speak of things rated in Rep Grids as "elements." In all of the studies we shall discuss, the elements were people, so that term will be adopted in this chapter.

important to the subject. Sometimes photographs of strangers, instead of names of acquaintances, are rated. The number of constructs used in the grid, how they are obtained, and whether they are the same for all subjects or unique to each one also vary from study to study. A final variation is in how people are rated on the constructs: Sometimes subjects simply check whether a construct applies to each person; sometimes they rank order the individuals on each construct; sometimes they rate the individuals on the continua that the constructs imply. The advantages and disadvantages of these variations are discussed by Bannister and Mair (1968), Fransella and Bannister (1977), Adams-Webber (1979a), and others. One result of the variation among different forms of the Rep Test is that it is impossible to generalize about its reliability. Whatever the differences in particular, the grids are analyzed by observing which constructs are used similarly to describe others.

Kelly (1955) invented a method of analyzing Rep Grid responses that yielded the locations of both individuals and constructs on the dimensions that it identified. With the widespread availability of electronic computers and of prepackaged programs, some form of factor analysis or multidimensional scaling of responses has since become the most common analysis technique. The structural properties identified include the number of dimensions that underlie the grid matrix, the proportion of variance that is accounted for by one or a few dimensions, how the dimensions are labeled, and what positions the constructs and the individuals occupy on those dimensions. Other ways of scoring responses to the Rep Grid have been used to define additional properties. Some of these measures are based upon manipulations so complex that it is next to impossible to decide what psychological processes they might represent. No attempt will be made to survey all these measures.

Use of Structural Measures in Psychotherapy

The most common use of Rep Grid analysis has been in the clinical setting. Constructs and the individuals to whom they are applied are selected specifically for each client. Rep Grid responses are factor analyzed to determine either which constructs are used similarly by the client, or which people are construed similarly, or both. The resulting patterns are often discussed with the clients to provide insight into how they construe themselves. The results are used to infer the kinds of problems that are likely to arise during therapy and the kinds of changes that are likely or desirable. Great disparity between a client's rating of Real Self and Ideal Self, or between ratings of Self, Mother, and Father have been shown to distinguish normal from neurotic individuals (Ryle and Breen, 1972). Comparison of patterns from the same client's grids at different periods in psychotherapy are used by the client and the clinician to assess the progress of therapy and its future directions. Such clinical applications are discussed at length elsewhere (Bannister and Mair, 1968; Fransella and Bannister, 1977; Ryle, 1975; Adams-Webber, 1979a).

Makhlouf-Norris, Jones, and Norris (1970) developed a method of identifying clusters of relations among constructs in an individual's Rep Grid. They reported two major types of patterns: articulated and nonarticulated. Articulated patterns contain several different clusters of intercorrelated constructs; these are connected by one or more "linkage" constructs, which are correlated with constructs in different clusters. Two types of nonarticulated patterns were identified: "monolithic" structures, in which the constructs formed one large interrelated cluster, and "segmented" structures, which contained several clusters with no linkage constructs. Obsessive-compulsive subjects gave nonarticulated patterns, normal subjects gave articulated ones. These results raise a number of intriguing questions: Are linkage constructs those that help perceivers account for inconsistency in the behavior of others? Do they serve as vehicles for drawing inferences from constructs in one cluster to those in another? Is change from a nonarticulated pattern to an articulated one part of the normal course of development? Does such change mark an improvement in personal adjustment? No doubt these and other questions will guide future research.

Bieri's Rep Grid Measure of Complexity

Bieri (1955) reasoned that when two constructs are applied in nearly the same way to describe the individuals in a Rep Grid, the two constructs do not discriminate among those individuals. Thus, a perceiver who applied a great many pairs of constructs nearly identically would not be differentiating very much among other people, especially as compared to someone who applied different constructs differentially to different people. Bieri set out to compare subjects according to how much their responses differentiated among others on the Rep Grid. In the first such measure, Bieri elicited 12 constructs from each subject, then had the subjects rate 12 individuals on those constructs. For each pair of constructs, a comparison was made of how similarly they were applied to the 12 individuals; a score of -2 was given when two constructs were applied identically to all 12 people, a score of -1 when there was only one discrepancy; and a score of 0 otherwise; scores were summed over all pairs of constructs. The resulting measure was called "cognitive complexity." Subsequently, Bieri et al. (1966) described a form of this measure in which ten bipolar constructs (the same ones for all subjects) were used to rate ten acquaintances. For each pair of constructs, the number of identical ratings is determined; these numbers are then summed over all pairs of constructs; a subject with a low total score is called complex, one with a high score is called noncomplex. For both measures, reliability coefficients are reported to range from about $+.65$ to about $+.85$.

Half a dozen studies have shown that this measure of "cognitive complexity" is unrelated to Crockett's measure, discussed above (Irwin, Tripodi, and Bieri, 1967; Crockett, Gonyea, and Press, 1967; Little, 1969; A. O. Miller, 1969;

O'Keefe and Sypher, in press). Both measures also seem to be unrelated to other measures that have been given the same name.*

In his first paper, Bieri (1955) reported that complex subjects were more accurate in predicting differences between themselves and others than were noncomplex subjects, but were not more accurate in predicting similarities. Subsequent research has found this measure not to be correlated with accuracy of impressions (Leventhal, 1957; Sechrest and Jackson, 1961; Honess, 1976). Instead, subjects who are defined as complex by the measure are less inclined than their counterparts to assume that others will agree with them (Bieri, 1955; Leventhal, 1957; Adams-Webber, 1969). Using a somewhat modified version of Bieri's measure, Adams-Webber (1969) found that complex subjects were better than noncomplex ones in picking from a large set of constructs those that were given by an acquaintance they had just met. Similarly, Adams-Webber, Schwenker, and Barbeau (1972) found that complex subjects, as defined by this measure, were better able than noncomplex ones to distinguish between the constructs that had been given by two new acquaintances. Olson and Partington (1977) found that a modification of the Bieri measure was significantly correlated with performance on Feffer's role-taking task.

Thus, some of the correlates of Bieri's measure are similar to those found with Crockett's measure of complexity as described above. However, other research shows different patterns. O'Keefe and Sypher cited four different experiments by Delia and his associates in which Bieri's revised measure of complexity was not significantly correlated with flexibility in perspective taking, with modification of communication style to address different individuals, or with sensitivity to others' feelings. It will be recalled that Crockett's measure correlated with all of those variables. Nor does it appear that scores on Bieri's measure of complexity increase with age in children (Olson and Partington, 1977; Barratt, 1977b; Alban Metcalfe, 1978; Vacc, Loesch, and Burt, 1980). The only report of a significant positive correlation between age and Bieri's measure was in a sample of adult college students (Goldstein and Blackman, 1977).

Irwin, Tripodi, and Bieri (1967) and Miller and Bieri (1965) reported that subjects were more complex (that is, discriminated more) in their ratings of people they disliked than of people they liked. They interpreted this result in terms of a "vigilance" hypothesis, proposing that subjects found it more important to distinguish among enemies than among friends. This was in apparent contradiction to a finding by Crockett (1965) that subjects employed more constructs to describe others they liked than to describe others they disliked; Crockett had interpreted this as evidence that people form more

---

*The term *cognitive complexity* has been a popular one. It has been applied to observations that are drawn from half a dozen or more different empirical measures. This chapter will not discuss similarly named measures — for example, those developed by Harvey, Hunt, and Schroeder, 1961; Schroeder, Driver, and Streufert, 1967; Scott, 1962; or Vannoy, 1965 — whose genesis and application were outside the framework of personal construct theory.

elaborate impressions of friends than of enemies. Crockett, Gonyea, and Press (1967) reconciled this discrepancy by an analysis of the processes that underlie judgments on Bieri's measure. They showed that subjects seldom give negative ratings on construct dimensions to people they like; however, they often give positive ratings to people they dislike. As a result, ratings of people the subjects like are concentrated within a narrow range on the construct dimensions; ratings of disliked people span the scale. Given this response bias, it is inevitable that there be more identical ratings of liked people than of disliked people.

It appears that increasing familiarity with others produces changes in responses to the Rep Grid that Bieri would define as a reduction in complexity. Bodden and James (1976) had college students rate a set of 12 occupational titles on 12 relevant constructs. Ratings were made on two occasions. Between testings, an experimental group received information about the occupations. Compared to subjects in a control group, those in the experimental group increased significantly in the number of identical ratings they made on the constructs (that is, they decreased in complexity by Bieri's definition). Two experiments that administered Bieri's measure before and after intensive sensitivity-training experiences also found an increase in the number of identical ratings given group members (that is, a decreased complexity by Bieri's definition) at the end of the group experience (Baldwin, 1972; Benjafield, Jordan, and Pomeroy, 1976). These results will be discussed below.

Measures Related to Bieri's

Bannister (1960) developed a way of scoring Rep Test responses that he felt reflected the "intensity" of relationships among constructs. Bannister's measure is approximately the inverse of Bieri's. In one version of the measure (Bannister, 1960), people who were known to the subject were used as the elements in the Rep Test; in a second (Bannister, 1962a), photographs of strangers were used. By both procedures, thought-disordered schizophrenics received lower scores (in Bieri's terms, showed greater complexity) than did other schizophrenics, depressives, neurotics, or normal subjects. McPherson and Buckley (1970), McPherson, Armstrong, and Heather (1975), and Heather (1976) have shown that differences on the measure between thought-disordered schizophrenics and patients with other diagnoses is much greater in judgments of people than in judgments of physical objects. Bannister interpreted these differences as indicating that thought-disordered schizophrenics have no consistent pattern of relationships among their constructs; this produces a loose form of construing that prevents them from taking stable, reasonably well-organized orientations in interpersonal relations.

Landfield (1971) developed a measure based on the Rep Grid that he labeled "functionally independent construction." Low scores indicate extensive interdependence among constructs; and high scores denote an absence of implicational relations among constructs. The measure is quite similar to Bieri's.

Landfield reported that clients who differed from their therapists' scores on this measure at the beginning of therapy seemed to show greater progress than those who did not differ much from their therapists' scores.

The similarity among the three measures has often been remarked in the literature, as has the incompatibility between their theoretical interpretations. Adams-Webber (1979a) offered a resolution of the incompatibility by proposing a curvilinear relationship between construct relatedness and effective construing, similar to the position outlined at the end of the preceding section. At one extreme, low scores on what Bannister termed intensity (or high scores on what Bieri called complexity and Landfield called functionally independent construing) would indicate a fragmented, chaotic system of constructs from which it is next to impossible for a perceiver to form a coherent set of expectations about others. At the other extreme, high scores on Bannister's intensity measure (or low scores on Bieri's and Landfield's measures) would indicate a massively interrelated system of constructs for which, as Crockett and Meisel (1974) showed, changes in one aspect of a construal require changes in many other aspects. By Adams-Webber's interpretation, it is in the middle range of relatedness among constructs that a perceiver is likely to show the most flexible patterns of construing.

This hypothesis accounts for the results obtained by Bodden and James (1976), Baldwin (1972), and Benjafield, Jordan, and Pomeroy (1976), all of whom found a decrease in complexity by Bieri's definition (that is, an increase in the magnitude of relations among constructs) as subjects came to know more about a set of occupations or became better acquainted with other members of a sensitivity group. By Adams-Webber's interpretation, subjects probably entered those experiments with little or no information about the occupations or the other people; therefore, their initial responses to the Rep Grid showed very little structure. With increasing knowledge, ratings on the grid revealed patterns of relationship among constructs that did not occur earlier. The increase in the extent of relationships among constructs could easily have occurred because subjects were making use of observed correlations among real events. Thus, instead of indicating less complex construing, the results probably indicated a reasonable increase in the patterning and structure of subjects' judgments.

Analyses of Implicit Personality Theory

The most sophisticated and systematic program of research into the organization of personal constructs has been carried out by Seymour Rosenberg and his associates. Detailed reviews of this research appear in Rosenberg and Sedlak (1972a), in Rosenberg (1977), and in Chapter 4 of this book. The work grew out of research into the implicit personality theories that perceivers use in person perception. Initially, subjects were asked to describe people by means of traits that the experimenters supplied; multidimensional scaling was performed on judgments that were aggregated over subjects. In later studies, subject-generated constructs were employed, again with judgments aggregated over subjects. Still later, multidimensional scaling and cluster analysis techniques were applied to the constructs of individual subjects. Most recently, instead of determining the relationships among constructs, analysis has been made of groupings of individuals who are important to the subjects.

In the first of these studies, Rosenberg, Nelson, and Vivekananthan (1968) had subjects describe other people in terms of 60 traits that were chosen by the experimenters. A measure of the distance between pairs of traits was obtained by assessing how often they occurred together and with other traits. The matrix of distances, aggregated over subjects, was analyzed by multidimensional scaling. Three factors were identified; they corresponded closely to the semantic-differential factors of evaluation, activity, and potency. Rosenberg and Olshan (1970) employed the same procedure with a different set of 60 traits, again chosen by the experimenters; they obtained essentially the same results.

However, the activity and potency factors seem to appear only in such analyses when the traits are chosen by the experimenter, not when they are generated by the subjects. Rosenberg and Sedlak (1972b) obtained traits from free descriptions by subjects. They took as their distance measure how often in those descriptions pairs of traits appeared jointly and with other traits. Multidimensional scaling of the aggregated distance measures yielded five dimensions. One of these was clearly an evaluative dimension. The others were not easy to interpret, but an activity factor did not appear, and potency was highly correlated with evaluation.

Multidimensional scaling looks for the basic dimensions in terms of which the distances between traits may be described. One might say that it identifies a small number of superconstructs (and their contrasts); individual constructs are then described in terms of their positions on those superconstruct dimensions. To obtain inferences about a different type of relationship, the hierarchic groupings of constructs, Rosenberg and his associates have applied cluster analysis procedures to subjects' sortings of traits. In the results of such analyses, a particular trait may, but need not, fall within clusters of traits at any of several hierarchic levels; traits that form clusters at one level may, but need not, separate into subclusters at some lower level.

In the first such study, Jones and Rosenberg (1974) aggregated the judgments of a group of subjects to obtain distance measures for 99 subject-generated traits. These were then subjected to cluster analysis. Six levels of clusters appeared. At the most general level was an evaluative clustering, which sorted a high proportion of the constructs into a good-bad classification. The other five clusters, at decreasing levels of generality, were interpreted as impulsive-inhibited, hard-soft, intellectual good-bad, active-passive, and dominant-submissive.

The first study in this series to apply the methods to the analysis of an individual's constructs was one by Rosenberg and Jones (1972) of Theodore Dreiser's descriptions of characters in *A Gallery of Women*. Distance measures were obtained among the 99 traits used most often in that book. Cluster analysis produced three clusterings: conforms-does not conform, male-female, and hard-soft. Multidimensional scaling identified four dimensions. Two of these, male-female, and conforms-does not conform, were approximately orthogonal and duplicated two of the levels in the cluster analysis; hard-soft was correlated with male-female in the four-dimensional space but was not redundant with it; an evaluative cluster also emerged. The authors interpreted these results in terms of salient aspects of Drieser's life.

Subsequently, Rosenberg (1977) obtained a detailed set of observations (requiring from 10 to 25 hours per subject) from 16 different individuals. Each subject described the traits of, and his feelings toward, at least 100 different people. Subjects rated each of the people on the traits and feelings that appeared in the descriptions; distance measures obtained from these ratings were subjected to cluster analysis and to multidimensional scaling. The results are much too complex to summarize adequately here. Suffice it to say that a general evaluative dimension appeared for every subject. That is, the constructs, feelings, and people could be arrayed on a continuum that varied from good-pleasant-liked at one end to bad-unpleasant-disliked at the other. Other dimensions of the subjects' judgments seemed to provide more specific contrasts within the larger, general evaluative dimension.

In the most recent publication in this series, Gara and Rosenberg (1979) applied a set-theoretical method to represent the similarities and differences among other people. Subjects spent 10 to 15 hours, first identifying a set of people, then describing the traits of those people and the feelings they aroused in the subject, and, finally judging whether each trait and feeling applied to each person. These judgments were analyzed to determine whether the traits attributed to one person were a subset of those attributed to another. Four classes of persons were identified. Supersets were people whose characteristics subsumed those of many others; subjects were concerned that supersets think well of them, they felt close to supersets and reported that they confided in them. Subsets were individuals who were described with only a part of the constructs attributed to the supersets; subjects were less concerned about the good opinion of subsets than of supersets. Disliked contrasts were people whom subjects disliked and about whose opinions they were unconcerned; such individuals were described by traits that were not applied to other people. Miscellaneous targets were those who did not fit into any of the other categories; subjects showed about the same amount of concern for the opinion of such individuals as of subsets. In commenting on these results, the authors suggested that supersets may provide the perceptual categories in terms of which subjects assess other people; they proposed that subjects monitor their own behavior in terms of the opinions of supersets.

Assessment

Questions have already been raised about the reliability and validity of direct measures of relations among constructs. Other questions can be raised about the meaning of indirect measures of relations. The different interpretations that Bannister, Bieri, and Landfield have given to very similar measures reflect disagreement about what those measures mean. Beyond this, it is not clear what it means when two or more constructs fall in the same cluster or occupy adjacent positions on the dimensions that are extracted by factor analysis or multidimensional scaling. The role such dimensions play in perception, cognition, and behavior has not been ascertained. Furthermore, the interpretation of such clusters or dimensions as superconstructs raises an important theoretical issue.

The nature of the issue is well illustrated by a quote from Rosenberg (1977, p. 203): "one of [one subject's] positive clusters consists of *faithful, understanding, sympathetic, warm, kind, intelligent, bright, responsible, admiration* (feeling) which might appear as two (or more) constructs in the Rep Grid, one referring to a concern for others and the other to intellectual competence." Rosenberg then remarks that differences in methods of data analysis probably result in some differences in the general construct-contrast "factors" that emerge, thereby affecting whether one considers the cluster to identify one, two, or more constructs.

The point of contention is that this approach treats the dimensions, not the attributes, as constructs. If one thinks of a personal construct as a discrimination that a perceiver makes about some aspect of the actions and character of other people, then for most perceivers the preceding cluster would include at least six different constructs (setting aside the feeling, *admiration*) not one or two. Many of those constructs may refer to closely related types of behavior; some or all of them may imply each other; but those possibilities constitute hypotheses to be tested, not a justification for collapsing different constructs into one or two constructs. To collapse them thus, I think, is to obscure the fact that most of us employ constructs to make highly differentiated discriminations and anticipations about our associates; frequently, all of the constructs in a cluster like the one above provide important and independent discriminations. Our constructs can often be classified along a variety of dimensions — good-bad, conforming-nonconforming, and the like — but they retain an independent identity; the discriminations they permit provide the routes along which a person's processes are psychologically channelized.

WHAT NEXT?

The preceding review makes it clear that there has been a good deal of research, and even more theorizing, into the organization of construct systems. The research sometimes reveals a great diversity in methods and an even greater diversity in interpretations. Even when the research is cast within the framework of personal construct theory, one sometimes finds a loose connection, at best, between concepts in the theory and observations in the field. Nevertheless, the results of this research have already led to important clinical and theoretical advances. Its continuance offers great promise for the extension and elaboration of the theory. In a few additional paragraphs, I will sketch out four directions in which I believe research and theory may profitably move in the immediate future.

Pursuing the Implications of Observations about Organization

The most obvious direction that research needs to take is set by the existing research results. For one thing, we need to know much more about how measures of the differentiation of constructs and of the pattern of relations among them correlate with the way people perceive and act toward others. It will be important to pursue the suggestion by Adams-Webber (1979a) that either too sparse or too extensive a pattern of relations among constructs is dysfunctional. It will also be important, on the one hand, to refine and simplify our measures of organization so as to tie them clearly to theoretical concepts and, on the other hand, to clarify and extend our theoretical concepts so that they make sense of our observations. An assessment needs to be undertaken of the reliability and validity of direct measures of implications among constructs; even more, procedures need to be developed that are less reliant upon the subjects' own insight into the implications among constructs. Furthermore, we need to determine what is represented by the proximity of constructs in clusters or in multidimensional space; as Rosenberg (1977) suggested, one promising line of research is to ask whether such proximity means that when perceivers identify one quality in another person, they infer the other.

The clinical implications of these concepts and methods need also to be examined. The protocols of many therapeutic sessions contain material that is similar to that from which Rosenberg and Jones (1972) obtained distance measures for the personal constructs of Theodore Dreiser; such protocols might be exploited to obtain an indication of the pattern of relations among clients' constructs and of how those relations change in the course of therapy. In addition, research that obtains repeated measures of the organization of clients' constructs, as in that by Fransella (1972) and Ryle (1975), can extend and exploit the clinical insights that seem to abound in these organizational concepts; at the same time, such research will test the usefulness of those concepts and suggest modifications and extensions of them.

The preceding lines of research extend directly out of developments within personal construct theory itself. I think theory and research will also profit from the merger of aspects of construct theory with recent developments in cognitive and social psychology. In particular, there are three new lines of development within the theory that I believe hold great promise: the relationship of constructs to patterns of behavior and action; the distinction between personal constructs and the psychological representation of events; and the analysis of sequentially related patterns of constructs, or schemata.

Constructs and Patterns of Action

A question that has received little or no attention in personal construct theory is how it is that one construct instead of another is evoked in a perceiver by a particular set of behaviors in another person. No doubt the question has been neglected because of the theory's emphasis upon the uniqueness of each individual's system of constructs; but the theory also emphasizes the role of constructs in anticipating events and the critical importance of errors in antici- pation for changes in constructs and construals. At some point, personal construct theorists need to find a way to relate constructs to concrete aspects of the individual's experience. A promising place to begin is to examine the patterns in other people's appearance and actions that are prototypic for par- ticular constructs.

The term *prototypic* is taken from Rosch (1973, 1975), who used it to describe the ordering of physical stimuli to semantic concepts. She found that certain patterns of stimuli are viewed as more typical of a semantic category than are others. Thus, some dogs (in particular, hounds) are considered to be "doggier" than others (for instance, bulldogs or Pekingese). Similarly, some articles of furniture (for example, chair, bed, and table) are viewed as prototypic for the higher-level category *furniture*, while others (for example, drapes, vase) are not. Rosch has shown that people of similar backgrounds agree as to which members of a category are prototypic. Judgments are made more rapidly, more confidently, and more consensually for prototypic members of a category than for nonprototypic members.

This approach can be applied in a straightforward manner to the construal of people. Constructs, in terms of which the actions of others are understood, may each be seen as tied to a particular pattern in the actions or appearance of others. That is, a given pattern of behavior by another person will evoke one or a few constructs in a perceiver, not any of a wide array of constructs. Conversely, the perceiver's attribution of a construct to another person forecasts a particular pattern of actions in the future behavior of that person.

An example may help to clarify these points. Consider the constructs help- ful and sympathetic. The attribution of either construct to a person, O, requires a context that involves O and another person, Q, who is experiencing some need and/or emotion. For the writer (and also for a sample of subjects in initial research on this topic) sympathetic is ascribed to O when O is perceived to be experiencing the same emotion as Q; helpful is ascribed when O assists Q to deal with a need or comforts Q in regard to unpleasant emotions. With care, it is possible to write anecdotes that follow those abstract patterns, which include only descriptions of concrete actions, and which evoke the attribution of one construct or the other by the great majority of subjects. Because evidence of mirroring another person's emotions is often accompanied by the offer of assistance, the two constructs are often applied to the same pattern of actions. However, most subjects find it easy to envision a person who is sympathetic but not helpful, or helpful but not sympathetic. The attribution to O of different combinations of the two constructs brings about substantial differences in a perceiver's anticipations of O's behavior and in the choice of strategies for dealing with O in situations that include the prototypic pattern of actions.

For most individuals, no doubt, those two constructs were differentiated out of a more global earlier construct, perhaps social good-bad. It seems likely that, for some people, such differentiation of the general construct into specific ones never occurs; it is even more likely that the two more specific constructs are given different names by different people. However, the point is that, for a substantial proportion of perceivers, two overlapping but distinct patterns of actions are prototypic for two related but distinct constructs. Furthermore, neither of these two patterns of actions is likely to invoke the ascription of such construct as intelligent, ambitious, or responsible, all of which are characterized by their own prototypic patterns of behavior-in-context. Any real situation (and most concrete descriptions) will include patterns that are prototypic for a large number of quite different constructs. Three research questions need to be addressed immediately: First, which patterns of actions are prototypic for commonly employed constructs? Second, are the patterns of relationship that exist among an individual's constructs paralleled by similarities in the patterns of actions-in-context that are prototypic for those constructs? Third, to what extent does the combination in a single description of patterns of action that are prototypic for several constructs lead perceivers to invoke a broader range of constructs than those for which the actions are prototypic? Other questions will become important as more is learned about the relationship between constructs and concrete events.

Dispositional Constructs and Constructs about Events

Dispositional constructs are not applied directly to the concrete characteristics of people and their behavior, they are applied to cognitive representations of such concrete characteristics. The two aspects of construal are not often distinguished, but I think they should be. The concrete representations are what is construed; the dispositional constructs do the construing. Dispositional constructs yield anticipations of future actions; concrete representations are checked against those anticipations and also against remembered actions of the past. A store of representations of concrete actions is accumulated in one's memory; as the nature of the store changes, perceivers may reexamine and revise the dispositional constructs that they apply to the other person.

This distinction parallels Tulving's (1972) differentiation of episodic memory — a person's stored representation of concrete events — from semantic memory — the semantic concepts in terms of which those experiences are given meaning and are understood. The distinction has been employed in the study of person perception by Carlston (1980); a similar viewpoint is presented in

Lingle and Ostrom (1979). The value of the distinction can be illustrated by an example: "Calvin Bower smiled when he saw me and held out his hand to shake mine. While we waited for the elevator, he inquired how my work was going and asked about my wife and family." Once an episode is over, such a description is about as close as a perceiver can come to the behavior itself. The description includes a dozen or more constructs: Calvin Bower-not Calvin Bower, smiling-not smiling, shake hands-don't shake hands, and so on; but the constructs that give meaning to the episode and provide the core of one's anticipations about Bower's future actions are dispositional ones like friendly, likes me, interested in my work, intelligent, perceptive. When Bower stops by my office two days later to ask for a contribution to a charity, and then two days after that looks the other way when he sees me on the street, those actions contradict my expectations and are added to the store of remembered behaviors about Calvin Bower. Changes must take place in the dispositional constructs that I apply to Bower. If feasible, they will make sense of all three of the behavioral episodes. Some constructs − intelligent and perceptive, perhaps − are likely to remain in my construal of Bower; others − friendly, likes me, interested in my work − may drop out; and still others − manipulating, glib, unreliable − are added and become the core of my reconstrual of Calvin Bower. When I describe him to a friend some time later, I am likely to include both dispositional and behavioral constructs in my account, but the essence of the construal will be captured by the former.

   If dispositional constructs provide the expectations about how another person is likely to act, those constructs are likely to affect which actions of the other person a perceiver will notice and represent in memory. However, when the expectations are unequivocally disconfirmed by the person's actions, those unexpected actions demand explanation in a revised construal. The new one will, if possible, account for all of the concrete events that are represented in memory, maintain continuity with the earlier construal, and provide an explanation of why the initial construal, and the expectations it generated, were incorrect. The manner in which this is accomplished remains to be explored in experimental research and clinical observations.

Personal Constructs and Schemata

   Not only are there implicational relationships among constructs, but sets of constructs are related to each other by a variety of organizing principles that may be called themes (Schank and Abelson, 1977) or schemata (Bartlett, 1932; Neisser, 1976). Many of these are socially shared; no doubt many others are idiosyncratic; for the present, we will restrict our attention to the former. Three different kinds of schemata will be reviewed.

   First, consider a commonly employed package of constructs and inferences that was described by Heider (1958) and that has been studied in detail by social psychologists: the processes involved in assessing ability in another person. According to Heider, perceivers make use of two subordinate schemata to make such assessments. One of these recognizes the intimate relationship between effort and ability: both are presumed to be necessary for effective performance. Without ability, perceivers assume, no amount of effort will suffice; conversely, without effort, even a high level of ability will not culminate in effective action. The other subordinate schema has to do with assessments of the effectiveness of the person's performance and of the demands of the task. Accomplishment of a reasonably difficult task requires a reasonably high level of performance; it may be achieved with a very high level of ability combined with moderate effort, or with a moderate level of ability combined with very great effort. Heider suggested that when perceivers observe someone carrying out a sequence of tasks, they continuously, and often without reflection, assess the amount of effort the person is making, observe the level of difficulty of the tasks the person faces, identify the level of success the person achieves, and arrive at a judgment of the person's level of ability. Once this level of ability has been attributed to the person, predictions can be made about his or her success or failure in other tasks.

This is not the place to review the extensive, and generally supportive, body of research into the attribution of ability; but the implications of this work for personal construct theory should be clear. It suggests that perceivers are likely to develop constructs about a considerable variety of abilities — intelligence, strength, physical coordination, logical reasoning, and so on; about motivation and effort and the cues by which they can be assessed; about environmental tasks relevant to those abilities and the cues by which task difficulty can be assessed; and about the cues by which one can determine whether, and at what level, a task has been accomplished. These constructs are neatly coordinated in one's observations of the actions of other people, and assessments of their ability are achieved. The assessments then enable one to anticipate how that person will act in other situations.

A second example of organizing schemata is the identification by Schank and Abelson (1977) of three different types of themes that are often invoked to understand the behavior of another person. These are role themes, in which the person's characteristics and goals are implied by his social role; interpersonal themes, such as "love," which define a person's relationship to someone else and carry with them implications about a host of other attitudes and behaviors the person will direct toward the beloved; and life themes, which describe the general position or aim that a person wants in life and imply that a whole array of abilities, opinions, beliefs, and other dispositional qualities will also character-ize the person. No doubt each such theme can be thought of as a construct — for instance, clergyman versus layman, loves versus is indifferent to, wants to get ahead versus doesn't care about getting ahead — but these constructs are superordinate to others in a different sense than that term has been employed previously in personal construct theory. Information about a person's role, about a relational theme, or about a person's aim in life carries inferences about an extremely large number of other constructs. Such "thematic" constructs are used to make sense of a variety of behaviors of other people; they, and the other constructs they imply, also provide more-or-less detailed anticipations about the behavior other people are likely to carry out in various kinds of situations.

As a final instance of schemata that organize constructs, consider the role that is played in construing by constructs about people's emotions and intentions. The sequence of actions of Calvin Bower, as described above, was interpreted in terms of his propensity to use others to further his own goals. The attribution of that intention carried with it a number of related dispositional constructs. Together, the cluster of constructs enables one to predict when Bower will behave positively and when negatively. For the perceiver, at least, the construal is definitive. Suppose, however, we learn that Bower's wife became critically ill just an hour or so before the last time we saw him. Now alternative schemata, involving other intentions and emotions, are available to account for the three behavioral episodes. Other information about Bower might implicate still other schemata. In any case, the constructs that are invoked to account for the behavioral episodes are likely to be dependent upon, and to be organized around, one or more constructs about Bower's intentions and emotions.

All of these examples demonstrate at least two points. The first point is that there are schemata that serve as the basis for ascribing constructs to other people. Some of them prescribe the actions that must be observed and the constructs by which those actions must be interpreted, in order for other constructs to be inferred. Others provide organizing themes for the application to a person of bundles of constructs. The second point is that theoretical concepts and research methods have been developed in cognitive and social psychology by which such schemata are being analyzed. A third point might be added: Personal construct theory has not tracked those developments. I believe that the assimilation of those concepts and methods into personal construct theory promises to increase substantially its explanatory power.

6

ASSIMILATION AND CONTRAST IN PERSONAL JUDGMENT: THE DICHOTOMY COROLLARY

Jack R. Adams-Webber

The Dichotomy Corollary: A person's construction system is composed of a finite number of dichotomous constructs.

Kelly's Dichotomy Corollary (1955, p. 59) asserts that "a person's construction system is composed of a finite number of dichotomous constructs." Each construct is assumed to represent a single bipolar distinction, for example, happy-sad. It serves as the basis of perceived similarities and differences among the events to which it is applied. The "nominal" pole of a construct represents a perceived similarity between at least two events, and its "contrast" pole represents the way in which at least one other event is specifically different from them. No construct can be understood fully without considering both of its poles, since contrast is as necessary as similarity in defining its meaning.

Kelly argued that the dichotomous nature of personal constructs is an essential feature of the way in which we conceptualize our experience. For example, given a group of at least three elements — A, B, and C — the minimum context of any construct, A and B may be viewed as similar to one another in some way in which C contrasts with both of them: "Alice and Betty are happy; however, Carol is sad." If the same behavior could be interpreted as simultaneously expressing happiness and sadness in the same respect, then this particular distinction would have no definite meaning. Thus, what it is that is assumed to be dichotomous in structure is the *form* of the distinction an individual makes whenever he applies the construct within a specific domain of events.

Kelly (1970a, p. 13) makes this point quite clear in the following terms:

A construct is the basic contrast between two groups. When it is imposed it serves both to distinguish between its elements and to group them. Thus, the construct refers to the nature of the distinction one attempts to make between events, not to the array in which events appear to stand when he gets through applying the distinction between each of them and all the others.

Thus, the same *act* of construing that establishes some basis of perceived similarity between two or more events also serves to distinguish them from other events (at least one). In this sense, each construct is fundamentally an integrating and differentiating operation. As Kelly (1969b, pp. 102-103) explains,

> it must be understood that the personal construct abstracts similarity and difference simultaneously. One cannot be abstracted without implying the other. For a person to treat two incidents as different is to imply that one of them appears to be like another he knows. Conversely, for a person to treat two incidents as similar is to imply that he contrasts both with at least one other incident that he knows. We intend this to be considered as an essential feature of the personal construct by means of which we hope to understand the psychology of human behavior.

According to Kelly, each construct is used to represent a single aspect of a specific domain of events. Outside of this "range of convenience" it is not useful (see Chapter 8). Whenever an individual employs a particular construct to interpret a person's behavior, for example, "Alice seems to be friendly," he is not only categorizing Alice's behavior in a certain way, that is, friendly, but also contrasting it directly with other behavior that is perceived as the opposite of friendly, for example, aloof. Very likely he has observed other actions that cannot be interpreted as either friendly or aloof. Such behaviors fall outside the range of convenience of this particular distinction.

INFORMATION AND UNCERTAINTY

Kelly (1955, p. 63) notes that "the Dichotomy Corollary assumes a structure of psychological processes which lends itself to binary mathematical analysis," for example, information theory.

Information can be defined as that which removes or reduces uncertainty (see Attneave, 1959). It follows that uncertainty is simply potential information. Thus, the same basic unit — the binary digit, or bit — can be used to operationally define both concepts. For instance, given an event E, which has m possible outcomes, each with the same probability of occurring; the amount of uncertainty associated with that event in bits (that is, the minimum number of binary digits into which that event can be encoded) will be equal to the logarithm, to the base 2, of the number of possible outcomes (that is, m). Thus, we can calculate the amount of uncertainty (that is, potential information) associated with that event by means of the following formula: $H = \log_2 m$ (where H represents the amount of uncertainty expressed in bits, and m the number of equiprobable outcomes).

Kelly assumed a priori that the probability that an individual will assign a particular event to one alternative pole of a given construct (p) is the same as the probability that he will assign it to the opposite pole (q), that is, $p = q = \frac{1}{2}$ (see Bonarius, 1965, pp. 10-13). Some specific implications of this assumption can be elaborated in terms of the basic principles of information theory outlined above.

Whenever all the alternative outcomes are equally likely, p — the probability of any one category of outcome — will be equal to the reciprocal of m (that is, $p = 1/m$). It follows that $m = 1/p$. Thus, our basic formula can be restated as follows: $H = \log_2 1/p$. Consequently, when all potential outcomes are equally likely, it is unnecessary for us to distinguish between the amount of uncertainty associated with each particular outcome and the average uncertainty of all outcomes. If Kelly's (1955) assumption were correct that the a priori probability that a subject will assign a given event to one pole of any construct is equal to the probability that he will assign it to the opposite pole, then the contribution of these two categories of response to average information would be the same, that is, one bit ($H = \log_2 1/\frac{1}{2} = 1$). As Garner (1962) points out, this is the maximum (or nominal) value of H for any dichotomous distribution. This seems consistent with Cochran's (1976) argument that a symmetrical distribution (that is, 50/50) of events with respect to the alternative poles of a construct yields the maximum degree of discrimination among these events.

THE GOLDEN SECTION HYPOTHESIS

It has been shown in a series of recent experiments that when subjects categorize acquaintances dichotomously on the basis of bipolar constructs (for example, pleasant-unpleasant), they tend to assign these figures to the "positive" poles (for example, pleasant) approximately 62 percent of the time (Adams-Webber, 1978, 1979a,b; Adams-Webber and Benjafield, 1973; Benjafield and Adams-Webber, 1975, 1976; Benjafield and Green, 1978; Romany and Adams-Webber, 1981). This finding has been generalized across a variety of bipolar constructs, different cultural groups, and alternative methods of measurement. It also has been replicated with the same subjects on different occasions. Its explanation may lie partly in early Greek philosophy and partly in modern information theory.

Pythagoras, the presocratic mathematician and philosopher, developed a complex system of numbers and geometric forms to which he and his followers ascribed great moral significance (Wheelwright, 1966). A central concept in this system was the "golden section," which can be constructed by dividing a line segment AB by a point C in such a way that the ratio AC:CB = CB:AB. If we assume that the entire line segment is of unit length, and let CB = $\emptyset$, then AC = $1 - \emptyset$. Therefore, $\emptyset^2 + \emptyset - 1 = 0$. If we solve this equation for $\emptyset$, we find that its positive root is equal to $(5^{1/2} - 1)/2$, which works out to approximately 0.62 (the negative root is extraneous, since this ratio is always positive).

The golden section has had a ubiquitous influence on Western science and art. This proportion occurs frequently in the patterns of growth of plants and animals (Thompson, 1942; Mitchison, 1977; Bateson, 1979). The Greeks based much of their art (for example, the statues of Phidias) and architecture (for example, the front of the Parthenon) upon it. Many painters, including Piero della Francesca, Bellini, Poussin, Vermeer, and Seurat, have proportioned their canvases on the basis of the golden section ratio.

At least since Fechner (1876) psychologists have studied the aesthetic properties of this proportion. Fechner himself measured many common rectangles, including windows, playing cards, book covers, and writing pads, showing that their proportions were often close to 1:$\emptyset$. More recently, Benjafield (1976) and Piehl (1978) have demonstrated that the rectangle that many people find the most pleasing is the "golden rectangle," whose sides are in the golden section ratio. Nonetheless, the advantages of alloting figures to the positive poles of constructs approximately 62 percent of the time in interpersonal judgment may not be entirely aesthetic.

FIGURE VERSUS GROUND

This strategy of applying bipolar constructs to persons may be optimal for allowing our negative judgments to stand out maximally as "figure" against a general background of positive information.

It was noted above that Kelly (1955) implies that the a priori probability that a subject will assign a given figure to one pole of a dichotomous construct is the same as the probability that this figure will be assigned to the opposite pole. On the other hand, the distribution we can expect on empirical grounds is not 50/50, but rather approximately 62/38. Whenever the alternative categories of response have, as in this case, different relative frequencies of occurrence, we must distinguish between the amount of uncertainty associated with any one response category and the average uncertainty of all responses. We can determine the amount of uncertainty associated with each response category separately and then obtain a weighted average of these two values. More precisely, the Shannon-Wiener measure of average information is based on the sum of the separate estimates of uncertainty, each multiplied by its associated probability of occurrence as a weighting factor, that is, $H = \Sigma \, p \log_2 1/p$ (Attneave, 1959, p. 8).

Frank (summarized by Berlyne, 1971) operationally defined the "strikingness" (salience) of an event in terms of two of its properties: its informational content, defined as $\log_2 1/p$; and its relative frequency of occurrence, that is, p. His specific index is the product of these two values: $p \log_2 1/p$. It follows that the strikingness of an event, as operationally defined by Frank, is equivalent to its contribution to long-term average information (H) in the Shannon-Wiener formula.

Berlyne (1971) points out that the expression $p \log_2 1/p$, as a function of p, reaches its maximum value when $p = 1/e$, which works out to approximately 0.37 (see Attneave, 1959, p. 117). This value is, as Berlyne notes, quite close to the minor element in the golden section ratio, that is, 0.38. He hypothesizes, in light of this relationship, that the golden section "allows the minor element to occupy that proportion of the whole that makes it maximally striking (Berlyne, 1971, p. 232). Benjafield and Adams-Webber (1976, p. 14) speculate, on the basis of Berlyne's "strikingness hypothesis," that we tend to assign people to the negative poles of dichotomous constructs about 38 percent of the time so as to render our negative judgments, considered as a whole, maximally striking as figure against a diffuse background of positive impressions.

This general strategy of interpersonal judgment seems to have developed fully by midadolescence (Davidson, 1970; Romany and Adams-Webber, 1981). Younger children tend to allot significantly more than 62 percent of their acquaintances to the positive poles of constructs (Romany and Adams-Webber, 1980). This suggests that as children mature, and presumably gain in social experience, the distribution of their positive and negative impressions of people tends to converge upon the golden section, having gradually progressed from distributions that are more lopsided in favor of the positive poles of constructs.

It is possible in light of these considerations that the golden section provides an optimal level of balance between the relative proportions of figures allotted to the positive and negative poles of dichotomous constructs. Obviously, a construct in terms of which all figures were relegated to a single pole (either one) would have no discriminatory power whatsoever. On the other hand, as we have seen, a construct in terms of which the distribution of figures with respect to its alternative poles is perfectly symmetrical will have maximal discriminatory power (see Cochran, 1976). The golden section hypothesis implies, however, that the distribution of positive and negative impressions that is theoretically optimal from the standpoint of allowing our negative impressions to stand out maximally, and to make the greatest contribution to long-term, average information, is approximately 62 percent positive and 38 percent negative (Benjafield and Adams-Webber, 1976). This distribution of positive and negative judgments may permit us to pay special attention to behavior we perceive as negative and potentially threatening.

Adams-Webber and Benjafield (1973, p. 235) speculate that the positive poles of dichotomous constructs are used typically in a somewhat global way to refer to commonplace or normal characteristics that we expect most of our acquaintances to exhibit to some extent in their everyday behavior; and the negative poles of the same constructs to mark deviations from these "norms" that are expected to occur relatively infrequently. Thus, our negative impressions may convey more specific information about people than our positive ones, because the former refer to events that are more atypical than those designated by the latter. In a similar vein, Kanouse and Hanson (1972) suggest that our negative judgments of people are generally more salient than our positive judgments because positive information about people is so common that it acts as the perceptual ground against which negative information stands out as figure. Also, Hamilton and Gifford (1976, p. 394) reason that "since for most varieties of behavior the norm is positive in value, undesirable (nonnormative) behavior is statistically less frequent than desirable behavior and can be considered distinctive."

Adams-Webber (1979a) argues in light of these considerations that a general strategy of encoding information about people that serves to render our negative impressions of them maximally salient could be very useful in adapting to a social environment in which it is deviant behavior that is more likely to pose a threat to us than is typical behavior. Indeed, there is ample evidence that behavior that we label with negative descriptors is more salient in impression formation than is behavior that we label with positive descriptors (Warr, 1974).

Thus, as Fisher (1978) notes, the "golden section hypothesis suggests that, while we construe most events positively, we attempt to create a harmony between positive and negative events such that the latter make a maximum contribution to the whole" (see Benjafield and Adams-Webber, 1976).

MARKING AND NEGATIVITY

The golden section hypothesis also relates logically to recent work in the psychology of language, which has implications for the Dichotomy Corollary.

A basic principle of linguistic analysis is that of minimal contrast. Minimal contrast occurs whenever two items differ in terms of a single feature that is relevant to a linguistic distinction. A second principle that operates in many cases of minimal contrast is linguistic marking. Marking occurs whenever a feature is added to a basic form in order to produce a new form that differs from the original by only one feature. The new form is said to be the "marked" version of the old one, and the old form is described as "unmarked" (Greenberg, 1966). Thus, the two forms, marked and unmarked, lie in a general relationship of minimal contrast (see Deese, 1973).

This marked-unmarked distinction can be indicated either explicitly or implicitly. An example of explicit marking occurs in plurality in English, such as when we add a special feature to a noun in order to make it plural, for example, duck is unmarked and ducks is marked. Explicit marking is also common in English among pairs of antonymous adjectives that represent bipolar constructs. That is, in many cases the difference in meaning between the marked and unmarked members of a given pair of adjectival opposites depends on a single morphological feature added to the unmarked member, for example, pleasant-unpleasant, relevant-irrelevant, marked-unmarked.

There are many other pairs of contrasting adjectives in English that include no explicit marker of this type but that nonetheless exhibit all the other semantic properties of linguistic marking, for example, long-short. The unmarked member of such pairs usually provide the names of bipolar constructs, for example, the name of the long-short construct is length (this point will be discussed further in the following section). In addition, the meaning of the unmarked member can be neutralized in certain contexts; for example, an unmarked adjective, when included in a question, does not bias the anticipated response (H. H. Clark, 1969). For instance, when a speaker asks, "How long was the meeting?" he seems to be simply requesting an estimate of its length. If, on the other hand, he were to ask, "How short was the meeting?" he would be implying something more. Rightly or wrongly, he would be assuming that the meeting was short and inquiring specifically about the degree of its brevity.

Thus, unmarked adjectives seem to have both nominal and contrastive uses, whereas their marked counterparts almost always are understood contrastively. Moreover, the unmarked member of pairs of adjectival opposites typically came into the language at an earlier date, are the first to be understood correctly by children, and are used more frequently (see Deese, 1973). Hamilton and Deese (1971) also report that adjectives that are marked, either explicitly or implicitly, are evaluated more negatively than their marked opposites. Thus evaluation (Osgood, Suci, and Tannenbaum, 1957) also seems to be a psychological correlate of linguistic marking (see Deese, 1971).

Furthermore, both evaluation and linguistic marking relate to frequency of usage. That is, not only are unmarked words used more frequently than marked ones, but also evaluatively positive (E+) words are used more often than evaluatively negative (E−) words. Zajonc's (1968) explanation of the latter finding is that we tend to regard whatever happens relatively often as good for the sake of adapting to our environment. On the other hand, Boucher and Osgood's (1969) "Pollyanna hypothesis" implies that unmarked words are used more frequently than their marked opposites simply because the former tend to be evaluated more positively and we generally prefer to communicate about the good things in life. Finally, Deese (1973) suggests that unmarked words are used more often than marked ones because the former usually refer to the typical state of affairs and the latter represent deviations from the norm that occur, by definition, relatively infrequently.

The results of a recent experiment by Eiser and Mower White (1973) shed further light on this problem from the standpoint of the golden section hypothesis. Sixty British schoolchildren categorized 20 nonsense words (for example, *johzan*) as if they were the "names" of real persons, on the basis of 20 bipolar constructs. Each construct consisted of a single trait adjective, such as happy, and the same adjective preceded by the single marker *not*. Every child judged ten names on constructs containing unmarked poles that were E+ and marked poles that were E—, for example, happy-not happy. The other ten names were judged on constructs containing unmarked poles that were E— and marked poles that were E+, for example, rude-not rude. Each name was judged on only one construct, and each construct was applied to only one name.

Eiser and Mower White developed this procedure partly in order to test Boucher and Osgood's (1969, p. 1) Pollyanna hypothesis, which asserts that "there is an universal human tendency to use E+ words more frequently, diversely and facilely than E— words." This hypothesis clearly predicts that subjects will allot more figures to the E+ poles of constructs than to the E— poles (see Warr, 1971). Contrary to this expectation, Eiser and Mower White found a marginal tendency to make fewer E+ and E— responses. On the other hand, our reanalysis of their data revealed that the children had assigned exactly 62 percent of the names to the unmarked poles of constructs and 38 percent to the marked poles. Although this is at best a post hoc interpretation of their results, the outcome is exactly what we should expect on the basis of the golden section hypothesis.

Adams-Webber (1978) replicated Eiser and Mower White's experiment with 60 Canadian undergraduates. The overall proportion of names allotted to the unmarked poles of constructs was 0.63 (SD = 0.13). We also administered a Repertory Grid task (Kelly, 1955; Fransella and Bannister, 1977) to the same subjects after they had completed the Eiser and Mower White questionnaire. In this grid task, each subject dichotomously categorized 11 personal acquaintances successively on the basis of 12 bipolar constructs. The mean proportion of figures assigned to the unmarked poles of constructs was 0.62 (SD = 0.07), which is comparable to that observed in previous Rep Grid experiments (Adams-Webber and Benjafield, 1973; Benjafield and Adams-Webber, 1975, 1976).

The fact that similar results have been obtained with both Rep Grids and Eiser and Mower White's questionnaire format seems to rule out the possibility that earlier findings could have been artifacts of Rep Grid procedure as such (see Benjafield and Pomeroy, 1978). Moreover, since only imaginary figures were used in these two experiments, it can be argued that the golden section hypothesis describes how subjects employ dichotomous constructs in general and not only how they characterize their personal acquaintances. It is also important that approximately 62 percent of the available figures are assigned to the unmarked poles of constructs that have been completely counterbalanced in terms of connotative meaning, thereby isolating the effects of marking from those of evaluation.

It should be noted that in all our Rep Grid experiments (summarized by Adams-Webber, 1979a), some pairs of antonymous adjectives representing dichotomous constructs contained explicit markers indicating the contrast pole, for example, fair-unfair, whereas others contained no such explicit markers, for example, strong-weak. In both Eiser and Mower White's experiment, and Adams-Webber's (1978) replication of it, half the constructs contained one pole that was marked explicitly (for example, not stupid) and an opposite pole that, presumably, was marked implicitly (for example, stupid). On these ten constructs, subjects allotted figures to the poles without an explicit marker 61 percent of the time in the first experiment and 64 percent in the second one. On the remaining ten constructs, where one pole was marked neither explicitly nor implicitly (for example, happy), the proportion of figures allotted to unmarked poles was 0.63 in both experiments. These results suggest that the influence of explicit marking can override that of implicit marking when they are opposed to one another in dichotomous judgment processes.

On the other hand, a 1972 experiment by Benjafield and Adams-Webber (summarized by Adams-Webber, 1979a) indicates that the presence of explicit marking is not a necessary condition for subjects to distribute their personal judgments in the golden section ratio on dichotomous constructs. In this study subjects used only three bipolar constructs to categorize personal acquaintances, the minimal number needed to represent all three dimensions of connotative meaning identified by Osgood et al. (1957): evaluation, activity, and potency. One pole of each construct was presumed to be marked implicitly (for example, cruel). The mean proportion of figures assigned to the unmarked poles across these three constructs was 0.61 (SD = 0.16).

Osgood and Richards (1973, p. 381) suggest that the distinction between positive and negative may be more basic than any of the three components of connotative meaning. Specifically they assume that "*strong* and *active*, as well as *good* are somehow positive as compared to their opposites" (see Osgood, 1979). The opposites themselves — weak, passive, and bad — are all presumed to be marked linguistically (Deese, 1973; Osgood, 1979). As Benjafield and Adams-Webber (1976, p. 11) point out, the model developed by Osgood and Richards implies that: cognition is organized along bipolar dimensions; one of the poles of each dimension is psychologically positive and the other negative; and dimensions are related in parallel, positives with positives and negatives with negatives.

Further support for the golden section hypothesis can be found in data reported by Osgood and Richards themselves. Their subjects completed a series of sentences of the form "X is (adjective) _____ (adjective)"; for example, "X is dangerous _____ empty," The task was to decide whether *and* or *but* should be used to fill the blank. Since *and* is positive and *but* is negative (Osgood and Richards) the golden section hypothesis predicts that the former should be used approximately 62 percent of the time and the latter about 38 percent of the time. Osgood and Richards report that *and* was used to complete 62.5 percent of the sentences, and *but* 37.5 percent (see Benjafield and Adams-Webber, 1976). Osgood (1979) replicated this study cross-culturally across 12 different languages including Belgian Flemish, Hindi, Iranian Farsi, Thai, and Japanese, among others. The grand mean for the proportion of *and* responses was 0.60.

Jaspars et al. (1968) submit yet another hypothesis to explain our general tendency to use positive words more frequently than their negative counterparts. They assume that the concept of positivity is a primary cognitive structure, whereas the concept of negativity consists of exactly the same structure plus some transformational rule (for example, marking). As Peeters (1971) notes, their hypothesis implies that positivity represents a simpler concept than negativity, and the former underlies the latter. In short, a relatively simple concept of positivity may underlie a more differentiated concept of negativity in a figure-ground relation with the latter serving as the figure and the former as the ground. The golden section hypothesis lends precise quantitative form to this general figure-ground explanation by specifying that subjects will allot approximately that proportion of events to the negative poles of dichotomous constructs that can be expected to make their negative judgments stand out maximally as figure against a background of positive judgments (Benjafield and Adams-Webber, 1976).

In this context, the golden section hypothesis goes considerably beyond Boucher and Osgood's (1969) Pollyanna hypothesis, which implies simply that "there is a universal tendency to communicate about the positive aspects of life" (Osgood and Richards, 1973; p. 410). This suggests, as Deese (1973) notes, that "we are all natural optimists." The Pollyanna hypothesis predicts generally that subjects will apply the positive (unmarked) poles of constructs to events more frequently than the negative (marked) poles (Warr, 1971); whereas the golden section hypothesis predicts specifically that subjects will, on average, apply the positive poles of constructs to events approximately 62 percent of the time.

The results of a recent experiment by Shalit (1980) suggest that the range of convenience of the golden section hypothesis is not confined to the sphere of interpersonal judgment. He asked 232 subjects working in various occupations (military officers, enlisted men, air traffic controllers, social scientists, and crane operators) to list those factors they perceived as typical of their job situations and to evaluate these as either positive, neutral, or negative in character. The average proportion of factors that subjects evaluated positively was 0.62 (SD = 0.02).

NOMINAL AND CONTRAST POLES

We have seen that the positive (unmarked) member of a pair of contrasting adjectives (for example, long) usually serves both a nominal function (it provides the name of the construct as a whole, for example, length), and a contrastive function (it also designates a specific pole of the construct). Its negative (marked) opposite (short), on the other hand, serves only the contrastive function of designating the other pole of the construct. In this respect the concept of linguistic marking parallels closely Kelly's own distinction between the nominal and contrastive poles of a personal construct.

It was pointed out above that Kelly (1955, p. 111) assumed that the minimum context of any construct consists of "at least two things which have a likeness and one thing which is, by the same token, different." He posited further that "any one of the like elements in the context of a construct may give the construct its name . . . [and] the symbol [name] of a construct is usually one of the like elements" (p. 149). Thus the nominal pole of each construct is viewed as subsuming the name of the construct itself in addition to a set of elements that are perceived as similar to one another in some respect, whereas the contrast pole subsumes only elements that are perceived as different in the same respect from those subsumed under the nominal pole (Adams-Webber, 1979a, p. 174).

A 1975 experiment by Adams-Webber, Benjafield, Doan, and Giesbrecht (summarized in Adams-Webber, 1979a) indicated that individual differences in terms of the relative frequency of usage of the nominal and contrastive poles of a given construct can affect memory for information encoded on the basis of that construct. Specifically, the more balanced the distribution of a subject's judgments between the alternative poles of a particular construct, the less difference there is between poles in terms of ease of recall. Conversely, the more lopsided the distribution of a subject's judgments in favor of the nominal pole of a construct, the greater the extent to which his memory for information encoded in terms of the nominal pole will surpass that for information encoded in terms of the contrast pole.

This finding may relate to the observation that the more lopsided the distribution of a subject's judgments with respect to the alternative poles of a set of dichotomous constructs, the less consistent from one situation to another he tends to be in characterizing self and others on the basis of those constructs (Benjafield and Adams-Webber, 1975; Clyne, 1975; Cochran, 1976). Since each judgment of a specific difference between two persons (including self) entails that one of them must be assigned to the contrast pole of a given construct, a subject with relatively lopsided constructs may be more likely to forget such contrastive information than a subject whose constructs are relatively balanced. It is interesting to note in relation to this possibility that the more lopsided the distribution of a subject's judgments in favor of the nominal pole of a particular construct, the more useful he tends to regard that construct for characterizing people in general, and the more definitely (extremely) he judges persons on it (Adams-Webber and Benjafield, 1973).

The observation that children's usage of the alternative poles of constructs becomes progressively less lopsided as they mature (Applebee, 1975, 1976; Barratt, 1977b; Romany and Adams-Webber, 1981) suggests, in light of the findings discussed immediately above, that children's memories for information encoded in terms of the contrast poles of constructs, and, by implication, their recall of specific differences between persons, may gradually improve with age until midadolescence when the distribution of their positive and negative judgments tends to converge on the golden section ratio. As we have seen, this proportion may be theoretically optimal from the standpoint of allowing our contrastive (negative) judgments to occupy that fraction of all impressions that could render them maximally salient (that is, 0.38).

Kelly's (1955) assumption that it is the more frequently used (nominal) pole of a construct that provides the name of the distinction represented by the construct as a whole also may have some psycholinguistic implications. If one particular pole subsumes the name of the construct, then the meaning of that (nominal) pole could be more fixed in terms of common usage than is that of the opposite (contrast) pole. This suggests that we might enjoy more degrees of freedom in employing the contrast poles of our personal constructs. Likewise, if positive (unmarked) adjectives usually serve the nominal function of providing the names of bipolar constructs (H. H. Clark, 1969; Deese, 1973), then we might expect subjects to keep their usage of positive (unmarked) adjectives as consistent as possible with what they understand to be commonly accepted public meanings while using the negative (marked) opposites somewhat more idiosyncratically in light of their own personal experience (Adams-Webber, 1979a).

By employing the contrast pole of a given construct more idiosyncratically than its nominal pole we may be able to rotate the meaning of that construct in terms of its axis of reference slightly away from what Mair (1967) calls the "logic of public language" so that its implications are more congruent with the overall structure of our own personal construct systems (Adams-Webber, 1979b). In Piaget's (1960) terms, we may accommodate to the dictates of the public lexicon more in our usage of the nominal poles of constructs and assimilate their meanings to the unique structure of our personal construct systems more in our usage of their contrast poles. In the language of construct theory, we may expect to observe more commonality (see Chapter 12) in the use of the nominal poles of constructs and more individuality (see Chapter 4) in the use of their contrast poles. In this way, each of us can try to bridge the gap between the common language system and our own private world of experience (Adams-Webber, 1980a).

The general model of construct usage outlined above, which is admittedly highly speculative, implies that we should expect to find more intersubject agreement concerning the meanings of the nominal poles of constructs than concerning those of their contrast poles. When Bannister (1962a) asked subjects to categorize people dichotomously on the basis of a set of unipolar constructs, he found a significant level of intersubject agreement concerning the specific pattern of relationships between constructs; however, there was little agreement concerning how particular figures were judged on each construct. Applebee (1975, 1976) showed also that the degree of consensus among children about relationships between constructs increases with age. As did Bannister, Applebee observed more intersubject agreement concerning relationships between constructs than concerning the ratings assigned to certain elements. In a recent experiment (Adams-Webber, 1979c) with normal adults, we observed significantly more intersubject agreement concerning the pattern of relationships between the nominal poles of constructs than concerning that between their contrast poles.

Insofar as the meaning of a particular construct is reflected in its specific relationships with other constructs (see Lemon and Warren, 1974), this finding is consistent with the hypothesis (stated above) that there is a higher level of consensus (commonality) concerning the meanings of the nominal poles of dichotomous constructs than those of their contrast poles. Some clinical significance may lie in the fact that deviations from the typical pattern of relationships between constructs are associated with the diagnosis and judged severity of thought disorder in hospitalized schizophrenics (Bannister, Fransella, and Agnew, 1971; McPherson et al., 1973).

It is tempting to speculate further that the development of personal construct systems involves the progressive integration of interpersonal judgments on the basis of certain normative prototypes (see Cantor and Mischel, 1979) defined in terms of various more or less agreed upon public meanings, for example, honesty, which can be referred to through the nominal function of the positive poles of constructs; and the increasing differentiation of one's personal world of experience in terms of specific contrasts represented by the negative (marked) opposite poles. There is at least some evidence that the contrast (negative, marked) poles of constructs are used more differentially in interpersonal judgment than their nominal (positive, unmarked) poles by normal adults and various clinical populations (Adams-Webber, 1977a). The hypothesis that the meanings of the contrast poles of constructs are more differentiated than those of their nominal poles also seems consistent with the observation that subjects tend to judge themselves and others more definitely on the former (Adams-Webber and Benjafield, 1973).

On the other hand, this hypothesis may apply only to psychological construing. Adams-Webber (1980b) found that although, as expected, normal adults showed significantly more functional differentiation between the negative poles of psychological constructs, such as happy-sad, this relationship was exactly reversed in terms of physical constructs such as physically strong-physically weak. A possible explanation of this finding is suggested by the consideration that the negative (marked) poles of physical constructs typically refer to the lack of some property named by their positive (unmarked) poles, for example, tallness or height (Clark, 1969), and therefore the former usually entail the notion of an absolute lower limit or zero point (see Harris, 1973). For example, a person can be only so short (in the ideal limiting case, a height of zero); whereas, at least in principle, there is logically no upper limit for a person's height. Thus, the negative poles of most, if not all, physical constructs can be viewed as related to one another through logical extension in the sense that they converge on the common reference point of absolute zero. This could help to explain why subjects tend to use the negative poles of physical constructs less independently of one another than the positive poles (Adams-Webber, 1980b).

In the case of psychological constructs, however, it may be the positive poles that entail the notion of limit. We seem to have a general ideal of perfection that serves to define the upper boundaries of the extensions of the positive poles of many psychological constructs, while those of their negative opposites are more open-ended. For example, the notion of perfect benevolence seems to define the absolute upper limit of kindness; whereas, unfortunately, cruelty has no such limits. On the basis of this consideration, we might expect subjects to use the negative poles of psychological constructs more independently of one another than the positive poles (Adams-Webber, 1977b, 1980b).

If it were the case that the meanings of the positive poles of psychological constructs tend to converge upon a general ideal, or halo, of perfection, while the logical extensions of their negative poles are not so restricted; then we might expect that the personal meanings that individuals assign to the negative poles of psychological constructs will be somewhat more specific, and perhaps more idiosyncratic, than those they assign to the positive poles (Adams-Webber, 1979a). Although this hypothesis is highly speculative, it is consistent with several observations: we tend to judge ourselves and others more definitely on the negative poles of psychological constructs than on the positive poles (Adams-Webber and Benjafield, 1973); there seems to be more intersubject agreement concerning the general pattern of relationships among the latter (Adams-Webber, 1979c); and we tend to allot that proportion of figures to the negative poles of psychological constructs that could serve to render our negative judgments maximally salient, that is, 38 percent.

SELF VERSUS OTHERS

Most of the evidence discussed above derives from experiments in which standard lists of bipolar constructs were supplied to all subjects alike, rather than personal constructs being elicited from each subject individually. Unfortunately, it is often difficult — if not impossible — to identify reliably the positive (or unmarked) poles of many of the constructs elicited from persons (for example, honest-kind). Thus, it is not clear how the findings reviewed so far apply to personal judgments based upon elicited constructs. One possibility is to approach this problem indirectly in terms of the structure of the self-concept. Kelly (1955, p. 131) argues that

the *self* is, when considered in the appropriate context, a proper concept or construct. It refers to a group of events which are alike in a certain way and, in that same way, necessarily different from other events. The way in which the events are alike is the self. That also makes the self an individual differentiated from other individuals.

It follows that each individual has a clear and distinct notion of his own identity only to the extent that he can discern a specific pattern of similarities and differences between self and others (Adams-Webber, 1979a). As Bannister and Agnew (1977, p. 99) point out, "the ways in which we elaborate the construing of self must be essentially those ways in which we elaborate our construing of others for we have not a concept of self but a bipolar construct of self-not self."

The proportion of figures that subjects assign to the same poles of dichotomous constructs as the self is highly stable over time (Benjafield and Adams-Webber, 1975; Jones, 1954; Sperlinger, 1976). It has been demonstrated also that normal adults tend to assign themselves and others to the same poles of constructs, both elicited and supplied ones, approximately 62 percent of the time (Adams-Webber, 1977b; Adams-Webber and Benjafield, 1976; Adams-Webber and Davidson, 1979; Benjafield and Adams-Webber, 1975; Romany, 1980). About the same proportion of like self judgments is observed when subjects describe strangers whom they have just met for the first time as when they characterize their own parents and siblings (Adams-Webber, 1977b). The distribution of like self-unlike self judgments seems to have stabilized at about 62/38 by midadolescence, having gradually decreased from more lopsided distributions at earlier ages. For example, children as young as 10 years of age construe others as significantly more similar to themselves than do 15 year olds (Romany, 1980). In contrast, agoraphobics, depressives, and other psychiatric populations have been found to construe others as significantly less similar to themselves than normal adults (Frazer, 1980; Space and Cromwell, 1980). A similar tendency was observed when normal university students role-played being depressed (Rodney, 1980).

This evidence suggests that the development of the self may also fall within the range of convenience of the golden section hypothesis. This would seem consistent with the relationship between the golden section and marking (discussed above) in light of the fact that marking occurs in many classifications of kinship relations to denote distance from self; for example, mother is unmarked, whereas mother-in-law is marked (see Greenberg, 1966). Lemon and Warren (1974, p. 123) speculate that a person's judgments of others "automatically involve a kind of self-comparison process . . . [in which] the self-construct will act as an anchoring point to produce the effects of assimilation and contrast familiar in psychophysics and from Hovland and Sherif (1952)." This seems quite plausible in light of the considerations that the self is probably an element within the range of convenience of most of an individual's personal constructs, if not the focus of convenience and, very likely, was one of the original set of figures used in the formation of many of them. Indeed, the importance of self-reference in encoding and remembering information has become an important focus of interest in current research in personal construct theory (Bannister and Agnew, 1977; Mancuso and Ceely, 1980).

Adams-Webber (1979a) suggests that our judgments of like self-unlike self may tend to be distributed in the golden section ratio because it is perceived differences between oneself and others that define the contours of the self as figure against a general background of perceived similarities. That is, we tend to organize our personal judgments in such a way that perceived differences between self and others will occupy approximately that proportion of all impressions that should, according to the golden section hypothesis, render them maximally salient. The potential importance of such a tendency in the organization of personal construct systems is reflected by the findings that the extent to which others are construed as similar to the self is not only one of the most stable characteristics of interpersonal judgment, but also it relates closely to the level of overall integration among constructs and the degree of differentiation between figures (Adams-Webber, 1970). Moreover, it relates to the ability to differentiate between others in terms of their own personal constructs, that is, sociality, which is the topic of Chapter 13 (Adams-Webber, Schwenker, and Barbeau, 1972).

An important problem for future research is the nature of the relationship (if any) between the way in which we structure our impressions of self versus others and our general propensity to assign people to the positive (unmarked) and negative (marked) poles of constructs in the golden section ratio. The tendency to assign the same poles of constructs to self and others approximately 62 percent of the time could be a side effect of the latter phenomenon; however, it could still have the effect of making perceived differences between self and others stand out as maximally salient (Adams-Webber, 1979c).

If we hypothesize that people employ a general strategy in interpersonal judgment that dictates that the negative poles of constructs will be applied to other persons approximately 38 percent of the time, and also that differences between self and others will constitute about 38 percent of all impressions, we can deduce several other consequences of employing such a strategy. The first of these is that whenever the self is assigned to the negative pole of a given construct, on average, half of the other figures will be assigned to the same pole and half to the opposite pole. In terms of the principles of information theory, this will tend to maximize the average informational value of all judgments on those specific constructs on which the self is assigned to the negative poles (excluding judgments concerning the self). Furthermore, positive and negative judgments about others will make the same contribution to average information on those particular constructs.

On the other hand, whenever the self is assigned to the positive pole of a construct, on average, the majority of other figures also will be assigned to the positive pole. Indeed, on constructs in terms of which the self is positive, the proportion of other figures assigned to the positive poles will exceed the proportion assigned to the negative poles by at least 24 percent. For the sake of convenience, we can refer to the overall proportion of positive characteristics attributed to the self as the self-esteem score. In the hypothetical strategy that we are considering, this index can assume any value between 0.24 and 1.00. That is, within these specific limits, the self-esteem score can vary independently of both the overall proportion of negative characteristics attributed to others or the proportion of differences between self and others.

In an earlier study (discussed above) we observed that relatively lopsided constructs have some theoretically interesting properties (Adams-Webber and

Benjafield, 1973). First, constructs that are unbalanced in favor of their positive poles are regarded as more useful for describing people in general than constructs with relatively balanced distributions of positive and negative impressions. Second, people tend to judge themselves and others more definitely (extremely) on the former than on the latter, which is consistent with the additional finding that rating extremity correlates positively with judged utility.

It is tempting to speculate in light of these considerations that we tend to regard our own negative characteristics as less important than our positive ones, and as more difficult to judge. This could make it much easier for us to attribute our own negative characteristics to about half of our acquaintances. It also seems plausible to assume that the precise number of constructs on which the self is relegated to the negative pole will depend primarily on the specific content of those constructs. Thus, it could make sense for people to adopt a general strategy of interpersonal judgment that allows the proportion of negative characteristics assigned to the self to vary fairly widely from one context of particular constructs to another while the basic structural features of social construing remain more or less stable, for example, the hypothesized tendencies to maximize the salience of perceived differences between self and other and that of the negative characteristics of others.

SUMMARY

In this chapter we have examined some of the theoretical implications of Kelly's Dichotomy Corollary in light of relevant experimental evidence. This corollary asserts that "a person's construction system is composed of a finite number of dichotomous constructs." Each construct represents a single bipolar distinction, such as happy-sad, which is seen as applicable to a limited range of events. One of its alternative poles is assumed to have a nominal, as well as a contrastive, function; that is, it provides the name of the construct (for example, happiness). The opposite pole is viewed as having only a contrastive use. Recent research indicates that the nominal poles of constructs are applied to events more frequently than their contrastive counterparts and also that there is more interjudge agreement concerning the meanings of the former. The contrast poles, on the other hand, are used more idiosyncratically and independently of one another and are applied to events in a more definite manner.

Perhaps the most significant finding that has emerged within this area of research to date is that we tend to assign people to the contrast poles of constructs, on average, approximately 38 percent of the time. It was suggested that this particular distribution of figures with respect to the alternative poles of constructs may allow our contrastive (marked) judgments to stand out as maximally salient. The implications of this finding were discussed in terms of the golden section, information theory, minimal contrast, linguistic marking, the Pollyanna hypothesis, and the development of self-concepts.

7

THE FLOW OF CHOICE:
THE CHOICE COROLLARY

Philip J. Boxer

The Choice Corollary: A person chooses for himself that alternative in a dichotomized construct through which he anticipates the greater possibility for extension and definition of his system.

The Fundamental Postulate is a construction of the individual as a "process in being." Like a flowing stream, the individual's behavior is construed as the dynamic choices implicit in his onward flow across the epigenetic landscape of his construing. The process of choice lies at the center of the development of the individual's construction system, and it is this system that forms the landscape that channelizes the onward flow of the individual's processes. Not only does the construction system construe its own extension and definition, thus setting itself apart as a self-referential system, but also the construction system produces alternatives, the experience of which varies the construction system itself: the construction system has the capability of being self-modifying. These two properties of the construction system have enormous implications (Varela, 1979) for the autonomy of the individual in relation to others that can only be touched on in this chapter. The individual also experiences himself as self-aware and conscious of the choices open to him within the context of that self-awareness. There is a duality in this consciousness in that the individual can both think about himself — the stream as seen from the point of view of the surrounding landscape — and he can also think as himself — the stream-in-being seen from the point of view of being the stream itself. This duality manifests itself to him on the one hand as a consciousness of choice and on the other hand as an aware-ness of choosing.

It is my intention to explore the Choice Corollary in this chapter from the point of view of choosing. The objective underlying this is to arrive at an understanding of what can go "wrong" with this process as construed by the individual choosing.

My reason for exploring the process of choosing as distinct from the nature of choice is that the former leads toward autonomy as a choice itself for the individual as opposed to the latter, which leads only to a consideration of the products of construction systems.

Throughout the chapter, I use the masculine gender in referring to indi-viduals. This is because of a limitation in my use of language, since the contents of the chapter are relevant to persons of either sex. This limitation raises an issue about the physical nature of the representational medium I am using: the printed word. When not referring to individuals in general, I also from time to time refer to managers and musicians. This is because of my particular experi-ence in working with managers on problems of development management and because I have some experience of being a musician. My use of these two different forms of experience, however, also reflects another issue: the relation-ship of the knower to that which is known.

If the physical nature of the representational medium I am using is examined, then it can be described as having a surface structure and a deep structure that can themselves be described in terms of syntactical rules and transformational grammar: laws governing the properties of the medium itself. As soon as the question of the meaning embodied in the use of the medium is raised, then another mode of description dealing with semantics can be used. The medium can be viewed as embodying syntagma forming syntagmatic struc-tures: structures of meaning that have no necessary correspondence with the syntactical structures through which they can be represented. In addition these syntagmatic structures can themselves be viewed as being embedded in paradig-matic structures of meaning. Thus syntactical structure describes the medium itself, and syntagmatic and paradigmatic structure describes the use of the medium, but in both cases the description is from the point of view of someone describing someone else expressing meaning — my use of my experience with managers reflects this point of view. These forms of description refer particu-larly to language and its use as a form of representation. If all forms of action are viewed as representation, then one adopts the same point of view as does Kelly in his Personal Construct Psychology. If one further adopts the view that not all that the knower experiences himself as knowing can necessarily be embodied in a form of representation observable as a whole by others, then one adopts the perspective of the knower as opposed to the observer — my use of my experience as a musician. It is from this point of view that I have elaborated the constructs of action structure, object structure, core structure, and implicate order in this chapter.

DOES HE KNOW IT IS HIS SYSTEM?

My work involves me with many managers who are concerned with their capabilities as managers. They desire to extract the greatest value possible from those activities for which they are responsible, although they rarely put it quite like that. I like to work alongside them in their own working habitat. They expect me to help them to be more capable. Naturally I ask them what they do, why they do it, and what it is about the anticipated consequences of their actions that leads them to do it that way rather than some other way. What I hear from a manager is his theory of action. What he tells me is self-referential, of course, and always has some form of coherence. Regardless of the theory's substance as reflected in its ability to predict, it is always possible to be critical of the theory's form of coherence. The manager can be pressed toward greater and greater coherence in what he says. Regardless of the degree of coherence to which he develops his theory, however, the manager can always make statements using it that do not make sense to him in its own terms. This follows from the theory's ability to be self-referential (Godel, 1962), and it means that the manager can never wholly rely on his theory to decide his choice for him: There will always be times when he will be thrown back to choosing directly for himself. The first question then is what determines the consequent choice if he cannot decide in terms of his own theory?

The second issue arises from the degree of incongruency that exists between the manager's "espoused" theory and his "theory-in-use" (Argyris and Schon, 1976). If I agree to a representation, with the manager, of his espoused theory, and then set about representing to him the coherence that I see implicit in how he acts, to the point at which he can recognize it for himself, we end up with two theories: one his espoused theory, and the other the theory he agrees as being implicit in his actions. As Argyris and Schon have shown, these two theories are frequently incongruent. For the manager this means that his own actions may become unmanageable from the point of view of his own consciousness. From the other's point of view, he will be construed as being unable to keep his word. The manager will be unable to identify those choices that extend and define his capabilities: He will experience himself as working in the dark. The second question then is what is it that leads to incongruency developing between the manager's espoused theory and theory-in-use?

Managers need to develop a kind of sixth sense about choosing — a form of awareness that enables them to make the "right shot in the dark." An awareness that Polanyi described as tacit knowledge (Polanyi, 1958). Developing this form of awareness is a necessary condition if the manager is to pick his way through the plethora of possibilities open to him. Let us assume that the manager's espoused theory and his theory-in-use are congruent; that he is capable of facing himself with propositions the truth of which he will be unable to determine in terms of his own theory; and that he has the capability to "take a shot in the dark" that he feels "right" in the sense that he anticipates that it gives him the best chance of extending and defining his construction system. Will he have the power to exercise that choice, or will others have the power to force him to make a choice he feels is not "right?"

The managers I work with frequently want to make things happen in areas over which they have no jurisdiction, and so they have to influence the choices of others, just as others will be trying to influence their own choices. There are a number of distinct "power styles" and corresponding "blocking responses" that goven this cross-flow of influencing. Some idea of the complexity of these crossflows particularly at higher levels of an organization can be gained from Mintzberg, Raisinghani, and Theoret (1976). It is not appropriate to pursue the nature of these blocking responses in this chapter, but the power styles correspond to the different forms of directive that are manifestations of "force" in the use of language. Kelly talks about this force in more general terms as "agressiveness" and the corresponding blocking response in terms of "hostility." I will be describing the nature of this force in greater detail later in the chapter, but even if the manager has a great deal of it, and he is well within his rights to make a particular choice, there is still one further problem he faces.

The manager will try to execute the choice he wishes to make through his ability to coordinate the development of resources to that end. If he has the appropriate resources within his control, then their deployment will "determine" the outcome. It may be, however, that there is no way within the current technology to secure the outcome he desires: It can't be done, and perhaps never can be done. He is thereby "overdetermined" as he experiences it in his ability to produce the outcomes he chooses, although he may be "underdetermined" in other areas in that he in fact has the ability to produce outcomes of which he has not yet dreamed. The experience of over- or underdetermination will be a function of the structure of resources accessible to him relative to his capacity to choose: What is overdetermining for one manager may be underdetermining for another. For the purpose of this chapter I will assume that the manager is underdetermined, but obviously the manager's ability to execute a choice he makes will affect the way in which his construction system develops.

Who Is It Who Chooses for Himself?

Managers frequently have to take shots in the dark. They call it making a judgment. For a long time it has been fashionable to believe that the decision-making process could be explained as a rational analytic process by reference to phenomena external to the decision maker (Newell and Simon, 1972). It could be made more rigorous and consistent and formalized into a decision science that could be subject to objectification through the familiar process of consensual refutation (Popper, 1959), just as is done in the physical sciences. If there are statements the manager can make that do not make sense in terms of his own rational analytic process, then by defining the rational analytic process as object-referenced, it can be distinguished from the "subject-referenced" process whereby the manager uses his "feel" based on the quality of his own experience of choosing (Boxer, 1978). This is a very difficult distinction to support, because subject-referenced knowing can be treated as a form of object-referenced knowing that only the manager can object-reference because only he has experience of it. It is not accessible to consensual refutation, because it belongs to a nonconsensual reality. A manager, however, is always working in a nonconsensual reality, so for him the issue is not one of others knowing what he knows, but rather the accessibility of his own knowing to himself: his experience of what Kelly referred to as his own construing process. For him this experience has object-referenced as well as subject-referenced aspects, and it is the latter that is the "feel" that enables him to make judgments and to take shots in the dark.

The manager experiences subject-referenced knowing as emanating from "within" and equally experiences object-referenced knowing as referring to "outside." The two will have become distinct to him at a very early age when his experience of one ceases to be coincident with the other. We have already discussed the possibility of incongruency developing between his theory-in-use (his construction system) and the espoused theory that is his consciousness. His consciousness will be "focal": it will represent to him that which he anticipates. The manager, however, will also be aware of himself as context to his consciousness, out of which context will emanate his "feel." He will experience himself, therefore, as existing between his "focal consciousness" of the outside as object-referenceable, including himself as object, and his "contextual awareness" of "within" as subject-referenceable.

The extrovert manager will draw his sense of himself more from focal consciousness. He will tend to identify himself with focal consciousness so that in choosing for himself he will have difficulty in recognizing any incongruency between himself and his construction system, but he will be very conscious of being overdetermined. When he presents himself with a choice that is undecidable in his own terms, however, he will be at a disadvantage in comparison with the introvert who will be able to identify himself more with his sense of himself within contextual awareness. The introvert will find it easier to explore his own feelings independently of the way in which the choice is presented: His difficulty will be in formulating a choice that is an expression of his sense of "feel."

There is an underlying problem, then, in disentangling the manager's sense of himself in choosing from the choices he might think about making. Whence the manager draws his sense of himself will affect the form of self for which he chooses. Kelly construed the person as construing the replications of events: the form of knowing that is object referenced and experienced as focal consciousness. It is also possible to see the person as construing the replications of his experience of himself as context to the construing of the replications of events: the form of knowing that is subject-referenced and experienced as contextual awareness. This construing by the construer of the replications of his own experience of himself as context itself can be construed as "propositional construing." This is structurally distinct from constellatory and preemptive construing: Collectively the person's propositional construing forms a "core structure" within his construction system, while the constellatory and preemptive contruing form an "object structure" (Boxer, 1980). Kelly made only a logical distinction between the different forms of construing. He also gave a different meaning to the word *context*. Before going on, therefore, to explore the implications of making a structural distinction between core structure and object structure, it is necessary to delve deeper into the meaning of contextual awareness.

The Nature of Contextual Awareness

In order to understand the nature of contextual awareness it is necessary to leave being a manager for the moment and to become a musician. All musicians have to have an instrument, just as creative artists need to work in a medium. To be effective, the musician must practice his technique, so that when he tries to play a particular piece of music, he will experience his ability to play the instrument as underdetermining. In this way he will be able to concentrate on his musical expression. By practicing, the musician is developing the "existential articulation" of his ability to play: He is developing his physical ability to act in more and more complex patterns of action that produce patterns of sound on his instrument. Skill in any medium involves the development of existential articulation, and this applies as much to the pronunciation of long words as it does to the movements of a ballet dancer.

Existential articulation will not be enough, however, for the musician to establish mastery over his instrument. He will also have to learn to read music. Music is written in another medium that is existentially articulated and that has acquired the special status of a "representational system." The existential articulation of the music will need to be at least as great as that of the musical actions he is to perform, and its purpose will be served if the choices of musical action he experiences from reading are those originally experienced and expressed by the music's composer. If you can imagine the composer writing down his own musical thoughts and then playing them, then the relationship between his thoughts and the consequent action will be one of "referential articulation." I am therefore defining referential articulation as the process that results not only in a separation of the actor from the action, but also in the experience of focal consciousness. The musician's ability to read the music in one key and to transpose it as he plays it into another key reflects the degree to which he is musically conscious and is referentially articulated between his musical thoughts and his musical actions.

Language is our most highly developed representational system, and its existential articulation can be described in terms of its syntactical structure, which gives the articulate speaker enormous choice in how he expresses meaning. When the speaker speaks, he creates a syntagmatic structure. A syntagma is a unit of meaning as experienced by the listener. Its meaning will be complicated by the fact that language is a self-referential representational system, but nevertheless the syntagma will ultimately acquire some meaning to the listener who is sufficiently referentially articulated. Language is in fact doubly articulated (Guiraud, 1975). The syntagma can acquire meaning independently from the meaning acquired by the way in which they are structured in relation to each other. The syntagma, therefore, represent the "substance" in the speaker's experience, and the syntagmatic structure represents the "form." Metonymy in the use of language results, then, from playing with the referential nature of language's substance; and metaphor results from playing with the substance itself in relation to the form within which it is embedded. The form, however, can also be played with, resulting in analogy.

Expressing form in language results in the experience of "figure" being lifted into the listener's consciousness in relation to the "ground" of what he is not conscious of. His attention will be focused on the figure. When the listener experiences an analogy, the representation of form that he has heard will be distinct from the representation he would be conscious of arising from his own experience. The listener can only be conscious of one syntagmatic structure at a time, so he will experience the possibility of creating another form as an awareness at the time he hears the one syntagmatic structure of a sense of its inappropriateness. The appropriateness of form can be represented as the paradigmatic structure implicit in the speaker's use of language. The experience of paradigmatic structure is contextual awareness.

Kelly defines the context of a construct as comprising those elements among which the user ordinarily discriminates by means of the construct. Elements clearly correspond to syntagma in speech, so that a construct is a way of structuring syntagma. Syntagma are embedded in syntagmatic structure, and syntagmatic structure is itself embedded in paradigmatic structure. Focal consciousness focuses on syntagmatic structures within which the Kellian notion of context is embedded. Contextual awareness is on the other hand the experience of paradigmatic structure within which focal consciousness is embedded. It is in this sense that the two uses of the word "context" are quite different.

Returning to our musician, therefore, he is existentially articulated: He has the ability to act in a variety of ways in the world and those ways can be extended by the use of various devices — in his case an instrument. This is the "creatura" that Jung (1967) conceived of: the world of causes and effects, which can be wholly object-referenced and about which statements can be made that can be consensually validated. The musician can also be conscious of a musical thought independently of its expression in his actions: He is referentially articulated, and he is able to represent those thoughts within a representational system capable of carrying "meaning" for him. This domain of consciousness, representation, and meaning is the pleroma (Jung, 1967), which contrasts with the creatura, and which exists by virtue of the existence of the subject and within which statements represent a form of coherence embodying the subject's (nonconsensual) experience of his reality. This view of representational systems in general, and language in particular, locates the representational system embodied in focal consciousness as the subject's consciousness of himself-in-the-world, but also embodies his awareness of the-world-in-himself (Coward and Ellis, 1977). The representational system thus becomes in focal consciousness "the Symbolic" through which the subject "knows" an "outer reality" ("the Real"), and which is itself embedded in contextual awareness through which the subject relates to an "inner reality" ("the Imaginary") (Lemaire, 1977). The possibility of incongruency between the subject's Symbolic and his construction system reflects the possibility that there will be "inner realities" that may be expressed through his actions directly in an "outer reality" without his consciousness. Mastery for the musician will, therefore, be the ability to express his "inner reality" directly in a musical "outer reality" through the Symbolic. The master will be underdetermined in his actions, congruent in his thoughts, self-determining in his choices, and he can act with force.

LEVELS OF STRUCTURE

This chapter is written using language as the representational system. In the act of writing it, I am subject to the same limitations described in relation to managers and musicians: I can be overdetermined in my ability to express myself by my lack of skill in the medium itself; and there can be incongruency between the meaning I experience implicitly in my actions (theory-in-use) and the meaning I represent through language (espoused theory). There is another limitation, however, derived from language's double articulation: There is a limit to the number of levels of structure that can be represented explicitly in the medium at any one time. What are these levels of structure, and what evidence is there that there are more levels than can be explicitly represented?

The composer making marks on his musical manuscript is acting in a way that is existentially articulated: The marks he makes are traces left through time of his existence in the world as a particular structure of actions. The manuscript, therefore, represents a particular "action structure." For the composer, however, there was a choice in what he wrote down in relation to his thoughts in focal consciousness: This experience of choice was described as referential articulation. The particular action structure can, therefore, also be construed as a representation of focal consciousness. Thus, language is both an action structure that has syntactical structure and that can be construed as a representation of focal consciousness; its structure is also a representational system reflecting the syntagmatic structure of meaning experienced in focal consciousness.

The structure of language embodies reference to particulars and predicate expressions concerning those particulars. The double existential articulation of language's syntactical structure enables its user to represent two "levels" of referential articulation: he can choose what particulars to which he refers (the first level of referential articulation between the individual and his experience of external "reality"), and he can choose the predicate expressions he uses to represent the relatedness he experiences between the particulars to which he has chosen to refer (the second level of referential articulation between the individual's contextual awareness of himself and his experience of focal consciousness). Thus, the double existential articulation of language allows particulars to be embedded in predicate expressions in which syntagma are embedded in syntagmatic structure, a way that represents the two levels of referential articulation resulting in the experience of focal consciousness. If congruency is assumed, therefore, the embeddedness of syntagma in syntagmatic structure reflects focal consciousness and can be represented by particulars embedded in predicate expressions in language, and it corresponds to action structures embedded in the object structure within the construction system.

If action structures are level 1 structures, and object structures experienced in focal consciousness as syntagmatic structures are level 2 structures, what then are level 3 structures? The double articulation of language makes it able to represent two levels of referential articulation, but to represent level 3 structures explicitly it would have to be trebly articulated. What evidence can there be, therefore, of level 3 structure?

In predicate expressions, there are two kinds of universals: categorizing universals and characterizing universals (Strawson, 1959). The particular represents the syntagma, which corresponds to preemptive construing. The categorizing universal is denotative in its use and represents a form of relatedness between syntagma that corresponds to constellatory construing. The characterizing universal, however, is connotative in its use and represents a form of meaning that is paradigmatic. Is the characterizing universal, therefore, the manifestation in a doubly articulated representational system of the third level of referential articulation?

The characterizing universal takes the form of an adjective pair. The individual's use of this pair is asymmetric, the "unmarked" one being used more frequently than the "marked" one for characterizing (Adams-Webber and Benjafield, 1973). Its use in language is such that it directs attention toward those phenomena that the individual experiences as unusual (Adams-Webber and Benjafield, 1976); judgments expressed in terms of the unmarked form show greater consistency with each other than those expressed in marked form (Adams-Webber, 1977b); the individual is better able to remember comparative statements when made in unmarked as opposed to marked form (Clark and Card, 1969); and the individual is able to make deductions faster from unmarked as opposed to marked information (H. H. Clark, 1969). The individual's use of language is thus riddled with marking, and this marking also affects the way in which language is used; the explicit representation of this marking in language as adjective pairs enables their use to be made manifest in syntagmatic structures;

and the way in which they occur as adjectives enables them to express propositional construing.

There is evidence, therefore, for a level 3 structure manifesting itself both within a doubly articulated representational system as characterizing universals and implicitly in the use of that system through marking. In the construction system a level 3 structure would be "core structure," and object structures would be embedded in it in the same way as action structures were embedded in object structure. Core structure would enable the individual to direct his attention toward those phenomena he experienced as unusual. Again assuming congruency, he would be conscious of those phenomena as striking, and by drawing out of his "feel" in contextual awareness ways of characterizing those phenomena, he could express what it was about them that was striking. Thus, contextual awareness would be the experience of core structure that would manifest itself in his actions as marked behavior and in his use of language would be described as paradigmatic structure.

Core structure serves to orient the individual in relation to his external "reality." In the terms used in stating the Choice Corollary, if object structure embodies "system" when choosing, then core structure embodies "his." Thus, from core structure would come the experience of "core" or "peripheral" construing. Why should not the individual be referentially articulated to three levels of construing? If this were the case, then he could choose how he was to value his experience of object structure in relation to himself. Not all of the structure at any level of construing need be articulated: The individual may never have developed referential articulation, or he may have chosen to "fix" his construing. Developing referential articulation at any level would, therefore, be "loosening," and fixing the articulation between levels would be "tightening." Thus, although much of an individual's level 3 structure might be permanently fixed for him, some areas might be articulated. In these areas he would become aware of a fourth-level structure. What evidence is there of a level 4 structure manifesting itself implicitly in language?

INTENTIONALITY AS SELF-DETERMINATION

The orientation the individual has in relation to his external "reality" may be described as his value gestalt. If the individual is underdetermined, congruent, and referentially articulated to three levels, then he will experience choice in the value gestalt that he can express through his actions. The choices will feel more or less peripheral within contextual awareness, and by "centering" himself within contextual awareness, he will make a choice that is least peripheral and, therefore, most likely to extend and define "his" system. The more centered his choice, the more inner "force" he will feel in its expression, and it is this sense of force that gives the clue to the nature of a fourth level of construing.

Austin (1962) first introduced the concept of illocutionary force. If language were viewed only as a propositional structure conveying sense and reference through some syntactical structure, then it could be treated as having only locutionary meaning that was object referenced and could be judged consensually as to its truth or falsehood. If, however, it was viewed as an utterance made by a particular individual, then it could also be said to have an illocutionary force that was more or less "happy" in the circumstances in which it was made. Austin identified five classes of utterance in terms of illocutionary force: exercitives, being the exercising of powers, rights, or influence; verdictives, being the giving of a finding as to something that is for various reasons hard to be certain about; behabitives, being the expression of attitudes and social behavior; commissives, being commitments to doing something or declarations or announcements of intention; and expositives, being expressions that make plain how the individual's utterances fit into the course of an argument or conversation or how he is using words in general. Examples might be voting, giving a verdict, congratulating, promising, and saying "I deduce that," respectively. The last class of utterance is self-referential in that it refers to the act of utterance itself. The other four reflect the nature of the speaker's relationship to the utterance he is making. The perlocutionary effects of an illocutionary act were then the effects induced through the other of the illocutionary force of the speaker's utterance, and the "happiness" of the utterance reflected the appropriateness or "fit" of the utterance that affected its perlocutionary effects in the circumstances in which it was uttered. The illocutionary force not only had a perlocutionary effect, but also expressed the force in the speaker's own actions. The hearer of an utterance could nevertheless block the perlocutionary effects of a speaker's utterance if he felt its illocutionary force to be inappropriate.

How then does the concept of illocutionary force relate to the other aspects of language discussed earlier, and is it evidence of the existence of a fourth level of construing? Searle (1969) developed Austin's ideas within a theory of language that was part of a theory of action and, therefore, particularly a study of speech acts. In addition to the study of the syntactical structure of the words used in uttering, there were two distinct semantic studies: one a study of the meanings of structures and one a study of the performances of speech acts. From this point of view two elements could be distinguished in the syntactical structure: an indicator of the presence of a proposition and an illocutionary force indicator. Even if these elements were not apparent on the surface, they were present in the syntactical deep structure. Thus, all speech acts bore some form of illocutionary force, even if not explicitly represented.

Thus it would seem that implicit in all speech acts there is not only some degree of marking but also some form of force. The marking became explicit through the presence of characterizing universals in the propositional content of speech acts and was evidence of the manifestation of level 3 core construing in language as a doubly articulated medium. It is now also apparent that the force becomes explicit in the form of exercitives, verdictives, behabitives, commissives, and expositives and thus provides evidence of the fourth level of construing. Why, though, are there five forms of illocutionary force?

A level 3 core structure could manifest itself in four ways: directly as a characterizing universal alone, as an adjective qualifying a predicate expression, as an adjective qualifying a particular, and as an adjective qualifying the statement as a whole. Examples would be "I feel happy," "that dog is running fast," "this is a red table," and "this is a stupid thing to say," respectively. Equivalently, therefore, level 4 structure manifests itself in five ways: directly as a commissive ("I will . . ."), as a behabitive, verdictive, or exercitive qualifying the content of a speech act ("I am sorry that . . . ," "It is my diagnosis that . . . ," and "I vote that . . ."), and as an expositive qualifying a speech act as a whole ("I repeat that . . ."). Thus, while the double articulation of language makes it possible to represent the first two levels of construing explicitly in the medium itself, the third and fourth levels of construing manifest themselves implicitly both in how the medium is used and also in parts of the medium itself.

The congruent individual who is underdetermined and aware enough to center himself will be aware of his own force as the manifestation in his own contextual awareness of his fourth level of construing. In focal consciousness this will become "intentionality." When expressed in language this will be classifiable as the illocutionary force of his utterance. Thus the self-determining individual is the individual who is capable of centering himself so that he can act directly from his own inner sense of force in extending and defining his construction system.

Is there a way of construing the fourth level of structure more clearly? Bohm (1980) argues that the explicate and manifest order of consciousness is not ultimately distinct from that of matter in general. Fundamentally these are essentially different aspects of the one overall order, so that the explicate order of matter in general is also in essence the sensuous explicate order in ordinary experience that is represented in focal consciousness. He develops the idea of a higher-dimensional reality that projects into lower-dimensional elements that have a nonlocal and noncausal relationship. This is the same idea as the concept of embeddedness of a lower-dimensional element in a higher-dimensional reality, which he calls enfoldment. The distinction between first- and second-level structure in the construction system follows from referential articulation between focal consciousness and the experience of action structures in the existentially articulated body. The distinction between the second and third levels of structure, however, follows from the identification of focal consciousness with the space-time bounded dimensionality of the individual's sensuous experience: The third level of structure is, therefore, the reality of higher-order dimensionality resulting from the individual's experience of himself as context to his experience of space-time bounded reality. This higher-dimensional reality is, however, limited by his experience of himself as context and still part of his explicate order. The fourth level is qualitatively distinct because it lies beyond the individual's experience of his explicate order, and it corresponds to Bohm's "implicate order." The projection of the implicate order into his contextual awareness is, therefore, a value gestalt, and he experiences as force the implicate order that lies beyond his contextual awareness. Can a fifth level be construed? My own sense of it is as the void.

CIRCUMSPECTION, PREEMPTION, AND CONTROL

The Choice Corollary is problematic because it introduces the idea that the construction system is "self-referential": unlike the other corollaries it necessitates construing the construer's own consciousness and self-awareness. All of the other corollaries can be understood solely in terms of the consequences of the construer's anticipations in his actions. From the self-referential nature of the corollary, therefore, flows the introduction of levels of embedded structure within the construction system: action structure, object structure, core structure, and the implicate order. The qualitative distinctions between these levels is not made in terms of the constructs' functioning at any level, but in terms of the nature of the construer's experience of his own construction system. The axis of distinction between levels is of increasing orders of "dimensionality" so that the here-and-now moment of experience is embedded in the space-time dimensionality in the quality of that experience of object structure that is itself embedded in the higher order dimensionality of the construer's experience of himself as context to his cumulative experience. Super- and subordinacy of constructs, therefore, vary along an axis that is orthogonal to the axis of levels: The constructs belong to the same order of dimensionality as the elements they construe, although their range, focus, and context (in the Kellian sense) will vary in terms of that to which they refer. Thought in focal consciousness moves between constructs along this axis of superordinacy and subordinacy, thus functioning at a level of construing in a way that is quite distinct from moving between levels through reflection (Boxer, 1979; Boxer and Boot, 1980).

The cycle of circumspection, preemption, and control, leading to a choice that precipitates the individual into a particular situation, is, therefore, not really a cycle at all, but rather a shifting of the focus of construing between levels. It is more useful to construe a cycle as occurring between each level as in Figure 7.1

The cycle at the level of object structure results in preemption. Kolb and Fry (1975) have described this cycle as an experiential learning cycle. Starting with reflective observation, depending on how referentially articulated or fixed object structure is in relation to action structure, the construer will be more or less able to loosen his construing of the situation as he experiences it. Construction in terms of more or less superordinate constructs within object structure will be experienced in focal consciousness as abstract conceptualization in some form. The choice to tighten construing in order to fix the relationship between object structure and action structure is, therefore, preemption resulting in active

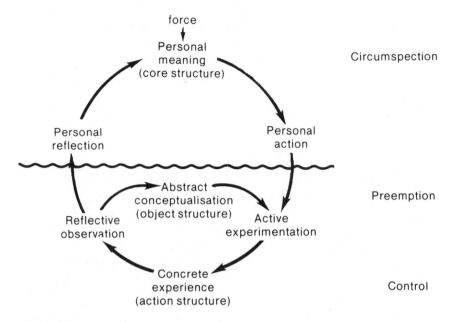

FIGURE 7.1
The Cycle Occurring between Levels of Construing and Experienced
as Circumspection, Preemption, and Control

experimentation. From this particular active experimentation will flow action within action structure experienced as concrete experience, that is, control. From this experience, the same cycle of reflective observation, and so on, can follow.

In Figure 7.1 the wavy line indicates the distinction between focal consciousness below and contextual awareness above. The process of abstract conceptualization will not only be in terms of constellatory constructs embodied in object structure; it will also be in terms of propositional constructs "projected" into focal consciousness from core structure and construed as if they were part of object structure. Constructions from object structure can be represented as a point of view, so that if the construer is able to be referentially articulated to three levels, then personal reflection becomes possible: the construing of a point of view as a particular value gestalt. Again there is the possibility of loosening or tightening the construction of a value gestalt, but again construction in terms of more or less superordinate constructs within core structure will be experienced in contextual awareness as personal meaning of some form. Any personal meaning felt in contextual awareness will project itself into focal consciousness as a point of view, although it will not necessarily follow that it can be expressed as an action structure. This process of exploring personal meaning is circumspection, and naturally, therefore, it is expressed in terms of propositional constructs.

The personal meanings explored will vary in how peripheral they feel. By being able to engage in circumspection, the individual can center himself by choosing that form of personal meaning that has the greatest force: personal action. It is this personal action that is self-determination and expresses intentionality. An individual who is either fixed or very tight in the referential articulation between his third and second levels of construing will be unable to center himself as effectively because his explorations of personal meaning will be foreshortened: He will tend to be impulsive. The ability to loosen or tighten construing at will is, therefore, essential at all levels if the individual is to construct alternatives between which he can choose. It is appropriate, therefore, that the loosening and tightening process is referred to as the creativity cycle.

SO WHAT IS THE BIG PROBLEM ABOUT CHOOSING?

It is said that a little knowledge is a dangerous thing. I agree with this statement, not because of what is known but because knowing implies consciousness, and it is from consciousness that the problems arise in choosing. Without consciousness, who is to say whether or not a person is choosing that alternative through which he anticipates the greater possibility for extension and definition of his system? For another person to say would be academic, because of his position as an outside observer, but for the person as knower to say it, he must be conscious. With consciousness comes perception, and it was this that led Kelly to say that "if one wished to state negatively the new position of the psychology of personal constructs regarding motivation, he might say that human behavior is directed away from ultimate anxiety. One would have to go further and say it is directed away from the 'perception' of ultimate anxiety" (Kelly, 1955, p. 894). Along with consciousness, then, enters anxiety with fear, guilt, and attachment. No wonder that eating of the Tree of Knowledge was seen as leading to the Fall.

Anxiety is the consciousness of events that lie outside the range of convenience of the individual's construction system: His referential articulation has no way of covering the situation. The creative response for the individual would be to construct through circumspection a point of view that felt centered, and then aggressively to set about personal action and active experimentation that extended and defined his construction system in such a way that the anxiety evaporated in the face of new experience. That would be self-determination. This does not always happen, however, for the reasons that follow.

First, the individual may be overdetermined, so that he cannot actively experiment in the ways he would choose. Without a physical action space in which to exercise the control he chooses, he will be unable to experiment actively. Some individuals appear to be more inventive than others, however, so that what might be overdetermining for one might be underdetermining for another. In circumstances where an individual can be overdetermined, however, it is not surprising that the anxiety can easily become threat or fear if, in addition to being unable to control the situation, the individual can himself be controlled in such a way that he is threatened or his own core structure is changed against his will.

When faced with anxiety, another response might be to form a dependent relationship with another individual. The whole education process is founded on the usefulness of this response. It too has a danger, however, which is less obvious than being overdetermined, but no less restrictive: disablement (Illich, 1971). For the knowledge the individual needs to be communicated in a way that is independent of the person communicating it, it needs to be expressible in object-referenceable form, and, therefore, in terms of object structure. A particular object structure, however, represents a point of view that reflects the value gestalt of the person who created it. This value gestalt may not be appropriate for the learner. No harm would be done if the learner carried on doing what he did anyway within his theory-in-use: He would only have developed an incongruency between his theory-in-use and his espoused theory as learned. If, however, he learned to control his actions from the espoused theory, he would be disabled in the sense that he would have learned a way of doing that was not an expression of his own core structure. He might, therefore, be unable to experience being centered. Knowledge learned in this way that was disabling would at least have the merit of being useful. If the knowledge learned was instead ritual, developed as part of a religious movement to enable the experience of a value gestalt that reflected force identified with religious process, then the ritual might become disabling insofar as it continued to be used after it had ceased to be appropriate in enabling the same experience of religious process in the worshipper (B. Reed, 1978). Such ritual could not only be disabling but also be bad ritual if it also induced guilt, which reinforced its disabling influence.

After overdetermination, therefore, comes disablement as the major source of restriction on self-determination. It is doubly effective in that it operates on consciousness itself, instead of through restricting experience. Both of these ways enable others to influence the choice the individual makes. There is, however, a third process restricting choice, namely attachment. If the individual is not overdetermined and is not disabled, he may have developed ways of acting that worked for him and even enabled him to feel centered. Thus, where he was originally very articulated in his ability to choose, success may have led him to become very attached to particular ways of acting to the point where he had lost his need for articulation and thus had chosen to become effectively fixed. Such a choice would follow from identifying the value with the action, and the resulting attachment would prevent the individual from considering a point of view as a whole value gestalt. The resulting impulsivity would also be a restriction on self-determination even more insidious than either overdetermination or disablement because of its being self-inflicted.

CONCLUSION

Society gives the individual no choice as to whether or not he has choice: It gives it to him. Even in the most totalitarian of societies the individual acquires a consciousness of choice. Finding the way from a consciousness of choice to self-determination is, however, a way strewn with the hazards of overdetermination, disablement, and attachment (Boxer, 1980). As the history of the religious movement has shown, even having found a form of self-determination, there is no guarantee that it is an appropriate way for the individual.

The Choice Corollary is primarily about consciousness gained through experienced choice. The elaboration of the corollary presented in this chapter is a way of construing the nature of that experience of choice. If the individual is more than a reaction to his physical situation, then he will at least develop a "head" way within focal consciousness to anticipate the greater possibilities for himself. The construing of core structure as distinct and the possibility of contextual awareness lead to a deeper way, however: the way of "heart," in which the individual anticipates the greater possibilities for himself through construing them in relation to his own experience of a value gestalt. Construing the implicate order as lying beyond core structure provides a still deeper way for the individual to anticipate the greater possibilities for himself: an anticipation based on an awareness of centeredness in his choice of value gestalt. This chapter is, however, my construction, so to conclude, it is only appropriate for me to suggest that you find your own way.

8

FITTING THINGS INTO SORTS:
THE RANGE COROLLARY

James C. Mancuso
Bruce N. Eimer

The Range Corollary: A construct is convenient for the anticipation of a finite range of events only.

A constructive process involves categorization. The convenience of employing a dichotomous construct depends on the success of anticipatory categorization. Convenient anticipation is achieved, overall, when one applies one or another construct to a finite range of events only. If a theorist postulates a system that has its fundamental base in the economics of anticipation, he would be disconcerted to find that a person would randomly apply any construct to any event. Only a certain range of events will "fit" successfully (in terms of anticipation) onto a particular construct.

SOME HISTORICAL BACKGROUND, DIRECTIONS, AND DEFINITIONS

Kelly's commentary on his Range Corollary (Kelly, 1955, pp. 68-72) suggests the origins of his statement. He wanted to be sure that his ideas would not be viewed within a framework that a reader might import from other psychological paradigms that were prevalent at his time. In his section on the Range Corollary, Kelly expressly warned against thinking of construct as being synonymous with ideas of concept, which were then in common usage. He was very specific in declaring that, at least, one must think of the bipolar character of a construct, as it had been defined in his exposition of the Dichotomy Corollary. One must see, Kelly stated, that the convenience of locating an event within a construct is limited, at least, by the contrast poles of the construct within which an event is located. One's anticipations are facilitated, at a minimum, by establishing the contrasts to the to-be-construed event.

By specifying the Range Corollary, Kelly was building an intrapersonal restriction on the range of events that might be subsumed by a construct. Recall that a person's processes are, according to the psychology of personal constructs, psychologically channelized by the ways in which he anticipates events. Other widely used behavior-explaining paradigms had adopted motivation principles that described channelization in terms of extrinsic energies (drives, impulses) that would be imported to build connections between events (stimuli) and the concepts imposed (responses) by a person onto those stimuli. From the perspective of this latter kind of mechanistic associationism, the range of a concept's applicability was determined by the level of force that had been built into the event-to-category association. By contrast, the motivation principle in personal construct theory describes motive as an intrinsic part of the cognitive context. Motive is not seen as an extrinsic parameter. Anticipation and psychological movement are taken to be synchronous.

In that Kelly seriously proposed to describe behavior from a contextualist paradigm, rather than from a widely used mechanist paradigm, he would sense the requirement to take a position on questions of why one particular construct, and not any arbitrarily imposed construct, would become involved in the anticipatory process. (The terms *mechanism* and *contextualism* are taken from Pepper's [1942] root metaphor analysis of metaphysical positions that have guided philosophical and scientific thought. The place of mechanistic and contextual world hypotheses in psychological thought is discussed in Jenkins [1974], Mancuso [1977], Sarbin [1977], and Sarbin and Mancuso [1980].) To start the search for contextualist explanation — that is, explanation that involves, among other things, a person's construct system — Kelly (1955, p. 68) lays down the Range Corollary: "A construct is convenient for the anticipation of a finite range of events only." Given this basic statement, one would need to proceed with investigations aimed at clarifying the ways in which convenience in anticipation could limit the range of events that are rendered equivalent to specific, previously anticipated events. Or, to describe the task in terms that appear in current discussions of cognitive processes, how would one describe the limits of a category's utility?

Direction of This Chapter

During the interval since Kelly presented his theory of personal constructs, the everyday science of psychology has become more receptive to constructivist solutions to psychological puzzles. This chapter shall demonstrate the clarity that accrues to the Range Corollary if one draws on the conceptions that have been developed by investigators who have used constructivist approaches to the study of cognition. To begin, there shall be a discussion of the ways in which definitions have changed as the result of considerations of constructivist ideas. We then propose that the issues addressed by the Range Corollary are those addressed by scholars who would study category assignment. Specifically, we will develop and endorse the proposition that, to anticipate successfully, a person locates an event at a particular point on a construct; that is, a person categorizes. Feature analysis models of category assignment contribute significantly to a theory of category assignment. This chapter will contain material that relates feature analysis to the process of limiting the range of events that are integrated by their assignment to one or another pole of a dichotomous construct. Techniques for assessing psychological similarity will be described briefly. In a final section we will cover two special aspects of categorization processes: the effects of context on category assignment, and metaphor as a special case of category assignment.

Some Clarification of Terms

As noted above, Kelly saw the possibility that the term *construct* would evoke the use of the then common idea of *concept*. In the American College Dictionary's (1948) definition of the term *concept*, we find the phrase, "A general notion; the predicate of a (possible) judgment." In contrast, Kelly (1955, p. 61) says, "In its minimum context a construct is a way in which at least two elements are similar and contrast with a third." In effect, then, the dictionary's definition of concept and Kelly's definition of construct both refer to predicating functions. Male-female may be taken as an example of a construct. Male predicates (in logic terms) John and Peter in the following proposition: John and Peter are male. The elements John and Peter are in contrast, by use of the construct male-female, to Mary who is predicated by the term female in the following sentence: Mary is female.

Note, however, that when one speaks of a construct one speaks simultaneously of two contrasting poles. Note also that a personal construct theorist would say, "Man looks at his world through transparent patterns or templates [given the name constructs] *which he creates . . .*" (pp. 8-9), italics added). Those who might use the term *concept*, on the other hand, are not obligated to think of concepts as being the specific, individualized construction of a construing person. One who would use the term *concept* may think of an isolated, unitary, externally shaped entity. By contrast, to use the term *construct* one best thinks of events being assigned to a two-poled, internally shaped entity that is hierarchically related to other constructs in the system.

When the notion of construct is used in the framework described above, one does not think of the process of categorizing as a process of "identifying", that is, of finding the "primitive," minimal, immanent category to which the event is to be assigned. For convenience in anticipation, many other constructs might be used to construe John, Peter, and Mary. One could say: "John and Peter are unsuitable sex objects, but Mary is a suitable sex object," or "John and Peter are hard, but Mary is soft." In diverse minimal contexts the range of convenience of one of many different constructs — for example, hard-soft — could be extended conveniently to anticipate the event that gave rise to the sensory input. No one construct would be regarded as the basic, irreducible dimension along which an event will necessarily be located. Construing is channelized by anticipation, not by the given nature of events.

When we speak of construing or imposing constructions we clearly speak of the process of imposing one's personal meaning on an event. We would not be adverse to using the terms *conceiving, cognizing, conceptualizing, perceiving, categorizing, instantiating.* Each of these terms can be taken to mean construing, if constructivist assumptions are consistently employed. By our use of the term *construing* we attempt to link our thinking to the fecund work of those who currently publish the voluminous material on cognitive processing (see, for example, Anderson, 1976; Just and Carpenter, 1977; Scott, Osgood, and Peterson, 1979).

Construing as Category Assignment

Specifically, it is convenient to see that the issues that Kelly tried to address by proposing the Range Corollary are the issues that are taken up in discussions of pattern recognition or of prototype matching. Studies of pattern recognition relate to questions such as: What influences a person to grant identity to a set of events that produce widely disparate sensory input? One identifies an E, for example, when there is a particular auditory input as well as when a particular visual input has been presented. What influences are at work to promote an input's location at a particular point along the particular construct all other letters of the alphabet-the letter E? Similarly, in a social cognition context, a person grants identity to widely disparate conduct by locating actions of self and others at a specific pole among a hostile-friendly construct.

A person, to anticipate successfully, must locate an event within a dichotomous construct that is hierarchically integrated with other constructs. By doing this, one fits an event into one's knowledge network and may thereby adduce extensive, inferred aspects to that event. In short, one then expects the located event to function in specific ways.

If a theorist accepts the foregoing propositions, he would find it satisfying to develop descriptions of the psychological channelization of the process of anticipation through construing. How does one best describe the process of locating an event at a point on a construct? If only a limited range of events is conveniently anticipated by a particular construct, how do the person's processes function to assign an event to a location on one particular construct and not on another, potentially less convenient, construct?

Investigators, applying information processing models to discussions of cognition and category assignment, frequently use the term *features*. A novice student might be at a standstill were he to demand a final integration of the many disparate definitions of the term *features*. Personal construct theory, however, leads to a specific definition. One first notes that dichotomous constructs are invented. A person extracts constructs through experiences involving (at least) two events that are similar in a way that makes them different from (at least) a third event. Constructs are somehow represented and stored in long-term memory. When one speaks of features he refers to assigning an event to one position at one pole of a stored construct. The event is then taken to "have the feature" that is the name used to label that pole. As tempting as it is to believe otherwise, one best believes that features are a product of a person's mind. One then better speaks of feature attribution than of feature detection. Feature assignment is to be regarded as one exemplar of the general process of category assignment — the process of locating an event on a construct.

The discussion of features and categorization will be resumed at a later point. This clarification is offered here in order to make the point that feature assignment is to be treated as construing, and, as such, it is channelized by anticipation. To attach this point to a concrete instance, consider the construing of a person with respect to the broad construct devious-honest. To achieve successful categorization and anticipation, a person would feature-analyze information input about that person-as-event. The parts of the input, then, are regarded as events whose appropriate construal would enhance anticipation. It would not do to construe the target person's clothing along the dimension deceptive-sincere. There might be some utility in construing his manner of smiling along that dimension. A record of a person's court appearances might be construed usefully along a fraudulent-trustworthy dimension. In the end, successful anticipation of this person, in the context of a business transaction, will depend on successful feature assignment. Arbitrary application of feature-defining constructs would decrease, rather than increase, the convenience of the feature-assigning parts of the categorizing process.

Recapitulation

The Range Corollary tells us that we need to consider convenience in anticipation if we are to develop a cogent explanation of why an event is construed within one or another category. Success in anticipation is some function of the construct that is used to construe, that is, to categorize, an event. To anticipate successfully, only certain constructs can be used in the categorization of certain events.

One might crudely say, "Convenient anticipation is enhanced by locating an event in the right place on the right construct." One would say this, however, only if he were prepared to exercise Kelly's expressed caution against considering rightness to be external to the person's construct system. Rightness develops from the person's success in anticipating events.

As a preparation for the ensuing discussion, the foregoing material contains an explication of features. The use of the term *feature* refers us to a person's having located an event, which often is a part of a larger event to be construed, at one pole of one of his stored two-poled constructs. The term *feature* directs us to a supremely contextual concept. By our usage, one cannot construe a feature without construing a personal construct within the context of a feature assignment.

CATEGORIES AS CONVENIENT ALLOCATIONS

Other workers, contemporary with Kelly, worked on the problem of defining ways in which an event would be classed as equivalent to other events. The investigator who would follow the metaphysics of formism (Pepper, 1942, Chapter 8) could believe that equivalence derived directly from the events. Accordingly, a person, as he acquired knowledge, would discover identities that were immanent to various events. On the other hand, a mechanist could explain the derivation of some equivalences by applying the classical conceptions of conditioning. A mother would become conceptually equivalent to a bottle of warm milk by the contiguous pairing of the mother and the milk through repeated presentation of the sequence, Mother (conditionable stimulus): warm milk (unconditional stimulus): comfort (unconditional response). Both mother and warm milk thereupon become predicated by comforting.

Bruner, Goodnow, and Austin (1956) made a vigorous early effort to bring to their research a contextualist/constructivist view of cognitive processing. They prefaced the presentation of their investigations with a discussion of the equivalence problem, as follows:

> The recognition of the constructive or invented status of categories changes drastically the nature of the equivalence problem as a topic for psychological research. The study of equivalence becomes, essentially, a study of coding and recoding processes employed by organisms who have past histories and present requirements to be met . . . the stimulus similarity that serves as a basis for grouping is a selected or abstracted similarity. There's an act of rendering similar by a coding operation, rather than a forcing of equivalence on the organisms by the nature of the stimulation (pp. 7-8).

Like Kelly, Bruner et al. assumed that a category was imposed so that an event could be anticipated successfully. "It is not simply that organisms code the events of their environments into equivalence classes, but that they utilize cues for doing so that allow an opportunity for prior adjustment to the event identified" (p. 14).

Obversely, to code an event by use of a construct whose range does not adequately extend to that event would not allow the use of an already-established adjustment to that event. The person would then find that an inappropriate assumption of equivalence would fail to produce convenient anticipation.

Consider a specific case of category assignment through pattern recognition. A professor scans a grade sheet, attempting to impose his constructs on information arranged in spatial patterns over the sheet. A particular arrangement of the spatial configurations will allow him to locate that arrangement at a particular point along the construct any letter-E. He scans the grade sheet, working toward successful anticipation, applying his construct any letter-E. Any of a wide variety of spatial arrangements will allow convenient anticipation in the immediate task of obtaining a match to the E pole of the construct. Yet, very few of those events that are taken as a match to that pole have three exactly horizontal lines that are precisely perpendicular to the vertical. Probably none of the events have horizontal lines of equal length; and so forth. Nonetheless, each of these many disparate events will be classed as E, allowing the professor's extensive implications network to function in anticipating a series of events. When the professor locates an event whose features are proximate to a prototype that would fit the E pole of the construct, he will relate that event, and the person designated by the sign identified as an E, to other constructs in his construct system. The many people who have been designated by the E have acted diversely, yet they all will be allocated to a particular pole of the professor's construct inept-able. They will have been categorized.

Feature Analysis Models of Categorization

Investigators have been at work to produce cogent models to describe the processes by which an event is taken to be an exemplar of an anticipatory construction. A feature analysis model, a model that is compatible to personal construct theory, has been widely used and advocated.

Feature analysis models begin with the overall assumption that a series of first-stage constructive processes precede any pattern recognition. The first-stage constructions serve to locate essential features to be used in achieving a more integrating construction. The visual display for the letter E, for example, can be analyzed in terms of the construct closed-open. The enclosed space is open to the right side. The construct curvilinear-rectilinear also can be applied. All lines are straight. The relationship of the lines can be analyzed in terms of the oblique-perpendicular construct. All line intersects form 90 degree angles. After these, and other features, are analyzed, the input may be construed at one pole of the any letter-letter E construct. The input is sorted into the category E.

Massaro and Schmuller (1975) more precisely described a feature analysis model. Their version of the model incorporates the concepts of storage areas and information processing stages. They postulate a visual input storage area — a "preperceptual" storage area — into which is placed a neural-based representation of the spatial pattern of the visual display. During a primary recognition phase, a synthesis is performed. This synthesis of the representation in the visual storage area involves constructs called up from long-term memory storage. During this active constructive stage, the feature analysis is performed. The features of a letter, for example, are defined in terms of judgment dimensions like those described in the above analysis of the E pattern. Following the synthesis and recognition of features, a search in long-term memory retrieves a letter pattern that matches the feature-synthesized pattern.

Massaro and Schmuller make specific predictions from their model. For example, they anticipated that where the ascribed features of syntheses of two different visual displays might overlap, the chances of inconvenient construing would increase. People frequently encounter such instances in separate visual displays that share common features. For example, the letters F and E share one vertical line, an opening to the right, and perpendicular cross-lines. The task of achieving a discriminating construction of the F and the E would be more difficult than would be the task of discriminating and E and a G., the latter letters having fewer shared features. Predictions from the model depend also on the assumption that an accomplished reader has stored a list of feature-defining constructs that are used to construe each letter of the alphabet, along with other information about the orthographic structures used in writing the language.

Numerous studies have demonstrated the utility of a features synthesis model. Mayzner (1975) reported a representative series of investigations completed by his group. This work involved presentation of alphabet letters through the use of a cathode ray tube display. A letter would be presented and then immediately thereafter a "noise pattern" could be "overprinted" in the same space in which the letter had appeared. The time interval of the letter presentation could be shortened or lengthened, thereby varying the time that a respondent could use to impose a construction onto the pattern. It is assumed that the noise pattern disrupts the construing process.

As expected, the correct recognition of all letters is enhanced by lengthening the presentation interval. Correct recognition of different letters, however, varies considerably. In 250 presentations of the letter C, across all presentation times, that letter was correctly recognized 7.4 percent of the time. The reasons for misidentifications are clear when it is noted that the presented C is construed as G in 29 of the 250 instances of presentations, and as the letter O 42 times. The character of the features analysis process is more clearly demonstrated, however, by noting that the letter T was identified correctly in 64 percent of the 250 presentations.

With another study, Mayzner and Habinek (1975) showed that whereas the letter T was identified correctly in 84 percent of the presentations, the nonletter character =, was identified correctly in only 8 percent of the presentations. The two symbols both contain two straight lines, so that their features can attain similarity on a number of lines feature. The perpendicularity of the two lines of the T, however, appears to be a major differentiable feature; and this feature is shared with a very small set of other letters.

To enhance some points to be made later in this chapter, we can note another way in which the validity of the features analysis model has been demonstrated. Gibson and Levin (1975) assessed the feature structures that children employ to analyze the letters of the alphabet. These investigators used hierarchic clustering analysis to structure the data from children's judgments. This technique produced easily interpreted results. It is no surprise that O and Q are judged to be very similar. Even a novice reader could assign shared features to these letters. O and Q soon join, in the hierarchic structure, the letters C and G, which also are judged to be similar, and which are differentiated from O and Q by the open-to-the-right construction. Farther up (or down) the structure these letters eventually join the cluster of letters containing B, P, R, and S. In the last joining of the hierarchically arranged clusters, these letters, all of which may be instantiated by the feature curvilinearity, join the set of letters that are defined by the feature rectilinearity. This final joining completes the set of all letters.

Rosenberg and his associates (Rosenberg, 1977; Gara and Rosenberg, 1979) have also demonstrated the utility of employing cluster analyses to study features in the process of categorizing. Their work has involved analyzing the feature structures of a person's implicit personality theories. In their application of the feature analysis model, these investigators first had people record names of persons with whom they interacted. Then the respondents recorded terms that named features they might attribute to the people they listed. Respondents rated every person on their list in terms of the features they had generated. Next, a similarity index was calculated to assess the cooccurrence in respondents' use of features for describing the individuals in their persons-by-features matrix. In this way these investigators were able to obtain an empirically derived measure of the similarity of each person. With these derived similarity measures, a hierarchic cluster analysis like that used by Gibson and Levin (1975) to reveal letter-defining constructs was used to establish the person-defining constructs — the features — used in the respondents' person perception systems. To illustrate the similarity, we can note that the last joining in the letter-defining system is taken to be representative of the curvilinearity-rectilinearity construct. In the findings of Rosenberg's group, the last joining, almost inevitably, in a respondent's system reflected the bad-good construct (Kim and Rosenberg, 1980). As Gara noted in Chapter 4, however, respondents create quite idiosyncratic person perceiving systems. Thus, although various studies have found a high degree of commonality across individual letter-perceiving structures, the expectation, following the Individuality Corollary, is that there is likely to be wide variation in commonality in the content of two different person-perceiving structures.

In summary, we may conclude that a feature analysis process is involved in construing an event. The assigning of features is regarded as a process by which an event is located on a personal construct. The feature analysis process is a part of the process by which a more inclusive event is located on a broader construct; that is, the event is categorized. For example, placing a person at the honest end of the devious-honest construct — that is, assigning him to the category honest — follows from having first attributed other features to him. We turn now to considering other issues relevant to determining the specific constructs applied to particular events.

Locating an Event

In a statement that echoes Kelly's exposition of his Dichotomy Corollary, Rosch (1978, p. 28) says that "to categorize a stimulus means to consider it, for purposes of that categorization, not only equivalent to other stimuli in the same category, but also different from other stimuli not in that category." In language being developed in this chapter, one would say that a categorization process involves the location of an event at one pole of at least one dichotomous construct.

For convenience in anticipating, it would be advantageous to a person were he *not* to differentiate one stimulus from others when that differentiation would contribute nothing to setting anticipations in that context. Thus, one event may fall into the range of convenience of one construct on one occasion and into that of another construct on an alternate occasion. Additionally, there is reason to believe that the "width" of a category can expand, to widen the range of events that can be construed by their assignment to a particular pole of a particular category-defining construct. The features concept along with the prototype concept are used cogently to explain the shrinking and expansion of the width of a category.

One speaks of prototype when referring to the clearest case of category membership, as defined by assessing people's judgments of the goodness of an event's fit to that category. To anticipate successfully one's psychological processes should lead to locating an event as an instance of its most proximate prototype. Prototypicality is related to features in that it is related to category structure. That is, one may formulate, on something of an a priori or empirical basis, the featural properties of a category and, thereupon, show that the rated degree of prototypicality of category exemplars will vary as some function of the degree to which exemplars share feature properties with other category members. To no one's surprise, at this stage of our game, there have been proposed alternative ways to model prototypes. Nevertheless, the basic strategy described here has logical appeal, and various investigators (Oden and Massaro, 1978; Rosch, 1978; Tversky, 1977) have produced data that help to advance the idea that people do establish prototypes and that events are located on constructs in terms of their proximity to category prototypes.

To describe extensively the use of prototypes in category allocation, one would want to explain the processes by which (a) critical features of a prototype are determined, (b) these features are weighted and combined to define the prototype, and (c) the boundaries are set to delimit the range of events that can be identified by reference to the prototype. The discussion of boundary setting relates to the Range Corollary, but propositions developed in that discussion must relate to those developed in clarifying points (a) and (b).

If we explored boundary setting in terms of features and prototypes, we would become aware that an event may be taken to be an exemplar of a prototype even though it does not contain all the critical features of the prototype, and the critical features in the event are not prototypical of those features. (Recall that feature assignment is also considered as construing.)

In actuality, it is Rosch's (1978, p. 40) position that "to speak of a prototype is simply a convenient grammatical fiction; what is really referred to are judgments of degree of prototypicality." Members of a category need not contain a singular set of maximally valid criterial features, but may share overlapping sets of probablistically assigned features. Thus, not all members of a category can be taken to be equally representative. In this way, the members of the category belong to a "fuzzy set."

What then is the process by which it is determined that an event-to-be-categorized has been assigned features that allow it to be put into a particular "fuzzy set?" Tversky (1977, p. 330) has offered a particularly cogent model for discussing categorization and contrast. He describes a set theoretical approach that accounts for psychological similarity "in terms of the notion of a (feature) matching function rather than in terms of the geometric concept of distance." He begins with the postulate that any event may have attributed to it a large set of features. Feature attribution is a product of prior feature formation, extraction, and compilation. Secondly, "the term *feature* usually denotes the value of a binary variable (e.g., voiced versus voiceless consonants) or the value of a nominal variable (e.g., eye color)" (p. 330).

Tversky then proceeds to establish five major assumptions for this theory of contrast. The first and second of these assumptions convey, for our purposes, the thrust of his theory. First, similarity, essentially, is viewed as a function of three values: the shared features of event A and event B; the features ascribed to A but not to B; and the features ascribed to B but not to A. Second, Tversky assumes that the similarity of events can be expressed as a monotonic function, in that the similarities of events are made greater or lesser by the addition or subtraction of common features, and/or by the deletion of those distinctive features that are ascribed to one event and not to the other.

Tversky's model is appealing. For example, by application of his five assumptions, Tversky develops elegant solutions for one of the most puzzling problems associated with judging the similarity of events: The problem of asymmetry. Event A can be more similar to event B than event B is similar to event A. To illustrate, 69 subjects were asked which of the following statements they preferred to use: North Korea is similar to Red China, or Red China is similar to North Korea. Sixty-six subjects preferred to use the former statement. Tversky explains this by appeal to one of his assumptions, which allows the deduction that the weighting given to the features of one of the events is greater than the weighting given to the features of other events that fit the category. Thus, the distinctive features of the "salient" event (in the above case the salient event is Red China) reduce its similarity to other events when the salient event is the variable event being compared to another event that has less saliency. The features of a less salient standard simply do not "add up" to the features of a salient standard.

Tversky also shows the relationships between his analysis of similarity and the quantitative processes involved in clustering techniques. He demonstrates that clustering analyses are dependent on classifying events in terms of common and distinctive features. A clustering analysis proceeds from a metric that indicates the similarity (or dissimilarity) of two events. These indexes of (dis)similarity are a quantification of the extent to which the two events share common features while these shared features are not shared with other events in the set of events. The result of comparing every event to every other event in a set is an N by N symmetrical matrix of (dis)similarity measures. An investigator may then use this matrix as input into an algorithm that assembles hierarchic arrangements of events. The output is a tree structure (dendrograph) that starts with a bifurcating trunk (an arc) that unites all subclusters in the set. The events come together at this arc because every event shares some subset of features that is shared by every other event. Thereafter the algorithm produces a consecutive breaking off of subclusters.

This partitioning has its basis in the greater and greater similarity of contrasted events, a similarity that is based upon the contrasted events having been assigned shared features that are distinctive, relative to other events in the total set.

To illustrate, Sattath and Tversky (1977) performed an additive clustering analysis on dissimilarity ratings of 30 animals. Participants had rated the dissimilarity of animals on a scale from zero to ten. Four major arcs, based on analysis of these dissimilarity measures, can be used to represent the four most overarching subdivisions of the set of all animals. The four most inclusive subsets of the population of animals are, of course, joined at the "bottom" by their sharing of those features common to all events (animals) above that "bottommost" arc. In contrast to other, nonanimal events, some of these shared features would be distinctive. These common features, in a contrast that might include other living forms, would contribute to categorizing these events at the animal end of a nonanimal-animal construct. Proceeding "upward" from this "bottom" category, the clustering analysis isolated major subsets that can be labeled herbivores, carnivores, apes, and rodents. The events in these subsets share features that are distinctive from other events included in the bottom category. The carnivores, for example, each share the meateater feature, and this feature distinguishes the included creatures from those in other major subsets. The major subset carnivore branches into three subsets: canine, feline, and bear. The role of feature assignments in the similarity judging process is further illustrated as the feline subset breaks down into two separate subsets: cat and lion/tiger/leopard. One would judge that these four felines break off as a separate cluster as a result of their having been assigned the distinctive features stealthy, quick, long tail, sleek coat. The cluster subdivides, however, since the cat was assigned the distinctive feature of small, a feature not shared by the three other felines. Then the leopard (assigned the distinctive feature spotted) breaks off from the lion and tiger, which share larger size and less distinction in coat color.

In that any set of events can be analyzed in this way, a hierarchic clustering can be shown to be a method of representing Tversky's (1977) contrast model of the categorization process. Gara and Rosenberg (1979) took a parallel position in the work that led to their analysis of persons as prototypes. These latter investigators built on the previous work of Rosenberg and his associates (see Rosenberg, 1977; and Chapter 4 by Gara, above), which involved the application of clustering analysis to assessing the structure of people's implicit personality theories. Rosenberg's work is built on a data base derived from having an individual produce a persons-by-traits matrix. People name, for example, 50 persons with whom they are acquainted. They then name a set of "traits" by which to describe these 50 persons. The similarity of any two persons in the matrix is calculated, essentially, in terms of their common and distinctive traits, ascribed to them by the participant. Obversely, the similarity of traits is calculated in terms of the sets of common and distinctive persons categorized by any contrasted pair of traits. It would follow, then, that by using these measures of similarity, one can perform a cluster analysis of persons in a participant's persons-by-traits matrix. The analysis would reflect the shared traits (features) ascribed to any subset of persons. Obversely, traits can be clustered in terms of the shared features (people judged by those traits) of the traits the participant put into his matrix. Two or more people will fall into a cluster if they are seen to share common traits and are assigned distinctive traits that differentiate all members of their cluster from all other persons in the matrix.

Gara and Rosenberg (1979) also showed that the persons in a participant's matrix can be clustered in terms of the extent to which they serve as prototypes in a person's implicit personality theory. To do this, they took into account Tversky's proposition that similarity judgments are asymmetrical. They proceeded on this assumption when they used an implications phi coefficient to quantify the similarity between two persons. The phi coefficient derived from contrasting Mary to Mother will differ from the phi coefficient derived from contrasting Mother to Mary. The phi coefficient indicates the extent to which features are coassigned to the more prominent and the less prominent members of the contrast pairs. Some persons are seldom assigned features that distinguish them from other persons. On the other hand, the features assigned to some persons never become a complete subset of the features assigned to any other contrast persons. In the participant's person perceiving system, these super-ordinate persons are seen to share common traits with each member of another particular set of persons and are seen to lack traits that are absent in other members of that particular subset of persons but are seen as having traits that are assigned to no other member of that particular subset of persons. These superordinate persons (or supersets) may be taken as "grand prototypes," that is, as prototypes of all those persons with whom they share common and distinc-tive traits, while retaining traits that are not ascribed to these similar persons. Mother, for example, may be a prototype, in that she shares common traits with Mary, Harry, Susan, and Rose, while being assigned traits that distinguish her from each of these exemplars of the "superset" person.

Gara and Rosenberg suggest that the appearance of the superset persons, as a structural property of an implicit personality theory, reflects a process similar to that which Sullivan (1953) discussed under the term *prototaxic distortion*. As Luchins (1959) observed when he related Sullivan's work to Luchins' (1942) previous studies of *einstellung effect*, behavior theories of all varieties have devised concepts that describe the ways in which people actively group persons-as-events, whereupon they may engage in anticipatory reactions to those persons categorized in the same subset.

Recapitulation

One may conceptualize the construing process in terms of locating events at a pole on a dichotomous construct. As such, construing is a matter of cate-gorizing. The Range Corollary addresses the matter of using, for anticipatory activity, one or another construct for locating an event in a valid category. Current work shows the worth of thinking of "successful" categorizing in terms of features and prototypes. Feature analysis may be taken as the basic case of locating an event on a construct. Such event location, or feature assignment, takes place as a part of the categorizing process.

The concept of prototype, hedged by the kind of cautionary statements described by Rosch (1978), can be used to describe the ways in which persons assign events, including other persons, to fuzzy sets. One speaks of prototype when thinking about the clearest case of a category. The boundaries of the fuzzy set that surround the prototype are demarcated by the extent to which the members of the set share features with each other and with the prototype.

Tversky's (1977) set theoretical contrast model of similarity is offered as a suitable guide to thinking about what events will be judged to belong to the same category and, thereby, to share the range of anticipatory convenience of a particular construal. Tversky's model, essentially, treats similarity in terms of a monotonic function of the set of features shared by two or more events and the distinctive, or nonshared, features of those events. By use of this model, one may conceptualize the similarity of two or more events, and then each of these events may be compared to a schematized prototype of those events. The prototype would be taken as the "ideal" of those events that may be located at one or another of the poles of a particular construct.

Sattath and Tversky (1977) illustrate the compatability of Tversky's (1977) model and cluster analysis techniques. Various clustering strategies are seen to be satisfactory quantitative methods for representing the nested features that account for hierarchic class inclusion. Rosenberg and his associates (Rosenberg, 1977; Gara and Rosenberg, 1979) have demonstrated that one's person categorizing processes may be analyzed in the same terms and by the same methods. Recent work (Gara and Rosenberg, 1979) presents a method for extracting prototypes from an individual's implicit personality theory.

In summary, one now finds a suitable literature from which to discuss the process of categorizing. To uphold Kelly's (1955) Range Corollary, one may borrow from current discussions of feature analysis, similarity, and prototype. Cluster analysis represents a satisfactory quantification of these kinds of concepts.

SOME ADDITIONAL CONSIDERATIONS: THE CHOICE COROLLARY, THE RANGE COROLLARY, AND DIAGNOSTIC VALIDITY

Investigators often speak of features or attributes in terms of their level of cue validity. As it is usually employed, the cue validity concept refers to the probabilistic frequency that a given attribute is included in the set of features that defines an exemplar of a given category (see, for example, Rosch, 1978). Other investigators (see, for example, Tversky, 1977) speak of the diagnostic value or classificatory significance of a given feature. In our terms, to assign a feature to an event is to assign an aspect of the event to a location along a two-poled construct. The convenience of such construing depends on its utility for anticipating the event under consideration. As such, convenience in anticipation functionally sets the diagnostic value of using a particular construct to achieve a particular schematic construction of an event. A similar notion is expressed by Rosch and Mervis (1975, p. 602) in the following statement: "Categories form to maximize the information-rich clusters of attributes in the environment, and thus, the cue validity of the attributes of categories; when prototypes of categories form by means of the principle of family resemblance, they maximize such clusters and such cue validity still further within categories."

The concept of diagnostic value is elaborated by considering the evidence that the diagnostic value of a feature may change, depending on the contextual surround of the event that is to be construed. Tversky and his associates (Tversky, 1977; Tversky and Gati, 1978), building on their studies, put forward the view that the diagnostic value, classificatory significance, or relevance of a given feature for allocating an event to a category is affected by the context of objects under consideration.

> For example, the feature "real" has no diagnostic value in the set of actual animals since it is shared by all actual animals and hence cannot be used to classify them. This feature, however, acquires considerable diagnostic value if the object set is extended to include legendary animals, such as a centaur, a mermaid, or a phoenix (Tversky, 1977, p. 342).

In one study, Tversky (1977) demonstrated that the addition of certain objects and the deletion of others from an object cluster had systematic effects on the diagnostic values of the features people used for grouping the objects. Participants were presented with quadruplets of faces; the sets were arranged so that one face was a "target" and the others represented a "choice set." The task was to select the choice set of faces judged to be most similar to the target, for each quadruplet. According to Tversky's analysis, participants performed the task by a feature matching process. So, for example, if there were two smiling faces and a frowning face in the choice set, and a neutral face as the target, participants generally grouped the smiling faces together, and the frowning face with the target. Thus, the diagnostic feature was assumed to derive from the not smiling-smiling dimension. However, when one of the smiling faces in the choice set was replaced with a frowning face, the process changed. Participants no longer grouped a frowning face with the neutral target face. Rather, the two frowning choice set faces tended to be paired, and the smiling face was grouped with the target. In this instance, the new diagnostic feature came out of the construct not frowning-frowning. In general, Tversky's experiments demonstrated that when the contexts of similarity judgments were altered, the nature of the similarities abstracted was also changed. As such, features defining constructs that were formerly diagnostically relevant were no longer so. "This account was supported by the experimental finding that changes in grouping (produced by the replacement or the addition of objects) lead to corresponding changes in the similarity of the objects" (p. 344).

Tversky's work on "feature diagnosticity" illustrates the connections between the Range Corollary and the Choice Corollary; it is in the context of the Choice Corollary that we see a major implication for the determinants of the range of any given construct at any given time. The likelihood of invoking any given construct is regarded as dependent on the implications it is judged to have relative to extracting validation for the rest of a person's system. Changing the context in which a set of events are construed leads to corresponding changes in the constructs that are deemed relevant to categorizing the events. Constructs that in a previous context might have been convenient for anticipating are no longer regarded as convenient. The person who is attempting to abstract the similarities among a set of events is faced with a set of decisions to make. First, what construct can be most useful for anticipating these events? Second, to which of the constructs' poles are the events to be allocated? Kelly's (1955, p. 64) Choice Corollary is an expression of the proposition that a person is guided in his choice by "that alternative in a dichotomous construct through which he anticipates the greater possibility for extension and elaboration of his construction system."

In Tversky's (1977) demonstration we see that the effort to understand the complete set of events can strikingly influence which feature is assigned to an event. In one context, the participating person achieves integration by locating a neutral face on the pole opposite to frowning faces. The neutral face is categorized with a smiling face. In another context, the same face is located opposite to the smiling pole. In this latter context, the participant classifies the neutral face with a face that, in the previous context, was an exemplar of the class (frowning faces) opposite to that now containing the neutral face. A choice of the construct by which to anticipate events depends also on anticipation of what will happen to events that surround the central event.

CONSTRUCT DIFFERENTIATION AND RATING EXTREMITY

From all of the foregoing, it would follow that a person would less successfully anticipate if he were to try to apply a construct to a range of events to which that construct had never been applied. If a person previously had developed the construct soft-hard to categorize only nonliving objects, he would not be expected to succeed immediately in an attempt to anticipate by categorizing another person with that construct.

Adams-Webber (1979a) reviews a body of studies that have addressed the issue of the meaningfulness of a construct. Overall, the research findings support the view that when a person uses a construct that he regards as relevant to, that is, has a range of convenience extending to, events under consideration, that person will be able to make more consistent and more discriminating categorizations.

Some examples can illustrate this point. Bonarius (1968) worked around issues associated with one's use of truly personal constructs, contrasted to that person's use of categorizing dimensions provided by an outside observer. Bonarius hypothesized that the former, that is, the personal constructs, would be more meaningful, particularly when applied to persons with whom the judge had interacted frequently. Personal constructs elicited from the judge himself would be more useful than would be provided constructs when the person attempts to construe himself, family members, and close associates. Bonarius predicted, among other things, that these frequently encountered persons would be rated at the extremes of elicited constructs, whereas less frequently encountered persons would be less clearly located at the extremes of a bipolar construct. The findings of Bonarius' study paralleled his predictions. When using the elicited constructs, a judge's "personal others" are rated at the extremes of a construct more than are people with whom he is less personally involved. If one were to take rating extremity as indicative of meaningfulness, one could say that a construct is more meaningful when it is used to construe the range of events that is more regularly anticipated by that construct.

One might also hypothesize that when a judge uses a construct as a bipolar rating scale he would think of the extreme ends of the construct as the location of the prototype. When a person, for example, uses the construct devious-honest, one would expect that the extreme of the honest end would be reserved for a person who has all the features shared by honest persons as well as other features that would be assigned to persons falling into the honest cluster. Considering Bonarius' work against the findings of Gara and Rosenberg (1979), we would expect that the familiar persons might be prototypical persons. Thus, in this case, as in other studies of meaningfulness and range, one could conclude that meaningfulness is associated with the availability of prototypes. If the features that define a construct are clearly organized in the judge's system, he will be more likely to have available a prototype against which to contrast the range of events that might be proximate to that prototype. He would then be better able to use that construct in a more consistent manner as he goes about the business of trying to differentiate objects that will or will not be successfully anticipated by locating them on that construct.

Metaphor: Stretching the Boundaries of a Construct's Range of Convenience

When one uses a metaphor, one acts as if the event being predicated is a thing of a different sort. The user sorts the subject of the predicate into a category that ordinarily would not include that object. To say, for example, "John is a tiger" is to use a metaphor. To say "John is a male" is to make a literal statement. One immediately expects consensus when one states that John is an event that falls within the range of events that are subsumed by the male pole of the female-male construct. Use of the literal statement ordinarily allows convenient predication of John, the subject of the metaphor. If one were to utter the statement, "John is a tiger," a listener would initiate a scan of his feature storage network to select features of the metaphoric term — the referent — that are applicable to the subject of the sentence. A search would extract the salient features of tiger that might be applicable to John. In this way the speaker would induce the listener to construe John in a way that is novel, perhaps subtle, and surely entertaining.

The volume of the current attention to and work on the psychology of metaphor (Cometa and Eson, 1978; Ortony, 1979; Ortony, Schallert, Reynolds, and Antos, 1978; Sarbin, 1980a,b) attests to the wide-ranging significance of this special form of category selection. A study of the metaphor-making process promises to provide special insights for one who would use constructivist concepts to explain human conduct.

Sociality and Metaphor Making

As Tversky (1977) notes, much needs to be done to develop explanations of the process of scanning a feature space to select features of the referent (the vehicle, the predicate) that are applicable to the subject of the metaphoric utterance. One important issue revolves around the influences that initiate this special search process. Why is the listener induced to conduct a special search rather than directly instantiating the subject by use of the predicating category given in the utterance? We propose, forthrightly, that the search is initiated on those occasions in which the literal use of the category does not allow convenient anticipation, and that contextual influences inform a person of the probable level of his anticipatory success. We would agree with Sarbin (1980b, p. 4) that metaphor is "an act that is not instantiatable given the interactional and/or linguistic context, but which can be instantiated through cognitive work."

One can see that it is important to consider the issue of the conditions that instigate the special search when one observes that nothing about the utterance itself informs the listener that a "sort-crossing" (Turbayne, 1962, p. 11) is required. Consider the example given by Sarbin (1980b, p. 6) as follows: " 'That man is a pygmy,' contains two terms from the same [hierarchically interrelated] domain, if the speaker and hearer are engaged in a conversation about African anthropology. The same terms are from different domains if the context leads the hearer to interpret 'pygmy' as an epithet for meager moral attainments." Sarbin proposes that the listener must construe the intent of the message in order to resolve the potential "strain-in-knowing" imposed by the anomalous statement. To do this as a part of his total construing activity, he categorizes the statement as metaphor, if he already has developed the construct literal-metaphor and if the use of this category is convenient for anticipation in the communication process. As Mair (1977, p. 254) points out, "in a sense, therefore, metaphor only exists where it is actively recognized, otherwise it is 'hidden' and likely to be taken for reality itself."

In a communication act involving metaphor, we have a solid example of sociality as conceived by Kelly (1955). The use of metaphor singularly demands that speaker and listener successfully engage in reciprocal construing of each other's constructions. According to Grice (1975), linguistic communication depends on the participants' beliefs that the process is governed by shared rules for conduct of the communication act itself. In a highly complex communication process a rule violation, in itself, is taken to be an adherence to a special rule about rule violation. Searle (1969) accepts this assumption and speaks of metaphor in terms of the following sequence: First, the listener schematizes the subject of the utterance in terms of the construct location given by the literal meaning of the predicate (the metaphor-to-be). Second, the context is searched for clues that affirm the convenience of using the literal construction. Third, where there is a low probability of successful anticipation, relative to the contextual surround, the listener deduces that a different communication rule — which he shares with the speaker — governs the utterance. At this point, the utterance might be taken to be a metaphor, and the special search is initiated. The listener might then "try out" the match between the features of the subject and the features of events usually located at the construct pole signaled by the metaphor. Again, if the match allows convenient anticipation, in that context, the metaphorized construction will hold.

Metaphor Making and Learning

Assume that the listener finds it convenient to anticipate through using the category named by the metaphor. Piaget (in Bringuier, 1980) might say that the subject of the metaphor has been assimilated to the schematization — the internally represented feature space — named by the metaphor. He would also say, "There is no assimilation without accommodation because the scheme of assimilation is general, and as soon as it's applied to a particular situation, it [the scheme] must be modified according to the particular circumstances of the situation. . . . That is what I call 'accommodation' — the adjustment of the scheme to the particular situation" (pp. 42-43).

It would follow that successful metaphor use would always bring about a revision of the construct used to locate the subject of the metaphor. The process by which this is achieved, we believe, would involve alteration of the feature set that defines the construct pole. Once the subject of the metaphor has been assimilated to the schematization, that schematization becomes capable of incorporating features that are distinctive to the subject. Those features then can become a part of the feature set that defines the construct pole to which the subject was assimilated. However, we do not aim to define the process by which accommodation alters the assimilating schemata. There is another point to be made.

We intend to develop further the metaphor of man-the-scientist that Kelly (1969) used to describe the psychologically functioning person. Sarbin (1980a, p. 2) extends this metaphor:

> The working conceptions of psychologists, like the working conceptions of other scientists, begin with metaphor. An event arouses the curiosity of a scientist (or layman); he has no literal term at hand to denote the event; he casts about for a way of talking about the perplexing events; the result of his casting-about is a metaphor.

Scientists are metaphor makers. Thus, if persons functioning in their perplexing worlds are to be treated as if they are scientists, then persons as they function to adapt to the world are to be treated as metaphor makers. We would say that when we speak of adapting, or learning, we speak of metaphor making. To do this, however, requires that our construction of metaphor contains features that are in accord with the foregoing discussion of category assignment.

CONCLUSION

In the immediately foregoing section, we stated that psychological adaptation and metaphor making would be interchangeable constructions. This is to say that the metaphors we have used to discuss the Range Corollary can usefully extend to construct psychological adaptation.

We began by specifying the important metaphors that we, as psychological theorists, have adopted to predicate the psychologically functioning person. We accept Kelly's Range Corollary, with the metaphors therein embodied: "A construct is convenient for the anticipation of a finite range of events only." Our discussion was directed toward showing that this corollary represented Kelly's efforts to explain why one puts an event into one category and not into another. To do this we, along with Kelly, relied on another assumption; namely, that a category is best represented as one of the poles of a two-poled judgment scale. From this point, one retrieves the constructs that schematize the Fundamental Postulate and the Choice Corollary. A range of events is construed as an exemplar of one or another pole of a construct when successful anticipation, in the total context of one's cognizing activity, is achieved by that construal.

In this chapter we extended the metaphor of the two-poled judgement scale by adopting the notion of features that is used extensively in current work on cognitive processes. Features, too, are discussed by talking about the immense set of two-poled judgment scales — constructs — that persons develop for use in construing. When a person interacts with the events in his world he assigns features to those events; that is, he assigns one or another pole of a particular construct to some sensory input from the event. On the basis of this feature assignment, one can determine if an event may be included in the range of those events that suitably match the prototypic event that acts as the "reference signal" (W. T. Powers, 1973), or standard, by which a category is schematized. A category, too, is considered to be a pole of a construct. If the feature-matching process allows the event to be regarded as a member of the fuzzy set that surrounds the prototype, then the event may be treated as if it is an exemplar of the category named by that pole of the construct. That category may become a metaphor for that event.

Any perplexing event may be construed successively by any of the constructs that a person has developed for use in anticipating events. One may say that learning is a matter of finding a construction that allows successful anticipation of an event. Finding a construction, that is, finding a useful category, is a process of metaphor making. Learning is like metaphor making. Metaphor making is a metaphor for learning.

The Range Corollary, however, which is to be regarded as an acceptable proposition, tells us that the construction named by the term *metaphor* might fail to be convenient for the anticipation of the events called *learning*. With a solid base in constructivist constructs, we believe that the construction labeled by the construct pole metaphor has a range of convenience to cover the events known as learning. Metaphor is a pregnant metaphor.

9

VARIATIONS IN DEVELOPING CONSTRUCT SYSTEMS: THE EXPERIENCE COROLLARY

James K. Morrison
Michael C. Cometa

The Experience Corollary: A person's construction system varies as he successively construes the replication of events.

At the Experience Corollary, personal construct theory best makes contact with developmental psychology. The infant becomes the person — the repository of a complex construction system. From infancy onward, that system undergoes the vast variation that reflects the successive construing of an immense diversity of event-associated information. To explain psychological development one explains the process of successively construing events and the product of that process, that is, a variation in a person's construction system. Yet, to speak of a person, one alludes to regularity, rather than to variation.

Kelly (1955, p. 76) said, "Construing is a way of seeing events that makes them look regular. . . . To be effective, the construction system itself must have some regularity." The very concept of regularity gives rise to the idea of person. It is the concept of regularity that has been at the core of a recent, heated psychological debate. Pervin (1978, p. 10), paraphrasing Mischel's (1968) critique of trait approaches to personality theory, says, "Since behavior depends on stimuli, regularities in behavior are to be explained in terms of regularities in external events, rather than in terms of internal characteristics." Kelly, having taken a contextualist position that diverges from the mechanistic thinking reflected in Mischel's position and from the formistic thinking of the trait theorists whom Mischel had criticized, would ascribe regularity to the person's ordered construing of the event. Kelly's conception of the development of the regularities are reflected in his discussion of psychotherapy, which he described as a cooperative learning experience. The therapist's adequacy in playing her role hinges on her ability to comprehend the manner in which the client views himself, his current situation, and the rest of his world; Kelly was quite clear in noting that interventions must be meaningful to the client and that alterations in overt behavior do not necessarily constitute, nor lead to, change in one's construct system. Practitioners of traditional, mechanistically oriented models of therapy find invalidation in Kelly's view that the client is best able to shed insight onto his condition and in Kelly's emphasis upon the client "doing the work" of revising his construct system.

Similarly, the perspective encouraged by Piaget's contextualist paradigm can be disconcerting to those educators who believe that knowledge can be "injected" into a child through lecture, drill, repetition, and reinforcement. Rather, a Piagetian approach to promoting children's learning emphasizes the need for a clear assessment of each child's unique level of conceptual development and stresses the view that children must invent and construct knowledge through their own active involvement in the learning process, that is, their own successive construing. As was seen to be the case with Kelly, a Piagetian emphasis does much to alert us to the point that we know little about a child's learning after we observed the child, for example, watching a demonstration, acting out the behaviors of "paying attention," sitting quietly in its seat, and then promptly vocalizing an answer when a cue is given. Both Kelly and Piaget view psychological development as inherent to the construction process, in that individuals are constantly seeking to extend their grasp of events. For both Kelly and Piaget, "learning," then, is equated with the individual's active construction of knowledge.

It was Piaget, however, who most completely carried out the task of upsetting formist and mechanist explanations of how regularities are established within the person. Piaget steadfastly looked at overt response as a manifestation of the person's construing of situations, and he convinced developmental psychologists to look to cognitive structure as a crucial strand in the context of psychological growth. Additionally, Piaget, unlike Kelly, devoted his professional life to explicating the qualitative variations in construct systems. As a biologist with a special interest in embryology, Piaget conceptualized the mind as a developing organism. The development of the mind, like the embryo, could not be conceptualized as an accretion of cells. The structure and functions of the cells vary as the embryo grows. The implications of this metaphor were reflected throughout Piaget's descriptions of the child's successive construing. Piaget, like Kelly, saw motivation as being intrinsic to the cognitive system (see Chapter 2 on the Fundamental Postulate). Furthermore, Piaget repeatedly stressed the epigenetic quality of psychological growth. Accommodative adaptations are just that — accommodations of existing structure (see Chapter 10 on the Modulation Corollary).

QUALITATIVE CHANGES IN CONSTRUING

Though Kelly did not center his study on issues of qualitative changes in construing, as did Piaget, he extensively used conceptions regarding quality of construing. Kelly described qualitative distinctions between construct groupings when he described permeable versus impermeable and propositional versus preemptive construing, and his early formulations gave rise to a large number of studies (see Adams-Weber, 1979a, pp. 75-77 for a review of research). With these concepts Kelly called attention to constructs that are flexible in their ability to embrace or admit new events (permeability) and in allowing for an event to be construed along a number of dimensions (a propositional construct). In contrast, some constructions are fixed and rigid in that they allow the person to impose only a single interpretation of an event.

Bannister and Fransella (1971) point out the parallel between Kelly's distinctions and Piaget's description of stage-related differences in the quality of thought, particularly as regards the contrast between preoperational and concrete operational reasoning. Piaget's (1932; Piaget and Inhelder, 1956) treatment of preoperational reasoning stresses the centrated, irreversible nature of thinking that characterizes younger (preseven-year-old) children. As such, preoperational thinking reveals not only the child's inability to "reflect back" upon events, a way of construing that would allow it to adopt a different perspective upon things, but also the child's proclivity for "locking onto" only one consideration, or aspect of a situation, so that the child is unable to deal with a multifaceted view of events. In general terms, the preoperational child sees the world in one, and only one, way and is unable to analyze events in terms of causal patterns or transitions leading up to a given outcome. Moreover, the preoperational child is seen as egocentric in that the child's own experiences and viewpoint serve as the sole standard by which judgments are made, thus clearly excluding the child's consideration of others' point of view.

The type of thinking that emanates from the use of impermeable, preemptive construct systems has much in common with that characterized by Piaget as preoperational. Kelly's descriptions of the flexible, multifaceted reasoning that ensues from propositional, permeable constructs is virtually synonymous with descriptions of the reflective, decentered, reversible quality of thought to which Piaget refers as "operational." One may conclude, then, that the adult who uses impermeable constructions in one realm of his world continues to use preoperational structures, even though adherence to Piaget's theory would lead us to believe that he might have abandoned such structures when he was in middle childhood.

YIELDING PREOPERATIONAL THOUGHT

To appreciate better the possibilities of elaborating personal construct theory through construing the work of current developmental psychologists, we shall present here some ideas about the child's transition from preoperational to concrete operational thought. To illustrate these changes in children's organizing cognitive structures we choose to discuss two areas of development: social cognition and the development of memory.

Construing Others

In his discussion of the Sociality Corollary, Kelly presents a point of view that is highly compatible to the framework Piaget (1932) used in discussing moral judgments and the development of interpersonal relationships among children. Piaget carefully details the manner in which the young child's egocentrism precludes his "putting himself in someone else's shoes," and he notes that it is only when the child becomes capable of seeing events from the perspective of others that equitable social relations emerge. Proceeding from these initial suggestions, developmental psychologists have elaborated the correlates of the major changes in cognitive organization upon which the "5 to 7 year shift" are built (see Brainerd, 1978, pp. 96-101, for an explication of these significant shifts) and have related general changes to changes in social cognitive function. As a result, there are now numerous reports of studies that describe the ways in which children develop skill in construing what others see, feel, think, or intend (see Broughton, 1978; Keasey, 1978, for reviews).

Selman and his coworkers (Cooney and Selman, 1978; Selman and Jaquette, 1978) have provided a well-constructed example of a progression of systematic variation in the child's construing of social relationships. Their analysis is built from an acceptance of a stage model of the development of social cognitions. Their stages are defined in terms of a child's developing awareness of how a person and another come to understand each other's point of view, a process they call social perspectivism. Selman and his collaborators interviewed large numbers of children in order to analyze the level of social perspectivism shown by each of the interviewed persons. For example, the assessment of a child's social perspectivism in the understanding of friendship began with the showing of a filmstrip or the telling of a narrated story describing an incident in the relationship between two people forming a new friendship. Following the story presentation the participants were asked a series of questions about such issues as trust and reciprocity. The interview served as the means by which the experimenters explored the children's naive theories of interpersonal relationships and gained access to the reasons underlying the expressed beliefs and opinions. By this process the investigators were able to categorize the participant's level of social perspective taking. They classed each participant's response pattern in terms of five progressive stages of perspective-taking development.

Their findings confirmed their initial expectations that at the earliest level, stage 0 (children ranging from age 2 years, 4 months, to 5 years, 11 months, showed stage 0 thinking), a child fails to distinguish social viewpoints of self and other. In thinking about friendship, stage 0 children characteristically think of shared physical space. Trust is equated with physical capabilities. "For example, four-year-old Alan said that he trusted his best friend because, 'if I give him my toy he won't break it . . . he isn't strong enough' " (Cooney & Selman, p. 30). At stage 1 (4 years, 6 months to 12 years, 4 months), children construe trust and loyalty in terms of the intentions and feelings of the participants. Participants at this stage show a concern with the uniqueness of the covert, psychological life of persons in a social relationship. There is not yet revealed in their reasoning a set of constructs by which the children can understand reciprocity. A child shows his use of stage 2 (age range 6 years, 9 months to 15 years, 10 months) constructions when he clearly expresses an understanding that trust in friendship is defined by reciprocal intentions and taking such reciprocity into account. By the use of these constructions a person can think of how they are construed by the other. At stage 3 (11 years, 3 months to adulthood) the participants can analyze a dyadic relationship from the perspective of a third-person observer. Finally, at stage 4 (17 years, 8 months to adulthood) the participants show the kind of sophisticated construing that would characterize the social scientist at work. At this level they show a contextualist, systems orientation.

Selman and his collaborators have collected and analyzed data that validates their stage approach to describing development in children's social cognition. Social perspective taking progresses through an invariant age-related sequence. There is no evidence that individual children regress to lower levels once a high stage is achieved. There are no misorderings of stages. The model is in accord with the kind of theory Piaget has advanced, in that children show ordered, qualitative changes in the ways that social information is organized. That is, new constructs emerge to allow the developing person to structure social information in new ways so that the person shows increasing awareness of, among other things, the psychological interdependencies in social relationships, the systemic aspects of social interactions, and the internal, psychological processes of the participants. As one also expects from following Piaget's assumptions, these constructions are applicable across a wide range of social events. Children at a particular stage show that they similarly construe group processes, friendships, and the nature of singular individuality or selfhood.

Damon (1981a and b), like Selman, used a stage approach to study aspects of children's developing social cognitions. Damon carefully analyzed the changes in his sample's responses to issues involving positive justice and authority relationships. He followed a sample of 34 children over the course of a two-year period. The children were first interviewed at time 0 and then on two other occasions, after one year and again after a second year. The children responded to questions about stories that had described situations involving social justice and authority relationships. Their responses were categorized in terms of a six-level system that Damon had found to be representative of the children's development of conceptions relative to these social interaction issues. When asking about a child's construction of authority, one is concerned about the child's understanding of the process by which a person pledges his obedience to someone who enacts respected leadership qualities. Damon found that at the lowest level (Stage 0-A, reflected in the majority of the responses of the youngest members of the sample), children think of legitimate authority in terms of an exchange of obedience for the loved leader's expression of desire for compliance. At the next level (0-B), the authority's ability to reward and punish is considered. At the next-to-highest level, 2-A, the children reason that obedience is offered on the basis of assessing experience and know-how. Repsect is no longer vested in persons, but in the role that is temporarily filled by the expert. At the highest level, 2-B, authority is flexible, consensual, and is based on an assumption of an underlying equality of the authority and the subordinate. The children's conceptions of positive justice develop along similar lines, reflecting the children's increasing abilities to differentiate, to take into account, and to consider the reciprocal interplay between the innerrepresented perspectives of the participants in the social interaction.

In that he used a longitudinal approach, Damon was able to draw some well-specified conclusions about the above-described course of variations in the children's ability to contrue social situations. Among other things, children's more advanced understandings appear to be anticipated by tentative forays into the next-achieved level. Because these anticipatory explorations are evident in their responses, it is possible to predict an immanent, full-blown variation in the construction system. Responses that reveal a "spread" of reasoning skill, toward the next level in the progression, are seen to be precursors of a consolidated mastering of those organizing constructions that are representative of the next level. Thus, the unstable use of more advanced constructs precedes their use as the dominant organizing features of the child's way of cognizing these social events. (Damon [1981b] notes that acceptance of this conclusion forces a developmental psychologist to consider the issue of fragmentation, which is discussed by Landfield in Chapter 11. Paralleling some of Landfield's comments, Damon says, "There is always a way, at some level of abstraction, to find uniformities in any array of phenomena, including human behavior. The issue in social science is always the heuristic value of the hypothesized uniformities in describing, explaining, and predicting human behavior" [p. 29]. In short, Damon reminds us of the history of the variations in our own constructions of how children's construct systems vary.)

Specifics in Construing Others

Flavell and his collaborators (see Flavell, 1978; Flavell, Everett, Croft, and Flavell, 1981) have used another approach to the analysis of the development of social cognition. Earlier work led Flavell (1974) to develop a description of a multileveled progression of perspective-taking skills, relative to understanding another person's visual perceptions. The work on the development of children's thought about what other people see began with Piaget and Inhelder's (1956) exploration of a child's ability to consider the perceptions of another person who looks at, from a different angle, a display the child is viewing. Piaget and Inhelder concluded that a preoperational child could not conceive of another person perceiving the scene in a way that diverges from the way in which he himself perceives it. Flavell (1974) concluded that Piaget and Inhelder's analysis required more careful elaboration and structure.

Flavell had been led to the proposition that a preoperational child (level 1, on average well achieved by age three years) "shows at least a minimal capacity for symbolically representing certain visual acts and experiences, for attributing them to others as well as to self, and for distinguishing between these two attributions (at least in some situations)" (p. 95). The level 1 child thinks of others seeing the *things* that he sees, but is not yet able to represent the *views* that others hold of these things. At level 2 the child can represent the fact that he and the other person "have particular, positive determined views (perspectives) of the things they see" (p. 96).

Flavell and his collaborators have completed a variety of investigations to clarify the specifics involved in the changes in construction that are apparent in level 1 and level 2 children. For example, one study explored the development of general rules about one's own visual input relative to the visual input of another person at another location who views the same scene observed by the participant. Salatas and Flavell (1976) studied the perspective-taking knowledge of six year olds and eight year olds. The children were given tasks to assess whether or not they satisfactorily used the following rules: If a person is at one particular position he has only one view of the scene, and different persons at different positions would have different views of the scene.

Analysis of their data led them to say:

> The results suggested that rule 1 may be acquired earlier in childhood than rule 2. Of the 32 subjects at each grade level, 22 kindergarteners and 28 second graders consistently recognized that no more than one depicted view should be attributed to any one observer. On the other hand, only 7 kindergarteners and 19 second graders consistently denied that one observer's depicted view could be seen by another observer at a different station point (Flavell, 1978, pp. 60-61).

This study, like others in the extended chain of studies developed by Flavell and his associates, shows that the child develops more and more sophisticated constructs for use as he tries to understand what another person perceives and thereupon experiences, at those times when he and the other person observe "the same" visual array. The studies corroborate the general proposition derived from social cognition studies; namely, skill in construing in social situations develops from the overt to the covert — from initial success in construing outer appearances and behaviors toward success in construing the inner aspects of another's world. Flavell's studies help to describe more precisely the variations in the child's construction system.

Memory and Construction System Variation

In Chapter 4, Gara discusses the relationship between a person's own construction of events and the memory for those events. He refers to the following general principle: When one employs an organization from his own construction system to process incoming information, that material will be better recalled than will material organized in terms of another's system. Piaget and Inhelder (1973; Inhelder, 1969) completed a series of studies in which this principle was invoked to explain the relationship between children's developed constructs and their memory for an event. The study also shows that the constructivist memory process deeply involves progressive variations in the child's construction systems.

A sample of children, ranging in age from three to eight years, was shown an array of ten sticks whose length varied from 9 to 15 centimeters. The smallest stick was placed on one end of the series, and the remaining sticks were arranged from that to the longest stick. The children were instructed to look at the sticks so that they could remember the array at a later date. No time limit was imposed on the viewing. After a week's interval the children were first asked to show by hand gestures what they had seen. They then tried to draw what they had seen. After another interval of six to eight months the children were again asked to draw what they had seen in the initial presentation. A subsample was instructed to give a verbal description of the array. None of the children had seen the original display at any time between the first presentation and the last testing. The children were, however, given a set of sticks and were asked to replicate the array after each of their attempts to draw a representation of the array.

The child's arrangements of the sticks were used to assess and to establish the level of construing the child had achieved, relative to the task of seriating the sticks by length. The child's memory performance, the dependent variable in the study, was assessed and classified as being representative of three levels of organization. The first-level participants, generally children of three to four years of age, were able to draw a series of aligned sticks, but there was no clear replication of the length gradations. Third-level memory performance was achieved when the children (aged six to seven years) represented an approximately correct seriation by length. Second-level performance produced an arrangement that showed an awareness of length considerations but lacked clear seriation. Table 9.1 shows the outcomes of the study. The percentage of children in each intersecting cell is displayed, so that one can see that there is a clear relationship between the child's cognitive organization level and his memory performance. For example, all of the children who could show operational seriation were able to give a level 3 memory performance. Furthermore, a review of the children's

TABLE 9.1
Distribution of Subjects by Memory Types and Operational Stages
(in percentages)

	Memory Types		
Operational Stages	*1*	*2(a-d)*	*3*
Preoperational	83	17	0
Transitional	0	65	35
Empirical seriation	0	27	73
Operational seriation	0	0	100

Source: B. Inhelder, "Memory and Intelligence in the Child," in *Studies in Cognitive Development: Essays in Honor of Jean Piaget*, ed. David Elkind and John H. Flavell. Copyright © 1969 by Oxford University Press. Reprinted by permission.

verbally expressed memories corrsponded to their performance in active arrangement. For example, the lowest-level children used only two words, long and short, to describe the array. They did not use the words shorter and longer that are used by the children who consider longness and shortness as locations along a unitary short-long construct.

Another result helps clarify the ways in which construct system variation is shown by this simple study. After the six- to eight-month interval, most of the children made drawings that showed "improvement of memory," in that the drawings at the time of the later testing were at a level above that shown in the first testing. Seventy-four percent of all the children showed an advance, and 90 percent of the children aged five to eight years showed an advance. The advance was generally from one level to the next higher level. If one accepts accurate replication as indicative of better memory, one is led to the counterintuitive conclusion that memory for the event had improved over a long time interval.

To interpret this work, Inhelder (1969, p. 343) says:

It is clear that the memory image is not a simple residue of the perception of the model, but rather a symbol that corresponds to the schemes of the child. . . . According to our hypothesis, the action schemes — in this particular case, the schemes of seriation [of length] . . . constitute the code for memorizing. This code is modified during the interval and the modified version is used as a new code for the next evocation. At each stage, the memory image is symbolized according to the constraints of the corresponding code.

The exemplary constructivist approach to memory that is embodied in the work of Piaget and Inhelder meshed well with the overall constructivist approach to memory that has emerged in recent psychological work (Jenkins, 1974; Greeno, 1980). Just as Piaget's work gave developmental psychologists a constructivist base from which to study the development of social cognition, Piaget and Inhelder's work similarly has inspired recent work on children's memory processes.

One cannot, in a short space, do justice to the complex and meaningful literature relating to the varied construction systems that children bring to bear as they process the new information that is integrated into and simultaneously alters their construct systems. We give an example from the work of Paris (1978). He and his collaborators studied the relationship between the (assumed) inference-building ability of children and their recall of presented material. In one simple study they read sentences to samples of children aged five, seven, and nine years. The sentences contain the format, actor-action-object of action, such as, "The boy cut the paper." Although the action in each sentence could involve the use of a tool, the instrument was not explicitly mentioned. Later, in a cued recall test, the children were given a prompt word, which could act to facilitate recall of the sentence. The cue word was either the implicated tool, the explicated subject, the verb, or the object of the action. The study was designed to allow comparisons of the successes of the different-aged children. The children's performance on a task requiring the recall of the specific sentences showed that five-year-old children more effectively recalled sentences when an explicit cue word, rather than the implicitly designated tool name, was used to prompt recall. Nine-year-old children used both the implicit and explicit cue words with equal effectiveness. It can be concluded, then, that at the time of storage the older children build a schema that includes constructions relative to inferred aspects of the event, and they then reflect the use of those inference-related structures when they recall the event.

The outcomes of the studies of Paris and his associates can be interpreted as follows: As the children develop psychologically, their experiences having prompted variation in their construct systems, they are better able to build a more elaborate construction of the presented sentences. These elaborate schemata "contain" settings, instruments, and consequences that can be related to events described. When they are then given a term that evokes a construction of one aspect of the stored representation of the episode, they construct a more complete representation of the episode. Younger children could only store those parts of the event that were evoked by the directly expressed verbal symbols, so that nonexpressed terms are not a part of the stored construction and will not aid in the recall of the episode.

Paris and other investigators have noted that these very useful studies have offered a ready solution to some important problems. Nevertheless, these studies, like those of Piaget and Inhelder, do not specifically explicate the nature of the construct system variation that facilitates the inference-making process. Furthermore, the studies do not allow confident inferences about the flow of experience that would bring about those variations in construction systems that are assumed to underlie the changes in the memory processing.

Myers and Perlmutter (1978) report a study completed by Staub (1973) that helps to illustrate the relationship between memory and the specific construction that the child is able to make at the time of input. Staub used a simple paired associate memory task. She worked with a sample of three-year-old children and a sample of four-year-old children. She had constructed a memory task involving 12 pairs of pictures. Three of the stimulus pairs depicted unrelated items. Three pairs depicted items related in a part-whole fashion; for example, tire-automobile. Three pairs depicted objects having a superordinate class relationship; for example, sock-hat. Three pairs of stimulus pictures showed a picture of an object in association with its habitat (fish-lake). The picture pairs were presented, as pairs, in random order. The children were asked to name each item as they were shown in one continuous presentation. During the test trial the children were shown one member of the original pair and then were asked to name the missing item.

As one would expect, the four-year-old children (compared to three year olds) correctly named more of the missing items. All the children showed better recall of related items, regardless of the kind of relationship embedded in the pair. Also, the children, like adults, more successfully recalled the missing item when the originally presented pair was successfully placed on a construct available to the learner. This point is made clearly when one considers that children least successfully recalled the items belonging to pairs that embodied a class relationship (four year olds correctly recalled 65 percent, and three year olds correctly recalled 56 percent). Items expressing part-whole and habitat relationships were better recalled. These straightforward results are totally compatible with repeated demonstrations that preseven-year-old children who, following Piaget's position, operate on the preoperational level and are unskilled in dealing with superordinate and subordinate class relationships. In that Staub's participants had yet to master the relevant cognitive structures, they are less able to organize the events along category class lines and, thereby, use that kind of organization to facilitate retrieval at the time of recall.

Recapitulation

Numerous investigations have followed from Piaget's original analysis of the development of concrete operational thought. A brief overview of some of this work serves well to illustrate several aspects of variation in construction systems. The examples reviewed above are drawn from studies of social cognition and from studies of changes in children's memory functioning. Two major themes have been developed, as follows: progressive changes in children's organizing cognitive structures can be inferred and illustrated, and the processing, storing, and retrieving of information is effected by the kinds of structure that the child can use to organize the input.

PLANNED CONSTRUCT SYSTEM CHANGE

Modern construct theorists will find a ready audience for their explanations of methods by which to prompt construction system changes. Recent publications (Stringer and Bannister, 1979; Landfield and Leitner, 1980) offer descriptions of a variety of planned change programs that have evolved directly out of Kelly's specific system. Other constructivist-inspired programs, less directly derived from personal construct theory, will be briefly described to illustrate the variety of ways in which workers have tried to bring about construct system variation.

The Harvard-Judge Baker Project

The work of Selman and his group, described above, has been conducted in tandem with the program at the Judge Baker Guidance Center in Boston. The Center serves children who are judged to be ineffective in their interpersonal relationships, particularly in their relationships with their age-mates. The program conducted with these children has been aimed at changing the constructions of their social relationships, so that the children, by their direct interaction with peers, may be prompted to alter their cognitions of conflict resolution, leadership, friendship, and so on.

Cooney and Selman (1977) report that the children's social reasoning has been studied in four main settings, as follows: interpersonal problem-solving sessions, conducted weekly — the children evaluate their activity relative to issues such as conflict resolution and cooperation; weekly group meetings to plan activities; classes to discuss current events; and irregular counselor-child discussions about classroom difficulties.

Discussions and interviews are recorded, transcribed, and analyzed. Children are interviewed, following procedures developed to assess their level of social cognitive development. Additionally, the investigators have accumulated a record of the actual social interchanges.

The goal of the program is, first, to demonstrate that the actual social interchanges can be categorized and described in terms of the cognitive structure levels that Selman's group has described. The capacity to think of children's social relational difficulties in terms of the cognitive structures they bring to bear on the events should allow more effective opportunity to assist the children in their development, this being a second goal of the project. For example, a child might find himself in a situation requiring at least a stage 3 understanding of peer group relationships; that is, he should at least understand that groups function as homogeneous communities. His development, however, has reached the stage 2 level (understands bilateral partnerships). When he is required to function with other children who expect a stage 3 level of functioning, he will be unable to function. It would be folly to require him to work with a peer group whose members spontaneously use stage 4 (understanding of pluralistic organization) structure.

A program in which the child will be prompted toward construct system change will require a full implementation of the Sociality Corollary (see Chapter 13 for a lengthy discussion of the Sociality Corollary and planned change). The most effective reactions to the child will be those that are at the proper "distance" (Mancuso and Handin, 1980, 1982; Sigel, 1970) from the child's current understanding of group functioning. It must be understood that when the experiences are not readily incorporated into the child's structures he will experience arousal, and he might then attempt to "extort validation evidence" (Kelly, 1955, p. 510) for his structuring of the situation. In such cases, those carrying on the program must be prepared to understand the child's arousal reaction as well as his failed construct system. In short, the total emphasis of a program of change will focus on the child's construction system, and the program will be directed toward supplying the child with events that he may successively and successfully construe, so that appropriate variation in his construct system may be achieved.

IMAGERY TECHNIQUES IN PLANNED RECONSTRUCTION

Kelly (1980, p. 24) said:

> As for the client, if he is one who regards his past as the successively emerging phases of his personal experience, each leading to a new outlook, he will make use of his therapeutic opportunities in a much different way than will one who recounts his past only to show what it has done to him and who looks at other men only to see who can tell him what to do.

If a psychotherapist has done his work properly, the client has been guided toward changing his constructs of self and others so that he takes some responsibility for the past and lays plans to shape the future. It is in this kind of psychotherapeutic venture that the application of construct theory, complemented by the developmental theory of Piaget, reveals itself in all its richness.

For Kelly, who held a life-long commitment to applying his theory, the focus of convenience of personal construct theory was psychotherapy. By thinking of psychotherapy against the background of current work in developmental psychology, one may broaden the understanding of how persons have organized the experiences that shape their adult constructions of the world.

According to Salmon (1970) the development of personality in the child can be viewed in terms of Kelly's concept of role. As Bannister and Fransella (1971, p. 87) have explained, the

> child's construing of his mother's construct system is the jumping off ground for the development of the child's construing system. He starts

out with this and uses it in his dealings with others. Soon he meets others like himself and finds that all the anticipations he makes do not always work out, so he develops new role constructs in relation to others of his age. So he goes on, gradually elaborating his role construing.

Consider these points relative to the experiences of adult clients who try to reconstruct their childhood. During the last eight years the senior author, working with adult clients, has used a type of psychotherapy that was developed to assist persons in the process of reconstruing themselves and significant others. Based on the cognitive theoretical assumptions of Kelly and Piaget, this psycho-therapy — emotive-reconstructive therapy (Morrison, 1979; Morrison and Cometa, 1977, 1980) — uses techniques, primarily of mental imagery, to encourage clients toward reviewing the events that prompted the overelaboration of some constructs and the underdevelopment of others.

Psychotherapists interested in the use of mental imagery techniques may now turn to a large literature on the relationship between cognitive processes and imagining (Ernest, 1977; Marks, 1977; Paivio, 1971; Paivio and Cohen, 1979; Piaget and Inhelder, 1971; Reese, 1977; Shepard, 1978; Singer, 1974; Yuille and Catchpole, 1977). Techniques, developed from this literature, can provide useful tools for psychotherapists whose prime goal is to help clients who persist in the use of simplistic, unelaborated, and impermeable construct systems. Having accepted the framework laid out in the early part of this chapter, we are in agreement with Reese (1977) in postulating that a visual image is inherently a memory process, and that it is dynamic and, therefore, is not always reconstructed in its original form. Images are not reproductions of reality or replications of sensory inputs. Rather, they are the products of transformations of inputs. They are regarded, similar to constructs, as schematic representations or interpretations of reality. The nature of the transformation and representation or interpretation depends on the entire situational and historical context in which the event occurred, including the cognitive structures of the client.

If, as Paivio (1971) postulates, the visual memory system does not make complete contact with the verbal system, it makes sense for a psychotherapist to help a client use new data (stored images not actively related to verbal aspects of the construct system) to confront the utility of a client's limited construct system. This is precisely the approach in emotive-reconstructive psychotherapy. Because at times imagery data, retrieved in therapy under the direction of the therapist, often contradict the verbally expressed constructs that clients apply to certain people, the clients experience arousal levels exceeding the optimum (Fiske and Maddi, 1961). Efforts to master this uncomfortable arousal, combined with the assistance and support of the therapist, are marshalled to prompt a substantial change in a client's construct system.

Frequently clients will succeed in reconstructing pleasant and/or unpleasant episodes that contradict long-cherished, simplistic constructions of an event.

For example, a client, who long maintained harsh negative constructions of his father, recalled an incident that happened when the client was nine. The first part of the incident had always fit neatly into his negative-weighted constructs of his father. In this reconstructed scene the client remembered having been severely spanked by his father. Another part of the scene was never included in a reconstruction of the event. When directed imagery reinvoked the experience the client remembered that, after the spanking, his father had come to apologize. The client had angrily and callously rejected his father and had told him never again to come near him or have anything to do with him. After recalling terrible feelings of guilt he had experienced when he then saw the "crushed look" on his father's face, the client began to remember pleasant memories associated with his father (for example, how his father used to take him bowling; how his father went to all his little league games).

Because of the "new" data, the client was forced to change his heavily biased and simplistic constructions of his father. The client could not, of course, simply wipe out the negative construings of his father. Such constructions were useful to understand many of his experiences with his father; but now the construct system had to be stretched to accommodate some positive constructs. Certainly now his superordinate constructs (for example, "Dad ruined my life") had to give way to a more permeable one ("Dad and I both contributed to what happened to me in life"). The client now understood why he had been "depressed." Focusing only on his father's blame, the client neglected his own role in the strained relationship between him and his father. The client cried profusely over the ways in which his constructions had sabotaged this relationship, and then, no longer "depressed," he proceeded to change his life dramatically. Long-term follow-up confirmed the predicted pre-post dramatic change in his constructs of mother, father, and self on a Semantic Differential analysis.

Another brief case study may help to clarify further how adults persist in using constructions built from the organizing constructs available in early stages of development. A female client, who always had been the favorite of her now-deceased father, was troubled by her very negative constructions of her mother, who had come to live with her. The client's negative views of her mother had begun to generate many problems in living with her mother. The client was guided toward reconstructing, from her early images, her home life at a young age. After first relating events that seemed to fit easily within the negative constructions of her mother, the client rebuilt images that told of events in which her mother "had been really nice" to her. The client began to become aware that she had evolved a one-sided construction of her mother as the client had doted almost exclusively on her father. As the client became more facile in construing her mother in positive terms, the client's construct system became permeable and complex enough to cope with an aging, lonely mother who needed her support and acceptance.

Research on Imagery Application and Construct Change

Our assumption that the theoretical propositions of Kelly and Piaget can be harmoniously integrated to acquire a clearer understanding of the development of personality leads to the strong conclusion that using induced imagery as a psychotherapeutic tool may enable a client to experience change in his construct system. Using the Semantic Differential as a measure of construct change, Morrison and Teta (1978) demonstrated, in a study of psychotherapy clients, that exposure in 15 sessions to the type of imagery techniques used in emotive-reconstructive therapy resulted in a significant positive change in those clients' constructs of self. Furthermore, positive self-construct change was found to be significantly correlated ($-.81$) with reduced symptom change on a symptom checklist (headaches, sleep problems, anxiety, and so on). These results suggest that to change a client's constructs through imagery induction can lead to client reports of reduced problematic symptoms.

Certainly further research needs to be done to clarify some of these tentative formulations about the relationship between imagery induction and construct change. However, for the present, there is enough evidence to entertain seriously the hypothesis that changing constructs can result in the kind of symptom relief that many clients seek from psychotherapy.

The Child and Death Imagery

The senior author has used imagery techniques with adult clients who have not yet properly grieved the death of a loved one (Morrison, 1978). Several of these clients had, when they were children, lost a parent through death. Some of these clients have experienced their reconstructions with such clarity that they begin to speak and sound like children. For example, one client, when relating her experience at the wake of a parent, spoke, uncharacteristically, in short sentences, using a limited vocabulary, a higher-pitched and more monotonic voice, and puckered her face like a child who was trying to keep from crying. In sessions with such clients one can obtain a good idea of how difficult it is to cope with events that evoke the levels of arousal associated with death.

A child who experiences death, especially during preoperational or concrete operational stages of development (in Piaget's framework), has but limited schemata within which to integrate a great many experiences (fear of death, death of parent, the wake and funeral, fear of future, loneliness, anger, sadness, crowds of people, and so on). One begins to realize that the simplistic, structured construct system available to the typical child can never adequately integrate all those data-producing experiences a child has to handle. Since the child does not have useful schemata into which to integrate these episodes, he necessarily develops a simplistic and biased view, and can recall the event only in these terms.

In therapy, imagery helps the client to construct more adequately the sensorial and cognitive data about life-changing events such as the death of a loved one. The process enables the adult client to use his more adequate construct system to understand better the myriad confusions of experiences surrounding the death he could not cope with as a child.

Events That Can Require Adult Reconstruction

Significant events that happen during childhood are, of course, construed with the child's constructions. The arousal reactions associated with these childish constructions often remain a central part of the adult's retrospective constructions of those events. The person's efforts to construe these often intense arousal-associated stimulations can intrude on the development of reconstructions that would be more in keeping with his adult system. The person then finds that he cannot assess his own role in those events. The senior author has found that persons who are trying to rearrange their outlook on their adult interpersonal relationships have profited from reconsidering these kinds of significant childhood events. Clients can develop a solid outlook on their construction systems by reconstruing childhood events like the following: death of a loved one, birth of a sibling, parental arguments, first day at school, sickness of a parent, and the separation and divorce of parents.

Depending on the level to which his construction system has developed, a child deals with such upsetting experiences in a variety of ways. Some children simply do not attend to the experience so that they do not modulate existing constructs to assimilate the situation. One client reported that when he was seven he would go up to the closet of his bedroom, close the door, and pretend he was on a spaceship going to the moon — all while his parents were arguing furiously downstairs. Because he did not have constructs to understand why his parents fought so bitterly, he simply tried to block out information.

Other children drawing on their limited system construe the events as best they can. For example, a client (mentioned earlier), at the age of nine, after being severely punished by his father, construed his father as "bad" because he could not process the complex circumstances (for example, the client had shot rubber darts at the television; it was the first time his father had spanked him; his father had tried to apologize) to include an understanding of his father's perceptions of the event. Additionally, he could not construe his own feeling (guilt?) at refusing his father's apology. He could see only that his father was culpable, and their relationship was permanently altered. A simplistic construction was used to assimilate the child's helplessness in trying to cope with a terrifying situation.

Still other children who face parental anger conclude, as do many preoperational children who view a reprimanded transgression (Mancuso and Allen, 1976) that they must be "bad." For many years thereafter such children may act out their purported "badness" and sabotage any efforts on the part of others to treat them as "good." Often adopted children, who know their natural parents gave them up for adoption, find themselves entrapped in this destructive and self-prophetic role.

According to Kelly, constructs modulate when events are projected on them. The case of the nine-year-old boy, mentioned earlier, comes to mind. When, as an adult, he recreated the spanking event, imagery connected with his rejection of his father's apology necessitated a shift in his simplistic construction of his father as "bad." This client's therapy work also shows that the alteration of a basic construction ("My father is bad") has effects throughout his system. For example, in therapy the client's imagery experience, in which he tried to assimilate all the circumstances of the event, led him to alter related constructions of self ("I wasn't so innocent after all") and his employer ("My employer and dad are really similar and maybe I've been dumping my somewhat unjustified anger at Dad on him").

SUMMARY

Developmental psychologists, following the constructivist/contextualist position explicated by Piaget, have provided a solid body of studies that support the proposition that "a person's construction system varies as he successively construes the replication of events" (Kelly, 1955, p. 76). Studies repeatedly show that the processing, storing, and retrieval of events are affected by the organizations that a child can impose on those events. It also has been shown clearly that children, at various levels of development, construe the "same" events from qualitatively different perspectives.

Behavior change interventions have been designed explicitly on constructivist principles. Such programs, especially those designed to affect younger people, illustrate the necessity of considering the person's current construction system, the input relative to those systems, and the possibilities of variation that may derive from that input relative to the person's existing system.

With a better understanding of the workings of imagery, behavior change specialists can use imagery techniques to induce variation in a client's reconstruing of early childhood events that can more adequately be integrated by use of the constructs he has available as an adult. Planned and directed experiences of this type can be useful in promoting changes throughout the person's construct system, so that he yields egocentric constructions and moves toward greater complexity and permeability. In the long run, the client can become aware of his own capacity to free himself from his previous history, and he can experiment independently with varying his constructions of replicated events.

10

EXPERIENCE — A CASE FOR POSSIBLE CHANGE: THE MODULATION COROLLARY

Brian C. Hayden

The Modulation Corollary: The variation in a person's construction system is limited by the permeability of the constructs within whose range of convenience the variants lie.

"Life may be seen through many windows, none of them necessarily clear or opaque, less or more distorting than any of the others."

Isaiah Berlin

Once an emphasis has been placed on the anticipating and predicting person, focus is placed on the process of his ability to invent and reinvent forms that give order and meaning to events. Human development is viewed as ubiquitous and may best be characterized as man's life-long attempt to construct increasingly meaningful, that is workable, representations of reality. Indeed several theorists — most notably Piaget (1954), Kelly (1955), and Werner (1957b) — propose such a view. Each of these theorists conceptualizes change as a process that is intrinsic to a person's attempt to give order and meaning to events. While there are differing emphases in each theorist's explanation of change, the spirit of their views, particularly as expressed in Piaget's concept of assimilation-accommodation and in the Modulation Corollary, are remarkably similar. These theorists view change as the elaboration and transformation of cognitive structures. Nevertheless, Kelly, more directly than do the other theorists, provides a conceptualization of change from which can be derived parameters of change in a person's construction system and most clearly articulates the predicament of every person's interpretation of reality: Any representation of reality delimits what he can, and can not, perceive. This chapter attempts to elucidate Kelly's ideas about change and to evaluate their heuristic value.

KELLY'S VIEW ON CHANGE

Kelly addresses two facets of change: Under what conditions can change occur and what, in fact, changes in the person's construction of reality? He does so in his Modulation Corollary. More specifically, "the variation in a person's construction system," Kelly asserts, "is limited by the permeability of the constructs within whose range of convenience the variants lie" (Kelly, 1955, p. 77).

The corollary specifies the conditions under which change can occur by alluding to a structural characteristic of theory building. A theory is vertically or hierarchically organized. Each level of the theory is subsumed by yet a higher and more integrative level. In the sense of structure, but not in content, the degree of abstractness of a construct refers to its relative position within this vertical organization of the comprehensive system. Some levels are thus more important than, or superordinate to, other levels that, in turn, are less important or subordinate to constructs of another level. Superordinate or "abstract" constructs have inferential links to various subordinate constructs. The more inferential links a construct possesses, the more extensive is the array of implicated constructs in which an event's interpretation is embedded. In effect, the more implications a construct possesses, the more meaningful is the construct (Hinkle, 1965). Additionally, the more inferences to be drawn from a single construct, the greater is its flexibility or plasticity in both subsuming or embracing a variety of events. Such a highly linked construct allows more subordinate predictions than does a less-implication-rich construct. This structural feature of the individual's construction system determines the relative "permeability of the constructs" at any level within the system. That is, a construct in a person's system may be more "abstract" or hierarchically inter-related; hence, that person can handle or embrace or perceive a new event with an existing form (a construct inferentially linked to a more superordinate construct) that another person's less "abstract" or hierarchically organized system prevents him from perceiving. What to one person is experienced as a "meaningful" event is not experienced by another.

The Modulation Corollary highlights each perceiver's predicament. He is a victim of his own construction system. There are limits to what he perceives. A construction system may effectively block the perceiver from interpreting or assimilating every aspect of reality. Thus, the person may need to modulate, adjust, or modify how he organizes an event so as to more effectively structure and predict it. For him to make variations or changes in how he structures experience, he is beholden to the structural characteristics of his construction system. Some permeable construct must be available to the perceiver to allow the assimilation of the event and thereupon to produce the change in the construction system.

In other words, he can not just change anything about his structuring of experience. Ultimately, the relative degree of permeability of his constructs delimits what can be varied or altered within the system. The modification or change in his structuring of an event can occur only within the context or "range of convenience" of some aspect of his existing framework, which after all allowed him to originally perceive, albeit unsuccessfully, the event. Within any construction system, even the most rudimentary, there will be some constructs that are relatively more meaningful (more implications) or superordinate than are others, thereby ensuring the possibility of change or variation occurring within the system's lower-level constructs.

Once Kelly stipulates the conditions under which change occurs, he must also address the issue of what actually changes in a person's representations of reality. In effect, how does a person's representation of reality become more predictive? To clarify what changes can occur so that a perceiver may experience or see some new event, but not all events, the Modulation Corollary must be placed within its theoretical context. The chapters of this volume extensively consider the meaning of each corollary and hence supply that context. The Modulation Corollary was derived from the Fundamental Postulate (Chapter 2), the Construction Corollary (Chapter 3), the Organization Corollary (Chapter 5), and the Experience Corollary (Chapter 9). A brief integration of paraphrases of these corollaries with references to recent research in the area of cognition and schema construction will indicate how a person gives order and meaning to events. In doing so, specific kinds of "variation in a person's construction system" can be derived from the proposed integration.

CONSTRUCTION SYSTEM CHANGE

In the process of giving order to the flux of encountered events, the person becomes emotionally aroused, he orients, and he attends to that which occurs. Extensive research in cognition demonstrates that people have a remarkable ability to ascribe features to recurring events (Posner and Keele, 1968; Reed, 1972; Hayes-Roth and Hayes-Roth, 1977). What is abstracted organizes what subsequently is perceived and experienced. In effect, there must be a concept (or hypothesis) available to the perceiver to direct attentional activity so that the event is perceived. Kelly suggested that these features or sets of constructs are used as if they are structurally bipolar.

Recent research on the nature of schema construction suggests the ways in which these sets or bipolar dimensions are organized. A schema is a general and large complex unit of knowledge that organizes what we know about general categories of objects, classes of events, and types of people. A schema, according to Neisser (1976, p. 54), is "internal to the perceiver, modifiable by experience, and somehow specific to what is being perceived. The schema accepts the information as it becomes available at sensory surfaces and is changed by that information. . . ." A schema is general since it is organized in terms of various representational features or dimensions. Besides encoding events, a schema includes both strategies to obtain information and rules to make inferences about what information is missing (Miller, Galanter, and Pribram, 1960; Neisser, 1967, 1976; Anderson, 1980). That is, the schema allows a perceiver to complete or fill in the pieces to analyze an event. Since a schema is taken to be an organization of various features, a schema can be conceptualized as a cluster of bipolar constructs. Basically, then, constructs are the building blocks of a schema.

The various representations or schemata of our past experiences form knowledge structures that organize and interpret new information. Hence, much of the information contained in a person's thought is provided by the actual structure he previously had imposed on the stimuli (Mischel, 1979; Markus, 1980). The complex schema used to organize the stimuli allows a person to make inferences from the information available by inferring or going beyond the given information. People have a keen sensitivity to extract and develop correlations between features in the environment often in disregard of available information. Thus, when an individual meets a person whom he perceives to be dull, he also infers, although without any evidence but a ready reliance on the previously construed correlations among dimensions, that this new acquaintance lacks intelligence, malice, a sense of humor, but is painfully sincere.

The more complex or elaborate is the schema, the more superordinate and meaningful it is within the existing comprehensive construction system. Consequently, some aspect of the system subsumes more experiences (more events can be matched with the existing less superordinate constructs in the vertical system), as well as distorts (misconstrues) them so as to maintain the integrity of the entire system.

The integration of the ideas of the personal construct theory and research on schema construction suggest how a person structures and experiences his environment. Within a person's theory or construction of self, others, and the world are a finite number of hierarchically organized schemata. Each schema is composed of specific personal constructs extracted from recurring events that are abstracted into matrixes of correlates among one another. These complex structures are continuously involved in the person's anticipating, thinking, and remembering of events. Each existing schema or cluster of constructs determines what gets encoded. Most importantly, each schema determines what is *not* perceived, encoded, and remembered. While each person is a victim of his construction of reality, the complex construction of each schema or cluster of constructs contains the seed of change. Schemata guide the extraction and organization of information, so that any construction of any event can fail to incorporate useful features and correlates among features. Hence, each schema is incomplete. In effect, a person always is engaged in the process of completing a more predictive structuring of reality.

Change, then, is a ubiquitous aspect of a person's psychological functioning. Within the context of a person's hierarchic construction system, four parameters of change can be derived. First, there can be change in the way in which a construct is used or applied as structure is imposed on an event (construct application). Second, change can occur in the number and variety of abstracted constructs used to impose structure on an event — a form of filling in the missing pieces of a schema (differentiation). Third, there can be change in the extent of the clusters or groupings of constructs and groups of schemata that are used to structure an event (interconnectedness). Finally, there may be changes in the different degrees of abstracted correlations among constructs, that is, in the degree of meaningfulness of constructs or the degree of ordinancy attained by constructs within the vertical system. Hence, change can occur in the increasing or decreasing degree of meaningfulness (that is, correlations or inferential links) that any given construct possesses within the vertical system (hierarchical organization).

This last parameter of change is most intricately involved in the successive changes within an evolving and more workable representation of reality. The permeable/more superordinate/more meaningful constructs within the existing hierarchic system serve as the framework for modulations in construct application, in the degree of differentiation, in the extent of clustering of interconnected constructs, and in some constructs becoming more permeable or superordinate. Each of these variations within a person's construction system contributes to his changing, and often increasingly elaborate, representation of reality. As the construction system becomes more complex and elaborate, the system becomes more hierarchically structured. Subsequently, the hierarchically structured system ensures even greater possibilities for each type of variation, or change, to occur. With such a system, the person has greater access to the flux of encountered events. In other words, the perceiver can experience and learn more about these events.

As a theoretical summary statement, a corollary proves valid to the extent that it is useful in organizing and predicting events. The Modulation Corollary addresses two issues pertaining to change: What does change, and what are the limitations on system change? Change or variation can occur in one's representation of reality when the change can be subsumed by a relatively more superordinate or more permeable construct within a person's existing hierarchic system. The crux of the heuristic value of the notion of variations in a construction system lies in the operationalization of these variations. Only after the variations are operationalized can there be an appraisal of the corollary's validity as a theoretical anchor for research findings. The next section includes an attempt to pull together and impose an order on the diverse measures of a person's construction system, hoping, thereby, to discern operationalizable variations in that construction system.

OPERATIONALIZING THE PARAMETERS OF CHANGE

Construct Application

A construct is used to structure and perceive events. The construct's effectiveness in organizing such events is assessed in terms of the construct's capacity to discriminate among the events that may be organized by using that construct. More specifically, a construct is envisaged as a bipolar dimension consisting of a continuum between end points on which a variety of possible demarcations may occur. The application of a perceiver's construct can be conceptualized in three ways: are both ends of the construct used to discriminate effectively between events, does the construct allow for differentiation or gradations among events, and does an event's location shift from one end point of the construct to the other?

With regard to the first of these three types of construct application, the perceiver can use either of both poles of a construct to structure any situation. The tendency to allocate events almost exclusively to one pole of the construct reduces the construct's predictive efficacy: Everything is seen as more or less the same. Researchers have used a variety of terms to describe the tendency to allocate most, if not all, events to one pole of a construct (that is, lopsidedness: Kelly, 1955; maldistribution: Bannister and Mair, 1968; and bias: Slater, 1972). The term *lopsidedness* will be used hereafter to refer to this one facet of construct application.

A construct possessing a number of demarcations along its continuum typically allows the perceiver to determine nuances or gradations among events. Basically, the number of intervals along a construct (for example, a seven-point scale) that a person applies to events permits him to perceive these various events as discretely different on the same dimension. Thus, a person's construct allows for more discriminations among a group of events to be discerned if all or most of the seven points on the scale are used rather than, say, only three points. The gradations (including the end points of a construct) permit new elements discriminately to be abstracted and added to the existing continuum. Consequently, the construct provides a way for a person to consider nuances in his interpretations of potentially varied events. A new element or event can be embraced by the construct either by it being organized by an existing gradation on the construct or by a new gradation being abstracted and then used to organize it. Several terms have been used interchangeably to describe this aspect of construct application: articulation (Harvey, Hunt, and Schroeder, 1961), number of intervals (Signell, 1966), precision (Scott, Osgood, and Peterson, 1979), and discrimination capacity (Hayden, Nasby, and Davids, 1977). The term *discrimination capacity* will be used hereafter to designate this second aspect of construct application.

The third aspect of construct application was suggested by Kelly (1955). He argued that the individual can shift from using one pole of his construct (for example, love-hate) to using the opposite pole to organize an element or event. One could shift from locating a friend at the love pole to locating him at the hate pole. The term *slot change* (Kelly, 1955) will be used to name this aspect of construct application.

Lopsidedness, discrimination capacity, and slot change are three aspects of one parameter of change: construct application. A construct can embrace within itself these variations or modifications in structuring an event. Because of these variations the new event is perceived and learned. The newly structured event may be a result of its being structured by use of a rarely applied construct pole, by use of a newly abstracted demarcation on the existing continuum of the construct, or by use of a contrasting pole or vantage point. For instance, a woman using the construct love-hate may perceive and interpret her lover's actions quite differently with experience (episodes of validation and invalidation of her view). Initially she may perceive almost everything he does by applying the love pole (lopsidedness). Gradually she may perceive and learn that his actions are best structured as representations of various degrees of love (discrimination capacity). Finally, she may interpret his actions in a very different way. She may come to perceive him by way of the hate pole (slot change). Though he is the same stimulus, she has modulated her structuring of her experience of that stimulus.

Differentiation

The number of constructs used to articulate an event indicates the extent to which the person more complexly interprets that event. Crockett (1965) defined differentiation as the number of constructs used to describe a class or domain of events. Differentiation refers to the number of discrete constructs brought to bear to any given event. The existence of some constructs allows for yet other constructs to be abstracted from the recurring pattern of imposed order. In effect, the existing framework of a schema allows for missing pieces (other constructs) to be abstracted and, thereby, improve the structuring of the experience of a particular event. Generally, the more constructs applied to an event, the more effective is the interpretation of that aspect of the perceiver's reality (Crockett, 1965). Some schemata or subsystems of constructs may be more differentiated than others (Fransella and Bannister, 1977). Hence, the effectiveness of a person's interpretations can vary within his comprehensive construction system. For a system to handle or embrace nuances, it would seem essential for the perceiver to have many constructs available to apply to an event and to use differing combinations of available intervals on these various constructs. Indeed, construct application (at least, discrimination capacity) and degree of differentiation are significantly related (Scott, Osgood, and Peterson, 1979).

The second variation, differentiation, represents the degree to which an event is discriminately perceived on many constructs. Returning to our example of the lover, she abstracts new constructs (reflecting increased differentiation) with which to structure and orchestrate an increasingly more elaborate way of predicting and making sense of her lover's motives, intentions, and actions. A schema, consisting of such constructs as her love-hate construct, serves as the framework within which she increases the degree of differentiation in how she structures her view of him. The more differentiation one can make as one structures an event, the more one experiences and learns from that event.

Integration

Unfortunately, there is considerable confusion in the area of assessing the organization of a person's construction system. In light of the importance of variation occurring in an organized construction system, it is essential that there be some order in how to assess organization. In an effort to impose an order on this assessment problem, two aspects of organization in a construction system are suggested: interconnectedness and hierarchic organization.

The measures most commonly used to assess organization of a construction system have been cognitive complexity (Bieri, 1955), intensity (Bannister, 1960), and a complexity measure derived from principle components analysis (Slater, 1972). Persons who perceive events in a similar way indicate a greater degree of functional similarity and hence appear to be "simple." Simplicity, in this framework, refers to the tendency of an individual to apply his unique set of constructs to a variety of events in a similar fashion. Zimring (1971), using Bieri's measure, found that such patterns of relationships among constructs simultaneously applied to events reflect concurrence in construct use or a kind of integration. Such a form of integration, Wyler (1964) suggested, would allow a person more easily to interpret diverse experience by means of a common orchestrating theme. In other words, it may be appropriate to view "simple" subjects as integrators. Concurrence in construct use allows a person to interpret more easily a variety of events in terms of their joint similarity, rather than in terms of their differences (Wyler, 1964). Thus similar (not identical because of the facets of each construct's application) use of a cluster of constructs by the perceiver allows events to be regarded as minor variations on an integrated theme (Langley, 1971). In contrast, cognitively "complex" subjects or those who have less of a pattern of construct relationships appear to be low on this kind of integration.

In line with this argument, Adams-Webber (1979, pp. 50-53) presented convincing evidence that the various measures of organization assess a kind of "integration" of construction systems. Indeed, Bannister (1960) originally assumed that the degree of statistical association between constructs indicated the level of integration of the person's system. Patterns of relationships among constructs reflect a kind of interconnectedness among the constructs available to the perceiver as to how the constructs are used to perceive and structure an event. Interconnectedness, the third parameter of change, reflects the extent to which the perceiver similarly uses a cluster of constructs to structure events. In effect, he construes similarity among a variety of events. For instance, the young lover may use one part of her comprehensive system in such a way as to perceive everything her boyfriend does as lovable, endearing, thoughtful, cute, and as a sign that he is the "right one" for her. This part of her construction system, in effect, allows her to see only similarity across his diverse expressions of sentiments, statements, gestures, and actions. With more experience (validations and invalidations of her particular view) her structuring of him may modulate or change. For example, the patterns of relationship among applied constructs either could become more interrelated (increased interconnectedness) or they could become more fragmented (decreased interconnectedness). In the latter case, the cluster of schemata that she developed to fill in the pieces (increased differentiation) of her many-faceted boyfriend may yet have proven an ineffectual predictive strategy when applied in a similar fashion. The change in a pattern of relationships among constructs reflects the third type of variation or change within a person's construction system.

The organization of a construction system is not unitary (Wyler, 1964; Scott, Osgood, and Peterson, 1979). If a person's interconnected cluster of constructs only allowed him to perceive everything as the same, then "organization" is a bit illusionary. To determine whether or not the person is perceiving events as functionally equivalent, that is as all the same, the degree of relative ordinancy among the constructs used to perceive some event or events must be assessed. The network of inferences among the constructs used to structure a variety of events needs to be known (A implies B, but B does not imply A). Another kind of organization exists in every perceiver's construction of reality: vertical or hierarchic organization.

The following is a brief description of two methods used to assess the degree of meaning or relative ordinancy of constructs (see Fransella and Bannister, 1977), that is, hierarchic organization. One method is derived from a cluster analysis of person perceptions, and the other method directly assesses the number of inferences possessed by each construct.

When Langley (1971) assessed hierarchic organization by means of a cluster analysis of a person's perceptions of others, he found the level of hierarchic organization to be unrelated to a measure of that system's degree of interconnectedness (Bieri's complexity measure). That is, the two proposed facets of organization — hierarchic organization and interconnectedness — are not measuring the same thing. Of note, Langley found that subjects low in interconnectedness (that is, cognitively "complex") are high in specific analytical skills, that is, the ability conceptually to take things apart (the subject does not have a highly interconnected construction system by virtue of his not using constructs similarly to structure events). Moreover, a person's analytical skill was unrelated to his integrative abilities, a finding later replicated (Epting, Wilkins, and Margulis, 1972; Smith and Leach, 1972). In contrast, the measure of hierarchic organization was shown to correlate significantly with a measure of intuition or integrative ability (the ability to "leap" from a limited clue to more integrative conclusions). With vertical or hierarchic organization, a person more rapidly can move up the system from the concrete event he had organized to other constructs that subsume the original structure imposed on the event. Subjects with low hierarchic organization were poor in the intuition task. In effect, these latter subjects apparently could not move away from a specific clue because they had no access to a hierarchically structured system that allowed them to move rapidly and vertically up the hierarchy to the more abstract, more inferential, constructs. As noted earlier, however, the subjects low in interconnectedness were quite adept at analyzing events, wherein perceiving differences among certain events was more predictive than perceiving similarities. In a more sophisticated but similar analysis, Smith and Leach (1972) confirmed these findings.

The other method of assessing hierarchic organization is to determine a construct's ordinancy by means of counting its number of inferences. This particular method has been used more extensively than has cluster analysis. Wyler (1964) suggested that a concept's level of abstractness is a function of the number of inferred attributes generated from the presence of the concept, a suggestion others adopted (Lemon and Warren, 1974; Warr and Jackson, 1977; Scott, Kline, Faguy-Cote, and Peterson, 1980). Wyler's measure of hierarchic organization was unrelated to interconnectedness (as derived from a principle components analysis), replicating the finding of Langley that the two facets of organization are unrelated. Of considerable importance Wyler found this measure of hierarchic organization to be a far more sensitive and reliable measure of change in a person's construction system than was the measure of interconnectedness. This finding of differential sensitivity in assessing change between the two facets of organization has been replicated (Honess, 1978, 1979; Kelsall and Strongman, 1978.

Hinkle (1965) similarly argued that personal constructs possess inferential links with other constructs within a conceptual system. Hinkle attempted to establish the relative meaning or ordinancy of individual constructs. Hinkle determined the relative meaning of a construct by establishing which constructs are conceptually related to other constructs within a person's system. To operationalize this version of "meaning," he developed an "Implications Grid" that enabled him to assess the level of hierarchic organization of any given construct and thereby determine which construct is superordinate to others and, perhaps, subordinate to others. Consistent with the Modulation Corollary, Hinkle demonstrated that the more superordinate constructs (more implications, hence more meaning) were less likely to change than were subordinate constructs (less implication, hence less meaning). Only the most superordinate constructs permitted change or modification of the less superordinate constructs that, consequently, permit the perceiver to experience and learn from an event. A person's more meaningful or superordinate constructs are less likely to change, because such a change would entail changes among all the inferred subordinate constructs. A kind of ripple effect would occur down the hierarchic structure. In addition to there being a differential degree of meaningfulness among constructs, it also can exist between the poles of any given construct (the "bipolar Implications Grid," Fransella and Bannister [1977]). The construct validity of the Implications Grid and modifications of it have been supported by other investigators (Fransella, 1972; Crockett and Meisel, 1974; Hayden, 1979). Also, Honess (1979) found Hinkle's method of assessing hierarchic organization to be a far more sensitive and reliable measure of change in a construction system than that of the measure of interconnectedness.

The really significant finding, in terms of the theoretical essence of the Modulation Corollary, is that the measures of hierarchic organization (a reflection of the extent of the permeability of the existing constructs) have been consistently found to be the most sensitive and reliable in detecting change in a person's construction system (Wyler, 1964; Honess, 1978, 1979; Kelsall and Strongman, 1978). As Kelly posits, change occurs when it can be embraced by existing permeable constructs. To exemplify this point, the previous example of the love-hate construct as it is used by two different lovers shows how each lover has different types of access to events. One lover may have a very hierarchic construction system, with the construct of love-hate being one of his system's most superordinate. The other lover may have a marginally hierarchic construction system in which the love-hate construct also is one of her system's most superordinate. However, each construct's degree of meaningfulness within the respective construction systems substantially differentiates their status as "superordinate" and, thereby, affords each lover with very different schematizations of their love relationships. Within the more vertical system, a greater variety of events (including episodes of invalidations) could be subsumed, as could many more variations in the construction of an event following such invalidations. The second lover's system would possess less flexibility or plasticity in subsuming a variety of events.

Integration, in conclusion, consists of two facets. One facet of integration reflects the patterns of relationships among constructs simultaneously applied to events (interconnectedness), whereas the other facet reflects the relative degree of meaningfulness (hierarchic organization) or ordinancy of constructs applied to the event. While the methods of assessing the two facets of integration are unrelated, interconnectedness and hierarchic organization must be viewed concurrently in order to assess the overall degree of integration in a person's construction system. For instance, extreme interconnectedness without hierarchic organization would suggest a system constituted of a homogeneous cluster of functionally equivalent constructs. The perceiver's view of reality would consist of everything seen as more or less the same.

A framework now exists so that we can appraise the heuristic value of Kelly's ideas on change: the Modulation Corollary indicates when change can occur, four types of variations within a construction system have been derived, and these variations have been operationalized.

The variety of variations in a person's construction system affects how bland and uniform, or how rich and varied, is a perceiver's view of reality. The variations in construction occur in how constructs are applied (lopsidedness, discrimination capacity, and slot change) to an event, in how many constructs are used (differentiation), in the extent to which constructs are "interconnected" and similarly applied to orchestrate a common theme or subset of themes (interconnectedness) across various situations, and in the relative ordinancy or meaningfulness (hierarchic organization) of each facet of the construction system. Each variation may entail either an increase or decrease. Moreover, such variations determine how restrictive or expansive is the person's view of events in his world. Any system necessarily delimits or determines what can be perceived and learned, and in turn, the system's structural characteristics determine what can be changed. Each change will then delimit what subsequently is perceived and learned, as well as what remains unperceived and unlearned.

The remainder of this chapter will review the research dealing with the four proposed parameters of change. The evolving system of the child will be reviewed first to provide a dramatic example of a potentially changing and increasingly elaborate construction of reality. Then the research on the four types of change in the adult's construction of reality will be reviewed. Review of the research on the child's and adult's construction of reality will document the modulations that can occur in a person's construction system and, therein, address the issue of the heuristic value of the Modulation Corollary. Simultaneously, we will consider Kelly's premise that a person's on-going construction of experience is structurally common to child or adult, whether neophyte or a well-seasoned interpreter of events, taking into account the existing research on the child's and adult's respective construction, and changes therein, of reality.

CONSTRUCTING AND RECONSTRUCTING: THE CHILD

Even in infancy the child is organizing, inventing, and reinventing the structures that form his experience. The infant and the young child have, and use, bipolar dimensions to make discriminations, such as like-dislike (Flavell, 1970; Zajonc, 1980), chance-nonchance, self-object (Piaget, 1926, 1954), boy-girl, familiar-unfamiliar, young-old, and self-other (Lewis and Brooks-Gunn, 1979). These forms are the building blocks of the child's construction of reality. Some of these dimensions may become his most important constructs (that is, superordinate) with which to structure reality. Regardless of which constructs remain as his most important, adults will be important collaborators in the child's effort to impose structure. The parent must attend to the child's existing level of organizing reality. In effect, the parent attempts to regulate the types of situations that can be embraced by the child's existing system of constructs.

The parent assists the child in discriminating and labeling events, as well as helps the child to "perceive" with his more permeable constructs the inter-relations among various events. The events will be embraced by his system only if the parent successfully presents a novel event that is accessible to him in that he has available constructs of sufficient permeability. By presenting new situations to the child, the parent can vary the degree of novelty relative to the child's existing construction. As any effective teacher (parent, psycho-therapist, or instructor), each parent helps the child use his own construction system to subsume that which he had not previously subsumed. In doing so the very existence of some of his original social constructs, such as self-other or self-object become more implicated with other constructs or become relatively superordinate. Such constructs form the basis of an evolving network of infer-ential links with other more recently invented constructs. Having developed relatively superordinate constructs, the child is better able to perceive and abstract new features (subordinate constructs) from events, as well as to extract correlations among them. In short, the parent-child interaction determines and, most likely, facilitates the likelihood of the child modulating his variations in construction so as to develop an increasingly more complex and hierarchically structured system.

Although adults are implicated in the variations of a child's developing construct system, the child's use of constructs may be quite different from that of the adult's. Many of the child's constructs will not allow him to interpret effectively some events. For example, the parent and child both may use the construct lie-truth, but the child may structure and learn from what his parent presents to him something quite different from what his parent's instruction had intended to achieve. There are several reasons for this. The child often creates idiosyncratic poles to discriminate events (see Wooster, 1968). Moreover, the use of poles may attain little consensual validation (relative to adults) before age six (Applebee, 1975), although the constructs are psychologically meaningful and recognizable to the child as his own (Bannister and Agnew, 1977). That is, some constructs will be incorrectly used (consensually rejected by others), such as living-not living, which is regarded as "animistic" thinking (Flavell, 1970). The meaning (the network of implications among constructs) of the child's constructs may, therefore, be limited or restricted compared to the adult's construct. Hence, in some contexts his construct may be quite sufficient to perceive the events his parent has construed and yet be insufficient to do so in other situations.

The process of variation in a child's construction system will occur since in many situations he uses an idiosyncratic, but necessarily limited, construction of reality. Often his anticipations are validated. At other times, they are incorrect or invalidated. In the latter case, the result is a lack of match between the stimulus and the organizing pattern (construct or schema). Such mismatch is the precursor of change; but any lack of match between the structure of an anticipation and the event creates anxiety (Piaget, 1954; Kelly, 1955; Hunt,

1971b; Epstein, 1973). In fact, the extent of anxiety is a function of the amount of discrepancy between the information presented and the schema available from the existing system. The greater is the success in meaningful anticipation achieved, the less the "cognitive anxiety" is experienced (Viney and Westbrook, 1976). Cognitive anxiety, then, signals the degree to which an event exceeds the structuring capacity of the system.

This lack of match between the imposed structure and the occurring event, the precursor of change in the construction of that event, brings into focus the essence of the Modulation Corollary. One such example of what changes in the child's construction of reality involves the child's encounter with a new event. He tends to structure the event in terms of an extreme position (Flavell, 1970). That is, he structures the event by means of one pole of an existing construct. Allocating the event to the extreme end of one pole reflects the child's initial stage of superimposing order. Successful anticipations are achieved, but the structure is also limited: It necessarily is restrictive. His overreliance on structuring events with only the extreme end of his construct, however, limits successful anticipation of other aspects of the environment that may be more effectively structured by the other pole. In short, the child's construction system undergoes some systematic modulations, which will be delineated below, as he attempts to create an increasingly more workable and effective representation of reality.

Construct Application

In terms of the first parameter of change, one would expect with increasing age that the child's applications of his constructs would become more effective in organizing experience. One such variation would be the use of either of both poles of any single construct to structure an event. Lopsidedness (one facet of construct application) should decrease with age since sooner or later overuse of one pole will lead to invalidation. Invalidation of the child's structuring attempt will occur despite the fact that the more extensively used pole permits far more efficient processing and storage of information, as well as better retrieval cues than does the less often used pole (Adams-Webber, 1979). A well-rehearsed, but limited, view affords the perceiver with only a limited anticipation of the future.

In a study assessing the constructs of children, Applebee (1976) found a significant decrease in the child's incidence of lopsided construct application with increasing age (6, 9, 13, 17). The incidence in use of lopsidedness leveled off by 13 and did not change thereafter. Similarly, Barratt (1977a) established that the older the child (8 to 14) the less he applied constructs in a lopsided manner. In other words with increasing age, and notably by puberty, the child appears to use both poles of his constructs.

A rather interesting finding of Benjafield and Adams-Webber (1975) — that lopsided use of socially relevant constructs is associated with interpreting the self as similar to others — may have implications for the child's application of constructs. As noted earlier, a child tends to structure a new event in terms of an extreme position (Flavell, 1970) on a new construct and to continue to apply a construct in a relatively lopsided fashion. It appears that the child initially is imposing the same pole of a construct to give order to and learn about himself and others. Hence the child's increased use of the opposite construct pole allows him at times to perceive himself as dissimilar to other persons. This structural variation in his construction may permit the child to now perceive his social world in a less unidimensional and restrictive way. In short, this change allows for the opportunities to learn yet more about himself and others. For example, as lopsidedness decreases with age, one would predict that the child would increasingly be able to differentially structure his experience of self and others. The child should, with increasing age, begin to perceive and experience others as being distinct from, or less similar to, himself. That is, the child would less often structure his experience of another person by means of the same pole of any given construct. Indeed, the elaboration in this distinction between self and other gradually does increase between age 8 and age 13 (Honess, 1980), a finding that complements the finding cited above regarding the decrease in lopsided application of constructs with children approaching puberty. The ability to differentially structure self and other intensifies by early puberty (Katz and Ziegler, 1967; Honess, 1980). Most importantly, the child's shift in how he uses his constructs toward the use of both poles might enhance the child's ability to predict not only that another person is different from him, but that he may not necessarily perceive things just as another person does. If a child exclusively uses one pole of a construct (wherein self and other are placed concurrently), the less likely he will be able to "decenter"; that is, he will be unable to imagine that the perspective or experience of another person can diverge from his own. As lopsided application of constructs gradually decreases, there will be an increase in the child's ability to structure other persons by means of construct poles other than those by which he structured his own experiences. Consequently he will learn that another's perspective is different from his. The evolving ability of construing another's perspective will be gradual since sometimes a failure of the young child to make the structured distinction between his own view and another's view does not lead to invalidation. For instance, a young child may correctly predict another child's feelings in situations with which he is familiar. What he may in fact have done is to simply state what he felt in that familiar situation, which coincidentally predicts correctly what the other child feels (Gruen and Doherty, 1977).

Implicit in any decreased lopsidedness in structuring events is a corresponding increase in another facet of construct application. More specifically, the child is shifting from the use of one pole to give order to that of the other to achieve order: slot change. The child is changing the means by which he perceives an element (self or other). Lumping everyone together with the same structure inevitably will result in some invalidation. There is a benefit to this change in structuring: Both poles of each construct now can be used and, there-after, elaborated into more efficient means to structure experiences. As the child more extensively elaborates each pole of a construct, the opportunities arise for yet other variations in construction of reality. His existing structure affords him the means by which to abstract intervening points or gradations between the poles. Finer discriminations begin to evolve within the context of a bipolar dimension. Indeed, using a modified form of Kelly's Rep Test, Signell (1966) found that among children aged 9 to 16 there was a progressive increase in the discrimination capacity of their constructs used to organize events. Older children have, and use, more gradations or intervals on their constructs than do younger children to organize their experiences of persons. Similarly, Applebee (1975) found an increase with age in a child's ability to use less frequently the extremes of the construct and instead to see more nuances in events.

In summary, the child's modulations in construction as evidenced in the decrease in lopsidedness and the increases in both slot change and discrimination capacity allow him to perceive more of the events around him. More specifically, the changes appear to account for a series of critical, but gradual, psychological events that occur in midchildhood. These events include the increasing differentiation of the child's structuring of self and others, the child's increasing ability to anticipate another's perspective, and his being able to perceive nuances and qualities in himself and other people. Moreover, these three changes result in increased elaboration in the child's interpretation of the environment that parallel the documented increases during latency in the child's efficiency in encoding, storage, and recall of information (Seamon, 1980).

In effect, the child's constructs are becoming functionally differentiated and hence more effective in handling information. There is a limit, however, to each facet of change in construct application. After all, effective handling of information is not enhanced only by creating, for example, innumerable intervals or using every existing interval of a construct for as many events (Miller, 1956). It is not the mere accumulation of intervals on a dimension that distinguishes the older from the young child. Experience is more than the structuring of more and more bits of information. It is what the perceiver "makes" of these bits. In part, this results from the possibility of variation in the second proposed parameter of change, differentiation. The missing pieces of the perceiver's schema gradually are abstracted. His evolving construction of reality allows him to perceive more and more of the particulars of the things he had structured originally with his existing system in a more global or general way. In the process, the child discovers unexpected features.

Differentiation

Applebee (1976) found a significant increase in the number of constructs used with increasing age (6 to 9). That is, differentiation in the construction system increased with a child's age. Analysis of the elicited descriptions of peers from some 320 children (age 7 to 15) revealed that the mean number of dimensions used to organize the experience of social relations increased with age (Livesley and Bromley, 1973). However, a significant increase in differentiation occurred between the ages of 7 and 8. The change in differentiation during one year actually equalled the magnitude of increase in constructs used by children between the ages of 8 and 15. Scarlett, Press, and Crockett (1971), who investigated developmental changes in the interpersonal perception of boys (age 6 to 12), found a significant increase with age in the average number of constructs used to describe their peers, with the greatest gain in the number of constructs occurring between 7 and 9. Using three rather disparate age groups (6/7, 12/13, and 18/19 year olds), Rosenbach, Crockett, and Wapner (1973) found a similar age-related increase in the average number of constructs used. The greatest difference occurred between the 6/7- and 12/13-year-old children. Between those aged 12/13 and 18/19 no significant change occurred in the average number of constructs used by a child to structure the behavior of his friends. It seems that a significant elaboration of a child's construction occurs in latency, particularly by age 9. Craig and Boyle (1979), using children in a lower age range (5 to 8), failed to confirm that young children's construction systems become more differentiated with increasing age (5 to 8).

Three other studies failed to replicate this finding of increased differentiation of person perception. However, these latter studies used samples of children who were older than the 7-9 level. Signell (1966), using children aged 9 to 16, found no increase in the number of constructs used to describe people using a modified Rep Test. Similarly, Little (1968) failed to establish any increased differentiation in the construction of peers among the children sampled (aged 10 to 18). A study of children in grades 3, 6, and 9 (ages 9 to 15) found no increases in a child's level of differentiation in describing others (Olshan, 1970).

A study by Cameron, Stewart, Craig, and Eppelman (1973) underscores the finding that it is during latency that a child begins to develop more ways to make increasingly more effective predictions and interpretations of that which most preoccupies him: learning how to organize and make sense out of the experience of peers. Cameron and his colleagues obtained a sample of the thoughts of some 4,420 persons and found that prior to age 7/8 children tend to think about objects or things, whereas by 8 and throughout life a person's thoughts predominantly center on people (self and others). In summary, increased opportunities to experience peers and increased thinking about people by the latency-aged child are paralleled by increased differentiation in their construction of peers. To deal with and think about people the child will need a more differentiated system. As he tests his system he will have experiences of validation, as well as of invalidation. These experiences will allow for an increased richness in the nuances of the child's interpretations of others and greater refinement of his construction system.

However, the evolving complexity in organization is a function of the opportunities to structure and organize specific types of events. Signell's (1966) study illustrates this point. She compared the construction system of two different types of events: people and nations. For children over age 9, she found no increase in the differentiation of a child's construction of peers. However, the children were relative novices in the domain of nation perception, hence increased exposure to information requiring the organization of features of nations resulted in a significant and positive increase with age in the differentiation of a child's construing of nations. In effect, the child abstracts more constructs specific to whatever schema and schemata permit a structure for an encountered domain.

While variation in the number of constructs used to perceive social events does occur, the rapid increase does not persist. There appears to be a kind of leveling off in the number of constructs used to perceive people. That is not to imply that after 9 the same constructs used to structure at age 9 will be used identically at age 15. The increasingly complex network of dimensions will modulate and evolve to permit him to perceive nuances of the social world; and, most importantly, his construction system will allow him to go beyond the perceived behavior and to infer an intention. Essentially, with increased differentiation one would expect there to be increased variations in the extent of interconnectedness, and hierarchic organization in a child's system should occur with age. That is, one would expect that the variations or modulations in the facets of integration presumably will become increasingly salient in the child's construction system.

Interconnectedness

Four studies investigated the interconnectedness of children's person perception. The children's age range in these studies was 6 to 17. Three studies found that there is a significant increase in interconnectedness with age (Olshan, 1970; Applebee, 1975, 1976). For instance, Applebee (1975) noted that the explanatory power of the first component (degree of interconnectedness of constructs) significantly increased with age (6 to 17). Contrary to his hypothesis, but consistent with the above stated expectation and research findings, Barratt (1977a) reported a significant and positive trend between age (8 to 14) and interconnectedness (that is, explanatory power of the first three components increased).

Prior to any significant development occurring in the degree of integration of the construction system, it would seem logical to expect that the child must extract a set of psychological discriminations to organize his impressions of others and that subsequently can be "interconnected." As noted earlier, the rise in differentiation occurred around age 9. Interconnectedness would be likely to increase around or just after then. That is in fact what Applebee (1975) found: Between 9 and 13 there was a significant increase in the degree of inter-connectedness of constructs used to perceive and experience people.

Many of these variations, as the Modulation Corollary posits, can occur only within the context of some existing relatively superordinate, abstract, or permeable construct. As each of the poles of the increasing numbers of available constructs becomes more elaborated and more interconnected, the hierarchic structure becomes more apparent. Such changes in construction permit the child to experience the increasing subtle social demands imposed on him, and from which he can now learn. In other words, with increasing age, the child's construction of reality will allow for the kinds of increased variations already reviewed because each variation can be subsumed by some existing relatively superordinate constancy.

Hierarchic Organization

Two studies have assessed directly the possible variation in the hierarchic organization of children's construction system. Applebee (1976) reported that "centrality" of a construct (the number of constructs inferentially related to it) increased with age (6, 9, 13), but not after 13 (at least up to 17). That is, the "abstractness," or permeability, of constructs increased as the interconnected network evolved. Using Hinkle's measure of hierarchic organization, Honess (1979) documented that with age there is an increase in the number of implications of children's constructs that permit them to perceive personality traits or psycholog-ical states. Moreover, all age groups (8.7, 10.2, 11.9, 13.3) have significantly high proportions of implications for the "abstract" constructs (allowing for the percep-tion of personality traits), while showing a lower proportion of less "abstract" constructs (for example, permitting for perceiving appearance, ability, activity, and preference in oneself and others). Honess' study indicates, as was earlier sug-gested in this section, that young children possess some relatively superordinate or "permeable" constructs. With increasing age the number of these permeable constructs' inferential connections with other constructs increased. The relative position of these constructs within the hierarchy may shift over time, depending on the extent to which each was used to structure various experiences. Of note is the finding that the relative permeability of some constructs does indeed increase and consequently such constructs are available to embrace the various structural changes and variations in the child's construction system that already have been described.

These studies on hierarchic organization indicate that late latency to early adolescence is the time when hierarchic organization greatly increases. The child's construction system is evolving a network of constructs by way of the modulations of structural changes. In effect, the structural changes facilitating elaboration of the child's construction system simultaneously ensures increases in some construct's degree of ordinancy within the system; that is, some aspect of the system is becoming more superordinate or permeable. The child has a system that allows him to move up or down the vertical structure and, in so doing, perceives his environment in terms as concrete and proximal or as inferential and removed from the immediate as is deemed more predictive. However, as was the case for the other three parameters, the parameter of hierarchic organization does not generalize to all the subsystems of the comprehensive system. Rather some hierarchic organization allowing for a more expansive vantage in one domain does not ensure that same opportunity in construing other aspects of his construction of reality (Kelsall and Strongman, 1978).

The modulations of each parameter of change afford the child an expanding effectiveness in perceiving and interpreting more and more about people. In addition, each change is complementary to each other. The pattern of variations in construction, moreover, intriguingly parallels Piagetian-based developmental research and theory. The postulated progression of stages, the number of stages and their age ranges, as well as the existence of stages, have been questioned previously (Gruen and Doherty, 1977; Selman, 1980). Instead, these changes delineated above in how a child organizes experience seem to occur within a contextualist perspective. The child's system affords a framework with which to ascribe increasingly more subtle aspects to social reality. The child becomes more aware of and learns more from his contact with the social domain. Variations in the construct application of his construction system occurs. For example, lopsidedness decreases, while both discrimination capacity and slot change increase with age (probably beginning around 6/7). Correspondingly, the child begins to organize his experience differently from how he interprets another person's experience, which enables him to anticipate that the other person may perceive the world quite differently than he, and to perceive that just about everyone, including himself, has both good and bad qualities. These variations continue until puberty. The latency-aged child is now able to perceive and has the cognitive structures to devote more thought and attention to people and less to things. A rapid increase in the differentiation of construction occurs during latency and may level off by 9, approximately when interconnectedness and hierarchic organization begin their gradual, but significant, increase until early puberty (12/13). The child's construction system is becoming more elaborate and allows for elaboration of existing construct poles. Moreover, constructs are becoming more inferentially elaborated within the system. Consequently, the relatively superordinate constructs become even more permeable as their relative ascendency increases relative to other constructs. Meanwhile, the actual use and meaning of any single construct may change considerably during this development toward more effective structuring of the environment. Invalidation of the child's construction often results in system change, but these changes occur within the framework of at least some relatively superordinate constructs. The process of the evolving construction system does not seem to reflect demarcated stages. Rather, the process involves a progressive differentiation and integration. Such variations in construction allow the child to restructure a stimulus and thereby provide opportunities to further experience and learn about that stimulus.

The Modulation Corollary suggests that variations can occur. The variations, however, can be elaborations toward either expansion or restriction in the view afforded by the perceiver's system. That is, the variations in a child's construction of reality lead to elaborations only of what he perceives and structures in his world. Although his system limits what is accessible to the perceiver, change can occur within the framework afforded by the existing construction system. For instance, the quality of a child's peer relations is closely related to the development of his social concepts; however, the development of physical concepts are unrelated to a child's popularity (Rardin and Moan, 1971; Reker, 1974). The more popularity a child enjoys, the more sophisticated and developed are his social concepts used to structure events. Popularity also is positively associated with the tendency of a child to anticipate positive intentions in others; whereas a child's unpopularity is associated both with his perceiving only negative intentions in others (Aydin and Markova, 1979), and with others anticipating the worst in him. The popular child's and the unpopular child's constructions of others delimit what can be perceived. In a sense, a child's reputation sets the stage for either a positive and pleasant cycle in his elaboration of structuring peer interactions or a negative and unpleasant cycle in elaboration of structuring to occur (Dodge, 1980). This limitation as to what the child can make sense out of begins a particular type of elaboration. In effect, this child is not able to perceive, experience, and learn more about people. Rather, he may perceive social events as functionally equivalent Hayden, Nasby, and Davids, 1977). Such a construction system places restraints on what a child could perceive and learn from those around him and the social demands that might arise. Much of the social world simply remains unperceived and inaccessible to the child.

The reviewed research on the child's construction of (social) reality substantially supports the specific assertions proposed in the Modulation Corollary. The child's construction system at any moment allows him access to some events, but not others. His system delimits what is perceived; however, change in his construction of reality can, and does, occur. Changes or variations in construction occur in the four proposed parameters; but there are two considerations about change that are fundamental to the corollary: First, changes (an increase and/or a decrease in one or more of the four parameters of change) occur within the context of some existing framework of the child's system and thereupon order is given to the change. Since the child originally created the forms that were the building blocks of his system, he can reinvent them. The opportunities for any change are determined not by desire alone to change, but by the nature (structural characteristic) of the construction system. Second, the child's system may become more expansive or more restrictive in the perspective it affords him. In either case, the change in his system depends on the opportunities the system makes accessible to the construing child, the frequencies with which such opportunities occur, and how he uses his system to structure experience. Change does not necessarily ensure a more rich and varied view of reality. Rather, the system allows the child to create some degree of orchestrated sense. Once the sense is created, does this mean that the process of creating an increasingly complex representation of reality, as evidenced so clearly in the child, ceases at some point? If change does occur in the construction of reality, then there are limits to the possible change. Moreover, the variations in construction create different effects within differently organized hierarchic systems. Sometimes the change would be subtle; sometimes the change would be dramatic. The following section offers some considerations about modulated variations in the adult's construction of reality.

CONSTRUCTING AND RECONSTRUCTING: THE ADULT

Some of the research on the four parameters of change occurring in an adult's construction system will be reviewed briefly. In doing so the review exemplifies how the nature of the adult's system makes him something of a victim of his previously created order and meaning. Also, the review delineates the ways in which the system necessarily limits the adult's attempts to reconstruct the system by which he experiences reality.

When the adult encounters new information or new events, his construction system allows him a particular way to structure the material or, alternatively, parts of his system can adjust or modulate to embrace such material. In the latter situation variations in construction are evidenced. For instance, investigations have shown that increased exposure to new information does indeed result in an increase in discrimination capacity of an adult's system (Scott, Osgood, and Peterson, 1979); in increased differentiation (Delia and O'Keefe, 1976) or "object complexity" (Scott, Osgood, and Peterson, 1979) of the construction system organizing the new material; and in increased "integration" or interconnectedness (seven studies in Adams-Webber, 1979) among the constructs used to organize and experience the events, as indicated by increased interconnectedness (increased cognitive simplicity/principal components analysis/intensity) in these studies.

These three variations (construct application, differentiation, and interconnectedness), however, can occur only when some degree of hierarchic organization allows these variations to be embraced. That is, change occurs only within the context of hierarchic organization. At the same time, the more meaningful or superordinate a construct, the more inferential links it has with various constructs within the entire system. In a system with relatively superordinate constructs, any change would cause an effect throughout much of the hierarchic system. A system with comparatively much less meaningful or superordinate constructs would allow for more changes (less of a ripple effect), as long as the change could be subsumed by its existing relatively superordinate constructs. For instance, Hinkle (1965) showed that when a perceiver's interpretation changed, it was a result of a change on subordinate constructs. The more superordinate is the construct, the less likely is the person to change how he uses it. Crockett and Meisel (1974) investigated the effect of varying degrees of disconfirmation in terms of whether a perceiver's hierarchic organization related to changes in his interpretation of events. They found that subjects with more hierarchically organized systems changed how they structured experience only in response to strong disconfirmation of their predictions. Only marginal changes occurred in response to slight invalidation of their predictions. Subjects possessing less hierarchically organized systems made dramatic changes in the ways in which they structured events, but in neither case were the changes in construction on the most central or superordinate constructs in the respective systems. That is, any change in how the person structured his experience was embraced or subsumed by existing relatively more central or superordinate constructs. This appeared to be achieved by means of his bringing to bear his more superordinate ("central") constructs to integrate information (Scott, Osgood, and Peterson, 1979). Moreover, Scott and his colleagues found that these superordinate constructs also possess fine discrimination capacity. That is, the superordinate constructs are used by a person to make fine discriminations among the events that can be embraced. The subject with such constructs tends to be more successful in integrating material than is the subject with less superordinate constructs (which also have less discrimination capacity). Moreover, contradictory information is resolved, or construed, by interpreting the information with a more superordinate ("more salient") construct (Delia, Gonyea, and Crockett, 1971; Little, 1972).

The more superordinate constructs allow the perceiver to "go beyond" the contradictions perceived and structured by the less superordinate constructs. He restructures and integrates the material with his more abstract and permeable superimposed forms. In effect, the person with relatively greater hierarchic organization possesses, by definition, more permeable constructs (more implications, more meaning, more abstract) and thereby permits the perceiver to modulate how these permeable constructs now are used to give order to and make sense of events. The less superordinate constructs used to structure those events are embraced by the more superordinate constructs and so subsume the invalidation or cognitive anxiety created by previously structuring the event by means of a less "permeable" construct. In the same way, variations in structuring are embraced by an existing relatively more superordinate construct. That is, the availability of such superordinate or permeable constructs ensures the greater possibility of new ways to structure events (construct application), of abstracting new constructs (differentiation), and of extracting new correlations among existing constructs (both facets of integration).

The previous discussion of the ways in which a child's system delimits his use of potentially available information pertains in parallel fashion to the adult's system. Although the adult's system may be rich in available constructs, the system necessarily may delimit that to which the adult has access. A few examples from the research literature can clarify this point: how failure to elaborate or some types of elaboration restrict his ability to perceive some things; how invalidation leads to a variation that delimits what can be perceived, and how the system prevents variation.

Perhaps it is recalled that the young child initially structures experience about himself and others by way of organizing all events by means of the same poles of each of his constructs. Consequently, this view limits him to an ego-centric perspective. Were an adult to so structure his world, then his construction of reality would provide a rather limited perspective. Indeed, that seems to be the case for an adult. Widom (1976), for instance, found that adult psychopaths in their efforts to perceive and structure events, unlike other adult psychiatric patients and normals, did so by structuring events exclusively with the same pole of every construct. As noted in earlier studies, lopsided construct application is associated with the perceiver's structuring the experience of another person in the same way as himself. Hence, the psychopath failed to anticipate how another person views the world. Or as Widom (1976) found, the psychopath simply thought that how someone else perceived and thought about the world was just as he thought. In other words, anyone, whether young child or adult, who relies on structuring the experience of self and other on the same pole of his variously used constructs (lopsidedness) is unable to "decenter" or imagine that the experiences of others may differ from those of his own. In effect the experience of the world is one wherein meaning or implications exist within a limited range compared to adults who elaborate both poles of a construct. The rigid reliance of one orchestrated sense imposed on experience prevents recognition of most types of invalidation of his social reality: It is simply beyond the scope of his created order to comprehend someone saying to him, "but that is *not* how I feel!" The elaborated system of the psychopath, then, does not allow for such an invalidation. The psychopath, in fact, is notorious for his relative absence of experiencing anxiety.

While the psychopath's way of perceiving social reality excludes perceiving another's perspective, his system nevertheless has been elaborated in other ways. His various constructs are just as interrelated (interconnectedness) as are other adults' construction systems. In other words, the psychopath's system allowed one variation or elaboration (interconnectedness) to occur, but not one that would have allowed for the elaboration in predicting another person's perspective. The resulting limitation in elaboration of the alternative pole on his many social constructs provides the psychopath with only one view. It may come as no surprise, then, that the psychopath's failure to elaborate one facet of his system provides a view of life that is "drab," "dull," and "unexciting" (Widom, 1976).

Modification or variation, due to some degree of invalidation of the perceiver's system, is typical if the perceiver is to achieve any degree of greater predictive efficacy in how he organized his experience of the environment. A person can structure events by way of either pole of his construct, although persons tend to locate more events at the positive poles (Adams-Webber, 1979). Although the existing construct does not restrict the perceiver to only one perspective, the more extensively used positive pole does ensure the present structuring of events along similar lines as the past. To this extent, the adult is a victim of his past perceptions. Mischel and his colleagues extensively reviewed research documenting that a person's past success (presumably as interpreted by means of several positive poles of several existing constructs) results in: his perceiving more often information available in a situation that pertains to his positive features, his doing more frequent benign acts, and his performing generally more frequent helpful acts toward others (Mischel, Ebbesson, and Zeiss, 1973). This represents what these authors called a "warm glow" effect. In light of this effect, the content of constructs may indicate what specifically the context of the "glow" is. The content analyses of social constructs yield several major factors: competency, intimacy, and sociability (Wish, Deutsch, and Kaplan, 1976; Rosenberg, 1977; Kim and Rosenberg, 1980). In other words, a person's constructs allow him to perceive things in terms of competency, intimacy, and sociability. A person's more frequent use of the positive pole on such constructs may well facilitate anticipating, thinking, and remembering things relating to his competency, likability, acts of sociability, and closeness to others. In effect, the range of convenience and permeability of these constructs consequently increase relative to other, less elaborated constructs. There is a perpetuation of the "warm glow" as the perceiver relies on the particular cluster of constructs to interpret his experience of self. The extensive use of and elaboration of the positive poles on his constructs allows the individual to perceive only the positive and competent quality of his actions. Nevertheless, the extensive elaboration of positive poles introduces a bias in the person's structure of experience. In a complex study in which self-ratings and judges' ratings of adults were compared, it was found that adults perceive themselves as significantly more positive than they were perceived by the judges (Lewinsohn, Mischel, Chaplin, and Barton, 1980). In other words, the vestiges of our past construction of self may be biased. The child's development of an increasingly more elaborate and more workable representation of reality may provide the adult with a conceptually tight but biased view of self.

So a construction pattern may not effectively interpret every aspect of reality. Eventually, some strong invalidation may occur in the perceiver. Consequently, he must modify how he applies his constructs to make sense of his experience of himself, but the modification occurs only in the context of the entire comprehensive system. In other words, the variation now creates a different affect within such a differently organized system. For instance, a person may attempt to reinterpret an event following invalidation by engaging in slot change (from positive to negative pole) on many constructs. In so doing, the person begins to elaborate and perceive only negative events (Sperlinger, 1976; Space and Cromwell, 1980). Indeed, the depressed patients' persistent elaboration of the negative pole on self-relevant constructs presumably increases the likelihood of their anticipating, thinking, and remembering feeling isolated, incompetent, and helpless. In fact, the depressed person attends to and recalls negative features about himself more often than he does positive self-features (Lewinsohn et al., 1980).

Invalidation of the perceiver's constructs often results in dramatic alterations or "loosening" among construct linkages (Higgins and Schwartz, 1978). In other words, interconnectedness may decrease. The resulting "loosening" of linkages allows the perceiver to organize things differently although with the same constructs. This type of variation in construction also allows the perceiver to generate different "meanings" from newly abstracted or already existing constructs and correlations among these constructs (Rehm, 1971). For instance, the perceiver can elaborate the network of "meaning" of such things as "verbal fluency," which, in turn, permits him to perceive and interpret what he had failed to structure: his own fluency (Fransella, 1972).

As the Modulation Corollary asserts, there are limits to these variations in construction. The very nature of the system prevents the construer to construe a change. For instance, the perceiver can not radically change his most superordinate constructs. In a study on the notion of self, Hayden (1979) reported that a person's willingness to make a variation (slot change) in the construction system by changing on one construct (ideal self pole-self pole) to a desired or ideal view of self was a function of the meaningfulness (number of implications) of that view of the pole. If the ideal view possessed greater meaning or more implications than did the present view of self, then the subject was willing to shift to the desired view of self. That is, the desired view of self was more permeable and thus could embrace the change. Apparently, he is willing and able (because of the meaningfulness of one pole) to change his view when the change is toward greater meaningfulness. Very often, in fact, the person knows how he would like to perceive his actions and thoughts, but the relative paucity of meaning possessed by that vantage point prevents a variation in his interpretation. In other words, the desired view is not sufficiently permeable within the existing system. The subject unable to change from his current view to his ideal view of self tended to have a less flexible or permeable construction system than did a subject able to change from the present self view to the desired view of self. Consequently, the subject possessing constructs with relatively less permeability must limit his construction process and cannot shift to the desired, but less meaningful, view of self.

The research on the adult's construction of reality demonstrates that the system that provided him with a way to give order and meaning to reality can be changed. As was the case with a child's construction of reality, these changes can occur in each of the four proposed parameters. Yet any variation in construction is affected by past interpretations. Change in the construction of a future event occurs within the context of the superimposed forms that gave meaning to his past experiences. His hierarchic system provides the context within which he can structure variations in construction. Such an organized system permits him to elaborate and thereby increase the network of implications or meaningfulness in his interpretations. Therefore, changes have differing effects on the integrity of the hierarchic system. A psychopath's construction of reality provides him with a "drab" perspective. Any change toward perceiving the possible "exciting" varieties of reciprocity in human relationships would jeopardize the integrity of his slowly built-up view of reality. In effect, there would be a loss in the degree of meaningfulness in the current view of social reality presently provided by his created construction. Nevertheless, other types of elaborations in his system could occur, giving him access to other aspects of reality and freeing him from his past constructions. Increased elaboration in some part of a construction system is no safeguard against further instances of invalidation of his interpretations or predictions. Indeed, elaboration of a system, as demonstrated in the above-cited research, allows vestiges of interpretations to enslave the perceiver further into, for example, an overly optimistic or overly despairing view of self. Either view necessarily delimits relative to some aspects of events what his system can allow him to interpret effectively. The perceiver elaborates what his already permeable constructs permit. It is the relative superordinancy of constructs in each component of his system that delimits the possibility and extent of change or variation in construction. For instance, one poignant restraint afforded by the construction of self is in a person's strivings to reach his self-defined ideal. That sought-after dream, constrained from access to the person's self-defining construct system, simply remains an old dream repeated in the future. In other words, his construction of self is used to structure and predict what is; his ideal view exists to structure what might be. A person's present construction of himself, however, does provide him access to that dream becoming a reality: His construction system did structure his dream.

CONCLUSION

The empirical research on the individual's construction of reality adds solid credence to what the Modulation Corollary implies: a person's construction of reality simultaneously sets the limits of both his freedom to create his uniquely orchestrated perspective and his bondage to his hierarchic system. His hierarchic system, in one sense, enslaves him to a set of his own constructed superordinate constructs. The superordinate and permeable constructs provide the restraining context within which modulations can be construed and, thus, occur. The perceiver, however, has the chance to change his construction of reality. While vestiges of the past constructions may partake in the anticipation of the future, the same constructs that appear to enslave him are the means by which he can reinvent his view of reality. Every variation in construction enjoys its existence by virtue of the permeability of some construct within his hierarchic system.

The significance of the findings and points that the reviewed research has documented about the types of changes and the conditions under which change in construction occur will depend, ultimately, on the careful charting of the child's and adult's future construction of some aspect of reality in terms of the simultaneous variations in their respective hierarchic system. The four parameters of change, as derived from research on schemata construction and the theory of personal constructs, indicate the complexity of the process of variation in a person's structuring of events. Unlike the research reviewed, the four parameters of change need to be assessed concurrently. After all, it is the nature of the hierarchic system that both determines the variation that can be entertained and the variation's relative success in providing comparable meaning to the newly structured experience. A person's construction system can be analyzed as he modulates and adjusts his application of constructs, the degree of differentiation (as assessed by Crockett's measure), the extent of interconnectedness (assessed by "intensity" or the measure derived from principal components analysis), and the degree of hierarchic organization (as assessed by the implication or bipolar Implications Grid) in the various components of his system as he structures the experience of new information, whether it is invalidated or validated.

Clearly the uniqueness of the construction process and the nature of the construction system stress the need for both an idiographic research approach and a constructivistic view of man's processing, organizing, evaluating, storing, and recalling of information. The approach and view invite and, indeed, require a link to be forged among cognition, memory, and the theory of personal constructs. In effect, what is required is an integration of the available research strategies from each of these areas in order to assess validly a person's idiosyncratic construction and reconstruction process.

The process of constructing and reconstructing reality as evidenced by child or adult appears to be parallel. Moreover, the normal and emotionally disturbed child's or adult's often confusing or even startling ways of interpreting and construing events may well be explained by reference to the similar ways people organize and structure events into their unique experiences and how that organization changes.

Variations in a person's construction of reality could be viewed as ubiquitous, yet they are limited by the permeability of constructs within the construction system. The structural characteristic of the construction system specifies the likelihood and type of change possible; therein the mystery in the process of change is removed. In doing so, the Modulation Corollary has most sharply defined the person as being free to construe and, yet, as being a victim of his constructions.

11

A CONSTRUCTION OF FRAGMENTATION AND UNITY: THE FRAGMENTATION COROLLARY

A. W. Landfield

The Fragmentation Corollary: A person may successively employ a variety of construction subsystems which are inferentially incompatible with each other.

What do you experience when confronted with the term *fragmentation*? Do you visualize a thin stemmed wine glass shattering on the patio deck? Do you see the blurring of crazy shapes and colors in the kaleidoscope? Do you remember the ambivalent cry of the unhappy child, "I don't care!" Have you experienced the unpredictability of your neighbor as he fails to return your greeting? Have you wondered how your colleague could know so much psychology yet make such a mess of his life? As a researcher, have you felt the pain of invalidation when confronted with the unexpected result? Have you encountered the bizarreness of a thought-disordered schizophrenic, the varied selves of the multiple personality, or the complained-about confusions of the psychotherapy client?

Have you observed the grin of ambivalence when a dependent person tells you he really wants to be more independent? Have you known the incongruous pairing of a smile with a profound statement of tragedy? How do you approach life and death? Do you understand them both as part of life? Conversely, do you separate them by the feeling that death is the supreme indignity to all creatures? Or, do you simply avoid thinking about this dichotomy of existence? Finally, how often have you felt the guilty sensation of your own inconsistency?

If these examples of fragmentation seem too vapid, you may resonate with the feelings of a distinguished anthropologist, Loren Eiseley (1971, pp. 193, 194):

> When I was a small boy I lived, more than most children, in two worlds. One was dark, hidden, and self-examining. . . . The other world . . . was external, boisterous, and what I suppose the average parent would call normal or extroverted.
>
> How I managed to exist in both I do not know. Children under such disharmony often grow sick, retire inward, choose to return to the void. . . . Yet the curious thing is that I survived and, looking back, I have a growing feeling that the experience was good for me.

If you cannot share in any of the above experiences, there certainly must be a host of other fragmenting possibilities that will be appropriate for your own life. Fragmentation of one kind or another seems as ubiquitous as order and unity. That this should be the case makes good sense within George Kelly's (1955) *The Psychology of Personal Constructs*. After all, how could one deeply sense unity without some reference base in fragmentation? Conversely, how could one profoundly experience fragmentation in the absence of a contrasting feeling for and understanding of unity? To comprehend fragmentation or unity, without even an implicit contrast, seems about as logical as contending that one can know night without day or life without death.

The remainder of this chapter is devoted to a limited, but possibly fruitful, theoretical thrust into the heart of a profound issue, one that psychologists find troublesome: how human beings create order from disorder, organization from confusion, harmony from conflict, single-mindedness from ambivalence, clarity from ambiguity, certainty from uncertainty, simplicity from complexity, and a sense of stability in a sea of change. Reversing the order of these events, we also have an interest in how human beings may create confusion from organization, and ambivalence from single-mindedness.

Since certain organizational terms will be used frequently throughout this chapter, a few definitions are in order. First of all, *fragmentation* will be defined by inferential incompatibility. *Integration* and *unity* will refer to the grouping of events on the basis of similarity and relationship. *Generalization*, although a type of integration, will be restricted to the perception of similarity and relationship over time. *Differentiation* will be understood within the contexts of contrast and oppositionality. Finally, contrasts and oppositionalities may sometimes be experienced by the person or an external observer as instances of inferential incompatibility and fragmentation.

A PERSONAL CONSTRUCT PERSPECTIVE

It was stated in the introduction that the focus of this chapter would be the issue of fragmentation-unity. Yet I was originally given the task of writing on Kelly's Fragmentation Corollary. Of course, the necessity of also writing about unity is built into Kelly's Dichotomy Corollary, which states that important understanding must involve contrast. Thus, there was no way of ignoring the Organization Corollary. Moreover, since construct theory functions as a whole, references to other theoretical statements began to intrude upon my writing. Finally, the decision was made to seek a better understanding of fragmentation-unity within many contexts of the theory, including references to constructive alternativism; the personal construct; the Dichotomy, Choice, Organization, Modulation, and Fragmentation Corollaries; and to such ideas as threat, organizational level, and the Rep Test. As a consequence, this chapter may be construed as a demonstration of how a variety of statements from personal construct theory have implications for understanding the contexts of fragmentation-unity and consistency-inconsistency.

CONSTRUCTIVE ALTERNATIVISM

Kelly first approached the question of personal meaning and its modification through his discussion of constructive alternativism, a philosophical position in which he assumed that whatever can be construed may be reconstrued. Rephrased, the world is open to interpretive revision if people are sufficiently venturesome. Thus, Kelly gave us the potential for change and defined the essence of life as interpretation and reinterpretation. As a consequence of this position, any attempt to comprehend human organization and disorganization would have to focus on the contexts, structures, and changes in personal interpretation. Even science would have to be seen as personal interpretation.

By stating that persons interpret their worlds, Kelly did not imply that there is no world other than interpretation. He did say that we slowly approximate reality through the process of interpretation and reinterpretation. This process of approximating reality was linked to anticipation. It is through the validation and invalidation of our anticipatory interpretations that we may better approximate reality. Moreover, he suggested that the world is of such a complexity and changeability that humans will not exhaust all possible alternatives for new interpretations in their lifetimes, or, for that matter, possibly in any lifetime.

These statements about constructive alternativism suggest both the hope of change and the great complexity of the process. That Kelly did hope for constructive change was most strongly brought forth in a manuscript entitled "Social Inheritance," a paper recently published by Stringer and Bannister (1979). In this paper, written while he was a student at the University of Edinburgh, Kelly took sharp dialectical aim at the elitist position of Cyril Burtt on the nature of intelligence. Perhaps Kelly's later conception of constructive alternativism was incubated at that time.

Returning to the theme of fragmentation-unity, the complexity of life suggested by constructive alternativism does imply that life fragmentation and confusion is inevitable for most of us. Also, the notion of successive approximations of reality suggests that we must constantly reach out for better understanding, the impetus provided by invalidational experiences associated with conflict and confusion, as well as new events that have never been experienced. Then, to emphasize the complexity of this "reaching out" for better understanding, Kelly stated that change can be dangerous. In sharp contrast to the potential for change seen in constructive alternativism, he spelled out the risk of change in his definition of threat as an awareness (at some level) of an imminent, comprehensive change in core structure. In other words, an anticipation of some fundamental change in ourselves, for good or bad, can be threatening. Thus, on the one hand, Kelly asserted the hope, the potential, and even the inevitability of change, but, on the other hand, suggested that human beings may try to avoid change with its inevitable uncertainties, doubts, and guilts. However, Kelly did not leave us completely without hope of resolving this conflict about change. He stated in his Modulation Corollary that certain superordinate structures of greater permeability might allow for some change and variation in our personal construct systems. As an example of a more permeable structure, he stated that a personal construction of change might facilitate change. More will be said about this later.

ORGANIZATION AND THE PERSONAL CONSTRUCT

The personal construct, described as a dimension of personal awareness, incorporated the idea of different levels of conscious awareness as well as the critical component of all dimensions — contrast. The "verbalized" construct used in Kelly's Rep Test procedures was formed by asking a person how two particular things are similar and different from a third. What distinguished Kelly's procedure from a typical concept formation task was the requirement that the person state a contrast. Thus, meaning is conveyed by more than what is similar. What is excluded from the grouping tells us as much about the concept as what is included. This can be readily illustrated by two persons, one of whom contrasted "liveliness" with "exhaustion," whereas the other person contrasted "liveliness" with "suicide." Clearly, the implications of liveliness are different for these two persons.

Now the structure of the personal construct ties together beautifully the concepts of integration and differentiation. It also provides a framework for the process of generalization, since personal constructs are employed in the anticipation of future events. Thus, the single personal construct, simple as it may seem, integrates three different themes of conceptual organization.

Moreover, the single personal construct also may even yield measures of fragmentation and excessively tight unity. Recently, Leitner (1980), working from a theory of literalism (Landfield, 1980), subdivided the personal construct into three component parts of feeling, valuing, and behaving. He then hypothesized that persons, who either "tightly" relate these components *or* "fragment" them by treating them as unrelated, will experience major problems in living. To illustrate this hypothesis, imagine the construct of friendship versus lack of friendship. Define the valued pole, friendship, by the components of (1A) I *feel* warmly toward people; (2A) I *value* intimate personal relating; and (3A) I *behave* toward others with interest, acceptance, and kindness. Define the contrast pole by the components of (1B) I feel cold and hating; (2B) I want to live at a distance from others because others are not worth it; and (3B) I actively avoid or hurt others.

Focus now on 1B, 2B, and 3B. Imagine what happens when these statements are linked together in an absolute, literal way. There is no distinction between any of them. Do you see how a momentary feeling of hating might trigger excessive guilt and an unreasoned acting out of hostility? Do you see how a momentary slippage into hostile behavior could trigger the notion that one's values have been lost? Conversely, imagine what happens when these statements are treated as though they are literally unrelated. Can you envision the chaos? Thus, we see how an excessive employment of tight unities or loose fragments can create problems of severe maladjustment.

ORGANIZATION AND CHOICE

Processes of differentiation and integration also are evident in the Choice Corollary in which "a person chooses for himself that alternative in a dichotomized construct through which he anticipates the greater possibility for extension and definition of his system" (Kelly, 1955, p. 64). This statement implies that the person chooses in the direction of unity, but a unity that can be elaborated through finer discriminations (differentiation) and future usefulness (generalization). Thus, we see the functions of integration, differentiation, and generalization in the process of unitary choice.

However, as we study the Choice Corollary, the nature of the personal construct should not be forgotten. In particular, one is reminded that the personal construct is defined importantly by contrast. This being the case, one must consider the contrast to the elaborating choice. At the same time, it must be recognized that elaborating choice may involve individuation or the development of different dimensions within the unitary choice. Thus, one may refer to contrasts of individuation within elaborating choice as well as contrasts between the pole of choice and its alternative. In other words, there may be contrasts *within* unity and contrasts *to* unity of choice. This may be illustrated.

Sally, a minister's daughter, employed the construct loyal versus disloyal. To show loyalty meant that one "does not displease persons whom you know well and like." Disloyalty meant that one displeases them. The loyalty pole was further differentiated. First, there is loyalty related to "flesh and blood," for example, parents. Such loyalty does not have to be earned. It is owed to one's parents. Loyalty that is "owed" was contrasted with loyalty to friends, husband, and others, who "earn" it. This contrast of loyalty owed versus loyalty earned was a positively construed dimension. There was no distinction between one pole being better than the other. They were just different. Then there was a second dimension of loyalty best described as in-sight, in-mind versus out-of-sight, out-of-mind. This dimension was critically applied to her husband in the sense that when he was out of Sally's sight, he was also out of mind. Moreover, there was no question of disloyalty when he was out of sight. And, as you correctly guessed, Sally was having an affair. However, she was becoming worried that she might "accidentally" be found out. She forcefully justified her affair by stating, "I am always home when my husband needs me." In other words, when he is in-sight, he is in-mind, and I am loyal to him. The solution that she was so desperately seeking was to find a way of successfully communicating her position to him. If he could understand, then she would not have to worry about being accidentally found out and "kicked out of the house."

This illustration not only emphasizes two kinds of contrast (that is, within a choice pole, and between a pole of choice and its alternative), but it also raises the question of "whose fragmentation?" Sally's conflict was "How can Harry, my husband, be such an intelligent and nice man, yet be so narrow minded about sexual matters?" The therapist's first thought was encompassed by two questions: "How can she be so blind to Harry's feelings? How can a person, brought up within a strict religious context, be so devoid of empathy for conventional modes of feeling?" Thus, as one can plainly see, Sally's experience of fragmentation was quite different from that of the therapist. Moreover, there was no easy way for either therapy participant to reconcile the two views. Sally did resolve her problem, at least for the moment, by elaborating her conception of Harry's strong feelings and by focusing on the reasons she married him. Although not understanding the basis for Harry's feelings, she decided to "cool" the affair. After all, she did like her husband better than the lover. Besides, she was getting bored with her lover's poetry.

Reflecting on this illustration, we see clearly how personal construing and choice can be most idiosyncratic. Also apparent is the difference between objective and subjective judging of what is fragmented, that is, inferentially incompatible. Whereas the therapist had no difficulty understanding Sally's husband, Sally could not understand how Harry could be such a nice guy, yet be so narrow minded. Then we see conflict resolution by means of superordinating the construct, Harry the nice guy over Harry the narrow guy in sexual matters. Likewise, she subordinated Sally's sexual freedom to constructs of relationship with Harry. Finally it was seen that the poles of constructs gathered under Sally's unitary choice of loyalty were more positively valenced than the contrast to her choice, that is, disloyalty. This positive and negative valuing of personal construct poles will be considered in the following section on value construction. In this regard, we next will apply the idea of fragmentation within the context of value preference and ambivalence about one's values.

CHOICE, THREAT, AND A PSYCHOLOGY OF VALUES

Using Sally's constructions as a base for our speculation, together with many experiences using the Rep Test, it is hypothesized that the pole of choice, at the moment of choice, tends to be positively valenced for the person, or, at least, more positively valenced than its contrast. Further, it is understood that a person may choose one pole of his construct within one context, then reverse his choice within a different context. Such reversals of choice and possibly even polar valence can be defined as fragmentation when such reversals are sudden and unpredictable to the person. An illustration may help in understanding the unexpected and fragmenting reversal of value choice.

It is not uncommon in therapy for an "improved" client to suddenly regress. There is the case of Henry who went to bed with another man at the point that he was beginning to experience sexual feelings for his female secretary. This client was highly motivated to change his homosexual behavior because he was out-of-phase. This engineering construct, in-phase versus out-of-phase, was a superordinate construction for him, but one that he had only recently begun to apply to himself. He was beginning to explore his life within the new construct. However, it was not easy to try out a new way of living. This was shown early in therapy by a momentary "fugue state" experience in which he lost track of his office building. The magnitude of his struggle was also shown later when he reverted to his older homosexual ways at a critical moment of anticipated change. Although being in "heterosexual phase" was highly valued, he nevertheless did regress to older values.

In order to comprehend this sudden reversal in construct behavior and possibly value, it must be recognized that Henry had found an active homosexual adjustment very meaningful in his life. He had elaborated it in a variety of ways. When he was confronted with new feelings, heterosexual ones, he was frightened of the very thing that, in theory, he wanted. That he did not know how to cope with the new feelings is exemplified by a dream, in his case a nightmare, about his secretary. He dreamed that he grabbed her by the hair and dragged her, kicking and screaming, to his cave. This dream and his short-term reversion to homosexual behavior came at the critical moment of asking his secretary for a date. He had carefully rehearsed the request for a date, then backed away from the experience. At this critical moment of decision, he envisioned failure and panicked. He did choose in the direction of the greater elaboration and definition of his system. For the moment, the security of tangible, experienced, and elaborated meaning overshadowed his more obscure and theoretical wish to be in phase.

After this regressive episode was interpreted to him within the context of threat (that is, the awareness of an imminent, comprehensive change in core structure), Henry began clumsily and fearfully to explore heterosexuality. He did ask his secretary for a date, and heterosexuality became easier as he experienced enlarged possibilities for himself when "in phase." Although his initial commitment to therapy had been strong, it was necessary for him to experience some elaboration in the heterosexual role before he could consistently choose that which he was determined to accomplish.

This illustration points up several issues. First of all, one must differentiate between established and elaborated values and those that have more recently arrived on the scene. In this latter instance, that which is more ideally preferred may take second place to that which is so well known. Thus, in any study of values, the investigator must be most careful in differentiating between values that have been highly elaborated and those that are inexperienced. Moreover, investigators concerned about the effects of "social desirability" would be encouraged to note the extent to which a "socially desirable" value has been elaborated. Highly experienced values, socially desirable or not, must be taken seriously.

This example also underlines the importance of threat in imminent, comprehensive change. Defining something as desirable does not necessarily mean that the person will easily choose in the direction of that value. After all, the person will be leaving well-trod ground for that which is unknown. Thus, the stretching out for new values may be a greater threat than remaining with past values and the known. Any psychology of valuing and value conflict must consider the threat of change and the extensive elaboration of older values.

CONSTRUCTS AND VALUE CODING

Continuing with the theme of valuing, it is hypothesized that social construction is heavily laden with value. My experience with Rep Tests, in which subjects value code the poles of their own construct dimensions, indicates that personal constructs can be readily coded for value. However, some constructs are not value codable. For example, one person did not value code the construct of introversion versus extroversion because it had no value other than as behavioral description. Nevertheless, the Rep Test tends to pick up the concerns of people, and areas of concern have important implications for how one values.

Of course, there are instances in which persons may deny any value, positive or negative, to construct poles that would seem to be of real value for them. Here we encounter another form of fragmentation, first seen by the psychotherapist and only later understood by his client. Three illustrations now will be used to demonstrate the functional significance of value denial.

First, there is Hank who used the construct intelligent versus dumb seven times on his Rep Test. When asked to rate himself, he stated that this dimension did not apply to himself. However, he had no difficulty in applying it to others. Hank's presenting problem was that he was having continual nightmares in which he was destroyed in a fatal accident. If you are a clinician, you have already predicted that therapy eventually focused on Hank's perception of himself as dumb, which included making mistakes to the degree of causing his own death. Therapy helped Hank reconstrue his life, and the construct of intelligence was reinterpreted in his repertoire of values.

Our second example focuses on Bill, who declined to value code his constructs of person perception. Why Bill declined to value code makes sense when you know that he is crippled. The implications of his own problems were so stressful that he actively avoided thinking about the "goods" and the "bads" of life. This kind of fragmentation might be called defensive behavior; however, within construct theory, one may speak of constricting his focus. Kelly defined constriction as a narrowing of the perceptual field in order to minimize apparent incompatibilities. In this case, Bill warded off an invalidation of his life. Within this reduced range of valuing, he could maintain his existence. He did not want to cope with how others valued him or with how he valued himself. Robots don't have values, and his life was a bit like that of a robot, but he did survive.

In the first two examples of value denial, one person refused to value code himself, and the other person failed to code his constructs for value. In the third example, a young psychotherapy client switches her focus from one pole of an important personal construct to another. In doing so, she completely reverses her previous value codings.

Ann is a severely disturbed woman. Her symptoms include withdrawal, hyperventilation, fits of screaming, the throwing of pots and pans at her husband, and periodic hallucinations. In regard to hallucination, she sometimes would see hair growing from the eggs she was frying. As one might expect, the early phases of therapy were like a fast ride on a yo-yo. At least this was the fragmenting experience of the therapist. One moment Ann would talk about the importance of being independent and her fear of trying; the next moment she would deny any value in independence. At one point she linked independence with her parents' boredom, fatigue, and unhappiness. Thus, what she had just said about the value of independence was completely contradicted. Ann did not seem to recognize these reversals. She was in dire conflict, but avoided confronting it by her all-or-none reversals of construct pole value.

In concluding this section, it should be pointed out that value coding is most highly visible on constructs that are self-derived, that is, where the person has been asked to characterize himself rather than others. One reason for this may be that people are less likely to use "peripheral" constructs in describing themselves.

CHOICE, THREAT, GUILT, AND PSYCHOTHERAPY

The concept of threat, introduced in a previous section, will be joined with a companion called guilt. Whereas threat can be applied to self-dislodgment from core role that *might* occur, guilt emphasizes self dislodgment that *has* occurred. It takes only one logical step from these definitions to hypothesize that a little,

actual self-dislodgment (guilt) might trigger the awesome possibility or anticipation of greater self-dislodgments in the future (threat). It is conceivable that
this hypothesis may explain why some persons overreact to guilts that are insig-
nificant and even ridiculous to the objective observer. These persons are experiencing threat as well as guilt. They are experiencing the larger events yet to
come. This hypothesis about the relationship between threat and guilt was also
observed by Willis (1961) in the context of a formal research investigation.

Careful consideration of the concepts of threat and guilt strongly suggests
that most of us have experienced being dislodged from a core role and also
have experienced the possibility of more comprehensive dislodgment. Such
experiences certainly are highlighted in the contexts of psychotherapy. It is
within the context of psychotherapy that the fragmenting possibilities of threat
and guilt will now be demonstrated. Specifically, this demonstration focuses on
the threatening and guilty choices of Joe, who verbalized his primary personal
construct as helping others versus only helping self.

Joe asked for help because his anger was "getting out of control," implying
both guilt and threat. He told the following story: He had volunteered to do
janitorial service in his church, free of charge. He enjoyed the work and the
opportunity to help, but now his minister wanted him to devote more hours to
this service. He had agreed, then wished he had not done so. He could not afford
the time. Additional service intruded upon other pressing demands. Joe
expressed increasing hostility toward his minister. He was angry because he
enjoyed helping others, but he was being pushed to the point of not helping
at all. He was being taken advantage of. He then elaborated on helping others,
giving numerous instances where he had "gone out of his way" to help friends
and even casual acquaintances. He demonstrated that he was really a helping person.

Now the minister's request can be interpreted as threatening to invalidate
Joe's view of himself as a helper. He did not want to increase his janitorial
efforts, did not want to admit to selfishness, but did begin to wonder whether
he might be better off as a selfish person. It was the minister who had forced
him into this bind. Joe had images of killing him.

After obtaining a clear statement that the "caring value" was of vital or
superordinate importance for him, the therapist asked Joe what he thought
about the following consideration: "If one always helps others and never
requests help for oneself, are you denying others the right to assume the
important helping role?" There was a deathly silence, followed by Joe's statement that "when I was twelve years old I was so strong that I could have taken
your hand in mine and crushed it." After Joe and his therapist had recovered
from this reply, Joe began to seriously wonder why he was the one who always
had to play the helping role.

Ending the story, Joe talked with his minister who gracefully assumed part
of the burden of guilt. Regarding Joe's core construct, he began to define
it differently. Helping others no longer precluded asking others to help him.

Moreover, he began to reconstrue the nature of his construct of independence-dependence. Joe's momentary confusion, brought on by the imminent invalidation of his helping choice, was resolved without his having to relinquish either his construct symbol or his preferred helping role.

In this illustration, Joe acted "as though" he had already made certain choices since his "bad" feelings were literally tied to both bad valuing and bad behavior (see Landfield, 1980). He felt guilty, that is, dislodged from core role structure because of his bad feelings. His feeling of being out of control signified threat or "worse things to come." The possibility that he would really become another kind of person (intense threat) was a responsibility that he attributed to his minister. It was the minister who forced him into his untenable position. Of course, the anger toward his minister only exacerbated his guilt and threat and heightened his experience of role fragmentation. In the context of his struggle to identify himself with either the helping or not-helping role, he sought therapeutic assistance. His solution was found in the redefinition of his core value, a redefinition that allowed him to both help and be helped by others. Previously, helping and being helped were seen as sharply contrasting and incompatible social roles.

This discussion of core valuing leads to the next topic: value hierarchies. In particular, the reader will be introduced to the fragmentation that may be experienced by the researcher as he tries to understand how construct systems can be measured.

SYSTEM HIERARCHY AND PROFESSIONAL FRAGMENTATION

Having made numerous statements about construct theory that carry implications for how persons organize and sometimes fragment their lives, we are ready to consider a corollary that includes organization in its title: "Each person characteristically evolves for his convenience in anticipating events, a construction system embracing ordinal relationships between constructs" (Kelly, 1955, p. 56).

In reading this corollary, the terms *anticipation* and *ordinal* stand out from the sentence. Beginning with anticipation, we are told that organization is "for the sake of" the better anticipation of events. Thus anticipation is given a role that is superordinate to organization and consistency. We do not organize for the sake of being organized or consistent. Organization enables us to better anticipate events, and the process of anticipation enables us to establish better (for us) interpretations of events. Reasoning upward in this manner takes us back to the fundamental issue of meaning and interpretation, which is stressed in the philosophy of constructive alternativism. Essentially, then, the human being is a creature that constructs meaning, a capacity not restricted to the scientist; and meaningful anticipation is an integral part of the constructive enterprise.

Turning now to the word *ordinal*, we are alerted to a primary feature of organization, namely that there is a hierarchic process in which something can be superordinated to something else. This interesting emphasis on super-ordinate-subordinate relating is a mixed blessing because it creates special problems in measurement, that is, fragmenting experiences for the scientist. Briefly stated, sometimes correlational statistics are not optimally useful for determining hierarchic relationships. This is the case because correlational statistics are most usefully applied where two variables are in a mutually influencing relationship (that is, when A changes, B also changes; when B changes, A also changes). However, in the case of hierarchic relating, one may find relationships that are more like one-way streets (that is, A influences B, but B has only a minimal influence on A). If one were to use a Pearsonian coefficient to represent this relationship, one could not expect to find a high relationship. Nevertheless, the relationship in hierarchy might be strong. This point can be demonstrated.

Using a Rep Test Grid procedure (Landfield, 1971), the following constructs, among others, were elicited from a subject: good teacher versus poor teacher; organized versus disorganized; humor versus lack of humor; imaginative versus unimaginative; and warmth of person versus distant. The subject then rated 15 of his acquaintances on 15 of his elicited constructs. Following this procedure, construct interrelationships were determined by the degree of direct or inverse overlaps between the rating patterns of the constructs. Now the curious thing about this analysis was the finding that good teacher versus poor teacher was unrelated to the other dimensions. It did not make sense.

Rather than accepting this lack of relationship as the best interpretation, a version of the Implications Grid was employed. The implications approach was first used by Hinkle (Fransella and Bannister, 1977) to determine relationships in hierarchy. Our particular instructions, differing from Hinkle's, began with placing the contrasting poles of 15 constructs at the ends of 13-point scales with zero mid-points. Scale points were numbered from 1 to 6 on either side of the mid-point. Thirty copies of these 15 scales then were made. Next, each construct pole was recorded at the top of a scale sheet, a procedure similar to that used by Osgood in his Semantic Differential. Finally, the subject responded to the following rating instruction: *"If* a person is described by the term at the top of your sheet, then what other characteristics would you expect to find? Circle one scale point on each of the 15 scales which best describes these other characteristics. If you are uncertain, use the mid-point of the scales."

Following this procedure, construct implications were analyzed by noting the placement of the 5- and 6-point ratings under each construct pole. In other words, greater rating scale polarization was used as a measure of meaningfulness. In this manner, it was possible to check out whether good teacher and poor teacher had any important implications for other constructs, and vice versa. Analysis of this Implications Grid revealed that the construct pole, good teacher, had strong implications for organization, humor, imaginativeness, and warmth.

However, there were no implications from these latter constructs to good teacher. This finding suggests why good teacher was orthogonal to other constructs on the initial Rep Test Grid.

Results of this study with one person, together with other Rep Grid experiences (Landfield, 1977), have interesting implications for future research, not only within construct theory, but also in relation to other work on cognitive structure. Specifically, in regard to studies of cognitive complexity, mostly done outside the framework of personal construct psychology, the mixed findings (professional fragmentations) and lower-order correlations may well be attributable to the presence of unexplored superordinate constructions on the protocols of subjects. For example, there certainly should be a significant difference between person A, with many dimensions of experience (complex) that are hierarchically unrelated, and person B with the same number of different dimensions, all of which are related in hierarchy. Kelly (1955, pp. 155-156) was most clear when he stated, "If a person attempted to use propositional (orthogonal) thinking exclusively, he might have considerable difficulty in coming to any decision as to what the relevant and crucial issues were in any situation."

In regard to construct theory, it seems obvious that we must develop new methodologies that will measure the superordinate-subordinate relations between constructs. It is hoped that these methods will not "just" depend on "insight" into what is related. In traditional Rep Test Grid analyses, no assumption is made that the person has insight into how his constructs will relate to one another. However, this assumption about insight is made when an Implications Grid is employed, the person being asked to state whether some characteristic implies another one.

This "relational" insight also is necessary in other procedures such as laddering, pyramiding, and ranking — methods reported by Fransella and Bannister (1977). Although these methods all have usefulness, one cannot assume that the particular insights of those who take these instructions are valid or useful within all contexts of interpretation. Even as it is important to discover how the person thinks about certain relationships, it must be recognized that construct theory does not assume that the person can verbalize accurately the relatedness among all his dimensions of experience. Dimensions of one's experience or personal constructs can be highly related, yet the person may not be able to articulate this relationship. Most of us who have taken Rep Tests have had the experience of not being able to accurately predict how certain of our dimensions will link together. Perhaps you have made the statement, "I would not have thought that there would be so much relationship, but it could be right. I'm not sure I like the idea, but it gives me something to think about."

The observation that what we expect to be true may not always match what happens on Rep Grid computer printouts should not alarm us. After all, sometimes the computer analysis is incorrect. Of course, sometimes we are incorrect. It is the sorting out of these divergent opinions that can lead to an improvement in our methods as well as challenging new awareness within ourselves. It is only when a measurement is treated literally that we are in trouble. This applies to both the test maker and his client. As long as we hold to hypotheses and interpretations that could change, the instruments of psychological science may improve and the subjects of science may grow into greater and more profound human beings. Fortunately, the nature of personal construct psychology allows the scientist the freedom to listen to both himself and his subjects.

Summarizing this section, the construct theorist and researcher must recognize the limitations of current methods for eliciting constructs in hierarchy. Moreover, there are limitations to the statistics that sometimes are employed with Rep Grids. Then it must be recognized that methods that rely solely on verbal description as a way of eliciting constructs may not exhaust possibilities of construction. Vital, superordinate structures of awareness may lie in other modalities of expression. Neimeyer (in Landfield, 1977, pp. 350-352) elaborated this point as he discussed tacit construing. Neimeyer (1980) then implemented this concern by developing a methodology for construct elicitation that does not depend on verbal articulation. Finally, it should be remembered that construct methodologies may vary in the amount of insight that is required of subjects.

That the personal construct researcher must live with fragmenting limitations of his methods seems obvious. However, the knowledge that methods may not meet one's intended reach will not become too depressing unless one loses hope. Hope provides a permeable structure within which to experience currently perceived and anticipated variations in one's system.

RESOLVING FRAGMENTATION

Having used the term *fragmentation* throughout the previous sections, it is time to introduce Kelly's (1955) Fragmentation Corollary in which he states, "A person may successively employ a variety of construction subsystems that are inferentially incompatible with each other" (p. 83).

This corollary states that a person may behave in ways which are inferentially inconsistent, specifying incompatible subsystems. In using this latter term, Kelly does imply that incompatible subsystems are part of a system; but what kind of system is he talking about? Is he saying that fragments only appear that way; that they actually are integrated at a higher level of theory?

Kelly (1970a, p. 39), in his elaboration of the Organization Corollary, stated that "some private paradoxes can be allowed to stand indefinitely, and, in the face of them, one can remain indecisive or can vacillate between alternative expectations of what the future holds in store for him." Kelly further stated that "we must be careful not to interpret the Modulation Corollary to mean that a construct system has to be logically intact." He then elaborated the idea that irrationality is not always a bad thing: "logic and inference can be as much an obstacle to his ontological ventures as a guide to them" (p. 40).

The above quotations clearly indicate that system does not necessarily refer to tightly or logically organizing ways of construing. Nevertheless, Kelly did want us to remain open to the possibility that seemingly incompatible subsystems might be integrated at some higher level of theory. This point will be elaborated in a discussion of permeable construction and the Modulation Corollary.

Returning to the statement of the Fragmentation Corollary, one should keep in mind that inconsistency also is a matter of interpretation. However, whose interpretation will prevail — the subject's or that of the external observer? Of course, it might be interesting to have both viewpoints, a position that fits with construct theory. After all, subject and observer might learn from each other. Moreover, the framework used by the observer is no more or less a personal construct system than that of his subject.

Beginning with the question of whose interpretation, it is helpful to refer to the case of Sally. As you remember, Sally's initially stated fragmentation was related to how she construed her husband. She did not understand how Harry could be such a nice guy, yet be so narrow-minded in sexual matters: "How can I change Harry so he will be more consistent — a broad-minded, nice guy?" In contrast, the therapist's interpretation of inconsistency focused on Sally's religious background, which should have helped her understand Harry's position. Although Sally did not answer her question about Harry's inconsistency, the therapist did manage to reduce his own fragmentation by creating several integrative interpretations of Sally's inconsistent behavior. He construed the religious orientation of her parents as primarily a matter of status. Her parents modeled the importance of being seen and acting well in public. Further, he construed the parents as most indulgent, allowing Sally to ignore the feelings of other persons, including the feelings of her parents. These constructions by the therapist were not shared openly with Sally. However, Sally and the therapist did focus on Harry's strong feelings. Sally, understanding that Harry would not compromise his stand, struggled with the fragmentation of imagining herself with Harry and without Harry. In this context of struggle, she decided that her liking for and dependency on Harry were more important considerations than her sexual freedom. Thus, she elevated liking and dependency into a superordinate position. At the beginning of therapy, sexual freedom seemed more important than any other construction.

Sally did experience insight in regard to the enhanced importance of liking and dependency. She also experienced a greater sense of unity in life as she focused less on the construct of sexual freedom. At the same time, she still did not have an understanding of Harry's position on sexuality. Perhaps a longer and more intensive treatment could have facilitated an appreciation of Harry's feelings and, of course, an understanding of the therapist's sense of fragmentation.

Further reflecting on the case of Sally, she resolved her sense of fragmentation about Harry's potential reaction through a process of reordering her constructs in hierarchy. This was done without confronting the apparent inconsistency of her behavior (that is, the fragmentation of the external observer).

However, she did experience a personal and emotional fragmentation when she first complained about Harry's inconsistency (that is, Harry the nice guy versus Harry the narrow fellow). Later she wrestled with the construct of living with Harry versus living without Harry. This sharp dialectic within herself resulted in the reordering of her constructs. In the language of the Choice Corollary, Sally chose Harry because she sensed a greater possibility for self-elaboration in relationship with him.

Now Sally's complaint about "the other" person can be contrasted with the initial fragmentation felt by Mark. In this case, Mark experienced a traumatic inconsistency within himself. His story begins in high school where he did brilliantly in math and chemistry. Students called him Mr. Science. Mark won numerous prizes, which led to a coveted scholarship at a prestigious university. During the first semester of his college year, he lived up to expectations by his "number two" standing in his science classes. Unfortunately, his norms were different from that of others. He was "only" number two. People argued with him, pointing to his illogicalness. Mark countered with "you don't understand" and shot himself. This tragic resolution to personal fragmentation points to many aspects of construct theory. First of all, there was guilt. He had fallen out of self role. Next there was threat. If one can fail once, one may fail again. Then there was a semantic problem. He had defined himself in a most simplistic way. Not only was success an absolute affair, but there also was nothing else. He had constricted his life to one dimension, then he had treated it in a most literal way. Mark had no superordinate ways within which he could understand himself within the shifting contexts of his life (see Kelly, 1961; Landfield, 1976).

Although Mark could not live with his inconsistency, most persons do cope, in some fashion, with the inconsistencies of their lives. Some persons behave with greater serenity as they live with their conflicts, mistakes, guilts, and inadequacies. Others attempt to obscure their fragmentations with integrative delusions and repressions or with frantic, distractive activity and unities "of the moment." How we live with our awareness of inconsistency and change, in ways both constructive and defeating, is related to Kelly's (1955) Modulation Corollary: "The variation in a person's construction system is limited by the permeability of the constructs within whose range of convenience the variants lie" (p. 77). In this corollary, Kelly is stating that how one copes with inconsistency and change must often be sought in those more open themes, abstractions, and superordinate aspects of the personal construct system. It is these more permeable structures that hold persons together and facilitate the encompassing of shifting contexts, behavioral change, conflicting experiences, and anticipations of the unknown.

Returning to the case of Sally, she was able to experiment with marital infidelity within the permeable construct of in-sight, in-mind versus out-of-sight, out-of-mind. She then shifted her position by upgrading the more stable yet elaborative construct of relationship with Harry. Eventually, the old construct in-sight versus out-of-sight would have failed in relation to Harry. In contrast to Sally's "reaching out" into the future, Mark was unable to create for himself an integrative life structure. Although there were numerous constructions that would have facilitated his continuing openness for new experience, he chose none of them. For example, tragedy might have been averted if Mark had defined his scientific life by interesting questions more superordinate than his competitive quest for greatness. Although curiosity may "kill the cat," a permeable curiosity could well have saved Mark's life. Of course, if he had defined his ideal as a logical impossibility, then employed it as a guiding star, he might have interpreted second place as a step in the right direction. Then again, he could have multiply defined his life, doing what Kelly called "spreading one's dependencies." He also could have superordinated a permeable "reaching out" for human relationships within his construct repertoire. He also might have construed life as a matter of coping with changing contexts and experiences. Kelly described this latter permeability when he stated that a construction of change may facilitate change. In other words, a superordinate or more general idea and conception of change may facilitate behavioral readjustments. This particular hypothesis was tested by Hass (1974) when he studied the ongoing, sharp, and sometimes bloody infighting within a branch of the Lutheran church. Hass successfully predicted that pastors, open to slow change, would reveal at least one elicited personal construct connoting closedness versus openness to change; whereas pastors of a demonstrated reactionary disposition would not employ dimensions of change.

The Multiple Personality

Anyone attempting to understand fragmentation in personality must confront, at some point, the phenomenon of multiple personality. Unfortunately, those who write novels about multiple personalities sometimes attempt to communicate two questionable messages to the reader. First of all, abrupt and sweeping change in social role is mysterious. Second, such change constitutes a special class of behavior, unrelated to normal personality. Both messages would be questioned by psychotherapists who routinely encounter sudden shifts in the behavior of their clients. Moreover, most of us can recognize instances of personality shift in our acquaintances, and sometimes even in ourselves. How often have you overheard such comments as: "What got into Margaret today?" "Why would he ever say that?" "That's not like Jim at all!" "He seemed like a different person." "I don't understand you at all!"

Understanding multiple personality within construct theory begins with the personal construct. By defining the human being as a system of organized dualities, the possibility of sudden change to the opposite is built into the personality of every human being. Then by understanding that persons may relate and cluster their dimensions of experience and behavior, it is possible to comprehend changes that may sweep across an entire construct system and those that are more limited to certain dimensional clusters. For example, a tightly integrated system of constructs might allow for sudden changes across all of one's dimensions at the same time. Changes that seem more limited in scope may be contained by a particular interrelating dimension (see Levy, 1956). In regard to construct clustering, it should be noted that a cluster may have special relevance for a particular situational context. Thus, one may employ a certain set of limited constructions for one's military role and other sets for "being the life of the party" and behaving as a loving father to one's children. Of course, there may be certain linkages among these more specialized clusters. For example, one's military, party, and fatherly dimensions might be drawn together by the superordinate dimension of commitment.

It seems quite obvious that the investigator will have some difficulties in judging whether a sudden shift in social role is a matter of "slot rattling" (that is, a sudden shift in construct sidedness), a shift in construct cluster focus, or both of these possibilities. The difficulties and complexities in understanding multiple personality are nicely elaborated by Neimeyer and Neimeyer in a recent book chapter (in press). They present the case of Janet, diagnosed as schizophrenic, who fluctuated among three distinct personality patterns. These three role patterns, which she referred to as Angela, Cynthia, and Cyn, were clearly perceived as behavior fragmented from herself. These fragmenting roles were described by Janet's therapist as: highly accusatory and domineering, aloof and condescending, and childlike and fearful.

A truncated Rep Test employed with Janet early in treatment yielded the following contrasting (for her) descriptions of combinations of 10 acquaintances: angry-passive, assertive-rejection, hating women-indifferent, suffered from parents-rejecting parents, powerful-intimidated, sensitive-scared, patriarch-matriarch, accepts anger-controlled by anger, manipulative-subdued, and superior-inferior. Relationships among these dimensions were measured by a grid procedure in which Janet described her ten acquaintances on 13-point scales within her ten elicited personal construct dimensions (Landfield and Barr, 1976). This grid analysis revealed that anger, power, and manipulation were highly related and stood in contrast to the pole passive, intimidated, and subdued.

Focusing on these contrasting poles, one may hypothesize that Janet's change from being highly accusatory and domineering to behaving in a childlike and fearful manner was a shift from one end of her construct cluster to its opposite. However, Janet's role of aloofness and condescension might better relate to the poles of indifference, matriarch, patriarch, and superiority.

That Janet's role and role construct transitions were not tightly controlled within her system can be inferred from her experienced confusion about her role changes, and also from the observation that she center-rated herself on her personal construct scales. In contrast to center-rating herself, she rated others in a more definitive manner, that is, employing the more extreme points on the 13-point scales. As it was pointed out previously, rating scale polarization has been used as a measure of meaningfulness by personal construct researchers. Thus it would seem that Janet's personal scales were meaningfully used, but not with respect to her own self-identity.

Speculating further about the significance of Janet's three fragmenting personalities, it would seem that her role of aloofness and condescension was a way of making sense of her domineering and subdued roles, defined by her related constructs of angry-passive, powerful-intimidated, and manipulative-subdued. Behaving in an aloof and condescending manner would seem to abstract both forcefulness and passivity from these contrasting role clusters. Unfortunately, such a reconciliation of opposite roles could not resolve Janet's problem of social alienation and suggests a further interpretation. Janet's sudden transitions within the role triad of Angela, Cynthia, and Cyn were a desperate experimentation with different social role alternatives.

In regard to this hypothesis about social role experimentation, it is interesting to note that Janet's therapist perceived her sudden shifts in role as only minimally related to changing external situational demands and expectancies. These role shifts were better interpreted as desperate and continuing attempts at self-expresison, all of which seemed unsatisfactory for her. Perhaps it is this lack of situational context that best defines the multiple personality.

In sharp contrast to Janet's self and role confusion, most of us have experienced sudden shifts in our social roles without a profound sense of fragmentation. Even as one may suffer guilt, there may not be any experience of having totally lost one's moorings. This point was highlighted in a research with high-ability college students recently undertaken by Page and Landfield at the University of Nebraska. Page first developed a Self Repertory Test that elicited only self-oriented personal construct dimensions. These self-dimensions then were used to explore self-ratings on a day-to-day basis. Page also asked for additional information, each day, about the context and content of the day. He found a surprising amount of self-shift, but these shifts did seem related to the reported changing contexts of experience. Moreover, these students did not seem to experience great difficulty in assigning unitary or general self-ratings to themselves. In other words, they were able to construe themselves as both changing and stable within their self-construct dimensions. In contrast to Janet, these students were able to link up changes in self-conception with changing conditions and contexts of their lives. In the words of the Modulation and Fragmentation Corollaries, the college students were able to encompass their somewhat inconsistent self-statements within broader, more permeable, generalized views of themselves.

Struggling to Encompass Change

Most of us understand the embarrassment and fumbling associated with acquiring new social roles, the anxiety of unknown and unpredictable situations, and the uneasy and even sharply conflicted transitions of increasing maturity. As we experiment with new feelings, behaviors, relationships, and beliefs, behavioral inconsistency and uncertainty are to be expected. The cutting edge of constructive change can be jagged, a point demonstrated by Mark's tragic failure, Sally's painful dialectic with egocentricity, the impulsive backsliding of Henry, and Joe's anger when confronted with a larger perspective.

Although there is much discomfort at the cutting edge of change, certain individuals experience greater difficulty than others when confronted with possibilities of change. One hypothesis accounting for this greater difficulty emphasizes how construct dimensions are organized. For example, imagine an adult who relates his dimensions on the Rep Grid so tightly that his system appears quite simple. In other words, there is an excessively tight unity of the system. Likewise, an Implications Grid on this same person shows little hierarchy of construction. Given these conditions, what happens when this person is confronted by the greater complexities of others? Again, what happens if this person is confronted by events that do not fit his preconceptions? The construct psychologist would state that this person might experience acute anxiety if he can not "force fit" the complexities and new events into his simplisitic framework. If he does force the relationship, one might speak of hostility since the person is extorting validational evidence for his system.

The bigot is an excellent illustration of one who makes things fit his simplified version of social reality. In this process of "force fitting," the bigot may try to simplify events by ignoring much relevant information. This ignoring of data could be called constriction. Kelly defined constriction as a narrowing of the perceptual field, which reduces one's sense of fragmentation. Now a casual reading of this definition might lead one to believe that constriction is all bad. This is not the case. After all, certain withdrawals from activities and people might provide a person with fresh perspectives. In the case of the professional, there are times when he or she may need to focus only on a few ideas. Sometimes the effort to integrate complex material must begin with a simpler structure. Then, in relation to our acquaintances, it may be better for us not to encompass all of their criticisms at one time. The experience could be too overwhelming. Although a professional might say that the person is defensive, such a term encourages one to ignore the potentially healthy properties of constriction as a way of preventing an overwhelming fragmentation.

Having introduced the idea of constriction, its opposite bedfellow, dilation, also must be considered. Dilation, as the term suggests, relates to an enlarging perceptual field. Moreover, just as constriction was seen in both beneficial and destructive contexts, dilation can be placed in both of these contexts. For example, a continual and sweeping dilation could well presage an acute confusion. However, the alternating employment of constriction and dilation, viewed within Kelly's Creativity Cycle, might result in most creative and productive behavior. Effective learning could be seen as the alternative opening of the system to new possibilities, then a partial closing of the system for the restructuring process. Interesting examples of dilation and constriction are found in the volume by Landfield and Leitner (1980).

Kelly referred to dilation and constriction as "diagnostic" constructs. He also referred to the joint idea of "tightening and loosening" in the same manner. However, constriction-dilation is defined by perceptual span, whereas tightening and loosening refers to clarity and stability of anticipation. Tight constructs have more clear and stable predictive consequences. Loose constructs have less clear and more unstable predictive consequences. Loose construing is seen in playfulness with the consequences of feelings, ideas, and behaviors. Tight construing can be exemplified by the careful predictions of scientists. Effective use of both loose and tight construing is the hallmark of great science. Ineffective use of these processes is associated with both poor science and social maladjustment.

Failing to Encompass Change

The most serious failure to encompass change is highlighted in those persons whose fragmentations prohibit effective communication with others and with themselves. Such extreme failure often is associated with excessive loosening of the construct system. This can be illustrated by the following quotation: "The fallacy of creating cohesion, the unthreatening control of togetherness, by intimate revelation by cohesion of exploiting needs to belong and be understood for purposes of sadism, inadequacy, and ability of leverage is not within condonability of educated professionals." Although this quotation does not suggest clear predictive aspects to the reader, someone might argue (with additional data) that this person is not confused within his idiosyncratic labels. How interesting! Imagine this person as tightly construing. However, such an interpretation presumes that the observer can translate these unclear conceptions into the language of a more public world. Clinicians and construct psychologists often attempt such a task. However, this effort to translate can meet with failure. Bannister (1960, 1962) discusses the problem in regard to thought disordered schizophrenics.

Bannister investigated conceptual loosening, using an experimental strategy in which repeated Rep Grid testings were done over short periods of time. He found that thought disordered schizophrenics tend to be most inconsistent in how they apply their personal constructs. He also observed that some of his patients were so loosely construing that they apparently had lost all sense of meaning. This observation by Bannister can be related to a hypothesis expressed by O'Donovan (1965). Writing on the topic of rating scale polarization as a measure of meaningfulness, he suggested that schizophrenics depolarize into meaninglessness; neurotics polarize into an undifferentiated and extreme meaningfulness; and normals are capable of both polarizing and depolarizing.

These observations by Bannister and O'Donovan not only suggest that thought disorder may involve loose construction, but also that looseness may deteriorate into a fragmented meaninglessness. This hypothesized relationship between extreme looseness of construction and meaninglessness should be pursued further. The methods for this kind of research are availble. Bannister certainly introduced an interesting measure of loose construction; and O'Donovan (1965), Bonarius (1970), and others have made a good case for employing rating scale polarization as a measure of meaningfulness, particularly when elicited personal constructs are employed. Adams-Webber (1979) provides an excellent survey of personal construct studies of fragmentation, thought disorder, and loose construction.

It seems obvious from the foregoing discussion that excessive loosening may be associated with serious problems of adjustment. However, is excessive tightening a better solution? Probably not. In order to live in a world of exact predictions, the person must restrict his activities to careful routines and even obsessive-compulsive rituals. The obsessive-compulsive ritual is illustrated by a desperately conflicted woman who defined her world by litter. She constantly picked up bits of paper from city streets. Her exacting and life-encompassing antilitter campaign could be seen as both constriction and tight construction.

INTEGRATING SOME BITS AND PIECES

The theme of this chapter has been fragmentation-unity as understood within personal construct theory. Throughout this discussion the reader has been exposed to many illustrations of social and intrapersonal fragmentation and unity, an exposure that has pointed up the complexities of both the theory and the phenomena being studied.

Many types of fragmentation and unity were described. For example, persons confronted with the possibility of a sharp change in core self-role may experience intense anger. This kind of fragmentation was highlighted in the case of Joe who was threatened by and guilty about a change to the nonhelping pole of his helping versus nonhelping personal construct dimension. In contrast to Joe, Sally experienced more anxiety than anger in her anticipation of change. Her fragmentation focused on the construct of understanding versus not understanding her husband, and trying to anticipate life with and without him. Sally's dialectic between the known and change to the unknown can be related to Kellian anxiety where one experiences a breakdown in the system for anticipating events. Whereas Sally was unclear about the nature of future events, Joe knew the outcome of flipping over to the other side of his constructs.

At the level of the individual personal construct dimension, it was observed that a person may shift from a preferred pole to its opposite and still perceive himself or herself as the same person. This awareness of being the same person in spite of shifts across personal construct dimensions suggests the presence of superordinate structures that encompass change in self-characterization. Then the personal construct dimension was broken down into three component parts of feeling, valuing, and behaving. In this context, it was suggested that a literal relating or a literal fragmenting of these construct components can lead to serious maladjustment.

Fragmentation also was described in terms of disharmony between whole subsystems or clusters of construct dimensions. A striking example of this fragmentation was provided by the "multiple personality." However, it was suggested that sharp changes in social role often may be explained by Kelly's concept of "slot rattling." In other words, a large-scale shift in social role does not necessarily mean that the person is functioning within a new system. Furthermore, a shift from one cluster of construct dimensions to another does not necessarily mean that these clusters are unrelated at a more superordinate level of personal theory. Kelly's Fragmentation Corollary left open the possibility that shifts from one subsystem to another could involve superordinate structures that bridge the gap between seemingly incompatible roles.

Regarding future research on fragmentation and unity, investigators of social understanding must provide greater opportunity for their subjects to share in the experimental enterprise. This may be facilitated by asking subjects to employ their own conceptions in the context of what interests them. Specific to the construct researcher, more effort should be devoted to exploring new methods — those designed to elicit information at varying levels of verbal awareness and hierarchy in meaning. Moreover, greater effort should be expended in designing formats within which to infer dimensions of experience within contexts of social interaction (Landfield, 1979).

A PROTOTYPE FOR EFFECTIVE PERSONAL ORGANIZATION

Kelly has given us the prerequisites for how we may better differentiate, integrate, and generalize our lives. First of all, it is essential to recognize that life involves interpretation and reinterpretation, a position related to observations made by other scientists. Einstein (Heisenberg, 1972, p. 77) stated that "it is the theory which decides what we can observe." Eiseley (1971) cautioned educators to remain open to "emergent novelty."

This assumption of interpretation may not feel so obvious. After all, most of us construe the lives of other persons, and our own lives, as seriously limited by a lack of social, physical, and historical opportunity. There seem to be "facts" that resist reconstruction, a point that Kelly would not have questioned. He did not offer any panacea of change. Instead, he offered the challenge of involvement and possibility in the context of risk, struggle, and pain.

A second prerequisite for effective personal organization is defined by propositional construction. A person may consider an event from different perspectives. Sometimes it is the integration of perspectives that can be most useful. However, the integrative decision or, alternatively, the choice of a particular perspective should be employed as an hypothesis. Functioning at the hypothetical level, our third prerequisite, the person relates situations and events in a manner that leaves him open to exceptions and new experience. Now there is a contrast to this open and interpretive hypothetical style. One may employ literal assumption and accumulations of absolute facts.

A fifth prerequsitie for effective personal organization refers to behavior. One should recognize the experimental opportunities in behavior. Behavior, more than just a reaction, provides a way of exploring new possibilities. Of course, there is risk in such exploration, a point that Kelly emphasized in his discussions of threat, guilt, and anxiety. A sixth prerequisite involves the duality of human nature. Each person should develop some recognition that his own life, as well as the lives of other persons, is a matter of contrast. To become more aware of personal contrasting may provide a clearer definition of one's choices, values, and possibilities for sudden transitions in behavior. Finally, the person needs some appreciation of priority in his life. Kelly (1970a, pp. 39-40) expresses this nicely:

> So it seems that each person arranges his constructions so that he can move from one to another in some orderly fashion, either by assigning priorities to those which are to take precedence when doubts or contradictions arise, or by arranging implicative relationships, as in Boolean algebra, so that he may infer that one construction follows from another. Thus one's commitments may take priority over his opportunities, his political affiliations may turn him from compassion to power, and his moral imperatives may render him insensitive to the brute that tugs at his sleeve. These are the typical prices men pay to escape inner chaos.

12

TWO INDIVIDUALS IN SEARCH OF AGREEMENT: THE COMMONALITY COROLLARY

Steve Duck

The Commonality Corollary: To the extent that one person employs a construction of experience which is similar to that employed by another, his psychological processes are similar to those of the other person.

It is always very refreshing to be encouraged to reread Kelly and to find how eloquently and concisely he could construct a view of some central point. What other recent psychological writer has shown such a stylish concern to create a psychology of the person rather than his circumstances, such a fluent recognition that statistical probability is not the same thing as psychological significance, or has been so magniloquently concerned with the behavioral expression of the wordless queries of our times? So I enjoyed rereading his comments on the Commonality Corollary, if only for the style, but I am supposed to be doing an evaluation piece on the Commonality Corollary itself, so enough of that literary stuff.

WHAT KELLY SAYS COMMONALITY IS

To the extent that one person employs a construction of experience which is similar to that employed by another person his or her

I am grateful to Martin Lea and David O'Hare for their most helpful comments on the first draft of this chapter.

processes are psychologically similar to those of the other person (Kelly, 1970a).

It is worth noting that Kelly gave two different definitions of the Commonality Corollary since he regarded his first (1955) statement as containing an error (namely, that "psychological" was used to qualify "processes" rather than "similar"). In the first, erroneous, version he seems to be emphasizing a construct theory definition of cognitive similarity ("similarly of psychological processes") whereas in the corrected version he emphasizes psychological similarity of processes — a subtle but important shift as shall become clear. In essence, however, it serves to make the corollary less cognitively oriented and more action oriented. Indeed, as Kelly (1970a, pp. 20-22) goes on to say:

> On the face of it, this corollary appears to assert pretty much what personal construct theory seems to stand for: the notion that behavior is governed by constructs. But there is more to it than such a simplified statement might be taken to imply. . . . I have used the expression "construction of experience," rather than "construction of events." I wanted it to be clear that the construction would have to cover the experience itself, as well as the external events with which experience was ostensibly concerned. At the end of an experiential cycle one not only has a revised construction of the events s/he originally sought to anticipate, but s/he has also a construction of the process by which s/he reached [the] new conclusions about them. . . . [The corollary] does not say that the two persons must have experienced "the same" events and it does not say their two experiential cycles have to be "the same." . . . The reason for this being so important is that the outcome of an experience is not merely a tendency to repeat or to avoid it thereafter, as reinforcement theory presumes, but that the conclusions reached through experience are likely to be in the form of new questions which set the stage for new ventures. . . . Thus personal construct theory further releases psychology from assumptions about the identity of events and [the person's] dependence upon them. It leaves us free to envision [the person] coping with "familiar" events in new ways and co-operating with other [people] to produce novelties which make their world a different place to live in. . . . What I especially want to make clear is that the extent of the psychological similarity between the processes of two persons depends upon the similarity of their constructions of their personal experiences, as well as upon the similarity in their conclusions about external events.

It just *looks* as if he's slipped back to the first, erroneous, emphasis here. He hasn't, as the rest of the passage makes clear.

This seems like classic Kelly in fine form. The flowing style, the precision, the breadth of vision, the humanitarianism, the concern with the person, the inventive revolutionary approach. But what exactly is he actually saying here, apart from the restatement of several important themes in personal construct theory (PCT) in the context of one new idea? It seems that, within the context of the rest of the system that is PCT, Kelly is asserting that the psychological similarity between two people is to be assessed by the extent to which they construe similarly. However, he is not *just* saying that psychological similarity equals similarity of constructs or relationships between them; he is implying that if people behave similarly they may have similar constructs and, to the extent that they have, then they are behaviorally and cognitively similar — that is, psychologically similar: They have come to a similar understanding of some part of the world as they act out this similar understanding in similar ways. Thus Kelly seems to be using "psychologically" in a broader sense than just cognitively as I had always thought he meant. The implication would be that the measurement of similarity in terms of construct similarity alone is somehow doing incomplete justice to Kelly's notion of "psychological similarity," although measuring it through constructs is the easiest way. (In passing, I note that in several other contexts Kelly's later work seems to have a more forceful emphasis on the ways in which behavior enacts constructs, rather than on constructs as disembodied, or disenacted, cognitive structures. I am sure that this represents no change of belief, but a reactive change of emphasis in response to the kinds of criticism that his early statements encountered.)

However that may be, most workers who have employed the Commonality Corollary in research have used construct similarity as the operational criterion of similarity (Adams-Webber, 1979). I still find Kelly's statement that bit puzzling, however. What I am not clear about from the above quotations is the part where he talks about construing similarly. Does he mean that two persons have commonality if the structure of their system is similar or if the content is similar or only if both are true? Furthermore, to what extent is Kelly insisting that similar events or experiences are a prerequisite for the reaching of similar conclusions? He seems to be denying that "the same" events are a prerequisite, and I take it that the quotation marks are simply a device to show that even sameness of events presupposes a similar construction of them in some other sense. If two people construe experience similarly, however, then it seems Kelly is saying that they are similar even if, in some sense, the events that prompt the conclusion are "different." Yet he does stress that the common construction must cover the experience itself as well as the external events with which the experience was ostensibly concerned. So it looks as if he is saying the two things together, but insisting that similarity of construing is the necessary condition for saying that two persons are psychologically similar. What troubles me is whether he is also saying that such construct similarity is alone a sufficient condition for psychological similarity, or whether some similarity of events or experience is essential before we can say that commonality exists. For, although he stresses that people need not have witnessed "the same" events, he does also talk about the outcome of *an* experience, and leaving a person free to cope with "familiar" events in new ways. Right at the end of the section that I quoted, he talks of two criteria for psychological similarity: the similarity of their constructions of their personal experiences and the similarity in their conclusions about external events. So presumably conclusions about external events are different from constructs of experience, yet both are included in the definition of commonality.

Anyway, it starts to get a bit clearer. Kelly is arguing that psychological similarity is to be seen primarily in terms of the structural and content similarity that exists between the construct systems but also in the conclusions about experiential cycles that constitute the persons' construct systems. Presumably, then, we could set about measuring this similarity as long as we can get to the right sorts of constructs and conclusions — and once we have decided whether these must be constructs and conclusions about some events that *both* persons construe, or whether the mere existence of the similarity (whether from construal of "the same" or "different" events) is a sufficient ground for saying that the persons are similar. So although there are some operational issues to be resolved, essentially Kelly's position seems clear enough once a bit of mental activity has been done.

However, what's this in Kelly (1955) on page 99? "Commonality between construction systems may make it more likely that one construction system can subsume part of another." What's all this about "subsume" and "may make it more likely that"? Wasn't commonality defined as *actually meaning* that the two systems are, in some respects at least, identical? Now he seems to be saying that it merely means "overlap" and "some of the time."

Well, of course we didn't think that he wanted to imply that the *whole* of both systems were identical. We know that the Individuality Corollary states that persons differ from each other in their construction of events (not, in this case evidently, of experience). Indeed, without individuality (and the Individuality Corollary) the issues of commonality and sociality would not be problematic. Without individuality, commonality would be universal; without sociality it would be meaningless. Equally, without individuality, sociality would not need definition. Further, Kelly recognizes that some commonality stems from people's feeble wit and incorporation in a cultural subsystem that presents them with some prepackaged commonality with other folk. So evidently he is most concerned about other sorts of commonality than these relatively trivial ones.

COMMONALITY OF WHAT SORT?

One important relevant issue concerns Kelly's view of the relationship of one person to another. For Kelly, individuals were inevitably dependent upon other individuals and should feel neither apologetic nor compelled to explain this dependency. He recognized that what the individual wants from others is broad, complex, and undifferentiated, but what the person has to offer in return is narrow, concrete, and specific (Kelly, 1969b). He also recognized that, while therapists may offer clients something very similar to the things that friends offer one another, people would prefer to be dependent on friends than on therapists and would find the dependency on a therapist a more fearsome recognition than recognition of others of life's dependencies. Those who have access to research literature published since Kelly wrote such insights would probably be inclined to feel that he had preempted, in this pithy piece of wisdom, the work on consensual validation that originated with Byrne and Clore (1967). These authors argue that social attraction is based on a human need for effectance (that is, a need to demonstrate capability in dealing with the world — perhaps, in Kellian language, a tendency to desire or create as elaborate and useful a construct system as is necessary best to anticipate the widest range of events, although "elaborateness" and "usefulness" need not be the same thing). In pursuit of this need, Byrne and Clore argue, individuals compare themselves with one another and are attracted to those individuals who share similar ways of mapping the world. In Kellian terms again, this suggests that the diffuse wants that we have of other people amount to a desire for confirmation that part, all, some, the whole, of our construct system is useful as a guide to the world. Recognition of commonality (a similarity of constructions of experience) is a brief way to recognize confirmation of construing. I note clearly, however, that Byrne and Clore's idea and Kelly's view are not identical and Kelly would have reacted against both the terminology and the theoretical framework of Byrne and Clore's statements: Kelly was certainly *not* a reinforcement theorist. He stressed the fact that the person actively anticipates events (rather than merely gravitating toward more and more comfortable organic states), attributing more significance to the outcome of such anticipations than to rewards, punishments, or drive reduction. So he would stress that commonality is a kind of confirmation of anticipations, rather than saying, as Byrne and Clore do, that it is reinforcing. There is another point, too: There is no need to suppose that commonality can occur only in respect of one sort of construct or one part of a system nor that people cannot discover different sorts of commonality as they gain a deeper understanding of each other. I am personally convinced that Kelly had deliberately left himself the option of exploring this possibility by means of the phrase "To the extent that . . ." with which he starts the Commonality Corollary, but that he had not fully worked out the implications for this corollary of different sorts of commonality that may exist.

COMMONALITY AT WHAT LEVEL?

Kelly clearly recognized that a far more important thing than the transaction between two people was the framework of understanding in which it takes place. As someone who saw lucidly the influence of time and change on human endeavors, Kelly would, I am sure, have realized that frameworks of understanding can shift dramatically (and undramatically) and that it may even be true that "to have said then what I say now" may have actually meant something different. Thus, I am sure that Kelly would have noted the changing commonalities that are made possible by the changing contexts, changing certainties, and changing uncertainties of human relationships. Change, in this context, means something. In this context it is related to knowledge about someone, although as a theorist who saw the clear relationship between knowledge and behavior, Kelly would also have recognized that, as people get to know one another better, so also they start to do different things with one another and that this in itself can indicate a shift in the style of commonality that is felt between them — an operational expression of another level of commonality, if you like.

Although Kelly does not actually say that different types and depths of commonality are possible, it would seem to be consistent with his views — especially if we look at this statement that "commonality between construction systems may make it more likely that one construction system can subsume part of another." What I still can't get clear, however, is whether "subsumes" means something like "incorporate" or "draw inferences about" or merely "understand" — and whether that distinction has any real significance in any case. However, it does seem to me to be an important point that commonality can be recognized at different levels, different types, and different degrees between two systems, whether or not one interprets Kelly to be hinting at this. Certain sorts of commonality are basic products of human experience in general and would be shared by almost all normal human beings from any culture (for example, anticipation of the sunrise each morning). Other sorts are more unusual and less easily attained (for example, explanations of why people do things). It is likely that *common* commonality is not particularly interesting, either to psychologists or to the pair of people who discover that they possess it (Lea, 1979; Lea and Duck, in preparation). Nevertheless it might become important to a person who discovers or comes to believe that it is absent when he compares his system with those of other people: Where a person finds little sharing of beliefs that his system holds to be basic, presumably that person will experience some extremely negative emotions and may even come to behave in a bizarre or deranged manner. By the same argument and from the same premises, unusual sorts of commonality should be treasured because they are rare and yet may be important all the same. But what exactly are "unusual sorts of commonality"?

Some types of commonality are likely to stem from the simple fact that the two relevant systems exist in the same cultural universe. Thus a common language gives people a common frame of reference for interpreting the world, and although there are differences in the ways in which individuals use that language to express themselves and understand their predicaments, there are many commonalities, not only in content but also in structure. For Kelly, I imagine that the important point would be the uses that were made of the language and the framework within which common uses or common constructs could be placed or understood.

My own interest is in the other sorts of commonality that may exist between people, for it is clear that the above, while significant in the general scheme of things, is ultimately of little interest to a social psychologist. On the contrary, the interesting commonalities are precisely those that render social attraction more probable, those that make people want to explore one another's systems further, those that create and embody the dependence on others that Kelly saw to be such a natural and necessary part of the human experience.

I have already argued at length elsewhere the ways in which personal constructs may be classified into subcategories (Duck, 1973, 1975, 1977a, b) as have other workers in the Kelly tradition (e.g., Landfield, 1971). Where I differ from some other workers is in my claim that there is a hierarchic structure to the types of constructs that may be identified, and that this represents a construct taxonomy (Duck, 1977a, b, 1979). Essentially the argument is that constructs may be about anything, and that in the infinitely complex system that this statement implies, constructs about other people are near the top of the hierarchy, since other people are more significant objects in the social environment than are other objects. I am simply drawing on Kelly's observations about dependency here and recognizing that people probably spend more of their time construing other people than they do construing other classes of objects.

Given the large and significant place occupied in construct systems by constructs about people (the Duck [1973] argument runs) commonality of constructs about people will be psychologically and personally more significant than commonality about other objects. However, this class of constructs can itself be subdivided and taxonomized. People can be construed as individuals at many levels simultaneously. Thus facts about them (married-unmarried), physical characteristics (tall-short), their behavioral style (talkative-quiet), their role-positions (teacher-pupil), and their style of characters (penetrating-obtuse) can all be seen as simple nonexclusive classes of constructs. Each can also be subclassified and each also branched into greater complexities of hierarchy. However, my point, heard many times before, is simply that these *can* be discovered and so, within each class, can commonalities between two systems. Equally, the classes can be structured hierarchically in terms of their ease of discovery: Thus some basic sorts of "facts" about someone are more readily discovered than are the details of that person's character.

Furthermore, it would be naive and simplistic to focus only on the fact that individuals may be construed as individuals at many levels. They may also be understood in terms of their relationships to one another, the kinds of relationships that they characteristically enter, and the ways in which they maintain their relationships. Also they may be construed — perhaps most significantly construed, as far as the person is concerned — in terms of their relationship to that individual specifically. A very significant influence on a person's perceptions of others is his belief about those others' liking or disliking for himself.

Such relational constructs do themselves represent a complex subclass of possible constructs. However, people's beliefs about relationships, their constructs of experiences based on relationships to other people, are themselves things that can be shared or held in common. They are different — that is, different in social significance — from other sorts of constructs, and to share them with other people represents an intriguing and valuable commonality with considerable significance for the conduct of relationships with the person whose view is common with it.

Given all these distinctions, my argument is simply that one's commonality to another person can be simultaneously measured at many levels and that those higher up the taxonomy will be more socially and psychologically significant to the persons concerned than will those lower down.

However, while I regard the suggestion of a taxonomy of commonality as an important development of Kelly's basic position (but of course, I would), it is old ground and will be familiar to many readers of these words from other sources (for example, Duck, 1973, 1977a, b, 1979). What really concerns me here is whether this view does justice to Kelly's notion of commonality — whether it and other workers' uses of the Commonality Corollary are consistent with his proposition of it. When Kelly talks about commonality is he really talking only about simple cognitive commonality as many of us seem to have presumed, or does he mean something more complex? Obviously the recognition of a taxonomy of potential commonality is one important way in which to extend his idea, but I think he knew this although he did not say it or develop the idea fully. I keep coming back to this phrase: "To the extent that. . . ." Somehow it seems to underline the possibility that extent of commonality may be a problematic concept and that we can expect to find not only different degrees but also different taxonomic levels and other differences of dimension.

COMMONALITY AT WHAT POINT?

Given the different typological and taxonomic sorts of commonality that are possible; given Kelly's views on the natural dependency of humans on each other; given that we choose to associate with some people, choose not to associate with others, have no choice in some cases, and are all members of at least one larger group sharing many simple types of understanding as well as complex ones; given all that, what use is Kelly's corollary? Kelly seems to take a very uncharacteristically unperson-centered view of commonality, don't you think? He is defining it from the outside; it is given a quasi-objective definition: "to the extent that one person employs," period. Not, we note, "to the extent that one person realizes that he employs," nor "to the extent that one person *thinks* that . . . ," nor "to the extent that one person discovers that . . . ." So it looks as if Kelly is simply saying that we are merely defining this from the observer's perspective; we are stating facts, defining the objective, giving verbal explanations to a reality. What if people do not realize they share commonality? What happens when they do realize their sharing?

I'm not being fair, however. As noted above, Kelly also spoke of the frames of reference and the interpersonal contexts in which people operate, and the changing nature of such things, the shifts in commonalities that are made realizable through changing contexts of unfolding events and the progress of time. Surely the psychological significance of commonality to the individual is precisely governed by the extent to which the persons realize that commonalities exist — and Kelly had the Sociality Corollary to explain that (see Chapter 13). For my money, the Commonality Corollary comes to life only in the context of the Individuality and Sociality Corollaries. This is where the meaning of commonality and its psychological significance come into vibrant being — at least from the perspective of the person. To anticipate the following chapter, I would argue that a person's capacity to understand his fellows, a person's capacity for social relationships with others (the iniquities, imbalances, and inequalities of them), is very much influenced by the commonalities and non-commonalities that exist between the two persons as well as by the relative sophistication or complexity of two comparable parts of the two systems.

Changes in the taxonomic levels at which there is commonality or in the structure of commonality are possible consequences of precisely those vagaries of time that Kelly recognized so clearly. They are not always passively attained, however, and can be a real part of the process of getting to know someone else and of getting to think that you know them, and of elaborating your construction of them and their construct processes.

So, given the taxonomic levels at which commonality can be detected, there is also the question of the points in a relationship at which growth of commonality (sorry, I mean growth of realization of commonality) may occur — or at which may occur the insights that a greater, broader, deeper extent of commonality than previously recognized is now available to the partners involved. Only one of the persons may realize it, or both of them might, but as the relationship grows along some other dimension of measurement (for example, intimacy), so, too, one may suppose that it grows in the depth and extent of the commonality that is experienced by the component partners.

Oh dear, here I am back emphasizing the words "To the extent that . . ." again; but extent is itself an ambiguous notion. It can mean depth or breadth for a start. In this context I wonder whether it ought not also say "to the degree that people realize that they share commonality" or "to the degree that they *construe* their commonality." Is Kelly saying that there may be different depths or types of realizations of commonality? Or is he wanting merely to emphasize its operational form and leave its social significance to the Sociality Corollary?

Whatever Kelly may have meant, we apostles have not been very consistent in our application of this corollary and have failed to distinguish the different points in relationship growth (or indeed the different types of relationships) at which commonality may take on different significance. Adams-Webber

(1979, pp. 102-126) gives a review of the work that has been done on commonality. (I nearly wrote, "aspects of commonality," but that would have been to negate my point. We actually have not perceived very clearly that commonality *does* have aspects to it.) Findings are confused not merely because Kelly probably had not worked out properly what commonality is, but because investigators have failed to recognize that commonality happens between people and that the people have a relationship to one another and that relationships are different both in type and in depth (Duck and Gilmour, 1981a, b). Thus the different investigators cited in Adams-Webber do not make clear the different personal importance of different sorts of commonality to different people at different points or in different types of relationship. Commonality either is or is not, as far as these investigators are concerned, and when researchers obtain different results using adult friends, marital pairs, client-therapist relations, adolescent friends, same sex friends, cross-sex friends, depressed patients – tomorrow the world – they question the notion of commonality, the measure of commonality, the validity of commonality, the statistical design, the operational definition of commonality, whether it is on provided or elicited constructs – everything. Everything except the nature of the relationship, the one point – the only point – that Kelly was making, in my view, when he spoke about the "extent" of commonality and hinted at its social significance in his other discussions.

COMMONALITY IN WHAT DEGREE?

We have already established that some minimal degree of commonality is probably inevitable between two people selected at random from the world's population. I have also argued that commonality of different sorts and extents can be differentially significant to people in their daily conduct of the human enterprise. If one can define, in personal terms, what is a significant sort of commonality and what is not, then one has the basis for deciding the extent to which a person may be affected by the discovery of that commonality between himself and another person.

A problem arises, however, from the fact that Kelly (1955, p. 99) says "commonality can exist between two people who are in contact with each other without either of them being able to understand the other well enough to engage in social process with him." Although the Sociality Corollary is fully discussed in the next chapter, it is clear that the Commonality and Sociality Corollaries, taken together, carry the weight of PCT's approach to social behavior. The weight seems to depend on the distinction between commonality and understanding, that is, that commonality may exist but not in a degree adequate to give good grounds for social interaction. Kelly does not, we notice, specify the limits by his magic phrase "To the extent that . . . ." In other words, he does not *say* that commonality can exist in a degree that renders an understanding degraded enough to be useless in social processes, but that is clearly what he means. The interesting possibilities, however, lie in those cases where the commonality level exceeds the threshold for useful social interaction.

Naturally, one assumes that Kelly is wanting to say that, as the degree of commonality increases and as the breadth, depth, extent increase, so, too, does the degree of understanding and so also does the basis for engagement in social processes. This is not to say that those who are similar *will* engage in social processes: Kelly was not naive, whatever else he was. He is saying merely that the extent of similarity defines or limits the type of social processes that are possible between them and that greater degrees of commonality may make it easier to communicate satisfactorily. Nor is this to say that commonality in one area means equality in the relationship. One system can subsume part of another — isn't that what Kelly said? — without the second system being equivalent to the first. It's like those Logic Circles that overlap: In some cases (that is, in some areas of construing) the smaller circle could lie entirely within the larger one such that one person (the larger circle) can subsume the other one without the same being true of the other person "in reverse" (the smaller circle).

Combination of the Commonality and Sociality Corollaries is thus a possible basis for some proposals on why people associate with one another — but I don't happen to believe that PCT satisfactorily explains that on its own in its formal structure anyway. One needs the fuller comments that Kelly made about human dependency as a basis for more complete explanation of human association. We can be fairly sure that Kelly would rest easy with the assertion that one implication of the Commonality Corollary, either on its own (given its original context in PCT), or together with the Sociality Corollary, is that to the extent that commonality exists between two systems, the common parts of the systems facilitate social interaction in relevant areas — and I put it no stronger.

"Being like" and "liking" are neither semantically nor psychologically equivalent. There are all the obvious reasons why it would be an absurdity to say otherwise (for example, one doesn't find it attractive to be shown to be similar to a lunatic, nor to be like a child or a fool, nor to have an uncanny resemblance to a criminal style of construing, if there is one, but an important point is also that, in some contexts, uniqueness (or at least a sense of difference) is an important thing. Individuality Corollary, art thou sleeping there below?

Crucially, however, given Kelly's views on the nature of commonality and subsumption of other people's construct systems, given also the psychological significance of commonality to the persons concerned as they conduct their different experiential cycles, sociality and commonality are inextricably linked in Kelly's theory. Commonality, I have argued above, facilitates sociality; but what else does sociality come from in Kelly's theory? How can one understand another's construct system without at least sharing many of its relevant parts? Commonality, I think, is perhaps, in Kelly's mind, the quickest route to sociality; but, in my view, it is an essential ingredient of it, and sociality without commonality just is not possible in the terms of Kelly's theory as stated by Kelly. Now don't get me wrong; I know that Kelly says that people can have commonality without understanding one another; what I am saying is that they can't understand one another without commonality of some sort. True, someone's understanding of another person will be improved by his ability to construe the construction processes of that other person, and sociality is more than commonality. I recognize that rather obvious point; but commonality is a necessary condition. The pair that employs a common construction of experience can play together if they choose and can then drink at the refreshing springs of one another's individuality. Association with other people who share experiences (sorry, constructions of experience) may lead the persons to a more elaborated common understanding of those experiences, simply because while they both bring to the relationship their common constructs, each person will have other unshared ones that may subsequently be communicated to the other person on the basis of those original commonalities. Thus sociality grows, liking grows, from the sharing of new constructions of experience just as it does of old ones. People come together in order to share; they share in order to prepare. What was it Kelly said earlier? "It leaves us free to envision [the person] coping with 'familiar' events in new ways and cooperating with other [people] to produce novelties which make their world a different place to live in . . ." (Kelly, 1970a, p. 22). An experience — a common construction of experience — is not simply an event but a construal of it also, a set of constructs about an occurrence. As Kelly realized, but no one has done much about since he realized it, a constant and important feature of human life is the recapitulation, revision, and repenting that people do (Duck, 1980). In the Commonality and Sociality Corollaries he is merely emphasizing that they can sometimes do it together.

So, as Kelly said, psychological similarity is more than just cognitive similarity, and construct similarity implies more than just cognitive similarities, since common construction of experience involves cycles of construal, cycles of behavior, cycles of repenting — as Kelly said, "experiential cycles."

I'm convinced that I wasn't clear about that until I began work on this chapter; but now I see that Kelly seems to be arguing that psychological similarity is more than just cognitive similarity and carries implications about behavior similarity to the extent that behavior is governed by constructs. Thus mere cognitive similarity is not what Kelly is spelling out here or defining. "Construction of experience" is the key phrase, and he is actually saying something much deeper and much wiser, much more insightful, much less mechanical, and much more social than at first appears. Indeed, the clearest way to summarize it is to say that, to the extent that one person employs a construction of experience that is similar to that employed by another person, his processes are psychologically similar to those of the other person.

Of course, that is exactly what Kelly said! Further, it even seems that he may have anticipated that someone might bother finding out, because I think we share a common experience of the problem (sorry, common construction of experience) and have both worked our ways through it to the same end, so that to that extent our processes are psychologically similar.

Yes, it is always refreshing to be encouraged to reread Kelly and to find how eloquently and concisely he could construct a view of some central point.

13

SOCIALITY, INTERSUBJECTIVITY, AND SOCIAL PROCESSES: THE SOCIALITY COROLLARY

Finn Tschudi
Ragnar Rommetveit

The Sociality Corollary: To the extent that one person construes the construction processes of another, he may play a role in a social process involving the other.

"All our present interpretations of the universe are subject to revision or replacement . . . there are always some alternative constructions available to choose among in dealing with the world" (Kelly, 1955, p. 15). This statement on constructive alternativism reminds us that it is a necessary cornerstone of our constructivist perspective, that our behavior theory reflexively applies to our theory building activity, and that we are about to explore alternative approaches to explicating sociality.

In explicating the concept of role, Kelly (1955, p. 97) wrote as follows: "A role is a psychological process based upon the role player's construction of aspects of the construction system of those with whom he attempts to join in a social enterprise." A dichotomous construction is suggested. Where one observes failure to play a role — "to join in a social enterprise" — one may invoke the contrast pole to social relating, namely, nonsocial relating. The quotations given below show how Kelly elaborated the two poles of the dichotomy.

Nonsocial relating (not play a role)	*Social relating* (play a role)
Q1. merely construe his behavior	construe the construction processes of another person (1970a, p. 23)

Nonsocial relating (not play a role)	*Social relating* (play a role)
Q2. only look at answers in arithmetic task	look at methods by which the pupil obtained his answer (1955, p. 320)
Q3. if immediate accuracy is what I must preserve, stick to the automaton behaving organism only, level of construction	if I am to anticipate you, I must try to sense what you are up to (1970, p. 24)
Q4. a psychopath is a stimulus response psychologist who takes it seriously . . . treat others as behaving mechanism or object . . . produce right stimulus in order to invoke accomodating behavior	creature with outlook . . . our interaction will be of a different order . . . have a construction of a creature who himself devises constructions (1969b, p. 220)
Q5. the kind of experience that gets the commonwealth work done	the sort that builds viable society (1970, p. 26)
Q6. adapt self to positions, play a part, deal with others as figures, construe relationships to other people as a matter of "social position"	adapt self to persons, construe relationships in terms of their unique identities and their personal viewpoints (1955, p. 877)

THE NORMATIVE ASPECT OF THE COROLLARY

A superordinate bad-good personal construct is easily detected in the above quotations. Social relating depicts "the good life," and nonsocial relating epitomizes those things that are transparently negative to Kelly as a person and as a theorist. It should be apparent, for example, that the second quotation, Q2 (a specification of Q1), opens a fundamental critique of psychometrically founded test interpretation — a critique that is in line with the tradition of Wertheimer (see Luchins and Luchins, 1977) and Rogers (1951, p. 219). Q5 may open a critique of capitalism. Q4 is Kelly's way of getting back at everything he found negative within mechanistic stimulus-response approaches. (The "psychopath" construction will be further discussed later in this chapter.)

The normative aspect is captured in the following simplified version of the corollary:

Version 1: To the extent that one person construes the construction process of another, he may join in a *viable* social enterprise.

However, the term *to the extent* diverts us from thinking of a strict dichotomy as in the above quotations.

Consider the core of the corollary: "construe (the construction processes of another)." The most succinct description of *any* one person's construction processes is, of course, found in the Fundamental Postulate. One may substitute the Fundamental Postulate in Version 1 to derive the following:

Version 2: To the extent that one person construes how another's processes are psychologically channelized by the ways in which he anticipates events, he may join in a *viable* social enterprise.

An Optimal Level of "the Extent" in the Sociality Corollary

Version 2 (or Version 1) suggests that the more extensive the construing of the other's construction processes are, the more viable the social process will be; but might there not instead be an optimal level, such that beyond that level social processes may in some sense be impeded? This possibility may call for revision of the corollary, yet the notion of an optimal level can (implicitly) be read from Kelly's (1955) first example of sociality. He uses driving on the highway to illustrate different levels at which we can construe what other people are thinking. "The orderly, extremely complex and precise weaving of traffic is really an amazing example of people predicting each other's behavior through subsuming each other's perception of a situation" (p. 95). This, however, seems to be at an extremely "low level"; indeed it seems almost indistinguishable from "merely construe behavior," "immediate accuracy is what I must preserve" (see above Q1 and Q3). The point here, however, is not just to emphasize variability in "degree of sociality," but to consider the implication of "if we are to understand oncoming drivers at higher levels, we must stop traffic and get out to talk with them" (p. 96). This certainly would be highly dysfunctional from the point of view of having smooth-running traffic! Different types of social situations entail different optimum levels of construing the construction processes of another. We are, for instance, all of us familiar with the embarrassment stemming from intrusion of too much "familiarity" in more formal situations. Furthermore, the optimum level concept puts into perspective Weber's classical arguments in support of bureaucracy. Formal handling of complaints, and so on, may be a guarantee against nepotism, bribery, and various forms of "injustice." That many of us have had occasion to wish for more "personal treatment" at the public level does not obviate the principal nature of the present argument; a further discussion of bureaucracy to buttress the present point is found in Berger et al. (1974).

This reasoning suggests yet another rewriting of the corollary:

Version 3: There is an optimal level, depending upon the type of situation, of the extent to which a person should construe the construction process of another in order for maximally viable and efficient social enterprises to take place.

Foreword

In the two sections to follow, Kelly's approach will be understood as a significant exemplar of an emerging, novel, person-explaining paradigm whose range of convenience extends far beyond traditional personality psychology. The Sociality Corollary paves the road toward an integration of personality theory and a general social cognitive theory of human communication and may indeed be conceived prospectively as a cornerstone for a general, though so far poorly elaborated, conceptual framework. Kelly (1970a, p. 22) himself maintains, "The implications of this corollary are probably the most far reaching of any I have attempted to propound. It establishes grounds . . . for envisionning . . . a truly psychological basis of society."

Much of the discussion in the next two sections is adapted from Rommetveit (1980, 1981; see also Rommetveit, in preparation). In thinking about the content in the section entitled "Constructive Alternativism," the reader might wish to regard the nonsocial-relating pole of sociality as an extreme case that would have little relevance for describing actual communication. Nevertheless, the mechanistic point of view, which this pole expresses, seems yet to dominate much current work. We may say that there is not only a normative dichotomy (bad-good) embedded in constructions of sociality, there is also (in principle) a "descriptive" dichotomy (faulty-adequate). Mechanistic theories of communication may simply be faulty description. They may describe atypical (if any) communication. Such theories, however, may readily yield beautiful formal edifices. We contend that such formalism should (at this point in time) be forsaken for admittedly more messy constructivistic conceptions.

In the section entitled "Construing Construction Processes . . . ," we make an analysis of some facets of social process intersubjectivity and shared social reality. We hope that this will encourage further specification of the as yet unanalyzed concept of social process. Furthermore, we detail ways by which to elaborate the process of construing construction processes to delineate the conditions for intersubjectivity. The preliminary nature of our endeavors will be further underscored when we try to analyze examples typical of the very best in current clinical psychology work in the section entitled "On Attaining Shared Social Reality."

In "Honoring and Violating Intersubjectivity" we carry further, from different vantage points, an argument from the previous section, showing how deep-seated sociality is much of the time, how difficult it may be to be completely nonsocial. In the last section we sketch some types of mainly nonsocial processes. If elaborating the social relation pole points to the good life, elaborating the other pole might be a contribution to the psychology of evil.

CONSTRUCTIVE ALTERNATIVISM: A PLURALISTIC APPROACH TO HUMAN COMMUNICATION

Human discourse takes place in and deals with a multifaceted, only fragmentarily known, and only partially shared social world. If one were to accept Version 2 of the Sociality Corollary one would be moved toward the conclusion that since another's processes form a system, complete sharing is theoretically impossible. A full grasping of anyone's construing of a situation would imply understanding the whole surrounding network of constructs, which in the limit involves the whole system — clearly an impossible task.

Vagueness, ambiguity, and incompleteness — and hence also negotiability, flexibility, and versatility — are, therefore, inherent and essential characteristics of the meanings of situations and the linguistic mediations of meanings.

Students of human communication who abandon basic monistic assumptions will accordingly have to redefine their trade in some important respects. A fully legitimate and important part of their task will be to try to explicate and be precise about rather than to evade life's inherent ambiguities and versatility. Meaning potentials of states of affairs (events, acts, or situations) may thus be systematically explored in terms of sets of experiential possibilities or aspects. Wittgenstein (1968, p. 212) maintains: "What I see in the dawning of an aspect is not a property of the object, but an internal relation between it and other objects." This seems to fit well with Kelly's (1955, p. 304) view: "Construing is never a single-dimensional proposition. There is always *the other respects* which are used in the application of a construct, it makes sense only as it appears in a network." A personal construct theorist might differ, however, from one who speaks of elaborations of meaning potentials. "Aspects" mainly refer to the event pole of the person-event-process, whereas "constructs" mainly refer to the person pole. There will be more about this difference.

The centrality of the playing-a-role pole of sociality explanation becomes evident when we consider the foregoing points relative to a crucial feature of verbal communication. The aspect(s) of an object that acquires saliency and is then put into words, in simple tasks of verbal labeling, is contingent upon the range of other objects from which the referent must be set apart. The psycholinguistic experiments reported by Olson (1970) and Deutsch (1976) demonstrate how differently such referential domains affect the linguistic encoding and decoding process. Olson points out that the answer to the question, "What is 'object S' surrounded by?" may be *bluebird* in the context of surrounding sparrows; *bird* in the context of surrounding mammals, and (perhaps) *creature* in the context of inanimate objects. Likewise the object S in Figure 13.1 will thus be unequivocally identified as the *white* one in Context II, the *big* one in Context III, the *triangle* in Context IV. Two persons — one with referential domain x, the other with domain y — will describe objects as *white* and *small*, respectively. But what about the single stimulus in Context I? This situation is discussed by Garner (1974, pp. 183-186). When people are asked informally to describe stimulus A in Figure 13.2 (where the rectangle is just a frame) they answer "a circle"; some say "a double circle." But if, in complete parallel to Figure 13.1, stimulus A is presented in the context of two larger circles, the description will change.

We could of course continue the process. Nobody for example thinks of mentioning the thickness of lines . . . or even the fact that lines forming

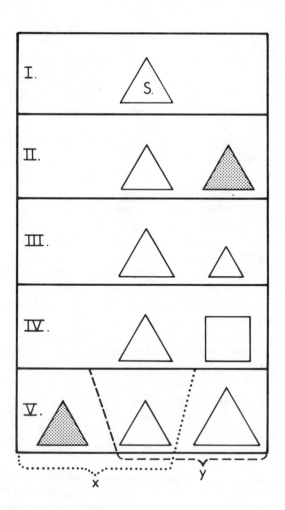

FIGURE 13.1

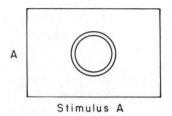

Stimulus A

FIGURE 13.2

Source: From W. R. Garner, *The Processing of Information and Structure.* Copyright © 1974, by Lawrence Erlbaum Associates. Reprinted by permission.

the circles are solid rather than broken. *The single stimulus has no meaning except in a context of alternatives.* When somebody uses the term circle, they infer that it could have been some other form. *Each descriptive term defines what the alternatives are, by defining what the stimulus is not.* Thus the organism infers sets of stimulus alternatives, and without these inferred sets no one can describe the single stimulus (Garner, 1974, p. 186, italics added).

However, Garner only partially endorses a constructivistic view: "We do not create the structure that makes the stimulus — we select it" (p. 186). This may be because his concern is rooted in the event pole, whereas Kelly is more rooted in the person pole. The main point here is that inferred sets of stimulus alternatives correspond to tacitly taken for granted referential domains or just personal constructs. So we may in some sense regard the description of a single stimulus, as discussed by Garner, to be the prototypical instance of how a situation is rendered meaningful. The difference between our perspective and Garner's would be that we are more interested in a privately provided range of possible alternatives, whereas Garner focuses on that which he believes the stimulus provides to persons for their selection.

As implied by our acceptance of constructive alternativism, we assume that every single person has the capacity to adopt a whole range of perspectives on objects, events, and states of affairs, and one is in that sense an inhabitant of many "possible worlds." Moreover, a person's perpsective and "private" domain of experiential alternatives, at that moment, sets the probabilities that one or another potential aspect will be ascribed by that person to that state of affairs. A major source of individual differences with respect to referential domains is superordinate concerns that can be described as interests and purposes. These correspond (in part) to different positions from which different alternatives become visible. The meaning of closing down a factory will, for instance, be radically different for a worker facing unemployment and for the manager considering the total economy of a multiplant corporation. The same point may be made even in Garner's simple example. The bride-to-be might describe a wedding ring, which is quite different from the mathematician's double concentric circles.

To describe the variety of possible worlds a person may entertain regarding a specific situation, one may invoke a variety of Kellian constructs, such as, for instance, C-P-C cycle (circumspection-preemption-control), the permeability of superordinate constructs, and the Modulation and Fragmentation Corollaries.

The enigma of the "real world as it is now" is subjectively resolved. Its potential aspects acquire saliency and significance in a process of comparison (see Tversky [1977] for a brilliant formal exposition of this basic Kellian view). Also, disparate meanings of situations, engendered by persons interacting in those situations, may thus be explored in terms of different tacit, taken-for-granted referential domains.

Generally different past personal experiences make for different tacitly presupposed referential domains (see Chapter 9 on the Experience Corollary). A major point, which will be further elaborated in the last section of this chapter, is that in any communication situation a major part of the referential domain is the general (or specific) constructs with which one participant approaches the other. Our position is simply that any real state of affairs is enigmatic; it must be construed. This point has been variously expressed in the literature. Schutz (1951, p. 167) maintains:

> If I, with respect to an element S of the world taken for granted, assert: "S is p," I do so because for my purpose at hand at this particular moment I am interested only in the p-being of S and I am disregarding as not relevant to such purpose that S is also q and r.

The assertion "S is p," in conjunction with the fact that aspects q and r are disregarded, implies, in the terminology of Mannheim (1952) and Hundeide (1980), that the state of affairs S (the situation) is experienced from some particular position — some particular referential perspective (Wertsch, 1980). In the terminology of Bateson, Goffman, and Minsky, S is enclosed within a certain frame. Its meaning, when experienced from that position at that particular moment, is thus generated from some particular premises for interpretation (Bateson, 1973, p. 60), a certain background understanding (Goffman, 1974, p. 22), a given collection of questions to be asked (Minsky, 1975, p. 245). Even the more narrowly defined linguistic study of presupposition is currently expanding so as to cope with dialogically and temporarily constructed "possible worlds" of actual conversations (Karttunen, 1974; McCawley, 1978). Modal logic is thus today in part replacing classical propositional logic as an auxiliary in the formalization of linguistic theory.

These philosophical and social scientific trends converge in a serious concern with dynamic, social-interactional features of linguistic communication. Together with the symbolic interactionism of Mead (1934), the theoretical framework for empirical semantic developed by Naess (1953), and the psychology of language and thought of Vygotsky (1962, 1978) and Piaget (1958), these developments constitute significant contributions toward the foundation of an interdisciplinary social-cognitive approach.

It may be illuminating in the present context to point out a contrast to constructive alternativism. When one consistently maintains a pluralistic perspective one is deprived of the opportunity to seek refuge in an unequivocal present tense reality that is uncontaminated by the repertory of possible human perspectives and the strategies of attribution and categorization that are inherent in ordinary language. The use of such a refuge is observed in the belief in literal meaning as a cornerstone in the study of communication, the attempts to dissociate ordinary language from actual use and to explicate its syntactic and semantic rules under stipulated ideal conditions.

A principal exponent of such an ideal/monistic view is Searle (1974) who, with his principle of expressibility, basically stipulates one-to-one correspondence between what is said and what is meant. Rommetveit (1979) argues in detail against this view and points out that what is said is an incomplete expression of what is meant. A similar concern for the distinction between what is said and what is meant is expressed by Kelly (1955, p. 200):

> If we utilize what our friend has *meant* as well as what he *said* as an element, that is, if we make his presumed personal construct as well as his behavior an element in our construing – then our *personal construct can be considered a version of his personal construct*. Thus communication at some more or less effective level has taken place . . . the sharing of personal experience is a matter of *construing* the other person's experience and not merely a matter of having him hand it to us across the desk.

The search for context-free meaning – literal meaning – of what is said is, we believe, doomed to failure. This approach must set aside as basically irrelevant the incompleteness, inherent ambiguity, and flexibility of language. What thus must appear chaotic to the believer in literal meaning may, however, be accounted for as orderly variance when we adopt a consistently pluralistic perspective (Rommetveit, in preparation).

The belief in literal meaning seems to correspond to Kelly's (1969b, p. 125) contrast to constructive alternativism; that is, "accumulative fragmentalism . . . that we discover nature a fragment at a time . . . like a piece in a jigsaw puzzle . . . capture an essence."

CONSTRUING CONSTRUCTION PROCESSES AND CONDITIONS FOR INTERSUBJECTIVITY

Traditional linguistics and psycholinguistics lean heavily upon Chomsky's aim at an analysis of language as a formal abstract system rather than as a social form of life. Thus Lyons (1977, p. 243) maintains:

> The synchronic language system is a theoretical construct of the linguist, and it rests upon the more or less deliberate, and to some extent arbitrary, discounting of variations in the language-behavior of those who are held, pretheoretically, to speak the same language. If pressed, we have to admit that there is a somewhat different language system (a different idiolect) underlying the language behavior of every individual and that this too changes through time.

The notion of individual language systems, however, is absurd. Linguistic codes, by definition, are embedded in interaction rather than in individual cognition.

Persons differ from each other in their construction of events; but ordinary language is clearly one of the most potent means for establishing states of inter-subjectivity between different "private worlds." Engaging in a dialogue implies a commitment to a shared reality. In fact, Habermas' (1979) analysis of speech suggests that the very construct reality emerges from linguistic acts. Truth — a claim that there is fact — and truthfulness — a claim that the speaker will not deceive — are prerequisite to language use; and the youngest speaker, accepting these claims, is egocentrically induced to accept reality as a given. The psycholinguist, however, is advised to eschew this view of reality and to adopt an outlook from which to see ordinary language as an open system, with inbuilt negotiability and reciprocal commitments. This outlook seems to be required to elaborate Kelly's Sociality Corollary as "a truly psychological basis for society" (1970a, p. 22).

Wittgenstein (1968), as a philosopher, has explored some of the underlying assumptions and focal issues of a dynamic, consistently pluralistic, and social-cognitive approach to verbal communication. He conceives of the incompleteness and inherent ambiguities of ordinary language as a necessary consequence of the fact that its semantic system borders on our fragmentary and imperfect knowledge of the world. Thus, any scheme of interpretation will have a bottom level and "there is no such thing as an interpretation of *that*" (Wittgenstein, 1962, p. 739). Utterances have meaning only in streams of life. Linguistic communication must hence be examined as embedded in more inclusive patterns of human interaction, as moves within language games. Ordinary language *is* a form of life. Allwood (1976) makes the related point that vagueness of ordinary language actually is a precondition for communication. An utterance may be seen as a "gestalt" where the context determines the parts and makes the utterance — more or less — precise.

Imagine now a situation in which two persons who engage in conversation about some state of affairs, S, differ with respect to what they believe S to be. The person, p_1, takes it for granted that S is A_i whereas his conversation partner sees S as A_j. How can we as linguists or psycho- or sociolinguists in such a situation transcend the private worlds of p_1 and p_2 and pass verdict with respect to the real nature of the state of affairs S? Granted that we from some carefully elaborated third epistemological-ontological position venture to claim that S is neither A_i nor A_j, but A_k, how can such a presumedly superior knowledge of the real world help us grasp what is being meant, understood, or misunderstood by p_1 and p_2 in that particular situation? The only alternative seems to be to take for granted the multiplicity of possible human perspectives on states of affairs.

A radical reformulation of assumptions and focal issues of research on human intersubjectivity and verbal communication follows from replacing a monistic outlook with a consistently pluralistic paradigm. The problem of what is being meant by what is said could no longer be pursued in terms of stipulated unequivocal literal meanings of expressions. The basic riddle within a pluralistic approach is, instead: How are states of intersubjectivity and shared social reality attained in encounters between different private worlds. Orderly negotiability and variance in what is meant by that which is said is clearly contingent upon some semantic invariance embedded in ordinary language. Some basic shared knowledge of the world appears indeed to be embedded as meaning potentials of ordinary words and expressions. Such potentials reflect at a very abstract level some minimal commonality with respect to experientially founded perspectives on and categorization of our pluralistic social world and may hence be conceptualized as a common code of potentially shared cognitive-emotive perspectives on talked-about states of affairs. What traditionally have been labeled "semantic rules," moreover, must, within our social-cognitive paradigm, be conceptualized as linguistically mediated drafts of contracts concerning categorization and attribution of meaning to states of affairs.

Consideration Regarding Intersubjectivity

The attainment of states of intersubjectivity in verbal communication is contingent upon contextually appropriate specification and elaboration of such abstract drafts of contracts. Such a state may be tentatively defined as follows:

A state of intersubjectivity with respect to some state of affairs S is attained, at a given stage of dyadic interaction, if and only if some aspect A_i of S at that stage is brought into focus by one participant and jointly attended to by both of them.

A dyadic state of (perfectly) shared social reality, moreover, may be described in the following way:

Some aspect A_i of a given state of affairs S constitutes at a given stage of dyadic interaction a (perfectly) shared social reality if and only if both participants at that stage take it for granted that S is A_i and each of them assumes the other to hold that belief.

Shared social reality is a stronger condition than intersubjectivity. The latter may be one-directional, but bidirectional intersubjectivity implies shared social reality. Role taking, construing the construction process of the other, will be seen to be an essential feature of human communication. Yet role taking does not constitute a state of intersubjectivity, unless constrained by reciprocal commitment and dyadic communication control.

Vygotsky (1978, p. 29) maintains: "Signs and words serve children first and foremost as means of social contact with other people." A primitive but possibly primary form of intersubjectivity is, according to Trevarthen and Hubley (1978, p. 184), attained at a very early stage in the sense that infants "share themselves with others." According to their observations, there emerges, at about the age of nine months, a secondary intersubjectivity in terms of a "deliberate, self-conscious and reciprocal sharing of focus with another" (p. 220). Newson (1978, pp. 36-37) describes the prerequisites for such a development:

> ... someone who is trying to communicate with the infant ... is bound to respond selectively to precisely those actions, on the part of the baby, to which one would normally respond *given the assumption that the baby is like any other communicating person.*
> ... It is ... only because mothers impute meaning to "behaviors" elicited from the infants that these eventually do come to constitute meaningful actions so far as the child is concerned.

A state of primary or secondary intersubjectivity in early mother-child interaction — whatever else such a state may entail — is thus inconceivable without naive, reciprocal faith in a shared experiential world. This is true, however, of any state of human intersubjectivity and indeed is a defining characteristic of ordinary language as a form of life. Only when one examines a breakdown of the process does one appreciate how unreflectively taken-for-granted and essential are such mutual confidences in normal verbal communication. Considerations about failure in the process will be taken up in the section entitled "Honoring and Violating Intersubjectivity" (see also the discussion of certain pathological conditions in Rommetveit, 1974, pp. 53-56). One may assert that intersubjectivity must, in some sense, be taken for granted in order to be attained. This semiparadox may indeed be conceived of as a basic pragmatic postulate of human discourse. It captures in a condensed form not only the insights achieved by observers of early mother-child interaction and students of serious communication disorders, but also convergent conclusions from ethnomethodological enquiries into the routine grounds of everyday adult conversation (Garfinkel, 1972) and the recent linguistic reflections on axiomatic features of normal speech. The linguist Uhlenbeck (1978), for example, refers to the basic "makes sense" principle of ordinary speech. He describes it as follows:

> It says that the hearer always takes the view that what the speaker is saying somehow makes sense. It is this certitude which makes him try to infer — on the basis of lingual and extra-lingual evidence available to him — what the speaker actually is conveying to him. This formulation implies that on occasion the hearer may be unable to do so or that he may make the wrong inferences. It is difficult to exaggerate the importance of this very general attitude. Awareness of its always being operative may keep us from entering into linguistically irrelevant discussions on the truth-values of sentences, or from participating in sterile debates about establishing a distinction between deviant and normal sentences (p. 190).

The significance of this "makes sense" principle can clearly be appreciated in conjunction with Piaget's theory of decentration and in the basic tenet of symbolic interactionism: An adult person's repertory of possible perspectives entails, as experiential possibilities, aspects that are immediately visible only from the position of her or his conversation partner; and an essential component of communicative competence in a pluralistic social world is the capacity to adopt the attitude of "different others." A mutual commitment to the same talked-about reality is, in ordinary discourse, endowed with naive confidence in "an intersubjective world, common to all of us" (Schutz, 1945, p. 534) on the part of communication partners. Reciprocal commitment, moreover, implies reciprocal role taking. A significant dynamic feature of ordinary language as a social form of life is thus a peculiar circularity. The speaker monitors what she is saying in accordance with what she assumes to be the listener's outlook and background information, whereas the latter makes sense of what he is hearing by adopting what he believes to be the speaker's perspective. But what is actually being meant, and which of the potential aspects of the talked-about state of affairs are in shared attention at any particular stage of a dialogue?

The mutual commitment and peculiar circularity inherent in acts of speech imply by no means, of course, that both participants in a dialogue assume equal or joint responsibility for what is being referred to and/or meant by what is said. The speaker — or, more generally, the participant who has introduced the focal events at any given stage of the dialogue — has the privilege of determining which aspect(s) is to be jointly attended at that moment. This is the case even if she fails to make herself understood. Only she — not the listener — is in a position to pass final verdict with respect to what she herself intends to make known by what she is saying. Understanding (and misunderstanding) is in ordinary verbal communication by definition a dyadic and directional affair, and vicious circularity is prohibited by reciprocal and intuitive endorsement of dyadic patterns of communication control.

The speaker, by taking the role of the other, enjoys the privilege of assuming that the listener temporarily is a "guest" in her (the speaker's) world. The speaker may thereupon legitimately act on the basis of assumed similarity; and her construct is (at least temporarily) socially validated to the extent the other person adopts her perspective and attends to the aspect of the event that she attempts to bring into joint focus of attention.

The listener's obligation to adopt the other's (the speaker's) perspective directs him to take the role of the other. He is committed to act on assumed differences. A computer simulation of the speaker's role taking would hence involve activation of memory of self in similar situations. The listener's role taking would involve memories of the other in similar situations. States of intersubjectivity are thus contingent upon the fundamental dyadic constellation of speaker's privilege and listener's commitment: The speaker has the privilege of determining the referent and the meaning of the event, whereupon the listener is committed to make sense of what is said by temporarily adopting the speaker's perspective. This view of the circularity inherent in acts of speech implies that both participants, to communicate, must in some sense engage the social process role described by the Sociality Corollary. In considering speech acts, one must rule out nonreciprocity, which Kelly (1970a, p. 25) otherwise clearly states as a possibility.

Symmetric and Asymmetric Patterns of Communication

Thus far we have outlined a basis for exploring the mastery of dialogue roles in normal and symmetric dyadic interaction. Symmetry/asymmetry with respect to dyadic communication control may now be defined as follows:

> An entire dialogue or a given stretch of discourse is characterized by a symmetric pattern of communication control if and only if unlimited interchangeability of dialogue roles constitutes part of the externally provided sustained conditions of interaction. An entire dialogue or a given stretch of discourse is characterized by an asymmetric pattern of communication control if and only if the interaction takes place under sustained constraints which are contrary to the basic or "prototypical" dyadic regulation of privileges and commitments.

Under such constraints one would expect to observe behaviors that are in violation of the implicitly understood rules of role taking. The speaker would be in breach of the normal role-defining rules if he were to watch the face of the listener to collect additional information about what the speaker means.

In the constrained infant-adult discourse, the situation changes. The interaction is directed by an overall pattern of dependency. The overriding constraints upon early adult-child communication, moreover, reside in the factual and reciprocally taken-for-granted adult superiority with respect to linguistic competence and knowledge of the world. It is hence not at all absurd for a one-year-old boy to watch his mother's face while uttering something in order to explore what is being meant by his utterance. It may indeed be essential to observe her response if he is going to make himself better understood on subsequent similar occasions. Some of the most well-established and significant findings in recent research on preverbal mother-child interaction and early language acquisition (Bates, 1976; Bruner, 1978; Lock, 1978) seem thus to converge into an apparently paradoxial conclusion: Adult-perfect interchangeability of the dialogue roles can develop only out of adult-child interaction with an initial consistently asymmetric pattern of communication control.

"Reality Control" and the Mastery of the Speaker Role

Berger and Luckmann (1967, p. 38) maintain: "It can . . . be said that language makes 'more real' my subjectivity not only to my conversation partner but also to myself." Bateson (1973, p. 167) defines ego weakness as "trouble in identifying and interpreting those signals which should tell the individual what sort of a message a message is. . . ." The issues of shared meanings of social situations, moreover, may in human interaction become an issue of whose private world is endorsed by others as well, accepted as the basis for joint or collective action, and hence in some very important sense made publicly valid.

Ego strength may under certain conditions of human interaction be seen as a question of which aspect (or whose personal meaning) of a given state of affairs is accepted as a temporarily shared social reality in an encounter between different private worlds. Let us not despair if we occasionally experience states of genuine uncertainty with respect to what is meant by what is said. Such states may signal transcendence of preestablished perspectives and the dawning of novel aspects of life, see pp. 246-248.

Social validation serves to confirm and sustain the basic assumption that "the world is . . . an intersubjective world common to all of us . . ." (Schutz, 1945, p. 53). Its subjective quality and contingency upon personal referential alternatives are brought to the foregound only under very exceptional conditions such as, for instance, when one of Kelly's clients attempts to account for some important aspect of people she knows well in terms of "Mary-ness" (Kelly, 1955, pp. 114, 125, 139). What is meant by that word is entirely bound to her subjective experience of one particular friend of hers, Mary. The bipolar nature of language as a bridge between different private worlds is reflected in its composition: The component "Mary" is intelligible only in terms of one particular referential alternative whereas the component "ness" is comprehensible to everybody, yet nearly devoid of experiential content. It is precisely in the interplay of such residuals of subjective experience and a common linguistic code that one's subjectivity can be made more real.

ON ATTAINING SHARED SOCIAL REALITY: A CLINICAL EXAMPLE

Some of the points made in the preceding two sections will now be illustrated by way of a clinical example taken from the influential recent work of Grinder and Bandler (1976). We wish to illustrate the thesis that failure to arrive at intersubjectivity and shared social reality is at the heart of clinical problems. In addition, we hope to demonstrate, the therapist plays her role by bringing to the situation her construing (explicit or implicit) of the complex construings of the participants (T = therapist, S = Son, F = Father).

    (1) T: Well, George (a ten-year-old boy), I've heard from all of the family members except you — tell me, what do you want.

    (2) S: I want respect.

    (3) F: (smiling broadly) Yes, that I believe.

    (4) S: (explosively) SEE! That's just what I am talking about. I don't get any respect from anyone in this family.

(5) T: Wait, George, you sound real angry to me. Can you tell me what just happened with you?

(6) G: I . . . I . . . oh, never mind, you wouldn't understand anyway.

(7) T: Perhaps not, but try me — did the way you just responded have something to do with something your father did?

(8) G: Yes, I ask for respect and HE (pointing at his father Matt) just laughs right out loud, making fun of me.

(9) T: George, tell me something: How specifically would you know that your father was respecting you?

(10) S: He wouldn't laugh at me — he would watch me when I say things and be serious about it.

(11) T: George, I want to tell you something I noticed and can see right now. Look at your father's face.

(12) S: Yeah, so what?

(13) T: Well does he look serious to you — like he, maybe respects you for what you are doing right now.

(14) S: Yeah, you know, he does look like he is.

(15) T: Ask him, George.

(16) S: What . . . ask him . . . Dad, do you respect me? Are you taking me seriously?

(17) F: Yes, son . . . (softly) . . . I'm taking you seriously right now. I respect what you are doing.

(18) S: (crying softly) I really believe that you do Dad.

(19) T: I have a hunch right now that Matt has more to say George, will you take him (indicating Matt) seriously and listen to him?

(20) S: Sure.

(21) F: You only saw the smile and did not hear what I said (crying softly) and then, when you became angry, I suddenly remembered how I never believed my father respected me and I'm grateful (turning to the therapist) that you helped me straighten this out with George.

(22) T: That's right — a message that is not received the way you intended it is no message at all. Matt, is there some other way that you can show George that you care for him and respect him (pp. 138-139)?

The example illustrates the complexity of actual messages. We here take the state of affairs to be the son's wish for respect and the intensity of the wish (its close relation to core constructs).

Consider now (3) — in light of the ensuing dialogue, see especially (21). At most this illustrates a quite limited intersubjectivity (see p. 245); the father understands the wish for respect, but not its intensity. It is as if (3) is addressed to two different worlds: On the one hand there is the smile, turned inwards, perhaps in memory of his own childhood where he may conceive of faded memories and resignation. On the other hand there are the words; probably honest, he has listened to the son and "understood" him. We might say that (3) communicates on different levels, the smile reflecting preverbal constructs. In, for instance, transactional analysis one could describe the smile as reflecting the wanton child; the words, the adult. Only in a very limited way does the father obey the constraints of sociality, that is, to speak on the son's premises, to adopt his emotional-cognitive perspective. He does not reflect on the fact that the smile refers to a unique background, which the son cannot possibly share. We may say that he is (partly) caught in his egocentricity.

In (4) we clearly see that even though there is a limited intersubjectivity for the father, there is no intersubjectivity for the son and thus no shared social reality. In the previous paragraph we attributed "the fault" to the father, but the son's anticipation was probably geared toward the disrespect pole, a pole that for him probably had been amply validated [see (6)]. So, might we not just as well have emphasized that the son did not listen on the father's premises? Is it possible to make general statements as to the fault when mutual intersubjectivity fails?

The therapist, however, wisely avoids any "attribution of fault." She asks for elaboration of the "unreceived message" (9), and helps the son to be more receptive to the relevant pole (11) to (13), while at the same time helping the father to focus better on *his* message (17) — see also (19). The therapist accomplishes "interchangeability of dialogue roles." Notice that bringing "respect" into focus for the son theoretically can be approached either in terms of permeability or complimentarily — how salient the message is made. Though this excerpt is meant to be a suitable illustration of attainment of shared social reality, it also underscores the improbability of achieving perfect sharing (see p. 238). We can pinpoint lack of intersubjectivity, but a positive diagnosis of intersubjectivity is difficult. The intensity of the wish for respect can probably not be approached by the conventional tools of cognitive psychology (see, for instance, the previously cited work of Garner [1974] and Olson [1970]) but must be approached by considering the speaker's complete construction system.

A primary therapeutic task is to provide data that unequivocally may serve to invalidate crippling beliefs, beliefs that are generalized beyond any reasonable range — see (4). This is a difficult task since we are too prone to disregard evidence contrary to our strongly held convictions (see Nisbett and Ross [1980] for extensive discussion of this point). It may be the case that bewilderment and uncertainty is a necessary step in a transition to new construction. Mancuso (1977; see also Chapter 2, on the Fundamental Postulate) discusses arousal and the behaviors instigated by failure to anticipate, concluding that persons seek optimum levels of discrepancy. In his terminology we may see the successful therapist as a "successful novelty moderator," just as he regards the successful parent (Mancuso and Handin, 1980).

It would, however, be much too optimistic to assume — even given therapeutic wizardry — that shared social reality is always a possible goal. Consider the following example from Perry (1977, p. 182): "the youthful, athletic father construes skateboarding with his adolescent son and his peers as 'sharing, demonstrating camaraderie,' whereas the son construes this as 'not only intrusive, but also embarassing.' " Perry takes this to illustrate "misconstrual of constructual implications . . . persons can provisionally share a construct, yet envision vitally different implications." One may, however, well imagine that the son can perfectly well construe the construction process of his father, but that this does not in any way change his construction of the state of affairs "father and son skateboarding." Kelly (1970a, p. 25) was quite aware of this: "My construction of your outlook does not make me a compliant companion, nor does it keep us from working at cross purposes . . . but there is . . . still a good chance of a social process emerging out of our conflict, and we will both end up a good way from where we started." In this quotation Kelly seems to imply something more by "social process" than just "construing construction system," perhaps what we have called "shared social reality" is implied. What can now be said about the ideal amount of movement in such types of conflicts? Generally we would suggest that both should seek for a joint goal that *does* imply shared social reality and that in some sense the amount of movement should be as small as possible for both participants — they should seek for some kind of "least common multiplum." This, of course, may not relieve the father from a rather painful awakening to a quite substantial generation gap. Indeed, the son may wish so little in the way of intimacy that perhaps the father would be better off nourishing some illusions. We have sympathy for Kursh's (1971) arguments on "the benefits of poor communication."

HONORING AND VIOLATING INTERSUBJECTIVITY

In the section on "Construing Construction Processes . . ." we discussed how deep-seated is our belief in a common intersubjective world. Reciprocal role taking provides the basic context in which one confirms and extends such an intersubjective world (see p. 247). In this section we illustrate, from quite different vantage points, our "inbuilt sociality," that is, the extent to which we are committed to sociality. First an analysis of the query, "What are you doing?" suggests how readily we are inclined to honor sociality. The amazing consequences of Milton Erickson's inimitable ways of violating intersubjectivity further illustrate the importance of taking intersubjectivity as a basic premise of our social actions. (We note in passing that Erickson was the chief inspirator of Grinder and Bandler's previously cited work.)

"What Are You Doing?"

The meaning of the query, "What are you doing?" obviously varies very much with context. In the context of a boss to a secretary it might signify a request to put other work aside in order to serve the boss' immediate wish. If the target of the question had been behaving in a nonstandard way, it might be taken as a demand for an explanation of the curious behavior, and so forth. Let us here suppose that there is no "obvious" contextual justification for the question and that the participants have a (roughly) symmetric relation. Furthermore, the questioner is genuinely interested in the answer. The main point to be observed is that the response will very probably vary according to the relation between the speaker and the listener. One obvious type of variation is level of generality/preciseness — what we may call a vertical dimension. Generally speaking, the closer the relationship between the questioner and the answerer, the more detailed is the account given by the respondent. If the questioner were someone whom the respondent has not seen since school days, 25 years previously, the response surely will be, "I am working as a university teacher." If the questioner is a colleague who is encountered several times each week, the answer might be, "I am struggling with some examples for the chapter I am writing with Ragnar."

We wish to suggest that for each specific relation between the questioner/ answerer there is an optimal level of preciseness. This implies that there are two different types of nonoptimal responses, each of which, though in different ways, will impede a smooth-flowing dialogue. One may answer on a too-general level: If one were to answer the colleague, "I am working as a university teacher," it would serve as a rebuff, irony, or refusal to engage in conversation. One may answer on a too-specific level: To speak of a very precise writing endeavor might be embarrassing to the questioner if she had been a former schoolmate; she would be at a loss about how to proceed with the conversation.

Generally we suggest that persons are very sensitive to whether the conversation is at an optimal level or whether it deviates. At signs of embarrassment one will move up to a more general level where the other can comfortably follow one's exposition. Conversely one will move down to a more precise level if one has underestimated the level of knowledge of the other. Monitoring the conversation to stay at an optimal level may well be a basic conversational skill; it is so well learned that pronounced (and repeated) departures from the optimal level, as already suggested, are taken to imply a different kind of message (for example, irony of being too general). This notion of optimal level of preciseness can be seen to have a general scope (see Version 3 of the Sociality Corollary). Consider Naess' (1953) notion of "depth of intention." The optimal depth of intention clearly varies with the context and the relation between the speakers. It is, for instance, hardly appropriate for the professor of political science to press the naive but enthusiastic local May 17th speaker (the Norwegian "Fourth of July") for a precise specification of what she or he implies by "democracy" and "freedom."

In a series of experimental reports on categorizing behavior, Rosch (1978) has attempted to explicate a notion of "basic level objects" independent of the social contexts of language. Tversky (1977, p. 348), in his more formal exposition of this notion, says, "Chair for example is a basic category, furniture is too general and kitchen chair is too specific. Similarly car is a basic category, vehicle is too general and sedan is too specific." Rosch suggests that there is a general principle of "cognitive economy" that accounts for formation of basic-level categories. These conceptualizations offer useful clarification of our idea of optimal level in precision of messages. The category level that one uses in a particular context should depend on other features of the context, as is suggested by Olson's (1970) previously cited work. We note that while Rosch's important work can be helpful in explicating the idea of optimal level, it does not completely serve as a basis for understanding conversations, since in our analysis the optimal level cannot be specified independently of the relation between the speakers.

Our point would be better made had we a systematic investigation of how people respond to the question, "What are you doing?" We would venture the hypothesis that the answer will generally be framed to give the questioner maximal information with a minimum of effort. In Kellian terms the answer will give a reply that optimizes the questioner's possiblities for anticipating the answerer. The process seems to conform to the following sociality inspired rewriting (in italics) of the Choice Corollary:

> A person chooses for himself *that statement* (that alternative in a dichotomized construct system) through which he anticipates the greater possibility for the elaboration of *the other's construction* of himself (his system).

This formulation should underscore how completely a person, in this analysis the person responding to the question, accepts the obligation to build a message on the other's premises; and it should be clear that this is a very effective mechanism for enlarging a shared social world. Furthermore, our sensitivity to departures from an optimal level inform us of the extent to which intersubjectivity is taken for granted.

This type of process, of course, follows from the necessary precondition that the answerer trusts that the questioner is genuinely interested in his doings. Only in this case will he effortlessly give an answer that provides the questioner with maximal opportunities for further getting to know him. If, however, the answerer suspects some manipulative intent, this "inbuilt sociality" will be replaced by a conscious review of one's doings, and the production of a guarded answer destined to minimize manipulation. ("Does the questioner try to find out if my current work is not important, so that I can be asked to serve on some [time consuming] committee?")

The Violation of Intersubjectivity

Generally we expect others to share our premises, and the strength of this expectation is best illustrated by considering the effects of seriously violating intersubjectivity. What happens when our naive faith in a shared experiential world (see above p. 246) is violated? Consider the following example, which is of special interest, since it inspired Erickson (1967) to develop one of his most powerful hypnotic techniques, the confusion technique.

Example (1)

The incident, one of spontaneous humor on my part, that led to its adaptation as a possible hypnotic technique was as follows. One windy day as I was on my way to attend the first formal seminar on hypnosis conducted in the U.S. by Clark L. Hull at the University of Wisconsin in 1923, where I reported on my experimental work and graduate psychology students discussed my findings, a man came rushing around the corner of a building and bumped hard against me as I stood bracing myself against the wind. Before he could recover his poise to speak to me, I glanced elaborately at my watch and courteously, as if he had inquired the time of the day, I stated, "It's exactly 10 minutes of two," though it was actually closer to 4:00 p.m. and I walked on. About half a block away, I turned and saw him still looking at me, undoubtedly still puzzled and bewildered by my remark (p. 131).

This illustrates what may happen when the speaker, here called the "agent," does not monitor what he does in accordance with what he assumes to be the premises of the other and, instead, acts from a position completely incompatible with that of the listener, here called the "victim." Erickson bars "a man" from acting from his position (bumping into a stranger) by acting from the incompatible position — a request for time. Erickson deliberately makes his own private world (thoughts about Hull, ever present intention to exercise his sense of humor) inaccessible to the victim. The importance of inbuilt circularity and reciprocal role taking is very clearly revealed when Erickson deliberately violates this and imposes an alien definition on the situation so that the victim is left gaping in confusion. Whereas ordinary communication can profitably be described as "drafts of contracts" and "potentially shared strategies of categorization" (Rommetveit, 1974, in preparation). Erickson in a sense offers a contract that cannot be accepted.

We may describe violations of intersubjectivity as varying in strength where some of the (overlapping) factors related to strength are: The ease with which the situation is construed in one specific way, and the implausibility of alternative constructions. In Kellian terms: How preemptive is the dominant construction? How strongly does the situation tend to elicit ready-made responses such as, for instance, "I'm sorry," "Look where you are going," and so forth. Put otherwise, how enmeshed, or engulfed, is the victim in the situation? Looking at the situation from the other point of view: How forcefully is the alternative ("violating") construction presented by the agent? Immediacy, exuded certainty, and definiteness are here important factors. There is a pronounced difference between the way a lay person might say, "It's exactly 10 minutes of two," and the way a highly accomplished hypnotist, like Erickson, would say it.

With weak violations of intersubjectivity one would scarcely expect more than a raised eyebrow or a puzzled glance. With very strong violations one would not be surprised to see open-mouthed befuddlement that would be comparable to a hypnotic trance. We do not have information about the state in which Erickson left the victim in Example (1). Consider, however, Example (2), which leads immediately to acceptance of the hypnotic role.

Example (2)

There was a physician who repeatedly manifested hostile aggressive behavior . . . when introduced to the author he shook hands with a bone-crushing grip . . . and aggressively declared that he would like to "see any damn fool try to hypnotize me." . . . As the man stepped up on the platform, the author slowly arose from his chair as if to greet him with a handshake. As the volunteer stretched forth his hand, prepared to give the author another bone-crushing handshake, the author bent over and tied his shoe strings slowly, elaborately and left the man standing helplessly with the hand outstretched. Bewildered, confused, completely taken aback at the author's nonpertinent behavior, at a total loss for something to do, the man was completely vulnerable to the first comprehensible communication *fitting to the* situation that was offered to him. As the second shoe string was being tied, the author said, "just take a deep breath, sit down in the chair, close your eyes, and go deeply into a trance" (Erickson, 1967, p. 153).

This the subject did, and it will be seen that "tying shoe strings" served a similar function as "it's exactly 10 minutes of two" in Example (1). In Example (2) tying shoelaces is incompatible with the physician's ritual/competitive greeting just as request for time is incompatible with bumping into a stranger in Example (1). Put otherwise, Erickson ignores the usual social conventions in these situations and provides a radically different answer to the basic question, "What is going on?" (Goffman, 1974).

These examples would suggest another (minor) revision of the Sociality Corollary. Notice first that in terms of mutuality one could hardly call the interactions in the examples social processes, (see p. 252). We emphasize in the corollary: *"to the extent* that one person construes the construction processes of another, he *may* play a role in a social process involving the other." Notice now that *may* seems to be ambiguous. Is it tied to *to the extent*; or is it a dichotomous choice, independent of the conditional *to the extent*? Our reading of Kelly suggests the first possibility; that is, the greater the extent, the more the conduciveness to role playing. However, our analysis of Examples (1) and (2) invites the second possibility. Even though "the extent" may be maximal, an agent may still choose to violate instead of honor intersubjectivity. The agent may just choose to bar a social process. This reasoning suggests the following (in italics) addendum in the corollary:

> Version 4: To the extent that one person construes the construction processes of another, he may, *if he so chooses*, play a role in a social process involving the other.

Varying levels of violations of intersubjectivity may be related to the previously mentioned optimal discrepancy hypothesis discussed by Mancuso (1977). Consider again the Fundamental Postulate: "A person's processes are psychologically channelized by the ways in which he anticipates events." Strong violations undermine intentionality by blocking off anticipations and may thus be expected to have profound effects on a person's processes. We trust that readers of this volume are fully aware that processes are not just information processing or some cognitive aspect, but involve the person in his or her total existence. Before considering this further we will take one more look at moderate violation. Humor may be regarded as an example of transforming a moderate violation to a definition that restores intersubjectivity. We are amused by the behavior of Sid Krassman, in Southern's (1970) novel *Blue Movie*, who:

Example (3)
stepping into a crowded elevator might intone with tremendous authority: "I suppose you're all wondering why I called you together."

The victims will be likely to apply the construction, a random assemblage, to the situation. Krassman deliberately violates this construction by acting from the contrasting position, a purposeful meeting. Since one rarely is deeply enmeshed in elevator riding, it is not difficult to enjoy temporarily the construction "a purposeful meeting"; it may provide a vastly more interesting trip. Moderate violations may alternatively be described as "being at the moving edge of assimilation" to repeat the fine phrase used by Eckblad (1981) in her Kelly-congenial account of "motivation for problem solving." Conversely, strong violations may be seen to exceed Mancuso's moderate discrepancy. There are then no superordinate constructions that readily can be invoked. (For a more complete analysis we would have to consider also the Modulation, Fragmentation, and, of course, the Organization Corollaries.)

Schematically we may ascribe two aspects to the social process of inducing hypnosis, illustrating from Erickson's work with cancer patients. (See Tschudi [1979] for a further discussion of how Erickson uses his confusion technique to alleviate cancer pains.) The patient is uprooted by violations of intersubjectivity and then redirected. The paradoxical injunctions make it impossible for the patient to uphold the ordinary state, and thus attention is diverted away from the pain: "an arrest of the patient's attention, rigid fixation of his eyes, the development of physical immobility, even catalepsy and an intense desire to understand what the author so gravely and so earnestly is saying to them." The special induced state paves the way for redirection: "There develops unwittingly in the patient a different state of inner orientation, highly conducive to hypnosis and receptive to any suggestion that meets his needs" (Erickson, 1967, p. 153).

We return now to previous allusions to the assumption that bewilderment and uncertainty may be necessary transitional steps to new constructions. Consider, in a Sullivanian mood, psychotherapeutic problems as failures of intersubjectivity. This suggests that in order to achieve a deeper intersubjectivity, previous intersubjectivity must first be renounced; uprooting must precede redirection. This may be seen as a paradoxical counterpart to our previous assertion that intersubjectivity must be taken for granted in order to be achieved. At present we can but touch on complex dialectic relations. Perhaps attainment of shared social reality should be regarded as a major accomplishment, something to be deeply cherished. All of us may have experienced situations in which the hold may seem to slip — the fragility of our existence. Violation of intersubjectivity may uproot us. Conversely, affirmations serve to root us. Bateson (1951, p. 213) expounds a view of everyday conversations that fits well with this point of view:

> When A communicates with B, the mere act of communicating can carry the implicit statement "we are communicating." In fact this may be the most important message that is sent and received. The wisecracks of American adolescents and the smoother but no less stylized conversation of adults are only occasionally concerned with the giving and receiving of objective information, mostly the conversations of leisure hours exist because people need to know that they are in touch with each other. They may ask questions which superficially seem to be about matters of impersonal fact — "Will it rain," "What is in today's war news," but the speaker's interest is focused on the fact of communicating with another human being.

This brings to mind Malinowski's (1923) emphasis on "phatic" communication. Analysis of human communication must consider the importance of providing mutual reassurance that we hold on to reality.

TYPES OF SOCIAL INTERCHANGES

In the outline below we attempt a preliminary classification of social interchanges. This is followed by some comments on types of interchange not previously discussed in this chapter. Our aim is to show how degree of construing of construction systems and honor-violate may serve as useful constructs. The incompleteness of our venture will be evident, but we assume, at least, to add some elaboration to Kelly's very basic proposition.

Type	Degree of Construing Construction Systems	Honor-Violate	Evaluation
1. love, dialogue, I-thou	high	highly honor	good
2. bureaucracy, usual meeting of strangers	medium		neutral/ good
3. humor (pranks)	medium, at best	medium violation	
4. cognitive imperialism	medium	medium violation	
5. sexism	medium/low	medium violation	evil
6. successful manipulation (seducer, "con man")	high	highly violate	
7. deindividuation, sadism, I-it	low	highly violate	

A beginning analysis of type 1, love, has been offered by Bannister and Fransella (1971, p. 38), who regard it as "elaborating core role structure." This phenomenon is readily seen to be high on all our dimensions. An intriguing analysis of love, one that is congenial to a Kellian, is found in Buber (1958) in his celebrated analysis of "I-thou" (contrasted with I-it). Types 2 and 3 have already been discussed (see p. 237, and p. 257), here we reiterate the point that deviations from the high degree of construing and honor poles need not be aligned with the bad pole of the evaluation construct. We now turn to our preliminary analysis of the psychology of evil, types 4 to 7, which is our attempt to go beyond Kelly's evaluations (see especially Q4 at the beginning of this chapter). Cognitive imperialism is a term borrowed from Berger (1976). He uses the concept in a highly critical discussion of experts who want to raise the consciousness of the poor and downtrodden. Cognitive imperialism is seen to occur when " 'inhabitants' of one world impose their particular modes of perception, evaluation, and action on those who previously had organized their relationship to reality differently" (p. 128). Cognitive imperialism is contrasted with cognitive respect, which "is based on the understanding that every human being is *in possession* of a world of his own, and that nobody can interpret this world better (or more 'expertly') than he can himself" (p. 60). "Cognitive respect, then, means that one takes with utmost seriousness the way in which others define reality" (p. 134). The argument for cognitive respect is based on "a postulate of the equality of all empirically based worlds of consciousness" (p. 127).

Consideration of the Kellian emphasis on reflexivity, as implied by the Fundamental Postulate, should enjoin one to see the world of the other as having the same epistemological status as one's own. We may see cognitive respect/imperialism as a highly superordinate or metaconstruct. To understand cognitive imperialism may well lead one to understand cultural imperialism. Why is it that so many seemingly well-intentioned attempts to help in the developing countries turn sour? Galtung (1978) has suggested that all such projects should be really bilateral, we should also be the recipients of help, not just benevolent senders. Perhaps this may turn out to be a necessary safeguard against the possibility of wrecking cultures through cognitive imperialism.

Sexism, type 5, may be seen as similar to cognitive imperialism in that it is another way whereby some humans see others as something less than themselves. Following Simone de Beauvoir's (1952) classical treatise, Johnsen (1979) sees the essence of sexism, exploitation, as denying transcendence for women. Women are then mainly regarded as immanent (as objects) and are not provided with the same opportunities for creative growth that are provided to men (see also Q6 at the beginning of the chapter). The tragedy of sexism is not only that it cripples women; sexism promotes a low level of construing and thereby bars the development of type 1, loving relationships. Kelly construes the psychopath as someone who "treats others as an object," see Q4 above. However, just placing such an unsavory actor at the nonsocial pole prompts us to overlook the insidious skill of the manipulator who understands our constructions all too well, but who does not honor our subjectivity. The successful manipulator does not grant us cognitive respect, but regards us exclusively as a tool for his or her own ends. A manipulator need not necessarily be concerned with mere immediate accuracy, but may well be out to "anticipate . . . sense what we are up to" (see Q3 above).

Returning now to the Erickson examples cited in the previous section, we highlight the insufficiency of the present analysis. While Examples (1) and (2) can be regarded as type 3 — humor — what about using hypnotism to alleviate pain? Should that be classified as type 6 — manipulation? It is necessary to emphasize that violation depends upon our level of construction. On some level such use of hypnotism could be regarded as high violation, but ultimately the behavior was completed under the aegis of deep concern. Uprooting at one level presupposes empathy with the hope of rerooting at another level. This is contrary to the act of the successful manipulator, which reflects a choice not to honor the interests of the other (see version 4).

Turning now to type 7, note first that the distinction between type 6 and type 7 seems to be missed by Kelly. To analyze type 7, we once again turn to Berger (1977), whose commentary parallels our thinking about sociality. Analyzing two well-known killers, Charles Manson (the Sharon Tate murders) and Lt. Calley (the My Lai massacre), Berger goes beyond the stultifying left/right distinction (Manson being the archvillain for the right, Lt. Calley for the left), and points out a deep-seated similarity between the two killers. For Lt. Calley the victims were (as for most Americans fighting in Vietnam) deprived of individuality: "I was ordered to go in there and destroy the enemy. That was my job on that day. I did not sit down and think in terms of men, women and children. They were all classified the same, and that was the classification we dealt with, just as enemy soldiers" (quoted from Berger, 1977, p. 119). Similarly Manson and his crowd were out to "get the pigs." Berger's formula for terrorism is "the victims must be dehumanized and the killers deprived of individuality" (p. 122). "Dehumanizing" is elaborated by Becker in his analysis of sadomasochism: "the sadomasochist is someone who has trouble believing in the validity and sanctity of people's insides — their spirit, personality and self" (Becker, 1968, p. 182).

We end by again referring to value implications. It behooves us to be utterly serious as we evaluate about consistently low levels of construing construction processes. Disregard of others' constructions may be associated with untold terror. Notice, as well, the other facet in Berger's formula — not only are the victims dehumanized, but the killers are also deprived of individuality. This raises the general question about the relation between construction of self and construction of others. If one reduces others, does this necessarily lead to a reduced conception of self? In Hegelian terms, is the master reduced when he subjugates the slave?

REFERENCES

Adams-Webber, J. Cognitive complexity and sociality. *British Journal of Social and Clinical Psychology*, 1969, *8*, 211-216.

Adams-Webber, J. An analysis of the discriminant validity of several repertory grid indices. *British Journal of Psychology*, 1970a, *61*, 83-90.

Adams-Webber, J. Actual structure and potential chaos. In D. Bannister (Ed.), *Perspectives in personal construct theory*. London: Academic Press, 1970b.

Adams-Webber, J. The organization of judgements based on positive and negative adjectives in the Bannister-Fransella Grid Test. *British Journal of Medical Psychology*, 1977a, *50*, 173-176.

Adams-Webber, J. The golden section and the structure of self-concepts. *Perceptual and Motor Skills*, 1977b, *45*, 703-706.

Adams-Webber, J. A further test of the golden section hypothesis. *British Journal of Psychology*, 1978, *69*, 439-442.

Adams-Webber, J. *Personal construct psychology: Concepts and applications*. New York: John Wiley, 1979a.

Adams-Webber, J. Construing persons in social contexts. In P. Stringer and D. Bannister (Eds.), *Constructs of sociality and individuality*. London: Academic Press, 1979b.

Adams-Webber, J. Intersubject agreement concerning relationships between the positive and negative poles of constructs in repertory grid tests. *British Journal of Medical Psychology*, 1979c, *52*, 197-199.

Adams-Webber, J. Empirical developments in personal construct theory. In H. Bonarius, R. Holland, and S. Rosenberg (Eds.), *Personal construct psychology*. London: Macmillan, 1980a.

Adams-Webber, J. Differences between physical and psychological constructs in repertory grids. *British Journal of Medical Psychology*, 1980b, *53*, 319-322.

Adams-Webber, J., and Benjafield, J. The relation between lexical marking and rating extremity in interpersonal judgment. *Canadian Journal of Behavioural Science*, 1973, *5*, 234-241.

Adams-Webber, J., and Benjafield, J. The golden section hypothesis. *British Journal of Psychology*, 1976a, *67*, 11-15.

Adams-Webber, J., and Benjafield, J. The relationship between cognitive complexity and assimilative projection in terms of personal constructs. *Bulletin of the British Psychological Society*, 1976b, *29*, 219.

Adams-Webber, J., and Davidson, D. L. Maximum contrast between self and others in personal judgment: A repertory grid study. *British Journal of Psychology*, 1979, *70*, 517-518.

Adams-Webber, J., Schwenker, B., and Barbeau, D. Personal constructs and the perception of individual differences. *Canadian Journal of Behavioural Science*, 1972, *4*, 218-224.

Alban Metcalfe, R. J. The validity, long-term reliability, generality, robustness, and inter-relatedness of selected rep grid indices of cognitive structure. *Journal of Experimental Education*, 1978, *47*, 134-139.

Allwood, J. Linguistic communication as action and cooperation: A study in pragmatics. *Gothenborg Monographs in Linguistics 2*, 1976.

Alvy, K. T. The development of listener adapted communication in grade-school children from different social-class backgrounds. *Genetic Psychology Monographs*, 1973, *87*, 33-104.

American College Dictionary. New York: Harper and Brothers, 1948.

Anderson, J. R., *Language, memory, and thought*. Hillsdale, N. J.: Lawrence Erlbaum Associates, 1976.

Anderson, J. R. *Cognitive psychology and its implications*. San Francisco: W. H. Freeman, 1980.

Anderson, J. R., and Bower, G. H. Recognition and retrieval processes in free recall. *Psychological Review*, 1972, *79*, 97-123.

Anderson, R. C., and Ortony, A. On putting apples into bottles — A problem of polysemy. *Cognitive Psychology*, 1975, *7*, 167-180.

Angyal, A. *Foundation for a science of personality*. Cambridge, Mass.: Harvard University Press, 1941.

Applebee, A. N. Developmental changes in consensus in construing within a specified domain. *British Journal of Psychology*, 1975, *66*, 473-480.

Applebee, A. N. The development of childrens' responses to repertory grids. *British Journal of Social and Clinical Psychology*, 1976, *15*, 101-102.

Applegate, J. L., and Delia, J. G. Person-centered speech, psychological development, and the contexts of language usage. In R. St. Clair and H. Giles (Eds.), *The social and psychological contexts of language*. Hillsdale, N.J.: Lawrence Erlbaum Associates, 1980.

Argyris, C., and Schon, D. A. *Theory in practice: Increasing professional effectiveness*. San Francisco: Jossey-Bass, 1976.

Asch, S. E. A reformulation of the problem of association. *American Psychologist*, 1969, *24*, 92-102.

Attneave, F. *Applications of information theory to psychology*. New York: Holt, Rinehart and Winston, 1959.

Austin, J. L. *How to do things with words*. Oxford: Oxford University Press, 1962.

Aydin, O., and Markova, I. Attribution tendencies of popular and unpopular children. *British Journal of Social and Clinical Psychology*, 1979, *18*, 291-298.

Baldwin, R. Change in interpersonal cognitive complexity as a function of a training group experience. *Psychological Reports*, 1972, *30*, 935-940.

Bannister, D. Conceptual structure in thought disordered schizophrenics. *Journal of Mental Science*, 1960, *106*, 1230-1249.

Bannister, D. The nature and measurement of schizophrenic thought disorder. *Journal of Mental Science*, 1962a, *108*, 825-842.

Bannister, D. Personal construct theory: a summary and experimental paradigm. *Acta Psychologica*, 1962b, *20*, 104-120.

Bannister, D. A new theory of personality. In B. Foss (Ed.), *New horizons in psychology*. Baltimore: Penguin, 1966.

Bannister, D. The myth of physiological psychology. *Bulletin of the British Psychological Society*, 1969, *21*, 229-231.

Bannister, D., and Agnew, J. The child's construing of self. In J. K. Cole and A. W. Landfield (Eds.), *Nebraska symposium on motivation*. Lincoln: University of Nebraska Press, 1977, 99-125.

Bannister, D., and Fransella, F. *Inquiring man: The theory of personal constructs.* Harmondsworth, Middlesex: Penguin, 1971.

Bannister, D., Fransella, F., and Agnew, J. Characteristics and validity of the grid test of thought disorder. *British Journal of Social and Clinical Psychology,* 1971, *10,* 144-151.

Bannister, D., and Mair, J. M. M. *The evaluation of personal constructs.* London: Academic Press, 1968.

Barratt, B. B. The development of organizational complexity and structure in peer perception (Unpublished manuscript, 1977a).

Barratt, B. B. The development of peer perception systems in childhood and early adolescence. *Social Behavior and Personality,* 1977b, *5,* 351-360.

Bartlett, F. C. *Remembering.* Cambridge: Cambridge University Press, 1932.

Bates, E. *Language and context. The acquisition of pragmatics.* New York: Academic Press, 1976.

Bateson, G. When validity depends upon belief. In G. Bateson and J. Ruesch, *Communication: The social matrix of psychiatry.* New York: Norton, 1951.

Bateson, G. *Steps towards an ecology of mind.* Suffolk: Paladin, 1973.

Bateson, G. *Mind and nature.* New York: Dutton, 1979.

Beck, A. T., Rush, A. J., Shaw, F. B., and Emery, G. *Cognitive therapy of depression.* New York: Guilford Press, 1979.

Becker, E. *The structure of evil.* New York: The Free Press, 1968.

Benjafield, J. The golden rectangle: Some new data. *American Journal of Psychology,* 1976, *89,* 737-743.

Benjafield, J., and Adams-Webber, J. Assimilative projection and construct balance in the repertory grid. *British Journal of Psychology,* 1975, *66,* 169-173.

Benjafield, J., and Adams-Webber, J. The golden section hypothesis. *British Journal of Psychology,* 1976, *67,* 11-15.

Benjafield, J., and Green, T. R. G. Golden section relations in interpersonal judgement. *British Journal of Psychology,* 1978, *69,* 25-35.

Benjafield, J., Jordan, D., and Pomeroy, E. Encounter groups: A return to the fundamental. *Psychotherapy: Theory, Research and Practice,* 1976, *13,* 387-389.

Benjafield, J., and Pomeroy, E. A possible ideal underlying interpersonal descriptions. *British Journal of Social and Clinical Psychology*, 1978, *17*, 339-340.

Berger, P. L. *Pyramids of sacrifice*. New York: Anchor Books, 1976.

Berger, P. L. *Facing up to modernity*. Harmondsworth, Middlesex: Penguin, 1977.

Berger, P. L., Berger, B., and Kellner, H. *The homeless mind*. Harmondsworth, Middlesex: Penguin, 1974.

Berger, P. L., and Luckmann, T. *The social construction of reality*. New York: Doubleday, 1967.

Bergson, M. *Time and free will*. New York: Macmillan, 1910.

Berlyne, D. E. *Conflict, arousal, and curiosity*. New York: McGraw-Hill, 1960.

Berlyne, D. E. *Aesthetics and psychobiology*. New York: Appleton-Century-Crofts, 1971.

Berlyne, D. E. Curiosity and learning. *Motivation and Emotion*, 1978, *2*, 97-175.

Bieri, J. Cognitive complexity-simplicity and predictive behavior. *Journal of Abnormal and Social Psychology*, 1955, *51*, 263-268.

Bieri, J., Atkins, A. L., Briar, S., Leaman, R. L., Miller, H., and Tripodi, T. *Clinical and social judgment*. New York: John Wiley, 1966.

Bodden, J. and James, L. E. Influence of occupational information giving on cognitive complexity. *Journal of Counseling Psychology*, 1976, *23*, 280-282.

Bohm, D. *Wholeness and the implicate order*. London: Routledge and Kegan Paul, 1980.

Bolles, R. C. Reinforcement, expectancy, and learning. *Psychological Review*, 1972, *79*, 394-409.

Bonarius, H. The interaction model of communication: Through experimental research towards existential relevance. In J. Cole (Ed.), *Nebraska symposium on motivation* (Vol. 24). Lincoln: University of Nebraska Press, 1977, pp. 291-343.

Bonarius, J. C. J. Research in the personal construct theory of George A. Kelly. In B. A. Maher (Ed.), *Progress in experimental personality research* (Vol. 2). New York: Academic Press, 1965.

Bonarius, J. C. J. Personal constructs and extremity of ratings. In *Proceedings XVIth International Congress of Applied Psychology*. Amsterdam: Swets and Zeitinger, 1968, pp. 595-599.

Bonarius, J. C. J. *Personal construct psychology and extreme response style: An interaction model of meaningfulness, maladjustment, and communication*. Groningen: University of Groningen, 1970.

Boucher, J., and Osgood, C. E. The Pollyanna hypothesis. *Journal of Verbal Learning and Verbal Behavior*, 1969, *8*, 1-8.

Bowers, K. S. Situationism in psychology: An analysis and critique. *Psychological Review*, 1973, *80*, 307-336.

Boxer, P. J. Developing the quality of judgement. *Personnel Review*, 1978, 7, 36-39.

Boxer, P. J. Reflective Analysis. *International Journal of Man-Machine Studies*, 1979, *11*, 547-584.

Boxer, P. J. Supporting reflective learning: Towards a reflexive theory of form. *Human Relations*, 1980, *33* (1), 1-22.

Boxer, P. J., and Boot, R. L. Reflective learning. In J. Beck and C. Cox (Eds.), *Advances in management education*. New York: John Wiley, 1980.

Brainerd, C. J. *Piaget's theory of intelligence*. Englewood Cliffs, N.J.: Prentice-Hall, 1978.

Bransford, J. D., Barclay, J. R., and Franks, J. J. Sentence meaning: A constructive versus interpretative approach. *Cognitive Psychology*, 1972, *3*, 193-209.

Bransford, J. D., and Johnson, M. K. Contextual prerequisites for understanding: Some investigations of comprehension and recall. *Journal of Verbal Learning and Verbal Behavior*, 1972, *11*, 717-726.

Bringuier, J. *Conversations with Jean Piaget*. Chicago: University of Chicago Press, 1980.

Broughton, J. Development of concepts of self, mind, reality, and knowledge. In W. Damon (Ed.), *Social cognition*. San Francisco: Jossey Bass, 1978, pp. 75-200.

Bruner, J. From communication to language: A psychological perspective. In I. Marlove (Ed.), *The social context of language*. Chichester: John Wiley, 1978.

Bruner, J. S., Goodnow, J., and Austin, G. A. *A study of thinking*. New York: John Wiley, 1956.

Bruner, J. S., and Tagiuri, R. The perception of people. In G. Lindsey (Ed.), *Handbook of social psychology*. Cambridge, Mass.: Addison-Wesley, 1954.

Buber, M. *I and thou*. New York: Charles Scribner's Sons, 1958.

Byrne, D., and Clore, G. L. Effectance arousal and attraction. *Journal of Personality and Social Psychology Monographs*, 1967 (6, Whole No. 638).

Cameron, P., Stewart, L., Craig, L., and Eppleman, L. Think versus self versus other mental orientation across the life-span: A note. *British Journal of Psychology*, 1963, *64*, 283-286.

Cantor, N., and Mischel, W. Traits as prototypes: Effects on recognition memory. *Journal of Personality and Social Psychology*, 1977, *35*, 38-48.

Cantor, N., and Mischel, W. Prototypes in person perception. In L. Berkowitz (Ed.), *Advances in experimental social psychology*. New York: Academic Press, 1979.

Carlston, D. E. Events, inferences, and impression formation, In R. Hastie, T. M. Ostrom, E. B. Ebbesen, R. S. Wyer, D. L. Hamilton, and D. E. Carlston *Person memory: the cognitive basis of social perception*. Hillsdale, N.J.: Lawrence Erlbaum Associates, 1980.

Carver, C. S. A cybernetic model of self-attention processes. *Journal of Personality and Social Psychology*, 1979, *37*, 1251-1281.

Chomsky, N. Review of B. F. Skinner's *Verbal behavior*. *Language*, 1959, *35*, 26-58.

Clark, H. H. Linguistic processes in deductive reasoning. *Psychological Review*. 1969, *76*, 387-404.

Clark, H. H., and Card, S. K. The role of semantics in remembering comparative sentences. *Journal of Experimental Psychology*, 1969, *82*, 545-553.

Clark, R. A., and Delia, J. G. The development of functional persuasive skills in childhood and early adolescence. *Child Development*, 1976, *47*, 1008-1014.

Clark, R. A., and Delia, J. G. Cognitive complexity, social perspective taking, and functional persuasive skills in second- to ninth-grade children. *Human Communication Research*, 1977, *3*, 128-134.

Clyne, S. The effect of cognitive complexity and assimilative projection on preference for the definitive or extensive role in an elaborative choice situation (M.A. thesis, University of Windsor, 1975).

Cochran, L. Categorization and change in conceptual relatedness. *Canadian Journal of Behavioural Science*, 1976, *8*, 275-286.

Cofer, C. N. Constructive processes in memory. *American Scientist*, 1973, *61*, 537-543.

Cofer, C. N. On the constructive theory of memory. In I. C. Uzgiris and F. Weizman (Eds.), *The structuring of experience*, New York: Plenum Press, 1977.

Collins, A. M., and Loftus, E. F. A spreading activation theory of semantic processing. *Psychological Review*, 1975, *82*, 407-428.

Collins, A. M., and Quillian, M. R. Experiments on semantic memory and language comprehension. In L. W. Gregg (Ed.), *Cognition and learning in memory*. New York: John Wiley, 1972, pp. 117-137.

Collins, J. T., and Hagen, J. W. A constructivist account of the development of perception, attention and memory. In G. A. Hale and M. Lewis (Eds.), *Attention and cognitive development*. New York: Plenum Press, 1979, pp. 65-96.

Cometa, M., and Eson, M. E. Logical operations and metaphor interpretations. *Child Development*, 1978, *49*, 649-659.

Cooney, E. W., and Selman, R. L. Children's use of social conceptions. In W. Darmon (Ed.), *Social cognition*. San Francisco: Jossey-Bass, 1978.

Coward, R., and Ellis, J. *Language and materialism*. London: Routledge and Kegan Paul, 1977.

Craig, G., and Boyle, M. The recognition and spontaneous use of psychological descriptions by young children. *British Journal of Social and Clinical Psychology*, 1979, *18*, 207-208.

Crockett, W. H. Cognitive complexity and impression formation. In B. A. Maher (Ed.). *Progress in experimental personality research* (Vol. 2). New York: Academic Press, 1965.

Crockett, W. H., Gonyea, A. H., and Press, A. N. Comparison of two measures of cognitive complexity. Paper delivered at 1967 meetings of the Eastern Psychological Association.

Crockett, W. H., Mahood, S. M., and Press, A. N. Impressions of a speaker as a function of set to understand or to evaluate, of cognitive complexity, and of prior attitudes. *Journal of Personality*, 1975, *43*, 168-178.

Crockett, W. H., and Meisel, P. Construct connectedness, strength of discon-firmation, and impression change. *Journal of Personality*, 1974, *42*, 290-299.

Cronbach, L. J. Processes affecting scores on "understanding of others" and "assumed similarity." *Psychological Bulletin*, 1955, *52*, 177-193.

Damon, W. The nature of social-cognitive change in the developing child. In W. F. Overton and J. M. Gallagher (Eds.), *Knowledge and development*. New York: Plenum Press, 1981a.

Damon, W. Patterns of change in children's social reasoning: A two year longi-tudinal study. *Child Development*, 1981b, *51*, 1010-1017.

Davidson, D. L. The golden section and interpersonal judgments. Paper pre-sented at the Tenth Annual Ontario Undergraduate Thesis Conference, University of Guelph, 1979.

De Beauvoir, S. *The second sex*. New York: Alfred A. Knopf, 1952.

Deese, J. Behavior and fact. *American Psychologist*, 1969, *24*, 515-522.

Deese, J. Semantic and syntactic processing are separate. Paper presented at the Annual Meeting of the American Psychological Association, Washington, D.C., 1971.

Deese, J. Cognitive structure and affect in language. In L. Pliner, P. Krames, and T. Alloway (Eds.), *Communication and affect*. London: Academic Press, 1973.

Delia, J. G. Dialects and the effects of stereotypes on interpersonal attraction and cognitive processes in impression formation. *Quarterly Journal of Speech*, 1972, *58*, 285-297.

Delia, J. G. A constructivist analysis of the concept of credibility. *Quarterly Journal of Speech*, 1976, *62*, 361-375.

Delia, J. G. Constructivism and the study of human communication. *Quarterly Journal of Speech*, 1977, *63*, 66-83.

Delia, J. G., and Clark, R. A. Cognitive complexity, social perception and the development of listener-adapted communication of six-, eight-, ten-, and twelve-year-old boys. *Communication Monographs*, 1977, *44*, 326-345.

Delia, J. G., Clark, R. A., and Switzer, D. E. Cognitive complexity and impres-sion formation in informal social interaction. *Speech Monographs*, 1979, *41*, 299-308.

Delia, J. G., and Crockett, W. H. Social schemas, cognitive complexity, and the learning of social structures. *Journal of Personality*, 1973, *41*, 413-429.

Delia, J., Gonyea, A., and Crockett, W. The effects of subject-generated and normative constructs upon the formation of impressions. *British Journal of Social and Clinical Psychology*, 1971, *10*, 301-305.

Delia, J. G., Kline, S. L., and Burleson, B. R. The development of persuasive communication strategies in kindergarteners through twelfth-graders. *Communication Monographs*, 1979, *46*, 274-281.

Delia, J., and O'Keefe, B. The interpersonal constructs of Machiavellians. *British Journal of Social and Clinical Psychology*, 1976, *15*, 435-436.

Deutsch, W. *Sprachliche redundanz und objekt identifikation*. Marburg: Lahn, 1976.

Dewey, J. The reflex arc concept in psychology. *Psychological Review*, 1896, *3*, 357-370.

Dodge, K. Social cognitions and children's aggressive behavior. *Child Development*, 1980, *51*, 162-170.

Dooling, D. J., and Lachman, R. Effects of comprehension and retention on prose. *Journal of Experimental Psychology*, 1971, *88*, 216-222.

Duck, S. W. *Personal relationships and personal constructs: A study of friendship formation*. London: John Wiley, 1973.

Duck, S. W. Personality similarity and friendship choices by adolescents. *European Journal of Social Psychology*, 1975, *5*, 351-365.

Duck, S. W. *The study of acquaintance*. Fernborough: Teakfield, 1977a.

Duck, S. W. Inquiry, hypothesis and the quest for validation: Personal construct systems in the development of acquaintance. In S. W. Duck (Ed.), *Theory and practice in interpersonal attraction*. London: Academic Press, 1977b, pp. 379-404.

Duck, S. W. The personal and the interpersonal in construct theory: Social and individual aspects of relationships. In P. Stringer and D. Bannister (Eds.), *Constructs of sociality and individuality*. London: Academic Press, 1979, pp. 279-297.

Duck, S. W. Personal relationship research in the 1980s: Towards an understanding of complex human sociality. *Western Journal of Speech Communication*, 1980, *44*, 114-119.

Duck, S. W., and Gilmour, R. (Eds.). *Personal relationships 1: Studying personal relationships*. London: Academic Press, 1981a.

Duck, S. W., and Gilmour, R. (Eds.). *Personal relationships 2: Developing personal relationships*. London: Academic Press, 1981b.

Eckblad, G. *Scheme theory. A conceptual framework for cognitive motivational processes*. London: Academic Press, 1981.

Eiseley, L. *The night country*. New York: Charles Scribner's Sons, 1971.

Eiser, J. R., and Mower White, C. J. Affirmation and denial in evaluative descriptions. *British Journal of Psychology*, 1973, *64*, 399-403.

Endler, N. S. The role of person-by situation interactions in personality. In I. C. Uzgiris and F. Weizmann (Eds.), *The structuring of experience*. New York: Plenum Press, 1977, pp. 343-369.

Endler, N. S., and Magnusson, D. Toward an interactional psychology of personality. *Psychological Bulletin*, 1976, *83*, 956-974.

Epstein, S. The self-concept revisited: Or a theory of a theory. *American Psychologist*, 1973, *28*, 404-416.

Epting, F. The stability of cognitive complexity in construing social issues. *British Journal of Social and Clinical Psychology*, 1972, *5*, 122-125.

Epting, F., and Wilkins, G. Comparison of cognitive structural measures of predicting person perception. *Perceptual and Motor Skills*, 1974, *38*, 727-730.

Epting, F., Wilkins, G., and Margulis, S. Relationship between cognitive differentiation and level of abstraction. *Psychological Reports*, 1972, *31*, 367-370.

Erickson, M. H. *Advanced techniques of hypnosis and therapy*. In J. Haley (Ed.), *Selected papers of Milton H. Erickson, M.D.* New York: Grune and Stratton, 1967.

Ernest, C. H. Mental imagery ability and cognition: A critical review. *Journal of Mental Imagery*, 1977, *2*, 181-215.

Fechner, G. T. *Vorschule der aesthelik*. Leipsig: Breitkopf and Hartel, 1876.

Fisher, R. The making of reality. *Journal of Altered States of Consciousness*, 1978, *3*, 371-389.

Fiske, D. W., and Maddi, S. R. *Functions of varied experience*. Homewood, Ill.: Dorsey, 1961.

Flavell, J. H. *The developmental psychology of Jean Piaget: With a foreword by Jean Piaget.* Princeton, N.J.: Van Nostrand, 1963.

Flavell, J. Concept development. In P. H. Mussen (Ed.), *Manual of child psychology.* New York: John Wiley, 1970.

Flavell, J. H. The development of inferences about others. In T. Mischel (Ed.), *Understanding other persons.* London: Blackwell and Mott, 1974, pp. 66-116.

Flavell, J. H. The development of knowledge about visual perception. In C. B. Keasey (Ed.), *Nebraska symposium on motivation: Social cognitive development.* Lincoln: University of Nebraska Press, 1978, pp. 43-76.

Flavell, J. H., Everett, B. A., Croft, K., and Flavell, E. R. Young children's knowledge about visual perception: Further evidence for the level 1-level 2 distinction. *Developmental Psychology,* 1981, *17,* 99-103.

Fodor, J. A. The mind-body problem. *Scientific American,* 1981, *244,* 114-123.

Fowler, W. Sequence and styles in cognitive development. In I. C. Uzgiris and F. Weizmann (Eds.), *The structuring of experience.* New York: Plenum Press, 1977, pp. 265-295.

Fransella, F. *Personal change and reconstruction.* London: Academic Press, 1972.

Fransella, F., and Bannister, D. *A manual for repertory grid technique.* London: Academic Press, 1977.

Frazer, H. Agoraphobia: Parental influence and cognitive structures (Doctoral dissertation, University of Toronto, 1980).

Galtung, J. Wither technical assistance: On the future of international developmental co-operation. In *Toward self-reliance and global interdependence.* Ottawa: Canadian International Developmental Authority and Environment, 1978, pp. 62-85.

Gara, M. A., and Rosenberg, S. The identification of persons as supersets and subsets in free-response personality descriptions. *Journal of Personality and Social Psychology,* 1979, *37,* 2161-2170.

Gara, M. A., and Rosenberg, S. Linguistic factors in implicit personality theory. *Journal of Personality and Social Psychology,* in press.

Garfinkel, H. Studies of the routine grounds of everyday activities. In D. Sudnow (Ed.), *Studies in social interaction.* New York: The Free Press, 1972.

Garner, W. R. *Uncertainty and structure as psychological concepts.* New York: John Wiley, 1962.

Garner, W. R. *The processing of information and structure.* Hillsdale, N.J.: Lawrence Erlbaum Associates, 1974.

Gergen, K. J. Social psychology as history. *Journal of Personality and Social Psychology*, 1973, *26*, 309-320.

Gibson, E. J., and Levin, H. *The psychology of reading.* Cambridge, Mass.: MIT Press, 1975.

Godel, K. *On formally undecidable propositions.* New York: Basic Books, 1962.

Goffmann, E. *Frame analysis.* New York: Harper, 1974.

Goldstein, K. M., and Blackman, S. Cognitive complexity, maternal child rearing, and acquiescence. *Social Behavior and Personality*, 1977, *4*, 97-103.

Graf, P. Two consequences of generating: Increased inter- and intraword organization of sentences. *Journal of Verbal Learning and Verbal Behavior*, 1980, *19*, 316-327.

Grandstaff, N. W., and Pribram, K. H. Habituation: Electrical changes in the visual system. *Neuropsychologia*, 1972, *10*, 125-132.

Greenberg, J. H. *Language universals.* The Hague: Mouton, 1966.

Greeno, J. G. Psychology of learning, 1960-1980: One participant's observations. *American Psychologist*, 1980, *35*, 713-728.

Grice, H. P. Logic and conversation. In P. Cole and J. L. Morgan (Eds.), *Syntax and semantics: Speech acts.* New York: Academic Press, 1975, pp. 41-58.

Grinder, J., and Bandler, R. *The structure of magic, II.* Palo Alto, Calif.: Science and Behavior Books, 1976.

Grossberg, S. Pattern formation by the global limits of nonlinear competitive interaction in dimensions. *Journal of Mathematical Biology*, 1977, *4*, 237-256.

Grossberg, S. Do all neural models really look alike? A comment on Anderson, Silverstein, Ritz, and Jones. *Psychological Review*, 1978, *85*, 592-596.

Grossberg, S. How does a brain build a cognitive code? *Psychological Review*, 1980, *87*, 1-51.

Gruen, G., and Doherty, J. A constructivist view of a major development shift in early childhood. In I. C. Uzgiris and F. Weizmann (Eds.), *The structuring of experience*. New York: Plenum Press, 1977.

Guiraud, P. *Semiology*. London: Routledge and Kegan Paul, 1975.

Habermas, J. *Communication and the evolution of society*. Boston: Beacon Press, 1979.

Hale, C. L. Cognitive complexity-simplicity as a determinant of communication effectiveness. *Communication Monographs*, 1980, *47*, 304-311.

Hale, C. L., and Delia, J. G. Cognitive complexity and social perspective-taking. *Communication Monographs*, 1976, *43*, 195-203.

Hamilton, D. L., and Gifford, R. K. Illusory correlation in interpersonal perception: A cognitive basis of stereotypic judgments. *Journal of Experimental Social Psychology*, 1976, *12*, 392-407.

Hamilton, H. W., and Deese, J. Does linguistic marking have a psychological correlate? *Journal of Verbal Learning and Verbal Behavior*, 1971, *10*, 707-714.

Harris, R. J. Answering questions containing marked and unmarked adjectives and adverbs. *Journal of Experimental Psychology*, 1973, *97*, 399-401.

Harvey, O. J., Hunt, D. E., and Schroeder, H. M. *Conceptual systems and personality organization*. New York: John Wiley, 1961.

Hass, L. Personal construct systems and theological conservatism (Doctoral dissertation, University of Nebraska, 1974).

Hayden, B. The self and possibilities for change. *Journal of Personality*, 1979, *47*, 546-556.

Hayden, B., Nasby, W., and Davids, A. Interpersonal conceptual structures, predictive accuracy and social adjustment of emotionally disturbed boys. *Journal of Abnormal Psychology*, 1977, *86*, 315-320.

Hayes-Roth, B., and Hayes-Roth, F. Concept learning and the recognition and classification of exemplars. *Journal of Verbal Learning and Verbal Behavior*, 1977, *16*, 321-338.

Head, H. *Studies in neurology*. London: Frowde, Hodder, and Stoughton, 1920.

Heather, N. The specificity of schizophrenic thought disorder: A replication and extension of previous findings. *British Journal of Social and Clinical Psychology*, 1976, *15*, 131-137.

Hebb, D. O. Drives and the CNS (Conceptual Nervous System). *Psychological Review*, 1955, *62*, 243-254.

Heider, F. *The psychology of interpersonal relations*. New York: John Wiley, 1958.

Heisenberg, W. *Physics and beyond*. New York: Harper Torchbooks, 1972.

Higgins, K., and Sherman, M. The effect of motivation on loose thinking in schizophrenics as measured by the Bannister-Fransella grid test. *Journal of Clinical Psychology*, 1978, *34*, 624-628.

Hinkle, D. N. The change of personal constructs from the viewpoint of a theory of implications (Doctoral dissertation, Ohio State University, 1965).

Hofstadter, D. R. *Gödel, Escher, Bach: The eternal golden braid*. New York: Vintage, 1979.

Holland, R. George Kelly: Constructive innocent and reluctant existentialist. In Bannister, D. (Ed.), *Perspectives in personal construct theory*. New York: Academic Press, 1970.

Honess, T. Cognitive complexity and social prediction. *British Journal of Social and Clinical Psychology*, 1976, *15*, 23-31.

Honess, T. A comparison of the implication of repertory grid techniques. *British Journal of Psychology*, 1978, *69*, 305-314.

Honess, T. Children's implicit theories of their peers: A developmental analysis. *British Journal of Psychology*, 1979, *70*, 417-424.

Honess, T. Self-reference in children's descriptions of peers: Egocentricity or collaboration. *Child Development*, 1980, *51*, 476-480.

Hovland, C. I., and Sherif, M. Judgmental phenomena and scales of attitude measurement. *Journal of Abnormal and Social Psychology*, 1952, *47*, 822-832.

Hundeide, K. Interpretative positions and perspectivity. Paper presented at Conference on Culture, Communication and Cognition. *Vygotskian Perspectives*. Chicago: Center for Psychosocial Studies, 1980.

Hunt, J. McV. Intrinsic motivation and psychological development. In H. M. Schroder and P. Suedfeld (Eds.), *Personality theory and information processing*. New York: The Ronald Press, 197b, pp. 85-117.

Hunt, J. McV. The role of situations in early psychological development. In D. Magnusson (Ed.), *Toward a psychology of situations*. Hillsdale, N.J.: Lawrence Erlbaum Associates, 1980.

Illich, I. *Deschooling society*. New York: Harper and Row, 1971.

Inhelder, B. Memory and intelligence. In D. Elkind and J. H. Flavell (Eds.), *Studies in cognitive development*. New York: Oxford University Press, 1969, pp. 337-364.

Irwin, W., Tripodi, T., and Bieri, J. Affective stimulus value and cognitive complexity. *Journal of Personality and Social Psychology*, 1967, *5*, 444-448.

Jacoby, L. On interpreting the effects of repetition: Solving a problem versus remembering a solution. *Journal of Verbal Learning and Verbal Behavior*, 1978, *17*, 649-667.

Jaspars, J. M. F., Feldbreigger, R., and Bongaerts, L. Het leren van sociale structuren. *Hypothese*, 1968, *13*, 2-10.

Jenkins, J. J. Remember that old theory of memory: Well, forget it. *American Psychologist*, 1974, *29*, 785-795.

Johnsen, K. M. *Hva er kvinnesak?* Oslo: Gyldendal, 1979.

Jones, E. E., Kanouse, D. E., Kelley, M. M., Nisbett, R. E., Valins, S., and Weiner, B. *Attribution: perceiving the causes of behavior*. Morristown, N.J.: General Learning Press, 1972.

Jones, R. A., and Rosenberg, S. Structural representations of naturalistic descriptions of personality. *Multivariate Behavioral Research*, 1974, *9*, 217-230.

Jones, R. E. Identification in terms of personal constructs. Unpublished Ph.D. thesis, Ohio State University, 1954.

Jung, C. G. *VII Sermones ad Mortuos*. London: Vincent Stuart and John M. Watkins, 1967.

Just, M. A., and Carpenter, P. A. *Cognitive processes in comprehension*. Hillsdale, N.J.: Lawrence Erlbaum Associates, 1977.

Kahneman, D. *Attention and effort*. Englewood Cliffs, N.J.: Prentice-Hall, 1973.

Kail, R. V., Jr., and Siegel, A. W. The development of mnemonic encoding in children: From perception to abstraction. In R. V. Kail, Jr. and J. W. Hagen (Eds.), *Perspectives in the development of memory and cognition*. Hillsdale, N.J.: Lawrence Erlbaum Associates, 1977.

Kanouse, D. E., and Hanson, L. R. Negativity in evaluations. In Jones et al. (Eds.), *Attribution: Perceiving the causes of behavior*. Morristown, N.J.: General Learning Press, 1972.

Karttunen, L. Presupposition and linguistic context. *Theoretical Linguistics*, 1974, *1*, 182-194.

Katz, P., and Zigler, E. Self-image disparity: A development approach. *Journal of Personality and Social Psychology*, 1967, *5*, 186-195.

Keasey, C. B. Children's developing awareness and usage of intentionality and motives. In C. B. Keasey (Ed.), *Nebraska Symposium on Motivation*. Lincoln: University of Nebraska Press, 1978, pp. 219-260.

Kelly, G. A. *The psychology of personal constructs*. New York: Norton, 1955.

Kelly, G. A. Suicide: The personal construct point of view. In N. L. Farberow and E. S. Shneidman (Eds.), *The cry for help*. New York: McGraw-Hill, 1961, 255-280.

Kelly, G. A. *Clinical psychology and personality: The selected papers of George Kelly*. (Ed. B. A. Maher). New York: John Wiley, 1969a.

Kelly, G. A. The autobiography of a theory. In B. Maher (Ed.), *Clinical psychology and personality: The selected papers of George Kelly*. New York: John Wiley, 1969b.

Kelly, G. A. Humanistic methodology in psychological research. In B. A. Maher (Ed.), *Clinical psychology and personality: The selected papers of George Kelly*. New York: John Wiley, 1969c.

Kelly, G. A. In whom confide? On whom depend for what? In B. Maher (Ed.), *Clinical psychology and personality: The selected papers of George A. Kelly*. New York: John Wiley, 1969d.

Kelly, G. A. A brief introduction to personal construct theory. In D. Bannister (Ed.), *Perspectives in personal construct theory*. London: Academic Press, 1970a.

Kelly, G. A. A summary statement of a cognitively oriented comprehensive theory of behavior. In J. Mancuso (Ed.), *Readings for a cognitive theory of personality*. New York: Holt, Rinehart and Winston, 1970b, 27-58.

Kelly, G. A. A psychology of the optimal man. In A. W. Landfield and L. M. Leitner (Eds.), *Personal Construct Psychology*. New York: John Wiley, 1980, pp. 18-35.

Kelley, M. M. The processes of causal attribution. *American Psychologist*, 1973, *28*, 107-128.

Kelsall, P., and Strongman, K. Emotional experience and the implication grid. *British Journal of Medical Psychology*, 1978, *51*, 243-251.

Kim, M. P., and Rosenberg, S. Comparison of two structural models of implicit personality theory. *Journal of Personality and Social Psychology*, 1980, *38*, 375-389.

Kintsch, W. *The representation of meaning in memory*. Hillsdale, N.J.: Lawrence Erlbaum Associates, 1974.

Kintsch, W. On comprehending stories. In M. A. Just and P. A. Carpenter (Eds.), *Cognitive processes in comprehension*. Hillsdale, N.J.: Lawrence Erlbaum Associates, 1977, pp. 33-62.

Koffka, K. *Principles of gestalt psychology*. London: Routledge and Kegan Paul, 1935.

Kolb, D. A., and Fry, R. Towards an applied theory of experiential learning. In C. L. Cooper (Ed.), *Theories of group processes*. London: John Wiley, 1975, pp. 33-57.

Kursh, C. O. The benefits of poor communication. *The Psychoanalytic Review*, 1971, *58*, 189-208.

Landfield, A. W. *Personal construct systems in psychotherapy*. Chicago: Rand McNally, 1971.

Landfield, A. W. A personal construct approach to suicidal behavior. In P. Slater (Ed.), *Explorations of intrapersonal space*. London: John Wiley, 1976, pp. 93-108.

Landfield, A. W. Interpretive man: The enlarged self image. In A. W. Landfield (Vol. Ed.), *Nebraska symposium on motivation: Personal construct psychology*. Lincoln: University of Nebraska Press, 1977, pp. 127-177.

Landfield, A. W. Exploring socialization through the interpersonal transaction group. In P. Stringer and D. Bannister (Eds.), *Constructs of sociality and individuality*. London: Academic Press, 1979, pp. 133-152.

Landfield, A. W. The person as perspectivist, literalist and chaotic fragmentalist. In A. Landfield and L. Leitner (Eds.), *Personal construct psychology: Psychotherapy and personality*. New York: Wiley Interscience, 1980, pp. 289-320.

Landfield, A. W., and Barr, M. A. Ordination: A new measure of concept organization (Unpublished manuscript, University of Nebraska, 1976).

Landfield, A. W., and Leitner, L. M. *Personal construct psychology: Psychotherapy and personality*. New York: Wiley Interscience, 1980.

Langley, C. W. Differentiation and integration of systems of personal constructs. *Journal of Personality*, 1971, *39*, 10-25.

Lazarus, R. S., and Launier, R. Stress-related transactions between person and environment. In L. A. Pervin and M. Lewis (Eds.), *Perspectives in interactional psychology*. New York: Plenum Press, 1978.

Lazarus, R. S., Averill, J. R., and Opton, E. M., Jr. The psychology of coping: Issues of research and assessment. In G. V. Coelho, D. A. Hamburg, and J. F. Adams (Eds.), *Coping and adaption*. New York: Basic Books, 1974, pp. 249-315.

Lea, M. Personality similarity in unreciprocated friendships. *British Journal of Social and Clinical Psychology*, 1979, *18*, 393-394.

Lea, M., and Duck, S. W. A model for the role of similarity of values in friendship development. In preparation.

Leitner, L. M. Psychopathology and the differentiation of values, emotions, and behaviors: A repertory grid study (Unpublished manuscript, 1980).

Lemaire, A. *Jacques Lacan*. London: Routledge and Kegan Paul, 1977.

Lemon, N., and Warren, N. Salience, centrality and self-relevance of traits in construing others. *British Journal of Social and Clinical Psychology*, 1974, *13*, 119-124.

Leventhal, H. Cognitive processes and interpersonal predictions. *Journal of Abnormal and Social Psychology*, 1957, *55*, 176-180.

Levy, L. H. Personal constructs and predictive behavior. *Journal of Abnormal and Social Psychology*, 1956, *53*, 54-58.

Lewin, K. A. The conceptual representation and the measurement of psychological forces. In D. K. Adams and H. Lundholm (Eds.), *Contributions to psychological theory* (Vol. 1). Durham, N.C.: Duke University Press, 1938.

Lewin, K. *Principles of Topological Psychology*. New York: McGraw-Hill, 1936.

Lewin, K. A. *Field theory in social science: Selected theoretical papers*. New York: Harper, 1951.

Lewinsohn, P., Mischel, W., Chaplin, W., and Barton, R. Social competence and depression: The role of illusory self-perceptions. *Journal of Abnormal Psychology*, 1980, *89*, 203-212.

Lewis, M., and Brooks-Gunn, J. *Social cognition and the acquisition of self*. New York: Plenum Press, 1979.

Lindsley, D. B. Psychophysiology and motivation. In M. R. Jones (Ed.), *Nebraska symposium on motivation*. Lincoln: University of Nebraska Press, 1957.

Lingle, J. H., and Ostrom, T. M. Retrieval selectivity in memory-based impression judgments. *Journal of Personality and Social Psychology*, 1979, *37*, 180-194.

Little, B. Factors affecting the use of psychological versus nonpsychological constructs of the repertory test. *Bulletin of the British Psychological Society*, 1968, *21*, 34.

Little, B. Sex differences and comparability of three measures of cognitive complexity. *Psychological Report*, 1969, *24*, 607-609.

Little, B. Psychological man as scientist, humanist, and specialist. *Journal of Experimental Research in Personality*, 1972, *6*, 95-118.

Livesley, W. J., and Bromley, D. B. *Person perception in childhood and adolescence*. London: John Wiley, 1973.

Lock, A. (Ed.), *Action, gesture and symbol*. London: Academic Press, 1978.

Luchins, A. S. Mechanization in problem solving: The effect of einstellung. *Psychological Monographs*, 1942, *54* (Whole No. 248).

Luchins, A. S. *Rigidity of behavior*. Eugene: University of Oregon Press, 1959.

Luchins, A. S., and Luchins, E. H. Wertheimer's seminars revisited: Diagnostic testing for understanding of structure. In P. N. Johnson-Laird and P. C. Wason (Eds.), *Thinking: Readings in cognitive science*. Cambridge: Cambridge University Press, 1977.

Luria, A. R. *The working brain*. Harmondsworth, Middlesex: Penguin Press, 1973.

Lyons, J. *Semantics*. Cambridge: Cambridge University Press, 1977.

Magnusson, D. The person and the situation in an interactional model of behavior. *Scandinavian Journal of Psychology*, 1976, *17*, 253-271.

Magnusson, D. Wanted: A psychology of situation. In D. Magnusson (Ed.), *Toward a psychology of situations*. Hillsdale, N.J.: Lawrence Erlbaum Associates, 1981.

Magnusson, D., and Endler, N. S. *Personality at the crossroads: Current issues in interactional psychology*. Hillsdale, N.J.: Lawrence Erlbaum Associates, 1977.

Mair, J. M. M. Some problems in repertory grid measurement, I. The use of bipolar constructs. *British Journal of Psychology*, 1967, *58*, 261-270.

Mair, J. M. M. Metaphors for living. In A. W. Landfield (Ed.), *Nebraska symposium on motivation: Personal construct psychology*. Lincoln: University of Nebraska Press, 1977, pp. 243-290.

Makhlouf-Norris, F., Jones, H. G., and Norris, H. Articulation of the conceptual structure in the obsessional neurosis. *British Journal of Social and Clinical Psychology*, 1970, *8*, 264-274.

Malinowski, B. *The problem of meaning in primitive languages*. Supplement to C. K. Ogden and I. A. Richards, *The meaning of meaning*. London: Routledge and Kegan Paul, 1923.

Mancuso, J. C. (Ed.). *Readings for a cognitive theory of personality*. New York: Holt, Rinehart and Winston, 1970.

Mancuso, J. C. Dialectic man as the subject in psychological research. In J. F. Rychlak (Ed.), *Dialectic: Humanistic rationale for behavior and development*. Basel: Karger, A. G., 1976, pp. 113-125.

Mancuso, J. C. Current motivational models in the elaboration of personal construct theory. In A. W. Landfield (Ed.), *Nebraska symposium on motivation: Personal construct psychology*. Lincoln: University of Nebraska Press, 1977, pp. 43-97.

Mancuso, J. Reprimand: The construing of the rule violator's construct system. In P. Stringer and D. Bannister (Eds.), *Constructs of sociality and individuality*. New York: Academic Press, 1979.

Mancuso, J. C., and Allen, D. A. Children's perceptions of a transgressor's socialization as a function of type of reprimand. *Human Development*, 1976, *19*, 277-290.

Mancuso, J. C., and Ceely, S. G. The self as memory processing. *Cognitive Therapy and Research*, 1980, *4*, 1-25.

Mancuso, J. C., and Handin, K. H. Teaching parents to construe the child's construing. In A. W. Landfield and L. M. Leitner (Eds.), *Personal construct psychology*. New York: John Wiley, 1980, pp. 271-288.

Mancuso, J. C., and Handin, K. H. Prompting parents toward constructivist caregiving practices. In I. E. Sigel and L. M. Laosa (Eds.), *Changing families*. New York: Plenum Press, 1982.

Mandler, J. M., and Johnson, N. S. Remembrance of things parsed: Story structure and recall. *Cognitive Psychology*, 1977, *9*, 111-151.

Mannheim, K. *Essays on the sociology of knowledge.* Oxford: Oxford University Press, 1952.

Marks, D. Imagery and consciousness: A theoretical review from an individual differences perspective. *Journal of Mental Imagery*, 1977, *2*, 275-290.

Markus, H. Self schemata and processing information about the self. *Journal of Personality and Social Psychology*, 1977, *35*, 63-78.

Markus, H. The self in thought and memory. In D. Wegner and R. Vallacher (Eds.), *The self in social psychology*. New York: Oxford University Press, 1980.

Massaro, D. W., and Schmuller, J. Visual features, perceptual storage, and processing time in reading. In D. Massaro (Ed.), *Understanding language*. New York: Academic Press, 1975, pp. 207-239.

Mayo, C. W., and Crockett, W. H. Cognitive complexity and primacy recency effects in impression formation. *Journal of Abnormal and Social Psychology*. 1964, *68*, 335-338.

Mayzner, M. S. Studies of visual information processing in man. In R. L. Solso (Ed.), *Information processing and cognition*. Hillsdale, N.J.: Lawrence Erlbaum Associates, 1975, pp. 31-54.

Mayzner, M. S., and Habinek, J. K. *Visual information processing of letters and non-letters*. A paper presented at the 16th Annual Meeting of the Psychonomic Society, Denver, 1975.

McCawley, P. D. "World creating" predicates. *Versus*, 1978, *3*, 77-93.

McFarland, C. E., Frey, T. J., and Rhodes, D. D. Retrieval of internally vs. externally generated words in episodic memory. *Journal of Verbal Learning and Verbal Behavior*, 1980, *19*, 210-225.

McPherson, F. M., Armstrong, J., and Heather, B. B. Psychological construing, "difficulty" and thought disorder. *British Journal of Medical Psychology*, 1975, *48*, 303-315.

McPherson, F. M., Blackburn, I. M., Draffan, J. W., and McFayden, M. A further study of the grid test of thought disorder. *British Journal of Social and Clinical Psychology*, 1973, *12*, 420-427.

McPherson, F. M., and Buckley, F. Thought-process disorder and personal construct subsystems. *British Journal of Social and Clinical Psychology*, 1970, *9*, 380-381.

Mead, G. H. *Mind, self, and society*. Chicago: University of Chicago Press, 1934.

Meltzer, B., Crockett, W. H., and Rosenkrantz, P. S. Cognitive complexity, value congruity, and the integration of potentially incompatible information in impressions of others. *Journal of Personality and Social Psychology*, 1966, *4*, 338-343.

Mihevc, N. Information, valence, and cognitive complexity in the political domain. *The Journal of Psychology*, 1978, *99*, 163-177.

Miller, A. D. Amount of information and stimulus valence as determinants of cognitive complexity. *Journal of Personality*, 1969, *37*, 141-157.

Miller, A. D., and Bieri, J. Cognitive complexity as a function of the stimulus objects being judged. *Psychological Reports*, 1965, *16*, 1203-1204.

Miller, G. The magical number of seven, plus or minus two: Some limits on our capacity for processing information. *Psychological Review*, 1956, *63*, 81-97.

Miller, G. A., Galanter, E., and Pribram, K. H. *Plans and the structure of behavior*. New York: Holt, Rinehart and Winston, 1960.

Minsky, M. A framework for representing knowledge. In P. H. Winston (Ed.), *The psychology of computer vision*. New York: McGraw-Hill, 1975.

Mintzberg, H., Raisinghani, D., and Theoret, A. The structure of unstructured decision processes. *Administrative Science Quarterly*, 1976, *21*, 246-275.

Mischel, T. Personal constructs, rules, and the logic of clinical activity. *Psychological Review*, 1964, *71*, 180-192.

Mischel, W. *Personality and assessment*. New York: John Wiley, 1968.

Mischel, W. Toward a cognitive social learning reconceptualization of personality. *Psychological Review*, 1973, *80*, 252-283.

Mischel, W. On the interface of cognition and personality. *American Psychologist*, 1979, *34*, 740-754.

Mischel, W., Ebbesen, E., and Zeiss, A. Selective attention to the self: Situational and dispositional determinants. *Journal of Personality and Social Psychology*, 1973, *27*, 129-142.

Mitchison, G. J. Phyllotaxis and the Fibonacci series. *Science*, 1977, *196*, 270-275.

Morrison, J. K. Successful grieving: Changing personal constructs through mental imagery. *Journal of Mental Imagery*, 1978, *2*, 63-65.

Morrison, J. K. Emotive-reconstructive psychotherapy: Changing constructs by means of mental imagery. In A. A. Sheikh and J. T. Shaffer (Eds.), *The potential of fantasy and imagination*. New York: Brandon House, 1979, pp. 133-147.

Morrison, J. K., and Cometa, M. S. Emotive constructive psychotherapy: A short-term cognitive approach. *American Journal of Psychotherapy*, 1977, *31*, 294-301.

Morrison, J. K., and Cometa, M. S. A cognitive, reconstructive approach to the psychotherapeutic use of imagery. *Journal of Mental Imagery*, 1980, *4*, 35-42.

Morrison, J. K., and Teta, D. C. Simplified use of the semantic differential to measure psychotherapy outcome. *Journal of Clinical Psychology*, 1978, *34*, 751-753.

Moruzzi, G., and H. W. Magoun. Brain stem reticular formation and activation of the EEG. *EEG Clinical Neurophysiology*, 1949, *1*, 455-473.

Myers, N. A., and Perlmutter, M. Memory in years two to five. In P. A. Ornstein (Ed.), *Memory development in children*. Hillsdale, N.J.: Lawrence Erlbaum Associates, 1978, pp. 191-218.

Murphy, G. *Personality: A biosocial approach to origins and structure*. New York: Harper, 1947.

Murray, H. A. *Explorations in personality*. New York: Oxford University Press, 1938.

Naess, A. *Interpretation and preciseness*. Oslo: Dybwad, 1953.

Neimeyer, G. J., and Neimeyer, R. A. Personal construct perspectives on cognitive assessment. In T. V. Merluzzi, C. R. Glass, and M. Geneset (Eds.), *Cognitive assessment*. New York: Guilford Press (in press).

Neimeyer, R. A. The structure and meaningfulness of tacit construing. In H. Bonarius, R. Holland, and S. Rosenberg (Eds.), *Recent advances in the theory and practice of personal construct psychology*. London: Macmillan, 1980, pp. 105-113.

Neisser, V. *Cognitive psychology*. New York: Appleton-Century-Crofts, 1967.

Neisser, V. *Cognition and reality: Principles and implications of cognitive psychology*. San Francisco: W. H. Freeman, 1976.

Newell, A., and Simon, M. *Human problem solving*. Englewood Cliffs, N.J.: Prentice-Hall, 1972.

Newson, J. Dialogue and development. In A. Lock (Ed.), *Action, gesture and symbol*. London: Academic Press, 1978.

Nidorf, L. J., and Crockett, W. H. Cognitive complexity and the integration of conflicting information in written impressions. *Journal of Social Psychology*, 1965, *66*, 165-169.

Nisbett, R., and Ross, L. *Human inference: Strategies and shortcomings of social judgment*. Engelwood Cliffs, N.J.: Prentice-Hall, 1980.

Oden, G. C., and Massaro, D. W. Integration of featural information in speech perception. *Psychological Review*, 1978, *85*, 172-191.

O'Donovan, D. Rating extremity: Pathology or meaningfulness. *Psychological Review*, 1965, *72*, 358-372.

Ohlsson, S. Competence and strategy in reasoning with common spatial concepts. A study of problem solving in a semantically rich domain. *Working Papers from the Cognitive Seminar*, Department of Psychology, University of Stockholm, No. 6, 1980.

O'Keefe, B. J., and Delia, J. G. Construct comprehensiveness and cognitive complexity as predictors of the number and strategic adaptation of arguments and appeals in a persuasive message. *Communication Monographs*, 1979, *46*, 231-240.

O'Keefe, B. J., Delia, J. G., and O'Keefe, D. J. Construct individuality, cognitive complexity, and the formation and remembering of interpersonal impressions. *Social Behavior and Personality*, 1977, *5*, 229-240.

O'Keefe, D. J. The relationship of attitudes and behavior: A constructivist analysis. In D. P. Cushman and R. D. McPhee (Eds.), *Method-attitude-behavior relationship*. New York: Academic Press, 1980.

O'Keefe, D. J., and Sypher, H. E. Cognitive complexity measures and the relationship of cognitive complexity to communication: A critical review. *Human Communication Research*, in press.

Olshan, K. The multidimensional structure of person perception in children (Doctoral dissertation, Rutgers – The State University of New Jersey, 1970).

Olson, D. Language and thought: Aspects of a cognitive theory of semantics. *Psychological Review*, 1970, *77*, 257-273.

Olson, J. M., and Partington, J. T. An integrative analysis of two cognitive modes of interpersonal effectiveness. *British Journal of Social and Clinical Psychology*, 1977, *16*, 13-14.

Ortony, A. Beyond literal similarity. *Psychological Review*, 1979, *86*, 161-180.

Ortony, A., Schallert, D. L., Reynolds, R. E., and Antos, S. J. Interpreting metaphors and idioms: Some effects of context on comprehension. *Journal of Verbal Learning and Verbal Behavior*, 1978, *17*, 465-477.

Osgood, C. E. Studies on the generality of affective meaning systems. *American Psychologist*, 1962, *17*, 10-28.

Osgood, C. E. From Yang to Yin to *and* or *but* in cross cultural perspective. *International Journal of Psychology*, 1979, *14*, 1-35.

Osgood, C. E., and Richards, M. M. From Yang to Yin to and or but. *Language*, 1973, *49*, 380-410.

Osgood, C. E., Suci, G. J., and Tannenbaum, P. H. *The measurement of meaning.* Urbana: University of Illinois Press, 1957.

Paivio, A. *Imagery and verbal processes.* New York: Holt, Rinehart and Winston, 1971.

Paivio, A., and Cohen, M. Eidetic imagery and cognitive abilities. *Journal of Mental Imagery*, 1979, *3*, 53-64.

Paris, S. G. The development of inference and transformations as memory operations. In P. A. Ornstein (Ed.), *Memory development in children.* Hillsdale, N.J.: Lawrence Erlbaum Associates, 1978, pp. 129-156.

Peeters, G. The positive-negative asymmetry: On cognitive consistency and positive bias. *European Journal of Social Psychology*, 1971, *1*, 455-474.

Peevers, B. H., and Secord, P. F. Developmental changes in attribution of descriptive concepts to persons. *Journal of Personality and Social Psychology*, 1973, *27*, 120-128.

√ Pepper, S. C. *World hypotheses.* Berkeley: University of California Press, 1942.

Perry, G. R. Construing interpersonal construction systems: Conjectures on sociality. In F. Fransella (Ed.), *Personal construct psychology 1977.* London: Academic Press, 1978.

Pervin, L. *Current controversies and issues in personality.* New York: John Wiley, 1978.

Piaget, J. *The language and thought of the child.* New York: Harcourt Brace, 1926.

Piaget, J. *The moral judgment of the child.* London: Kegan Paul, 1932. (In paperback: New York: The Free Press, 1966.)

Piaget, J. *The origins of intelligence in children.* New York: International Universities Press, 1952. (In paperback: New York: W. W. Norton, 1963.)

Piaget, J. *The construction of reality in the child.* New York: Harcourt Brace, 1954.

Piaget, J. *The child's construction of reality.* London: Routledge and Kegan Paul, 1958.

Piaget, J. *The psychology of intelligence.* New York: Harcourt Brace, 1960.

Piaget, J. The problem of common mechanisms in the human sciences. *The Human Context*, 1969, *1*, 163-185.

Piaget, J. *Psychology and epistemology.* New York: Viking, 1971a.

Piaget, J. *Structuralism.* London: Routledge and Kegan Paul, 1971b.

Piaget, J., and Inhelder, B. *The child's conception of space.* London: Routledge and Kegan Paul, 1956. (In paperback: New York: W. W. Norton, 1967.)

Piaget, J., and Inhelder, B. *Memory and intelligence.* New York: Basic Books, 1973.

Piaget, J., and Inhelder, B. *Mental imagery in the child.* New York: Basic Books, 1971.

Piehl, J. The Golden Section: The "true" ratio? *Perceptual and Motor Skills*, 1978, *46*, 831-834.

Polanyi, M. *Personal knowledge: Towards a post-critical philosophy.* London: Routledge and Kegan Paul, 1958.

Popper, K. R. *The logic of scientific discovery.* London: Hutchinson, 1959.

Posner, M. I., and Keele, S. W. On the genesis of abstract ideas. *Journal of Experimental Psychology*, 1968, *77*, 353-363.

Posner, M. I., and Keele, S. Retention of abstract ideas. *Journal of Experimental Psychology*, 1970, *83*, 304-308.

Powers, W. G., Jordan, W. J., and Street, R. L. Language indices in the measurement of cognitive complexity: Is complexity loquacity? *Human Communication Research*, 1979, *6*, 69-73.

Powers, W. T. *Behavior: The control of perception*. Chicago: Aldine, 1973.

Powers, W. T. Quantitative analysis of purposive systems: Some spadework at the foundations of scientific psychology. *Psychological Review*, 1978, *85*, 417-435.

Press, A. N., Crockett, W. H., and Delia, J. G. Effects of cognitive complexity and perceiver's set upon organization of impressions. *Journal of Personality and Social Psychology*, 1975, *32*, 865-872.

Press, A. N., Crockett, W. H., and Rosenkrantz, P. S. Cognitive complexity and the learning of balanced and unbalanced social structures. *Journal of Personality*, 1969, *37*, 541-553.

Pribram, K. H., and McGuiness, D. Arousal, activation, and effort in the control of attention. *Psychological Review*, 1975, *82*, 116-149.

Rardin, D., and Moan, C. Peer interaction and cognitive development. *Child Development*, 1971, *42*, 1685-1699.

Reed, B. *The dynamics of religion: Process and movement in Christian churches*. London: Darton, Longman and Todd, 1978.

Reed, S. K. Pattern recognition and categorization. *Cognitive Psychology*, 1972, *3*, 382-407.

Reese, H. W. Toward a cognitive theory of mnemonic imagery. *Journal of Mental Imagery*, 1977, *2*, 229-244.

Rehm, L. Effects of validation on the relationship between personal constructs. *Journal of Personality and Social Psychology*, 1971, *20*, 267-270.

Reker, G. T. Interpersonal conceptual structures of emotionally disturbed and normal boys. *Journal of Abnormal Psychology*, 1974, *83*, 380-386.

Richardson, A. *Mental imagery*. New York: Springer, 1969.

Riegel, K. F. *Foundations of dialectical psychology*. New York: Academic Press, 1979.

Rodney, Y. The effects of moods on self and person perception (Unpublished manuscript, Brock University, 1980).

Rogers, C. R. *Client centered therapy*. New York: Houghton Mifflin, 1951.

Rogers, T. B., Kuiper, N. A., and Kirker, W. S. Self-reference and the encoding of personal information. *Journal of Personality and Social Psychology*, 1977, *35*, 644-688.

Rogers, T. B., Rogers, P. J., and Kuiper, N. A. Recognition memory for personal adjectives: Some evidence for self-reference as an aspect of memory (Unpublished manuscript, University of Calgary, 1977).

Romany, S. The Golden Section hypothesis: A cross-cultural, developmental perspective. Paper presented at the Tenth Annual Ontario Undergraduate Thesis Conference, University of Guelph, 1980.

Romany, S., and Adams-Webber, J. The Golden Section hypothesis from a developmental perspective. *Social Behavior and Personality*, 1981 (in press).

Rommetveit, R. *On message structure*. London: John Wiley, 1974.

Rommetveit, R. On negative rationalism. In R. Rommetveit and R. M. Blaker (Eds.), *Studies of language, thought and verbal communication*. London: Academic Press, 1979.

Rommetveit, R. Language acquisition as increasing linguistic structuring of experience and symbolic behavior control. Paper presented at Conference on Culture, Communication and Cognition. *Vygotskian Perspectives*. Chicago: Center for Psychosocial Studies, 1980.

Rommetveit, R. On the dawning of different aspects of life in a pluralistic social world. In E. Wright (Ed.), *Irony: An interdisciplinary reader. Essays on ambiguity in intersubjective encounters*. London: Harvester Press, 1981.

Rommetveit, R. Ordinary language as "a form of life." Book in preparation.

Rosch, E. On the internal structure of perceptual and semantic categories. In T. M. Moore (Ed.), *Cognitive development and the acquisition of language*. New York: Academic Press, 1973.

Rosch, E. Cognitive representations of semantic categories. *Journal of Experimental Psychology: General*, 1975, *104(3)*, 192-233.

Rosch, E. Principles of categorization. In E. Rosch and B. B. Lloyd (Eds.), *Cognition and categorization*. Hillsdale, N.J.: Lawrence Erlbaum Associates, 1978.

Rosch, E., and Mervis, C. B. Family resemblances: Studies in the internal structure of categories. *Cognitive Psychology*, 1975, *7*, 573-605.

Rosenbach, D., Crockett, W., and Wapner, S. Developmental level, emotional involvement, and the resolution of inconsistency in impression formation. *Developmental Psychology*, 1973, *8*, 120-130.

Rosenberg, S. New approaches to the analysis of personal constructs in person perception. In A. W. Landfield (Ed.), *Nebraska symposium on motivation* (Vol. 24). Lincoln: University of Nebraska Press, 1977, pp. 179-242.

Rosenberg, S. A theory in search of its Zeitgeist. (Review of *Personal construct psychology: Concepts and applications* by J. R. Adams-Webber). *Contemporary Psychology*, 1980, *25*, 898-899.

Rosenberg, S., and Gara, M. A. Conceptual and methodological dimensions in the history of personality and social psychology: An empirical approach. Paper presented at the meetings of the American Psychological Association, Montreal, 1980.

Rosenberg, S., and Jones, R. A. A method for investigating and representing a person's implicit theory of personality: Theodore Dreiser's view of people. *Journal of Personality and Social Psychology*, 1972, *22*, 373-386.

Rosenberg, S., Nelson, C., and Vivekananthan, P. S. A multidimensional approach to the structure of personality impressions. *Journal of Personality and Social Psychology*, 1968, *9*, 283-294.

Rosenberg, S., and Olshan, K. Evaluative and descriptive aspects in personality perception. *Journal of Personality and Social Psychology*, 1970, *16*, 619-626.

Rosenberg, S., and Sedlak, A. A structural representation of perceived personality trait relationships. In R. A. Shephard, A. K. Romeny, and S. Nerlove (Eds.), *Multi-dimensional scaling: Theory and application in the behavioral sciences*, Vol. 2: *Applications*. New York: Seminar Press, 1972a.

Rosenberg, S., and Sedlak, A. Structural representations of implicit personality theory. In L. Berkowitz (Ed.), *Advances in experimental social psychology* (Vol. 6). New York: Academic Press, 1972b.

Rosenkrantz, P. S., and Crockett, W. H. Some factors influencing the assimilation of disparate information in impression formation. *Journal of Personality and Social Psychology*, 1965, *2*, 397-400.

Rotter, J. B. *Social learning and clinical psychology*. Englewood Cliffs, N.J.: Prentice-Hall, 1954.

Rotter, J. B., Chance, J., and Phares, J. *Applications of a social learning theory of personality*. New York: Holt, Rinehart and Winston, 1972.

Rumelhart, D. E. Notes on a schema for stories. In D. G. Bobrow and A. Collins (Eds.), *Representation and understanding: Studies in cognitive science.* New York: Academic Press, 1975.

Rumelhart, D. E., and Norman, D. A. Accretion, tuning, and restructuring: Three modes of learning. In J. W. Cotton and R. L. Klatzky (Eds.), *Semantic factors in cognition.* Hillsdale, N.J.: Lawrence Erlbaum Associates, 1978.

Rumelhart, D. E., and Ortony, A. The representation of knowledge in memory. In R. Anderson and W. Montague (Eds.), *Schooling and the acquisiton of knowledge.* Hillsdale, N.J.: Lawrence Erlbaum Associates, 1977, pp. 99-135.

Russell, B. *History of western philosophy.* London: George Allen and Unwin, 1961.

Ryle, A. *Frames and cages: The repertory grid approach to human understanding.* London: University of Sussex Press, 1975.

Ryle, A., and Breen, D. Some differences in the personal constructs of neurotic and normal subjects. *British Journal of Psychiatry,* 1972, *120,* 483-489.

Salatas, H., and Flavell, J. H. Perspective taking: The development of two components of knowledge. *Child Development,* 1976, *47,* 103-109.

Salmon, P. A psychology of personal growth. In D. Bannister (Ed.), *Perspectives in personal construct theory.* London: Academic Press, 1970, pp. 197-221.

Sarbin, T. R. Contextualism: A world view for psychology. In A. W. Landfield (Ed.), *Nebraska symposium on motivation* (Vol. 24). Lincoln: University of Nebraska Press, 1977, pp. 1-41.

Sarbin, T. R. A preface to a psychological theory of metaphor. Unpublished paper, 1980a.

Sarbin, T. R. The root metaphor of metaphor: Application to psychological problems (Unpublished paper, 1980b).

Sarbin, T. R., and Mancuso, J. C. *Schizophrenia: Medical diagnosis or moral judgment.* Elmsford, N.Y.: Pergamon, 1980.

Sarbin, T. R., Taft, R., and Bailey, D. E. *Clinical inference and cognitive theory.* New York: Holt, Rinehart and Winston, 1960.

Sattath, S., and Tversky, A. Additive similarity trees. *Psychometrika,* 1977, *42,* 319-345.

Scarlett, H., Press, A., and Crockett, W. Children's descriptions of peers: A Wernerian developmental analysis. *Child Development,* 1971, *42,* 439-453.

Schank, R., and Abelson, R. *Scripts, plans, goals, and understanding.* Hillsdale, N.J.: Lawrence Erlbaum Associates, 1977.

Schmidt, R. A. The schema as a solution to some persistent problems in motor learning theory. In G. E. Stelmach (Ed.), *Motor control.* New York: Academic Press, 1976, pp. 41-65.

Schneider, D. J. Implicit personality theory: A review. *Psychological Bulletin,* 1973, *79,* 294-309.

Schneider, D. J., Hastorf, A. H., and Ellsworth, P. C. *Person perception.* Reading, Mass.: Addison-Wesley, 1979.

Schroeder, H. M., Driver, M. J., and Streufert, S. *Human information processing.* New York: Holt, Rinehart and Winston, 1967.

Schutz, A. On multiple realities. *Philosophical and Phenomenological Research,* 1945, *5,* 533-576.

Schutz, A. Choosing among projects of action. *Philosophical and Phenomenological Research,* 1951, *12,* 161-184.

Scott, W. A. Cognitive complexity and cognitive flexibility. *Sociometry,* 1962, *25,* 405-414.

Scott, W. A., Kline, J., Faguy-Cote, E., and Peterson, C. Centrality of cognitive attributes. *Journal of Research in Personality,* 1980, *14,* 12-26.

Scott, W. A., Osgood, D. W., and Peterson, C. *Cognitive structure: Theory and measurement of individual differences.* Washington, D.C.: V. H. Winston, 1979.

Seamon, J. R. *Memory and cognition.* New York: Oxford University Press, 1980.

Searle, J. R. *Speech acts: An essay in the philosophy of language.* Cambridge: Cambridge University Press, 1969.

Searle, J. R. *On speech acts.* Cambridge: Cambridge University Press, 1974.

Searle, J. R. Metaphor. In A. Ortony (Ed.), *Metaphor and thought.* Cambridge: Cambridge University Press, 1980, pp. 92-123.

Sechrest, L. B., and Jackson, D. N. Social intelligence and accuracy of interpersonal predictions. *Journal of Personality,* 1961, *29,* 167-181.

Selman, R. L. *The growth of interpersonal understanding.* New York: Academic Press, 1980.

Selman, R. L., and Jacquette, D. Stability and oscillation in interpersonal awareness: A clinical-developmental analysis. In C. B. Keasey (Ed.), *Nebraska symposium on motivation: Social cognition*. Lincoln: University of Nebraska Press, 1978.

Shalit, B. The golden section relation in the evaluation of environmental factors. *British Journal of Psychology*, 1980, *71*, 39-42.

Shepard, R. N. The mental image. *American Psychologist*, 1978, *33*, 125-137.

Shikiar, R., Fishbein, M., and Wiggins, N. Individual differences in semantic space: A replication and extension. *Multivariate Behavioral Research*, 1974, *9*, 201-210.

Shweder, R. A. Likeness and likelihood in everyday thought: Magical thinking in judgments about personality. *Current Anthropology*, 1977, *18*, 637-657.

Sigel, I. The distancing hypothesis: A causal hypothesis for the acquisition of representational thought. In M. R. Jones (Ed.), *Miami symposium on the prediction of behavior, 1968: Effects of early experience*. Coral Gables, Fla.: University of Miami Press, 1970.

Signell, K. Cognitive complexity in person perception and nation perception: A developmental approach. *Journal of Personality*, 1966, *34*, 517-537.

Singer, J. L. *Imagery and daydream methods in psychotherapy and behavior modification*. New York: Academic Press, 1974.

Skinner, B. F. *The behavior of organisms: An experimental analysis*. New York: Appleton-Century-Crofts, 1938.

Skinner, B. F. *Science and human behavior*. New York: Macmillan, 1953.

Skinner, B. F. *Verbal behavior*. New York: Appleton-Century-Crofts, 1957.

Skinner, B. F. *About behaviorism*. New York: Alfred A. Knopf, 1974.

Slamecka, N. J., and Graf, P. The generation effect: Delineation of a phenomenon. *Journal of Experimental Psychology: Human Learning and Memory*, 1978, *4*, 592-604.

Slater, P. Notes on INGRID 72 (Unpublished manuscript, London Institute of Psychiatry, 1972).

Smith, S., and Leach, C. A hierarchical measure of cognitive complexity. *British Journal of Psychology*, 1972, *63*, 561-568.

Sokolov, E. N. *Perception and the conditioned reflex*. New York: Macmillan, 1963.

Southern, T. *Blue movie*. New York: Signet, 1970.

Space, L., and Cromwell, R. Personal constructs among depressed patients. *Journal of Nervous and Mental Disease*, 1980, *168*, 150-158.

Sperlinger, D. A repertory grid and questionnaire study of individuals receiving treatment for depression from general practitioners (Doctoral dissertation, University of Birmingham, 1971).

Sperlinger, D. Aspects of stability in the repertory grid. *British Journal of Medical Psychology*, 1976, *49*, 341-347.

Spiro, R. J. Remembering information from text: The "state of schema" approach. In R. C. Anderson, R. J. Spiro, and W. E. Montague (Eds.), *Schooling and the acquisition of knowledge*. Hillsdale, N.J.: Lawrence Erlbaum Associates, 1977.

Spiro, R. J. Accomodative reconstruction and prose recall. *Journal of Verbal Learning and Verbal Behavior*, 1980, *19*, 84-95.

Staub, S. The effects of three types of relationships on young children's memory for pictorial stimulus pairs (Doctoral dissertation, Graduate School of Education, Harvard University, 1973).

Stolorow, R., and Atwood, G. *Faces in a cloud: Subjectivity in personality theory*. New York: Jason Aronson, 1979.

Strawson, P. F. *Individuals: An essay in descriptive metaphysics*. New York: Methuen, 1959.

Stringer, P., and Bannister, D. *Constructs of sociality and individuality*. London: Academic Press, 1979.

Sullivan, H. S. *The interpersonal theory of psychiatry*. New York: Norton, 1953.

Swanson, D. L., and Delia, J. G. *The nature of human communication*. Chicago: Science Research Associates, 1976.

Thompson, D. W. *On growth and form*. London: Cambridge University Press, 1942.

Thorndyke, P. W. Cognitive structures in comprehension and memory of narrative discourse. *Cognitive Psychology*, 1977, *9*, 77-110.

Tolman, E. C. Cognitive maps in rats and men. *Psychological Review*, 1948, *55*, 189-208.

Tolman, E. C. A psychological model. In T. Parsons and E. A. Shils (Eds.), *Toward a general theory of action*. Cambridge, Mass.: Harvard University Press, 1951.

Trevarthen, S., and Hubley, P. Secondary intersubjectivity: Confidence, confiding and acts of meaning in the first year. In A. Lock (Ed.), *Action, gesture and symbol*. London: Academic Press, 1978.

Tschudi, F. On violating intersubjectivity. Manuscript, 1979.

Tulving, E. Episodic and semantic memory. In E. Tulving and W. Donaldson (Eds.), *Organization of memory*. New York: Academic Press, 1972, pp. 282-402.

Tulving, E., and Thomson, D. M. Encoding specificity and retrieval processes in episodic memory. *Psychological Review*, 1973, *80*, 352-373.

Turbayne, C. M. *The myth of metaphor*. Columbia: University of South Carolina Press, 1970.

Tversky, A. Features of similarity. *Psychological Review*, 1977, *84*, 327-352.

Tversky, A., and Gati, I. Studies of similarity. In E. Rosch and B. B. Lloyd (Eds.), *Cognition and categorization*. Hillsdale, N.J.: Lawrence Erlbaum Associates, 1978.

Uhlenbeck, E. M. On the distinction between linguistics and pragmatics. In P. Gerver and H. W. Sinaiko (Eds.), *Language interpretation and communication*. New York: Plenum Press, 1978.

Uzgiris, I. C. Plasticity and structure: The role of experience in infancy. In I. C. Uzgiris and F. Weizmann (Eds.), *The structuring of experience*. New York: Plenum Press, 1977, pp. 89-113.

Vacc, N. A., Loesch, L. C., and Burt, M. A. Further development of the adapted modified role repertory test. *Measurement and Evaluation in Guidance*, 1980, *12*, 216-222.

van Dijk, T. A. Semantic macro-structures and knowledge frames in discourse comprehension. In M. A. Just and P. A. Carpenter (Eds.), *Cognitive processes in comprehension*. Hillsdale, N.J.: Lawrence Erlbaum Associates, 1977, pp. 3-32.

Vannoy, J. S. Generality of complexity-simplicity as a personality construct. *Journal of Personality and Social Psychology*, 1965, *3*, 385-396.

Varela, F. J. *Principles of biological autonomy*. New York: Elsevier North Holland, 1979.

Viney, L., and Westbrook, M. Cognitive anxiety: A method of content analysis for verbal samples. *Journal of Personality Assessment*, 1976, *40*, 140-150.

Vygotsky, L. S. *Thought and language*. New York: John Wiley, 1962.

Vygotsky, L. S. *Mind and society*. Cambridge, Mass.: Harvard University Press, 1978.

Warr, P. B. Pollyanna's personal judgments. *European Journal of Social Psychology*, 1971, *1*, 327-338.

Warr, P. B. Inference magnitude, range and evaluative direction as factors affecting relative importance of cues in impression formation. *Journal of Personality and Social Psychology*, 1974, *30*, 191-197.

Warr, P. B., and Jackson, P. Salience, importance and evaluation in judgments about people. *British Journal of Social and Clinical Psychology*, 1977, *16*, 35-45.

Warren, N. Constructs, rules and the explanation of behavior. Paper presented to the Symposium on Personal Construct Theory and Repertory Grid Methodology, Brunel University, 1964.

Watson, J. B. *Psychology from the standpoint of a behaviorist*. Philadelphia: J. B. Lippincott, 1919.

Wegner, D. M., and Vallacher, R. R. *Implicit psychology*. New York: Oxford University Press, 1977.

Weizmann, F. Praxis and interaction: The psychology of J. McVicker Hunt. In I. C. Uzgiris and F. Weizmann (Eds.), *The structuring of experience*. New York: Plenum Press, 1977, pp. 1-23.

Werner, H. *Comparative psychology of mental development*. New York: International Universities Press, 1957a.

Werner, H. The concept of development from a comparative and organismic point of view. In D. Harris (Ed.), *The concept of development: An issue in the study of human behavior*. Minneapolis: University of Minnesota Press, 1957b.

Wertsch, J. V. Semiotic mechanisms in joint cognitive activity. Paper presented at Conference on Theory of Activity, Moscow, 1980.

Wheelwright, P. *The presocratics*. New York: Odyssey Press, 1966.

Widom, C. Interpersonal and personal construct systems in psychopaths. *Journal of Consulting and Clinical Psychology*, 1976, *44*, 614-623.

Wiggins, N., and Fishbein, M. Dimensions of semantic space: A problem of individual differences. In J. G. Snider and C. E. Osgood (Eds.), *Semantic differential technique*. Chicago: Aldine, 1969.

Willis, F. The movement interpretation of threat and level of self-acceptance (Doctoral dissertation, University of Missouri, 1961). *Dissertation Abstracts*, 1961, *22*, 17-19.

Winograd, T. A framework for understanding discourse. In M. A. Just and P. A. Carpenter (Eds.), *Cognitive processes in comprehension*. Hillsdale, N.J.: Lawrence Erlbaum Associates, 1977, pp. 63-88.

Wish, M., Deutsch, M., and Kaplan, S. Perceived dimensions of interpersonal relations. *Journal of Personality and Social Psychology*, 1976, *33*, 409-420.

Wittgenstein, L. The blue book. In W. Barrett and D. H. Aiken (Eds.), *Philosophy in the twentieth century, Vol 2*. New York: Random House, 1962.

Wittgenstein, L. *Philosophical investigations*. Oxford: Blackwell, 1968.

Wooster, A. D. Testing the ability to respond to verbal instruction. *British Journal of Disorders of Communication*, 1968, *3*, 156-160.

Wyler, R. Assessment and correlates of cognitive differentiation and integration. *Journal of Personality*, 1964, *32*, 495-509.

Yuille, J. C., and Catchpole, M. J. The role of imagery in models of cognition. *Journal of Mental Imagery*, 1977, *1*, 171-180.

Zajonc, R. B. Attitudinal effects of mere exposure. *Journal of Personality and Social Psychology*, 1968, *9*, 1-27.

Zajonc, R. B. Feelings and thinking-preferences need no inferences. *American Psychologist*, 1980, *35*, 151-175.

Zimring, F. Cognitive simplicity-complexity: Evidence for disparate processes. *Journal of Personality*, 1971, *39*, 109.

AUTHOR INDEX

SUBJECT INDEX

ABOUT THE CONTRIBUTORS

Editors/Authors

James C. Mancuso is Professor of Psychology at the State University of New York at Albany. He received his B.A. from Dickinson College and Ph.D. from the University of Rochester. His edited volume, *Readings for a Cognitive Theory of Personality* (Holt, 1970), is well known to students of personal construct psychology. More recently, he has published *Schizophrenia: Medical Diagnosis or Moral Verdict* (Pergamon Press, 1980) in collaboration with Theodore R. Sarbin.

Jack Adams-Webber received his B.A. from Haverford College, M.A. from Ohio State University, and Ph.D. from Brandeis University. He is currently Professor of Psychology at Brock University in Ontario. He was previously Principal Psychologist with the British Medical Research Council Unit for the Study of Clinical Thought Disorder at Bexley Hospital in London, England. He is the author of *Personal Construct Theory: Concepts and Applications* (Wiley, 1979).

Contributors

Philip J. Boxer received his B.Sc. in electrical engineering from King's College and M.Sc. in business administration from the London Business School, where he is now a member of the associate faculty. He has published several papers dealing with issues in personal construct theory.

Michael C. Cometa completed his undergraduate study and his Ph.D. at State University of New York at Albany. He currently is on the faculty at Radford University, Virginia, and is a consultant at Saint Alban's Psychiatric Center, Adolescent Unit. His publications relate to developmental psychology.

Walter H. Crockett's seminal research on cognitive complexity and related topics has played an integral role in the development of personal construct psychology. He is Professor of Psychology at the University of Kansas, where he earned both his B.A. and M.A. His Ph.D. is from the University of Michigan.

Steven W. Duck earned his B.A. and M.A. from Oxford University and his Ph.D. from Sheffield University. He is now senior lecturer in the Department of Psychology at the University of Lancaster. He has published several books, including *Personal Relationships and Personal Constructs* (Academic Press, 1973).

Bruce N. Eimer completed his Ph.D. at the State University of New York at Albany, where he explored and wrote about constructivist explanations of reprimand. He is entering his career as a child development specialist at the Louisville University School of Medicine.

Michael A. Gara published several innovative explorations of implicit personality theory before he completed his Ph.D. at Rutgers, The State University of New Jersey. He has been examining the utility of implicit personality theory technology in psychiatric settings at the Rutgers University School of Medicine.

Brian C. Hayden completed his B.A. at New York University and his M.A. and Ph.D. at the University of Florida. Currently an Associate Professor of Psychology (Adjunct) at Brown University, he has published several articles dealing with developmental issues in personal construct theory.

Alvin W. Landfield received his B.A. from the University of North Carolina and his M.A. and Ph.D. from Ohio State University, where he was a student of the late George Kelly, the originator of personal construct theory. Dr. Landfield is Professor of Psychology at the University of Nebraska-Lincoln. His most recent book is *Personal Construct Psychology: Psychotherapy and Personality* (Wiley, 1980).

David Magnusson is head of the Unit of Applied Psychology at the University of Stockholm, where he completed his Ph.D. and Docent. His distinguished scholarly record has been recognized by his election to membership in the Swedish Academy of Sciences. His most recent books are entitled *Personality at the Crossroads* (L. Erlbaum Associates, 1977, with Norman S. Endler) and *Toward a Psychology of Situations* (L. Erlbaum Associates, 1981).

James K. Morrison maintains a very active practice as a psychologist, while holding a post as Clinical Associate at Albany Medical College, Albany, New York. Since completing his Ph.D. at State University of New York at Albany he has published dozens of papers on public conceptions about mental illness, emotive reconstructive therapy, and imagery in psychotherapy. A recent book bears the title, *A Consumer Approach to Community Psychology* (Nelson Hall, 1980).

Lars B. I. Nystedt is Director of Graduate Studies in Psychology at the University of Stockholm, where he received both his B.A. and Ph.D. His many papers on topics in person perception represent an important contribution to personal construct research.

Ragnar Rommetveit, Professor of Psychology at the University of Oslo, has been a visiting professor at Michigan, Minnesota, and Cornell Universities. He has published more than seventy books and articles dealing with a wide range of issues in psychology. His recent book, *On Message Structure* (Academic, 1976), is a landmark in the field of psycholinguistics.

Finn Tschudi completed his Ph.D. at the University of Oslo, where he has recently served as Acting Chairman at the Psychologist Institute. He was a visiting scholar at Cornell University and has been an active proponent and elaborator of personal construct theory.